THE ETHICS RUPTURE

Exploring Alternatives to Formal Research Ethics Review

*Edited by Will C. van den Hoonaard
and Ann Hamilton*

For decades now, researchers in the social sciences and humanities have been expressing deep dissatisfaction with the process of research ethics review in academia. *The Ethics Rupture* builds on ongoing critiques, such as those presented in Will C. van den Hoonaard's *The Seduction of Ethics* and *Walking the Tightrope*, to evaluate the failures of ethics review systems and offer a series of proposals on how to ensure that social practices are ethical and effective rather than merely compliant with institutional requirements.

Comprising twenty-five essays written by leading experts from around the world in various disciplines, *The Ethics Rupture* is a landmark study of the problems caused by our current research ethics systems and the ways in which scholars are seeking solutions.

WILL C. VAN DEN HOONAARD is a professor emeritus in the Department of Sociology at the University of New Brunswick.

ANN HAMILTON holds a PhD in human communication from the University of Oklahoma.

The Ethics Rupture

*Exploring Alternatives to Formal
Research Ethics Review*

EDITED BY WILL C. VAN DEN HOONAARD
AND ANN HAMILTON

UNIVERSITY OF TORONTO PRESS
Toronto Buffalo London

ISBN 978-1-4426-4832-6 (cloth)   ISBN 978-1-4426-2608-9 (paper)

Library and Archives Canada Cataloguing in Publication

The ethics rupture : exploring alternatives to formal
research ethics review / edited by Will C. van den Hoonaard
and Ann Hamilton.

Includes bibliographical references and index.
ISBN 978-1-4426-4832-6 (cloth).—ISBN 978-1-4426-2608-9 (paper)

1. Social sciences—Research—Moral and ethical aspects.
2. Qualitative research—Moral and ethical aspects.   I. Van den
Hoonaard, Will C. (Willy Carl), 1942–, author, editor   II. Hamilton,
Ann, 1955–, author, editor

H61.E85 2016   174'.930072   C2015-908170-X

University of Toronto Press acknowledges the financial assistance to its
publishing program of the Canada Council for the Arts and the Ontario
Arts Council, an Ontario government agency.

Canada Council   Conseil des Arts
for the Arts   du Canada

ONTARIO ARTS COUNCIL
CONSEIL DES ARTS DE L'ONTARIO
an Ontario government agency
un organisme du gouvernement de l'Ontario

Funded by the   Financé par le
Government   gouvernement
of Canada   du Canada

Contents

Part II: Outside the Comfort Zone: New Methodologies

Part III: Analysis of Change: When Superficiality Displaces Substance

Part IV: Solutions: Renewal, Reform, or Dismemberment?

Final Thoughts

Acknowledgments

We can confidently exclaim that any attempt to organize, analyse, or critique research ethics regimes leads to better protection of research participants. If one were to aver that any protest against such regimes implies the abandonment of any ethical stance in research, one could not be further from the truth. As the authors in this volume clearly testify, researchers have as much vested in doing ethical research as the administrators and agencies who are formally appointed to oversee ethics in research. Only attempts by those administrators and agencies to exercise a measure of control within an irrelevant bureaucratic framework countervail the desires of social researchers.

Exploring the many dimensions of research ethics regimes – their weaknesses and their strengths, their failures and their invested hopes – requires a panoply of thinkers and researchers. A number of the authors in this volume have dedicated their lives to this task, and we wish to thank them for their generous scholarly contributions. We are grateful to the 25 contributors to this volume who found time to produce their thoughtful offering to the discourse that has been streaming through the research ethics community for some two decades, involving more than 325 scholarly articles, book chapters, and books that have fairly opposed, reconsidered, or reformed research ethics regimes around the world.

As editors, we are also grateful to the Social Sciences and Humanities Research Council of Canada for a grant that allowed us to organize the Ethics Summit that took place in Fredericton, New Brunswick, Canada, in October 2012. The grant permitted us to publish this volume, in addition to creating an opportunity to develop the "New Brunswick Declaration on Ethics in Research and Governance." Our other institutional supporters of both the Summit and the resulting volume include St Thomas University, in Fredericton, its Atlantic Centre for Qualitative Research and Analysis (ACQRA), and the University of New Brunswick. Their support was unflagging. Deborah van den Hoonaard, as Canada Research Chair and Director of ACQRA, was enthusiastic in her support, ably assisted by Lehanne Knowlton whose talents to direct the many resources related to organizing the Summit were indispensable. Through Donna Safatli, a graduate student in the Department of Sociology at the University of New Brunswick, much of the preparatory groundwork for the Summit was accomplished. We also offer our thanks to the staff at the Wu Conference Centre at the University of New Brunswick, and to Karen Spinning.

We owe a particular debt to Paul Burnett who at the time of our grant application was the formal applicant for the grant. His administrative and presentational skills and enthusiasm were a delight to behold. We are also grateful to Rena Lederman of Princeton University who, in addition to writing a chapter for our volume, has been most helpful in helping us improve our introductory and concluding chapters.

Our acknowledgment and thanks would not be complete without paying a special tribute to Douglas Hildebrand, social science acquisitions editor at the University of Toronto Press, whose support for the volume was so welcoming.

Will C. van den Hoonaard and Ann Hamilton
Fredericton, New Brunswick, and Logan County, Oklahoma

THE ETHICS RUPTURE

Exploring Alternatives to Formal
Research Ethics Review

Introduction

The Ethics Rupture Summit in the Context of Current Trends in Research Ethics Review

WILL C. VAN DEN HOONAARD AND ANN HAMILTON

The theme at the 2012 "Ethics Rupture" Summit in Fredericton, New Brunswick, expressed a near-collective dismay, discomfort, and disorientation about the process known to social science researchers as "research ethics review." Even members of ethics review committees, as "guardians" of ethics review processes, are not entirely happy. Mandating researchers to submit their research plans to ethics committees before gathering any data involving humans is often not a joyful or productive one for either party.

It would be a grave mistake to assume that members of research ethics committees are the sole source of these discomfiting times. Similarly, we cannot attribute such a state to only ourselves as researchers who might go wild or rogue without the external restraints of moral dictates. Members of ethics review committees are, for the most part, dedicated to the tasks at hand and are often displeased, or even distressed knowing that researchers perceive their work and efforts as unnecessary, careless, lacking in caution, overly confining, or even dangerous. However, in contrast to researchers, members of ethics committees are neither restrained nor overseen by others – they can and do summarily dismiss criticisms and suggestions. Approximately 325 scholarly publications and presentations about the shortcomings of this system have been put forth since the late 1990s, but it is clear that policymakers have ignored them (van den Hoonaard, 2013). When policymakers read these articles, "they come up with conclusions quite different from ours," says Rena Lederman (personal communication, 29 Jan. 2014). However, it is not only about "misreading" or even ignoring the criticisms put forward by researchers. It is about two veritably different world outlooks.

Research ethics review trawls all research involving humans into the same net. Just as fishing trawlers scour the ocean floors and have a by-catch that contains species not germane to the purpose of the trawlers, the system of research ethics review implicates all research involving humans regardless of the levels of imputed risk or harm induced by the research. All are caught in this mighty trawl. A deep satisfaction settles on those who see a great benefit in demonstrating public accountability that the ethics review system allegedly serves, but there are those who bewail the plight of researchers who must now conform – often contort themselves – to an ethics framework that is far removed and often quite alien from the ethics of their discipline.[1] It is no exaggeration to say that we are witnessing, through the mandatory process of ethics review, the unmooring of social science research from its original prominence. The process entails the use of paradigms too frequently unfamiliar to researchers in the social sciences.

Consisting of papers presented at the Ethics Rupture Summit,[2] our volume reveals that the current plight can be traced to an uncanny confluence of circumstances feeding the adversarial culture within the research ethics regime, controlling social science research, disempowering research participants, exaggerating the perceptions of risk, increasing financial burdens on universities, placing social science research at a disadvantage, striking undue fear among generations of graduate students, contorting the natural world under study, and potentially shifting moral agency from the individual researcher to a bureaucracy. A number of contributors in *The Ethics Rupture* express deep concerns about the mandatory, hierarchical, and gatekeeping features of research ethics review. Despite the force of these worries, the contributors to this volume have articulated myriad responses that reflect their personal circumstances, social context, and discipline. The uniqueness of each vision is contingent on each author's experiences with formal research ethics review, on the extent to which his or her discipline has been affected by ethics review, and on the stage of his or her career.

Regardless of where one stands, there is virtually no researcher in this volume who is not prepared to offer viable and helpful advice about how ethics committees can or should proceed, perhaps realizing at the same time that abolishing the regulatory system remains a pipe dream for now. Certain misgivings, however, hang as a cloud over social science researchers who involve themselves in addressing issues arising from research ethics review, whether they support the process, advocate the reform of it, or resist the regulatory system. Social science researchers may look askance at "believers" (supporters) of the system; others believe that reformers have not gone far enough, while still others see resisters as negative or too critical in their approach. Throughout it all, scholars studying the regulatory system are taught they must take into account the impact of their stance on their careers, publications, reputation, and scholarship. Resistance in such a system frequently does not pay off, regardless of how right one is.

It is helpful to remind ourselves that regardless of the position researchers take towards research ethics review, the interests and protection of research participants, research subjects, interlocutors, or whatever term is used within a given discipline, are foremost. The contributors to this volume are deeply engaged in the ethics review debate, and they care deeply about research participants. Opposition to formal research ethics review does not entail a lack of concern for the well-being of research participants. The opposition is also concerned with the paucity of actual problems in social science with respect to harms inflicted on participants in survey, interview, observational research, and similar methods. These harms pale into insignificance when compared to such medical experiments as the notorious Tuskegee study (Reverby, 2009) when the US Public Health Service between 1932 and 1972 studied the evolution of untreated syphilis in 600 in African-American men in Alabama. They were told that they were receiving free health care from the US government, but the researchers withheld administering penicillin. Neither did the researchers inform the subjects what the "treatment" was about. The "Common Rule" in the United States is one of the means to ensure that researchers do not overlook informed consent in research. The Common Rule consists of 15 sets of regulations of which 45 CFR 46 is the best known one (see http://www.hhs.gov/ohrp/humansubjects/commonrule/).

In assembling and editing the presentations at the 2012 Ethics Rupture Summit, we have tried, whenever possible, to retain their fresh and engaging tone. For the convenience of the readers, we have grouped the chapters into the following four sections: "Strains in Research Ethics Review Processes," "Outside the Comfort Zone: New Methodologies," "Analysis of Change: When Superficiality Displaces Substance," and "Solutions: Renewal, Reform, or Dismemberment?"

Strains in Research Ethics Review Processes

The contributors to the first section of this volume (Robert Dingwall, Rena Lederman, Patricia and Peter Adler, Laura Stark, Marco Marzano, and Patrick O'Neill; chapters 1 to 6, respectively) find themselves at odds with any regulatory system that, they argue, is unhealthy for the future of the social sciences. Their worries about the current system of research ethics review stem mainly from the following three areas of concern: the biomedical roots of research ethics regulation, the ethics mission creep into non-medical research, and the surrender and compliance of social science researchers with the demands of ethics review committees.

Robert Dingwall, in chapter 1, makes the case that, "the social costs of ethics regulation in the social sciences have been massively underestimated " and that "the benefits attributed to these ethics regimes are wholly disproportionate to the losses," which consist of the obstruction of innovation, the creation of areas of ignorance, and the infantilization of human beings participating in research. If we value a democratic society, then we should be aware that research ethics review regimes use societal resources that are "inefficient, ineffective, inequitable, and inhumane."

Researchers in the social sciences universally agree that research ethics review has deep roots in *the biomedical model of research*. Thus, ill-fitting rules continue to significantly shape the social sciences, the rules having been extended far beyond their original function by local research ethics boards. Faced with vast paradigmatic differences, Rena Lederman (chapter 2) underscores the problem of ethnographers who must translate their research into a language understood by biomedical researchers. She relates this situation to the pluralism/hegemony problem concerning the dominant culture folks, that is, those on ethics committees who use the ethics of biomedical paradigms to gauge the work of researchers in the social sciences. They do not see the world the same way minority culture folks do, namely, researchers in the social sciences. Fieldworkers thus bear a heavy "burden of translation" when they undergo formal ethics reviews because of their minority-culture status within a hierarchy of knowledge cultures dominated by biomedical terminology. Lederman explains how disciplinary diversity is effaced in research ethics regulations and notes the impressive depth of disciplinary tone-deafness. The burden of translation rests with the researcher, and especially with students who are still in the process of acquiring their "native tongue" of social science research. It is no small irony that the most affected are graduate student researchers who occupy a vulnerable position in the scheme of things.

Some researchers undertake this translation work by taking refuge in subtexts and carefully devised terminologies. A researcher who conducts interviews will avoid claiming that his or her interviews are "therapeutic" in the event a member of the ethics committee is a professional counsellor and objects to others describing their work as having "therapeutic" content. Will C. van den Hoonaard, in his *The Seduction of Ethics* (2011), shows that researchers employ a variety of other strategies, partly to bypass translational problems. Some try to be as vague as possible when presenting their research plans to ethics review committees; others couch their application in a language understood by members of ethics committees. Ethics committees are more likely to respond favourably when researchers plan to conduct interviews, as opposed to ethnographic fieldwork. Ethics committees, on their part, are prone to use the passive voice in their missives to researchers to depersonalize their message as if to speak with incontrovertible authority.

Inter alia, ethical failures in biomedical research have come to weigh heavily on the evaluation of risk in the social sciences. Kate Holland (later in chapter 18), concludes that "even though the risks of qualitative, non-medical research are minimal compared with the physical or psychological harm brought on by biomedical procedures, drug trials, and other experimental conditions, abuses or failures in the biomedical realm contribute to a disproportionate level of largely irrelevant processes of ethics review."

Mission creep constitutes yet another striking aspect of the formal process of ethics review. Patricia Adler and Peter Adler (chapter 3) proclaim that as research ethics committees are nestled within academic and governmental bureaucracies, they "have followed the sociologically well-known tendency to sustain themselves and grow by entrenching and expanding their mission and reach." They point out that "Institutional Review Boards [IRBs] have quantitatively and qualitatively absorbed more kinds of inquiry into their domain" while at the same time tightening the standards for researchers, they have relaxed the procedural restraints governing the IRBs, and they have expanded IRB authority.

Some researchers, however, have achieved success in freeing researchers in their discipline from the academic constraints of research ethics review. Linda Shopes, a main proponent to liberate oral history scholarship from formal processes of research ethics review (2013: para 7) writes that when IRB requirements for human subjects review in biomedical research have not been met, several major institutions have had to suspend research. With the fear of litigation or bad press over dangerous or controversial research, IRBs have become very vigilant, "extending review to forms of minimal risk research in the social sciences and humanities that previously had escaped their purview."

This regulatory hypervigilance has other consequences. No less weighty than placing an unjust burden on social science research is the "contamination" of the natural world each time an ethics committee requires the use of written (and signed) informed consent documents, or disallows any form of covert activity or other kind of masking that is so critical to ethnographic research, as Marco Marzano explains in chapter 5. People being observed know they are being observed, which is just common sense, and the Hawthorne Effect comes into play if the researcher must announce that research is being conducted.[3] Nor do researchers need to gain consent from people to be viewed while in a public place: it does not make sense to approach persons in a mall and formally request their consent or to ask them to sign a document that says, essentially, "other people can see you and a very few of them may write about it and very few of those writings will be read by very few people." A frustrating irony for all involved is that this mission creep creates situations in which researchers often would know the identity of "participants" *only* because of written (and signed) informed consent documents.

Laura Stark in chapter 4 opens our eyes to how ethics review committees operate with significant biases and that "board members' monolingualism is a structural barrier to the equitable protection of language minorities in research and assessment of research." Based on a year of ethnographic fieldwork of ethics review committees in the United States (2012), Stark explains that "the review process results in unequal treatment of research participants who do not share the dominant language of IRB members," contributing, subsequently, to inequities in the treatment of scholar-researchers. One could migrate the idea of monolingualism to what Patrick O'Neill, in chapter 6, has learned about ethics committees, namely, that committees see the concept of risk only through one lens, namely, harm will be done unless committees intervene on "behalf of" research participants. The *nature of risk* or harm is another term subject to variable definitions and interpretations. These definitions are contingent on the kind of research that is being proposed, notions about past research such as Zimbardo's famous prison simulation study and Milgram's obedience study,[4] and on how one defines *vulnerability*. O'Neill's concerns are not only confined to defending past controversial research, but also include challenges that ethics committee members face when assessing risk or harm.

Mission creep is a global trend. Originally, economic forces were at work to establish formal regimes of ethics review around the world. Mark Israel, Gary Allen, and Colin Thomsen, in chapter 15, explain that medical researchers in Australia were eager to secure access to research funds from the United States, especially from the National Institutes of Health. To access those grants, a national system of ethics review must be in place. We can attribute the initial spread of similarly flawed systems of ethics review to other countries wanting access to American funds for research.

Taking in the broad landscape of how faculty and students alike have responded to research ethics review, one is struck by what seems like a purposeful resignation among researchers. This resignation expresses a dismay that traditional forms of research are no longer in the cards and that the regimes regulating research ethics seem immutable to change. Researchers do not have much leverage to challenge the system, even within the legal realm. As Robert Dingwall notes, "Litigation requires deep pockets, a thick skin, and a willingness to be unpopular with all those who have an interest in the status quo. Bringing a lawsuit presents significant career and professional risks for individuals and political risks for any professional association attempting to confront the institutions that demonstrate ill treatment of its members." It is therefore highly unlikely that researchers will involve themselves in litigation. Fear and a judicial system stacked in favour of institutions win. Besides, who among us wants to be singled out as a troublemaker?

A central problem is that ethics review processes and faculty members who inform students about them instill and entrench self-censorship. The ability to mount legal opposition to these processes is beyond the reach of all but a few researchers. The power of the inhabitants in this ethics world is, however, unequal. A legal framework underpins ethics review committees and infiltrates numerous layers of control. A system of "vertical ethics" (van den Hoonaard, 2011) influences academic units, graduate schools, journals, and funding agencies. Researchers are often aware of these layers of ethics approvals. As Ann Hamilton reminds us (in chapter 17), all these layers are active in the mind of the researcher with IRB experience. She also argues that the fact that researchers have rarely been granted access to study the ethics review process itself is also frightening, frustrating, ironic, and ridiculous.

Even so, one should not claim that all social sciences experience the same fate in terms of research ethics review. Rena Lederman, a contributor to this volume, says there is no question that lots of researchers – in particular, sociocultural anthropologists – "are continuing to do what they've been doing either with their ethics board's approval or without worrying their boards about the details of their work" (personal communication, 29 Jan. 2014).

Marco Marzano, in chapter 5, follows a similar argument, namely, that the particular mentality of ethics review committees has inflicted serious harm on the quality and freedom of social science research: "The result of this Orwellian climate of obsessive control over the activities of scholars in the field," citing Katz (2007), he says, "has been that the social studies have too often succumbed to the triumph of rhetoric, to a wave of fine sentiments and hypocrisy."[5] Robert Dingwall concurs when he concludes that ethics review has "considerable value as rhetorical cover for extensions of command-and-control management in universities."

Outside the Comfort Zone: New Methodologies

In addition to the problems discussed above, pauperization sets in when researchers believe they are bound to study people who are not in protected classes, or where ethics review committees believe that risks (of liability) are high, namely, research involving children, prisoners, people with disabilities, members of vanishing cultures, or the elderly. And when social science researchers do engage with these populations, the encounters have not been shown to be harmful; rather the more we know, the better the chances vulnerable members of society will benefit from research. We can surmise that when ethics committees need to balance the protection of studied populations with risks of institutional liability, the balance, it seems, gives more weight to the latter. In chapter 17, on *compliatorianism*, Ann Hamilton stares this issue right in the face. She describes the invisible chilling effect on the part of faculty "to acknowledge to students and colleagues that many a research proposal would produce a great study, involve excellent methodologies, would be timely, and deal with an important topic, but they would *never* get past the IRB" (Hamilton's emphasis). As a consequence researchers avoid some topics and populations. While it is true that such journals as *Qualitative Research, Qualitative Inquiry,* and *Action Research* do not hesitate to cover sensitive topics or vulnerable populations, some embedded ideas dictated by ethics review committees compromise the goals of researching these topics or populations (such as the need to report any illegal behaviour of prisoners to the warden).

Some research practices are impossible for researchers to effectively describe within the current framework of ethics review, and they are also impossible for members of ethics review committees to respond to as the system is now. Ethics regimes, for example, barely acknowledge the place of covert research in most of the practices of social research. There are references in ethics codes to doing deception, but that is not the same as doing covert research. In deception, the research participant knows that research is going on, knows the researcher is a researcher, etc. But in covert research, research participants are not aware that research is being conducted and are probably unaware of the presence of a researcher in their midst. Covert methods and the use of confederates in social research, for example, have nearly vanished in the face of ethics review mission creep, though harms have not been found.

At least three authors in our volume, however, have highlighted the discomfort ethics review committees have with relatively new or less frequently used methodologies, namely, Internet research, auto-ethnographies, and community research.[6] In chapter 7, Heather Kitchin Dahringer deconstructs the notion of *privacy* and questions whether privacy is a misnomer when exploring Internet activities. Today, researchers are entering a "new frontier of research ethics laden with ambiguous privacy rules." Research ethics committees must reframe the notion of "privacy" to accommodate cyber life. In view of the permanency of material on the Internet, Dahringer concludes, "privacy may be nothing more than an illusion." She seeks to reframe "privacy" more appropriately as a form of performance.

Often, too, ethics review committees greet a whole arena of research, such as auto-ethnography, with reluctance. Auto-ethnography, according to B. Lee Murray (chapter 8), "requires a new way of looking at research and our intentions for research." It asks researchers to examine knowledge from a subjective position – clearly a major counterpoint to positivism as the basis of the biomedical paradigm prominent in processes of ethics review. She further notes this method often involves "hearing and telling difficult knowledge gained from difficult experiences." If the proposed research involves inquiries into secrets and difficult topics (developmental disabilities, sexual abuse, divorce, accidents, and illness) ethics committees then demand to see more of the research plans. Often uncomfortable with that methodology, they even hesitate to explore the different ways to address anonymity and consent. It is ironic, as Lee Murray reminds us, that according to the Canadian *Tri-Council Policy Statement: Ethical Conduct for Research Involving*

Humans (TCPS 2), "REBs [research ethics boards] should not reject controversial research proposals including those that offend powerful or vocal interest groups" (CIHR et al., 2010: 24). Yet, these rejections are common. And researchers, especially novice ones, gravitate away from certain controversial topics, protected classes of participants, or more obscure yet highly useful, low-risk methods.

In research involving Aboriginal communities, Julie Bull (chapter 9) argues that a paradigm shift within the existing REB structure is needed in order to produce ethics committee members better suited to review community-based research, especially with Aboriginal people. It is the community that defines the research, rather than an ethics board or even the researcher. Contemporary review boards, Bull avers, are still vested in the idea of the "individual" as opposed to working through the idea of what "community" consent looks like. This situation also demonstrates what Rena Lederman discusses about translation. It is likely that most members of ethics review committees come from individualistic cultures, and Bull is studying collectivistic cultures, and so it is not difficult to see why committee members might require processes, such as written informed consent documents that individuals must sign, that make no sense in the community-research context.

Analysis of Change: When Superficiality Displaces Substance

Aside from some researchers in disciplines such as anthropology and oral history trying to go their own way (more or less), it is no less disturbing to note, as Kirsten Bell (chapter 10) does, that "academic passivity and our tendency to accept systems of audit and accountability" persist despite their poor fit with social research. She also explains that especially in light of "growing moves to quantify research output based on positivistic models," these models have "noticeably corrosive effects on social science scholarship," corroborating points raised by several contributors to this volume, including Marzano, Dingwall, Hamilton, van den Scott, and others.

Kirsten Bell asserts that despite the substantial round of consultations within the country to change Canada's *Tri-Council Policy Statement* (CIHR et al., 1998, 2010), there are no fundamental changes from *TCPS 1* to *TCPS 2* in spite of the 12-year span between them. She avers that many of its well-intentioned efforts to become friendlier to social science actually contribute substantially to mission creep in the ethics review system. Bell describes the current system in Canada as having "taken on a life far beyond what was initially anticipated by its creators" and that "no one is more cognizant of this than social scientists." She also points out that "changes to Canadian human research ethics guidelines have done little to curb the excesses of institutional research ethics oversight." In short, mission creep in this already hyper-regulatory context has constrained the production of knowledge and, alarmingly, has muted the possibility of substantively challenging the ethics review regime.

Natasha Mauthner (chapter 11) stresses that our ethical responsibility is less about implementing ethical guidelines and more about researchers themselves taking responsibility for our ethical practices. She argues that mandatory data sharing exposes research participants to harm.

Many researchers, especially students, according to Lisa-Jo Kestin van den Scott (chapter 12), live in fear of the heavy hand of ethics committees. Van den Scott discusses the self-censorship operating in the world of graduate students and other researchers. Whether this heavy hand is imagined or real, the fear is still real in its consequences. Much-needed research on special groups and subcultures now occurs less frequently, in large part because members of ethics boards are reluctant to approve studies involving vulnerable populations. Researchers – especially novice ones – avoid these groups precisely because they know (because they are taught by professors and other students) that getting the proposal approved by the ethics board will be much more difficult, encroaching on the limited time and financial resources students have to complete their graduate work.

The ramifications on students are serious. Van den Scott reiterates that ethics review committees influence the formative years in a young researcher's career, not only what the researcher chooses to study, but also how the student-researcher thinks about the work at hand, as well as possibilities for research in general. Students are researchers-in-training, as Laura Stark (2012) has said, so the evaluations of their research should not be different based on whether the researcher is also a student. One might suggest that faculty should speak against the sense that Institutional Review Boards are natural or inevitable. This shortcutting of academic apprenticeship is particularly felt in ethnographic research. Lise Dobrin and Dena Plemmons (2012), in their paper delivered at the Ethics Rupture Summit, find that ethics review committees exercise serious gatekeeping when it comes to ethnographic research. They find that the "present regulatory framework provides anthropologists with little by way of guidance as they work through the ethical challenges inherent in such open-ended protocols."

In searching for "a more workable and ethically productive model of human research protections for anthropological research," they realized that the process should be "collaborative and educative rather than gatekeeping in character." This perspective is particularly consistent with the expressed views of Julie Bull, Robert Dingwall, Kate Holland, and other contributors to this volume.

Kirsten Bell (chapter 10) calls the change from "human subject" in the *TCPS 1* to "human participant" in *TCPS 2* superficial. Similarly, Igor Gontcharov (chapter 13) is reluctant to consider the terminological change from "human subjects" to "human participants" a significant shift from the biomedically based ethics code to one less hostile to social science. Gontcharov is calling for a critical assessment of the current universalist framework that "can be described as a euphemistic spiral: When a word becomes offensive, a taboo, it is necessary to substitute it with a new one in order to be able to continue referring to the same thing." This trend to the adoption of the term "research participant," moving away from "human subjects" has become near universal, except for its appearance on the occasional research ethics application form.

Iara Coelho Zito Guerriero, a Brazilian psychologist serving on Brazil's National Ethics Commission, writes in chapter 14 about the system in Brazil where approximately seven hundred committees govern ethics in research. She explains how research ethics policies disadvantage social science researchers in Brazil and describes how the National Commission has engaged in the process of consultation with researchers (a positive point) and is in the process of developing a uniform application system for social science researchers (a negative one). One must wonder whether Guerriero's observations about Brazil's national system of ethics review fit into the growing awareness about the inadequacies of ethics review regimes that focus on standardization. The visual and political imagery that underlies this strategy is powerful: on the one hand, the Brazilian system will be highly standardized, centralized (and computerized) – perceived as efficient; on the other hand, the diversity of research and of the social science community of researchers does not lend itself to standardization, as expressed consistently by the contributors to this volume.

Solutions: Renewal, Reform, or Dismemberment?

Plenty of good sense resides in this volume that is pertinent to the future unfolding of the research ethics review system. Some of the contributing authors have turned dismay into a positive force for renewing or reforming the current codes for research ethics into a framework that accommodates the goals of protecting participants in research that involves risk, while also recognizing the needs of social researchers, the agency of participants, and the potential benefits to society.

Although the regulatory system is cohesive in its authority, it remains uneven in places – and we hope that resolving this unevenness will provide a better space for social research. The world offers diverse regulatory systems of research ethics review. In the United States, the legal ramifications are quite pronounced. Canada follows a set of guidelines, rather than national and local legal codes as found in the United States. In the United Kingdom, one finds the prevalence of local and professional bodies that also fall within a national ethics framework. Australia and New Zealand are similar to Canada. Throughout all of these national structures there remains the presence of local university ethics committees, and these committees vary enormously in their decision-making authority and power. For all the efforts to standardize and solidify the system of research ethics review, it remains, as Ann Hamilton says (cited in chapter 17), a "liquid and local" system, that is, "specific researchers give specific power(s) to specific regulators at specific times" (2002: 216) in an adversarial system that has adverse effects on social science, as Robert Dingwall argues in chapter 1.

Mark Israel, Gary Allen, and Colin Thomson (chapter 15) declare that "the growth of the adversarial culture should not have surprised anyone – its origins were identified by senior academics engaged in developing regulations – and was a predictable result of a failure to consult with researchers, a lack of regulator resources, and a gap in expertise in key parts of the regulatory structure."

Zachary Schrag (chapter 16) claims that because the prevailing ethics regime is based on biomedical parameters, it has no actual relevance for the social sciences. It is better to dispense with the system. Schrag points out that "one long-standing grievance among social scientists is the concept of informed consent embedded in the *Belmont Report* and comparable documents based on bio-medical ethics. Many social researchers have complained that formal criteria and procedures for obtaining informed consent ... can destroy needed rapport between researcher and participant and can effectively silence those defined as 'vulnerable' because they do not conform to an imagined norm."

The bending of research towards the demands of ethics review committees means that some social science methods are becoming homogenized while also pauperizing the social sciences as a whole. Because standardization is at the core of any bureaucracy, the system of research ethics review fails to differentiate among the social sciences, as mentioned in the context of proposed changes in the Brazilian system.

These disturbances are not new to historian Zachary Schrag who produced a history of ethics review in the United States (2010).[7] Research ethics committees offer very little, if any, opportunity for the critical inquiry that many social science scholars take "to be their duty in the pursuit of the truth," he writes. What is more, "the reliance on institution-level ethics committees, which historically arose in response to medical research abuses, all but guarantees that many such committees will be unfamiliar with the ethics of specific disciplines and approaches, even hostile to and suspicious of them" (Schrag and Dreger, 2012: 1). These ideas are consistent with those expressed by Rena Lederman in chapter 2.

Ann Hamilton (chapter 17) urges local ethics review boards to follow federal rules for exemption, thereby freeing all social science involving surveys, interviews, fieldwork, and observational methods from ethics review. Kate Holland (chapter 18) sees community-based research as one area that holds much promise, a place where change can be more easily envisaged. It is reasonable to assume the received code of ethics excludes consideration of community-based research. Policymakers are more open to such a new venue of ethics in research. If one were cynical one could claim that the new venue offered a new means for ethics review committees to stretch their powers and bureaucratic control. Still, this approach holds out hope that formal recognition can be forthcoming for such a welcome change in research ethics codes.

Many authors in this volume are optimistic that the current system of ethics review can adapt to the needs of social scientists. Emma Tumilty, Martin Tolich, and Stephanie Dobson (chapter 19) and Ron Iphofen (chapter 20) have been working on a modus vivendi trying to reconcile conflicting demands, and ultimately acknowledging that the research ethics regime is a worthy one to follow, demonstrating the importance of keying the ethics of research into existing formal structures of national or federal policies. They seek piecemeal solutions to reforming the ethics regime, tinkering with proposals to change some foundational features, whether they pertain to mandatory informed-consent forms or the need for researchers to specify in advance of their research the precise nature and purpose of their data collection plans and analysis.

Consistent with the idea of collaborative review, Emma Tumilty, Martin Tolich, and Stephanie Dobson (chapter 19) and their colleagues have created The Ethics Application Repository (TEAR), an open-access online repository of ethics applications donated by scholars. They express hope that TEAR will "aid student researchers facing enrollment deadlines and academics constricted by funding timeframes." They established TEAR in response to delays caused by conditional board approval or even rejection (requiring full resubmission) of ethics applications of researchers in the social sciences. TEAR can be useful to ethics committee members, too, by providing examples of studies that have been approved at other institutions.

With the focus revolving around institutional attempts to bring researchers to account, Ron Iphofen (chapter 20) argues "for acknowledging the integrity of researchers and their ability to conduct research in a responsible manner." This is an entirely reasonable approach to take, we believe, and, in the spirit with which we put forth this volume, an effort to repair the Ethics Rupture. We concur. With no direct oversight of researchers, this trust is all we have, on the most practical level. It is all we need given the lack of participant harm in social science research.

Our concluding chapter in *The Ethics Rupture* offers an amalgam of ideas about researchers and policymakers who envision a different dynamic within the current system. They touch upon ethics committees' allowing for more research exemptions, being more knowledgeable about community-based research, detailed explorations of research settings before an application is made to the ethics committee, being sensitive as far as language is concerned, developing educational presentations about ethics in the field, insisting on using the narrative approach in the ethics approval process, fostering ethical relationships between researchers and ethics committees, having ethics committees stop interfering with researchers' proposed method(s), allowing researchers to publish their experiences with ethics committees, discouraging ethics committees from using flawed research practices as not-how-to-do lessons, finding ways to trust researchers, and, finally, not to employ default settings when adjudicating applications (e.g., not to insist that signed consent forms must be used). A restructured system would promote the use of covert methods, and welcome research projects that embody controversial ideas, challenge mainstream thought, and dare to offend even highly powerful groups.

NOTES

1 In the case of one of the most recent and egregious use of the "ethics trawl," the spokesman at the University of Colorado at Boulder let it be known that its Institutional Review Board should have a say about what happens in classrooms. He offered this comment as a reaction to allegations about what was transpiring in a classroom. The University quickly retracted this inadvertent pronouncement, but it revealed an urgent desire by University officials to have their IRB exercise a control that would extend beyond research. The University was prepared to bully Professor Patricia Adler (who was a participant in the 2012 Ethics Summit) into retirement or into ceasing to teach her popular course, "Deviance in U.S. Society," which she had taught for 25 years. Her course involved the use of skits where teaching assistants would each portray a particular type of prostitute (street hooker, call girl, escort, etc.).

2 Patricia Sikes, a presenter at the 2012 Ethics Summit, already published her paper on critical research ethics in *Compare* (2013).

3 The Hawthorne Effect, sometimes called "observer effect," is what happens when individuals modify or improve an aspect of their behaviour in response to their awareness of being observed.

4 See Philip G. Zimbardo (1971), "The Power and Pathology of Imprisonment," in *Congressional Record. (Serial No. 15, 1971–10–25). Hearings before Subcommittee No. 3, of the Committee on the Judiciary, House of Representatives, 92nd Congress, First Session on Corrections, Part II, Prisons, Prison Reform and Prisoner's Rights: California* (Washington, DC: US Government Printing Office), and Stanley Milgram (1974), *Obedience to Authority: An Experimental View* (New York: Harper and Row).

5 Marco Marzano has found no less worrisome accounts in Italy where notions of protecting "privacy" serve to protect the interests of the privileged from undesired research.

6 It was not possible for the Ethics Summit organizers to have David Calvey present at the Summit. We would have gained much from his expertise in doing covert research (see Calvey, 2008).

7 While editing *The Ethics Rupture*, we have learned of *Protecting Research Confidentiality*, a fourth empirical book on the processes of research ethics review (Palys and Lowman, 2014).

REFERENCES

Calvey, David. (2008). "The Art and Politics of Covert Research: Doing 'Situated Ethics' in the Field. *Sociology* 42 (5): 905–18. http://dx.doi. org/10.1177/0038038508094569

CIHR et al. (Canadian Institutes of Health Research, Natural Sciences and Engineering Research Council of Canada, and Social Sciences and Humanities Research Council of Canada). (1998, with 2000, 2002, 2005 amendments). *Tri-Council Policy Statement: Ethical Conduct for Research Involving Humans.* Ottawa, ON: Interagency Secretariat on Research Ethics.

– (2010). *Tri-Council Policy Statement: Ethical Conduct for Research Involving Humans.* 2nd ed. Ottawa: Interagency Panel on Research Ethics.

Dobrin, Lise M., and Dena Plemmons. (2012). "Cultivating Ethics Before, During, and After the Field: Alternatives to Gatekeeping Ethics in Anthropological Research." Paper presented at the Ethics Rupture Summit, 28 Oct.., Fredericton, NB, Canada.

Hamilton, Ann. (2002). *Institutional Review Boards: Politics, Power, Purpose, and Process in a Regulatory Organization.* Doctoral dissertation, University of Oklahoma.

Katz, Jack. (2007). "Toward a Natural History of Ethical Censorship." *Law & Society Review* 41 (4): 797–810. http://dx.doi.org/10.1111/ j.1540-5893.2007.00325.x

Palys, Ted, and John Lowman. (2014). *Protecting Research Confidentiality: What Happens When Law and Ethics Collide.* Toronto: Lorimer.

Reverby, Susan. (2009). *Examining Tuskegee: The Infamous Syphilis Study and Its Legacy.* Chapel Hill, NC: University of North Carolina Press.

Schrag, Zachary M. (2010). *Ethical Imperialism: Institutional Review Boards and the Social Sciences, 1965–2009.* Baltimore: Johns Hopkins University Press.

Schrag, Zachary M., and Alice Dreger. (2012). "Ethical Pluralism: The Importance of (Self)Discipline in the Regulation of Research Ethics." Paper presented at the Ethics Rupture Summit, Fredericton, NB, Canada, 28 Oct.

Shopes, Linda. (2013). "Oral History, Human Subjects, and Institutional Review Boards." Oral History Association. http://www.oralhistory.org/ about/do-oral-history/oral-history-and-irb-review/

Sikes, Patricia. (2013). "Working Together for Critical Research Ethics." *Compare: A Journal of Comparative Education* 43 (4): 516–36. http://dx. doi.org/10.1080/03057925.2013.797765

Stark, Laura. (2012). *Behind Closed Doors: IRBs and the Making of Research Ethics.* Chicago: University of Chicago Press.

van den Hoonaard, Will C. (2011). *The Seduction of Ethics: Transforming the Social Sciences.* Toronto: University of Toronto Press.

– (2013). "The Social and Policy Contexts of the New Brunswick Declaration on Research Ethics, Integrity, and Governance: A Commentary." *Journal of Empirical Research on Human Research Ethics* 8 (2): 104–9. http://dx.doi.org/10.1525/jer.2013.8.2.104

PART I

Strains in Research Ethics
Review Processes

1 The Social Costs of Ethics Regulation

ROBERT DINGWALL

The rise of ethics regulation in the social sciences has been extensively discussed and analysed since the 1980s (Dingwall, 2012). A model developed for the governance of biomedical research in the United States has been extended to the social sciences and exported throughout the anglophone world; its adoption elsewhere has been more limited. There is now a broad consensus among those who have examined the workings of this model that it is not fit for purpose in its application to the social sciences. However, the growing documentation of these failings has had little impact. Two main reasons for this are apparent: (1) there are strong interests vested in the system itself that constitute a lobby against reform, and (2) the case for reform has been too easily dismissed as self-serving. This chapter focuses on the second issue, namely, the social costs of research ethics regulation in the social sciences have been massively underestimated. Consequently, the benefits attributed to these ethics review regimes are wholly disproportionate to the losses that are generated for all citizens. The regulation of research ethics must be reformed because it obstructs innovation, creates profound areas of ignorance, and infantilizes human subjects. All of these obstructions contribute to the use of societal resources in ways that are inefficient, ineffective, inequitable, and inhumane. These are not desirable outcomes for social science research.

Why "Regulation"?

The use of the term *regulation* can provoke discomfort in discussions of research ethics. Its introduction links the analysis of research ethics review to a well-established interdisciplinary literature. Even if current systems of pre-emptive review were founded on explicit ethical principles, such general statements would still need to be translated into practice by means of operating rules and organizations to interpret, administer, and enforce these. Ethical principles are not self-enacting: they always have their effects through human decisions about what they mean. It is appropriate to evaluate the (in)consistencies between these human interpretations, implementation processes, and the founding principles of ethics on which the systems are said to be based.

What questions might regulation researchers pose about a system of ethics review? They would probably begin by asking about the stated goals and justifications for having such a system at all. Why do we need to use social, economic, or legal resources to intervene between researcher and research participant? The next questions would address the proportionality of the system. Are the costs or burdens of the review process proportionate to the risks or benefits to any of the parties involved? Is the system effective in managing those risks and benefits? Does it strike an appropriate balance among stakeholders? Which areas of research and which methods should be reviewed? Do benefits or risks present themselves to the actual participants in the study proposed? What should be done in the case of observational methods? Surveys? Finally, there would be a set of questions about procedural justice. Does the system provide for a fair hearing in cases of disputes between researchers and regulators? Between participants and researchers? Is there a protocol for review of decisions at first instance, made by the first committee to consider them? Does the ethics review system have institutionalized ways of learning from its mistakes or misjudgments to avoid repeating them? Is the system accountable to its stakeholders, both those who bear the costs and those who derive the benefits?

What Are the Arguments for Regulation?

When faced with a claim about the existence of a social problem that requires a particular solution, the classic sociological response is to ask, "What interests are involved in formulating that problem such that this proposal is a credible response?" (Waller, 1936). Social problems are the result of successful claims that frame particular social groups, institutions, or events as troubling to the claims makers and therefore requiring an intervention to prevent, remedy, or resolve them. One of the first questions we should ask about any proposal for regulation, then, is "Who says there is a problem?" "Where is the evidence of need for regulation?" We should follow this by asking why they think regulation is the solution, specifically, why *this* regime in *this* form at *this* time is required. Reviewing work by Laura Stark (2012), Zachary Schrag (2010), Adam Hedgecoe (2008; 2009), and others, I found it clear that the drivers for systems of research ethics regulation generally owe more to reputation management and legal issues than to concern for human subjects (Dingwall, 2012). The approach in the United States, for example, has become increasingly hegemonic: it originates in the National Institutes of Health (NIH) with attempts to deflect litigation risks in relation to subcontracted research, which were extended to protect NIH from similar legal claims in relation to grant-funded work as well. Researchers outside the United States have been forced to adopt similar models as a condition of research collaboration with researchers in the United States.

The model of ethics review has been extended outward from the biomedical science centre where it originated, initially through uniform requirements by biomedical funding agencies that had, occasionally, supported social science projects under their programs in health and mental health. More recently, this model has become the basis for a claim of distinctive expertise and authority in ethical matters by the biomedical world, through pressure on other funding agencies and academic publishers. It is now very difficult to conduct or publish social science research in health care anywhere without meeting these requirements, although their relevance to the social sciences has never been demonstrated. No historical evidence of the abuse of human subjects exists that is in any way comparable to that perpetrated by biomedical researchers during the past 150 years (Dingwall and Rozelle, 2011). Indeed, from the start, empirical social science researchers have consistently shown concern for the protection of human subjects (Dingwall, 2012). Some part of the extension of ethics regulation, then, is bound up with the relative prestige of various academic disciplines and their struggles to influence the agendas of both public and private organizations engaged in funding or disseminating research.

If ethics regulation is centrally about reputation management and legal protection, previous critics may not have presented arguments that precisely hit the target. In essence, these criticisms derive from claims about the costs and obstructive nature of regulatory compliance, and about interference with academic freedom and the rights of researchers. Both of these are significant issues. Will C. van den Hoonaard (2011: 75) has estimated that, just considering the United States, United

Kingdom, and Canada, the current system costs Cdn$432 million at 2010 prices, without allowing for committee members' salaries. This may seem a large sum, but it should be put in the context of the total research income to universities: for Canada alone, this was Cdn$6.46 billion in 2010.[1] It might be argued that the cost of regulation is actually quite modest, whether for the protection of research participants or of institutions. More sophisticated arguments can be developed about the opportunity costs from tying up experienced researchers in committee work, but these seem unlikely to inflate van den Hoonaard's figures to the point where they become significant in system terms, except insofar as institutions should consider the efficiency of all their activities.

Persuasive arguments have been offered, particularly from the United States, demonstrating that ethics regulation is an infringement of researchers' fundamental constitutional right to freedom of speech (Hamburger, 2004; 2007). It is one thing, however, for lawyers to argue for the existence of a right and another to secure that right, particularly when important stakeholders are opposed to granting it. Litigation requires deep pockets, a thick skin, and a willingness to be unpopular with all those who have an interest in the status quo. Bringing a lawsuit presents significant career and professional risks for individuals and political risks for any professional association attempting to confront the institutions that demonstrate ill treatment of its members. Moreover, it is hard to see how narrow legal actions could halt wider mobilization of unreasonable and ill-fitting regulation. Does anybody really care about the free speech rights of academics other than academics themselves?

Ultimately, such arguments are vulnerable to being dismissed as self-serving. A little bureaucracy is a small price to pay for public safety, and academic freedom is just about folks who do not like to have their ivory towers invaded by a supposedly more real world. There may, though, be better arguments aimed at generating wider leverage. These establish, in particular, that the regulation of research ethics imposes costs on everyone, not just researchers and universities. If the balance has been misjudged, everyone loses. Four such arguments are explained here – the first two elaborate and reframe the existing case; the last two are new.

1 The justification for academic freedom is the promotion of innovation by academics, not the indulgence of academics.
2 The allocation of resources to research ethics regulation is part of a wider movement of resources, within universities, from delivery

to control systems; this is detrimental to the ability to deliver innovation.

3 Research ethics regulation encroaches on participants' rights to self-determination.

4 Research ethics regulation interferes with the processes by which we hold each other mutually accountable for the benefits of living in society.

Why Do We Have Academic Freedom?

As Ralph Fuchs (1963) notes, the concept of academic freedom has its roots in nineteenth-century Germany. Enlightened authoritarian states created a protected space within their universities that liberated professors to pursue ideas wherever they might lead, to seek truth and disseminate findings as they develop them, without penalty: "The idea of the university as a place where scholars are to pursue truth, as well as to formulate and transmit it to students, who at the same time learn to pursue truth for themselves, came to be dominant there [Germany]. Especially in an age of science, knowledge grows as individuals ferret it out; and the free interplay of ideas is the means of purifying it. Intellectual discipline over the members of the university community is excluded, lest it distort their search" (435).

The results were impressive. By the mid-1800s, German universities were internationally acknowledged as research leaders, attracting a wide variety of young scholars who took the culture and organizational model back home, particularly in the late nineteenth-century expansion of university systems in England, the British Empire, and the United States. Peter Byrne (1989) notes how this was driven by the evolving nature of science and the vision of a university as a site for the production of new knowledge rather than the transmission of faith or authority: "Science provided ... a strong rationale for freedom: Scientific endeavor presupposes a progressive conception of knowledge. Understanding at any one moment is imperfect, and defects can be exposed by testing hypotheses against reality, through either adducing new data or experimentation. The process of hypothesis–experimentation–new hypotheses improves knowledge and brings us closer to a complete, more nearly objective truth about the world. Error is not dangerous so long as the process is continued, because acknowledged means will expose it; in fact, it is actually beneficial (and inevitable) as part of progressive discovery" (273–4).

Freedom of inquiry, at least when practised by those recognized as competent by their peers and committed to the impartiality of science, has been integral to progress, discovery, and innovation. Fuchs (1963) quotes from a 1902 book, *The German Universities and University Study* by Friedrich Paulsen, a professor at the University of Berlin: "a people, [who establish and maintain a university], cannot as such have an interest in the preservation of false conceptions. Its ability to live depends in no small measure upon its doing that which is necessary from a proper knowledge of actual conditions. And hence the people and the state ... can have no desire to place obstacles in the way of an honest search for truth in the field of politics and social science, either by forbidding or favoring certain views" (436).

Although Fuchs's focus is on scholars and politics, the implications are as relevant to science, engineering, and medicine as to the humanities and social sciences. Academic freedom is not about self-indulgence; it is about innovation. There is no point in a country funding universities that are not capable of expanding knowledge and progressively enhancing understanding of the natural and social worlds.

One might object that these arguments rest on an old-fashioned theory of research as a pursuit of truth, although this goal is still widely held in the natural sciences. However, even if we might be more cautious about claiming that we can achieve perfect knowledge of an objective world, there is a persuasive argument that the free pursuit of knowledge is critical to a society's adaptive capacity. Although it is a reasonable proposition that the laws of physics have not changed since the Big Bang, biomedical and environmental sciences are dealing with phenomena that are as complex and fluid as those addressed by the human sciences. Where we are dealing with change and instability, a society's ability to respond will be strongly influenced by the degree to which its institutions can successfully innovate. Academic freedom is one of the preconditions of that adaptability.

Freedom should not be confused with licence, however. This is not a case for never asking academics to account for their use of the time and resources supplied to them. Nor is this a case for saying that human experimentation should never be regulated. Clearly, bad things happened in nineteenth-century universities, although these were criticized at the time and generated attempts at regulation (Dingwall and Rozelle, 2011). Regulation may, classically, be justified where there is a marked asymmetry of knowledge between parties, creating an incentive for the more knowledgeable party to minimize communication about risks to the less knowledgeable (Akerlof, 1970; Leland, 1979; Breyer, 1982). The point here, however, is that excessive regulation of research ethics obstructs innovation and delays potential benefits to society.

An increasingly prominent issue in the biomedical sciences deals with determining the number of lives lost as a result of delays and obstruction by Institutional Review Boards (IRBs) in the United States (Whitney, 2012). Such computations are more difficult in the social sciences and humanities, but they do recognize the importance of proportionality in regulation. Biomedical sciences involve potential risks of death and serious injury that participants are not well equipped to assess. However, successful research may significantly reduce those risks for future research participants (or, in this case, patients). The risks to human subjects must be balanced against the wider societal benefits to sick people in the future. If a regulatory system becomes preoccupied with risk at the expense of benefit, it is failing to perform its proper function of managing, rather than obstructing, innovation. On the whole, social science projects do not create comparable risks; where they do, participants are often better placed to assess those risks than either researchers or regulators. If we are studying drug trafficking in a developing country, for example, local dealers are better placed to estimate the risk of being shot for indiscretion than are fieldworkers or a regulatory committee thousands of miles away. The benefits of social science research are more diffuse and difficult to quantify – but this may not be particularly important given the greater symmetry of knowledge and the limited nature of harms in social science research.

Command and Control

The expansion of ethics regulation also needs to be seen as part of a package of structural changes within universities. In principle, according to Michael Tushman and Charles O'Reilly, III (1996), universities are ambidextrous organizations:

> The real test of leadership, then, is to be able to compete successfully by both increasing the alignment or fit among strategy, structure, culture, and processes, while simultaneously preparing for the inevitable revolutions required by discontinuous environmental change. This requires organizational and management skills to compete in a mature market (where cost, efficiency, and incremental innovation are key) *and* to develop new products and services (where radical innovation, speed, and flexibility

are critical). A focus on either one of these skill sets is conceptually easy. *Unfortunately, focusing on only one guarantees short-term success but long-term failure. Managers need to be able to do both at the same time, that is, they need to be ambidextrous.* (Tushman and O'Reilly III, 1996: 11, emphasis added)

Ambidextrous organizations face the challenge of maintaining stability in some aspects of their business, while simultaneously sustaining instability in others. Historically, universities have been able to achieve this by separating teaching and research missions under funding arrangements that have only led to contestability at the margin. Undergraduate teaching has been a relatively secure income stream, without high demands for innovation, and a certain amount of research activity and infrastructure has been underwritten by generic funding, whether from governments or endowments. This has provided a base for competitive engagement with other income streams, where adaptability has been more important. These income streams have often been associated with more flexible types of business units, like research centres, that have protected the stability of the core through the use of short-term employment contracts, temporary space allocations, and looser organizational controls. However, recent changes have increased the contestability of university funding streams by placing greater emphasis on competition for student enrollments, against a tightening demographic supply in many countries, and on reducing the guaranteed floor for research funding in favour of competitive grants and contracts (Ginsberg, 2011; Martin, 2012; McGettigan, 2013). These changes have been accompanied by an increase in external control, by government regulatory interventions, and public or private ranking tables in the case of students (Sauder and Espeland, 2009), and by contractual terms, in the case of research funding.

An unstable environment and external controls have increasingly prompted universities to seek stability and predictability by strengthening internal management. They have drifted away from the traditional model of worker co-operatives to resemble more conventional machine bureaucracies. As Henry Mintzberg (1979: 288–92) notes, this is a predictable, although inappropriate, result of these external contingencies. Bureaucracy can promote internal stability, which is valuable in certain types of public sector organizations (Boyne and Meier, 2009), but it is not conducive to ambidexterity. This is a significant challenge for universities (Ambos et al., 2008). Although there are possible structures that would allow business units (academic departments, in this case) to operate more flexibly and closer to their markets, these do not fit with the demands of external control and institutional performance management by predetermined metrics, adapted from business. Although detailed institutional responses vary, ethics regulation is an important tool for influencing individual research agendas, alongside other internal regulatory processes required in the name of research integrity, grant demand management, the pre-screening of research grant applications, and open access publishing. Having engaged in the kind of strategic planning required to maintain external legitimacy, university managers have acquired internal tools to impose conformity without the outright directing (i.e., close supervision) of labour (colleagues) that would directly challenge the organization's professional culture.

The regulation of research ethics, then, is not just a tool for institutional reputation management and legal protection, but also potentially a tool for performance management. Ethics review committees favour particular topics or styles of research. These bodies have a record of preferring research that is easily regulated by prior approval of designs and questionnaires. This should not be pitched as quantitative versus qualitative: many ethics committees have adapted to complaints by qualitative researchers and accepted the looser format of qualitative interviewing, treating interview agendas as equivalent to questionnaires in terms of risk. The problems come with participant observation (and other methods), where pre-emptive controls are genuinely difficult (Murphy and Dingwall, 2007). If an organization is committed to a strategy that shapes its research performance for external audiences, simply allowing staff or students to go out and hang around until they find something to write about is not a viable institutional practice. Research ethics regulation adds to the tools for institutional stabilization, a conservative response to an unstable environment that is inimical to innovation. Safe topics and safe methods are preferred, delivering predictable results that translate easily into application or impact.

Participants' Rights

I have already noted the argument for regulation where there are marked asymmetries in knowledge and understanding between the parties to a transaction. Regulation of research ethics, in theory, ensures that research can be sustained by promoting trust between participants and researchers: participants can assume that the study has been reviewed by people with appropriate expertise and declared to be sufficiently safe. This is a prominently stated purpose for the regulation of professional work – to avoid potential market failure through lack of trust in an area of individual or social importance (Dingwall and Fenn, 1987). One bad study can damage the entire "brand" of the university and tarnish research in general. In the social sciences, such asymmetries are less common; indeed, they often operate in the reverse direction, with participants being better informed about potential risks than those researching them.

The power relationship is also reversed in many contexts. Researchers are guests in the lives of the people they are investigating, and as with any other guest, inappropriate behaviour leads to a request to terminate a conversation or leave a research site (Murphy and Dingwall, 2007). There are some exceptions, particularly in psychological experimentation, where participants may find it difficult to leave a closed environment. Pre-emptive ethics review may not, however, be an effective means of managing these risks. It may create a false sense of security, as with the Stanford Prison Experiment: Philip Zimbardo, the principal investigator, has admitted that he was blinded to abuses that were obvious to others because he had prior approval from an ethics review panel (Zimbardo, 2008; Dingwall, 2012). Ethics regulation, then, implies that research participants are not capable of making judgments for themselves about the risks and benefits of cooperation with researchers, even though the methods often used simply replicate behaviours demonstrated by ordinary people in everyday life. How do we learn about anything? By watching what happens, by asking questions, by reading documents, by counting events, describing them, etc. Google Glass allows every user to record, with video and audio, all the people, interactions, and events he or she encounters without obtaining consent – especially in written form. Insistence on informed consent in research appears anachronistic, unless its role in organizational and public surveillance is understood.

The common requirement for informed consent forms extends institutional surveillance of researchers in ways that undermine the trust of research participants. There are documented cases of consent forms provoking hostile reactions from participants who indicated they were insulted by the lack of trust shown towards them (Dingwall, 2008). However, the greater harm may be the signal to participants that the institution does not fully trust the researcher asking them to participate. Researchers must prove they are in compliance with absent regulators rather than being respected as professionals. Again there is an issue of proportionality. Where knowledge is highly asymmetric or the environment is closed, it may be reasonable to require written informed consent documents, by analogy with (written) consents to surgery. Where knowledge is not asymmetric, and the methods of inquiry and risks are entirely within the competence of the research participant to evaluate, disproportionate levels of surveillance question the ability of participants to make judgments for themselves and trust in the researcher as a professional. Is such a level of paternalism reasonable? Are we participating in the world of institutional risk management rather than the protection of research participants?

In general, ethicists are fairly hostile to paternalism: autonomy is thought to be a critical characteristic of respect for another person. In this mainstream view, we should be reluctant to encroach on a participant's right to self-determination unless we have strong arguments for doing so. There is debate among ethicists about when regulation is appropriate. It is a philosophical equivalent of the debates about market failure or the "tragedy of the commons," that is, the pursuit of self-interest destroying a community resource that would benefit the collective more than any individual gains from exercising a right (Hardin, 1968). One example might be the way in which the pretense of carrying out market research by companies seeking to sell products over the telephone has compromised the ability of social science researchers to achieve decent response rates. Marketing practices are, however, entirely outside any ethics review system.

A wider argument, then, might be that ethics regulation is ineffective in dealing with abuse, like telemarketing, and trespasses on the rights of individual participants to make their own judgments about which projects to participate in and to what degree. Projects are preselected, both directly by the regulators, and indirectly by the decisions of researchers to avoid topics that are presumed likely to meet regulatory disfavour:

> I discourage students from studying any group that might be construed as a "special population." That means school observations or youth group observations are automatically out. But I have come to learn that the IRB also raises its eyebrow at more nebulous categories, such as gays and lesbians, or poor workers. It basically makes me worried about [studying] any population that is not adult, well-adjusted, crime-free, middle class, heterosexual, white (i.e., do not study immigrants as some of them might

be undocumented or do not study black workers because some of them may fear reprisal from their white employers), and male (i.e., women might report domestic violence). This is, of course, an exaggeration, but the layers of fear that IRB creates leads to this kind of [faculty] policing of student projects. (Bledsoe et al., 2007, 622–3)

There may be an objection that the current system works for the robust adults in full possession of their faculties assumed by utilitarian thinkers, but it is less appropriate for those people who are defined as "vulnerable." One problem here is the lack of consensus about which groups are defined as vulnerable. Ronald White (2007) notes the lack of any rigorous conceptualization of vulnerability and the disparate groups swept into the regulatory net through ad hoc reasoning including prisoners, children, fetuses, pregnant women, the mentally ill, the elderly, disaster victims, prostitutes, homosexuals, disgruntled employees, primitive tribes, and people with developmental disabilities.

For prisoners or hospitalized people, for instance, it may be a question of context, although there is abundant evidence that many such groups are well capable of protecting their own interests in spite of their incarcerated status. Individual trust must still be negotiated, regardless of any institutional agreement, and may well be obstructed by regulatory interventions. Similarly, the insistence on regulatory paternalism sits uneasily alongside the increasing assertions by many vulnerable populations (as established by regulators rather than by the individuals themselves) for recognition of their capacity for self-determination. People living in the community and in institutionalized care, with a wide range of intellectual, physical, and chronological disabilities have asserted their rights to make decisions about their own lives rather than to have others make decisions for them. So, we come back to the nature of the decisions that people are asked to make when agreeing to participate in social science research. The guest/host relationship is at its heart. Ethics regulation shows no respect for traditionally disadvantaged groups when it casts a wide net of vulnerability with very little specific justification for the determination that certain groups are incapable of assessing their own interests and judgments in relation to everyday problems about what questions to answer in what way with what consequences for their interests and reputation. Regulation demeans those individuals it professes to protect.

Mutual Accountability

John Harris (2005) argues that citizens have a moral duty to participate in biomedical research. He notes that ethicists have traditionally
treated research with suspicion, reflected in a precautionary presumption that risks are more likely than benefits, and that no individual
should participate unless safety is assured by regulation. Empirically,
Harris concedes, this assumption is well founded in the biomedical
field. The result, however, has created an imbalance between the interests of research participants and those of the wider community. Two
ethical principles have been interpreted in an overly narrow fashion:
(1) the obligation not to harm others where we can reasonably avoid
this, which is denied by excessive regulation of research, and (2) the
commitment to basic fairness, that it is wrong to "free ride" on the benefits of research without contributing to them. These principles may
require participation even where there are no direct benefits to the individual participant. Although Harris does not propose compulsory participation, he does identify ethical arguments that could justify it. In so
doing, he suggests that it should be assumed that moral persons would
wish to participate in minimal risk research: "It is crucial that the powerful moral reasons for conducting science research are not drowned by
the powerful reasons we have for protecting research subjects" (245).
Burdensome rules obstruct moral action.

These arguments also apply to social science research where, as we
have seen, the rules have even less empirical justification. Harris's critique of "free riding" requires no elaboration: to the extent that we all
enjoy the benefits of social research, then it will normally be unethical
to regulate participation in ways that encourage refusal.

John Rawls (1971: 4) defines a society as a "cooperative structure for
mutual advantage." Within this, there is both an identity of interests,
in the benefits from cooperation, and a conflict of interests, in the distribution of those benefits. His work develops a theory of justice that
is intended to maximize the gains from cooperation while minimizing
the conflicts about distribution. Although his model does not explicitly
address the place of social science research, it can be argued that this
is an essential element in egalitarian societies, both in informing citizens about institutions and in holding institutions accountable. In John
Dewey's (1927: 184) words, "free social inquiry is indissolubly wedded
to the art of full and moving communication" contributing to "a life of
free and enriching communion." Rawls, for example, explores the kinds

of inequalities that might be justifiable and how these would relate to equitable opportunity to enjoy the resulting distribution of outcomes. These justifications will necessarily rest on empirical evidence to inform the reasoned debate that Rawls, like Dewey, regards as fundamental. The rich may be able to justify their wealth if they can show that this also raises the living standards of all, by directly creating employment, and funding investment in institutions that increase opportunities available to the poor, including providing primary goods. What Rawls and other social democrats may have neglected, however, is the argument for a corresponding obligation on the poor to justify the wealth transfers through their use of them to contribute to the general welfare.

Everyone derives benefits from a society to which everyone contributes. The social sciences are part of an institutionalized system of audit by which those contributions and receipts are evaluated. They are not the whole of that system – creative artists, journalists, and other social commentators also contribute (Strong, 1983). Nevertheless, they are a particularly important part because of their grounding in supposedly disinterested organizational environments and their regulative discipline of fidelity to data. Checks and balances come from the competition among these diverse sources of information. Films and novels tell one kind of truth about society and ethnographers tell another.

Most of the social sciences' competitors are lightly, if at all, regulated. The freedom of creative artists and journalists is a central pillar of democratic societies. In practice, of course, this freedom is constrained by the nature of the markets for their services and by the laws of libel and obscenity. Nevertheless, their entry costs are relatively low, particularly with new media, and pre-emptive review is rare and in many countries unlawful. For social scientists, entry costs are rising with the spread of pre-emptive regulation. The ecology of societal audit is being disrupted in ways that may not be beneficial. As ethics regulation directs research away from "difficult" populations, topics, and methods, it creates systematic areas of ignorance about social conditions. Without such knowledge, however, it is difficult to create the transparency among people that promotes better lives.

Conclusion

These arguments are less straightforward than those often advanced in favour of research ethics regulation but together they constitute a case for a more proportional approach to ethics regulation that fits the level of risk. In particular, the arguments identify a range of costs or harms arising from regulatory intervention that have been neglected by the "do no harm" claims for regulation. Who could be opposed to ensuring the greater safety of research participants? The result of over-zealous regulation, though, may be a society that is less adaptive, less respectful of human rights, and less secure in its social order. These are real consequences of actions that may originally have been well intentioned but were imposed on the social sciences with inadequate consideration and justification. None of this, of course, prevents universities from creating reputation management structures – but calling a thing by its proper name is the first step to understanding its nature. Reputation management is not research ethics; regulation is not protection.

If our concern is to protect participants in research, then it is not difficult to discern the criteria that we might use to define a proportionate approach. First, an ethics review system should exclude all research that presents no more than everyday risk to research participants (AAUP, 2013). It is not a question of reviewing everything "just in case": social science research participants are generally better placed than research ethics regulators to determine what is likely to damage them. Second, a system should recognize that social science research participants are normally in a more powerful position than researchers because of their ability to grant or withhold access to information. No individual can be compelled to participate in research or to give truthful answers to questions. The system should, then, presume the competence of participants and should only intervene where there is clear evidence of a lack of capacity to consent. Third, and related to this, all citizens should be assumed to have a right to participate in research as part of their demonstration to others of their good faith membership in a particular society. Any research ethics regulatory system should demonstrate preference for approving research, and allowing people to decline participation, rather than to disapprove research so that individuals are not offered the choice of participation. Finally, any regulatory system should conform to minimum standards of due process. Researchers have a right to a clear statement of the grounds for disapproving a project, which should be restricted solely on matters of ethics: if an institution is concerned about reputation management, employer's liability, or offence to patrons, these are management decisions that do not bear on the integrity of researchers or their projects. Due process also requires proper standards of peer review, opportunities to appear in person, and to have decisions reviewed independently.

The regulation of research ethics has a powerful, if naive, appeal backed up by a growing body of people and organizations with direct material interests in its expansion, including university administrators, lawyers, and ethics board members themselves. It also has a considerable value as rhetorical cover for extensions of command-and-control management in universities. Neither of these drivers will easily be resisted by rational argument or evidence. The challenge is to reach beyond our immediate environment to those wider interests that will be damaged by depressed levels of innovation and by the disrespect for human rights and a prominent lack of trust embedded in the present system.

NOTE

1 According to the inflation calculator at the Bank of Canada, this same Cdn$432 million would be $555,686,520 in 2013. The $6.46 billion become $8.31 billion. – Eds.

REFERENCES

AAUP (American Association of University Professors). (2013). *Regulation of Research on Human Subjects: Academic Freedom and the Institutional Review Board*. Washington, DC: American Association of University Professors.

Akerlof, George A. (1970). "The Market for 'Lemons': Quality Uncertainty and the Market Mechanism." *Quarterly Journal of Economics* 84 (3): 488. http://dx.doi.org/10.2307/1879431

Ambos, Tina C., Kristiina Mäkelä, Julian Birkinshaw, and Pablo D'Este. (2008). "When Does University Research Get Commercialized? Creating Ambidexterity in Research Institutions." *Journal of Management Studies* 45 (8): 1424–47. http://dx.doi.org/10.1111/j.1467-6486.2008.00804.x

Bledsoe, Caroline H., Bruce Sherin, Adam G. Gallinsky, Nathalia M. Headley, Carol A. Heimer, Erik Kjeldgaard, James Lindgren, Jon D. Miller, Michael E. Roloff, and David E. Uttal. (2007). "Regulating Creativity: Research and Survival in the IRB Iron Cage." *Northwestern University Law Review* 101 (2): 593–641.

Boyne, George A., and Kenneth J. Meier. (2009). "Environmental Turbulence, Organizational Stability, and Public Service Performance." *Administration & Society* 40 (8): 799–824. http://dx.doi.org/10.1177/0095399708326333

Breyer, Stephen. (1982). *Regulation and Its Reform*. Cambridge, MA: Harvard University Press.

Byrne, J. Peter. (1989). "Academic Freedom: A 'Special Concern of the
First Amendment.'" *Yale Law Journal* 99 (2): 251–340. http://dx.doi.
org/10.2307/796588

Dewey, John. (1927). *The Public and Its Problems*. New York: Holt.

Dingwall, Robert. (2008). "The Ethical Case against Ethical Regulation in
Humanities and Social Science Research." *Twenty-First Century Society* 3 (1):
1–12. http://dx.doi.org/10.1080/17450140701749189

– (2012). "How Did We Ever Get into This Mess? The Rise of Ethical
Regulation in the Social Sciences." *Studies in Qualitative Methodology* 12:
3–26. http://dx.doi.org/10.1108/S1042-3192(2012)0000012004

Dingwall, Robert, and Paul Fenn. (1987). "'A Respectable Profession'?
Sociological and Economic Perspectives on the Regulation of Professional
Services." *International Review of Law and Economics* 7 (1): 51–64. http://
dx.doi.org/10.1016/0144-8188(87)90006-8

Dingwall, Robert, and Vienna Rozelle. (2011). "The Ethical Governance of
German Physicians, 1890–1939: Are There Lessons from History?" *Journal of
Policy History* 23 (1): 29–52. http://dx.doi.org/10.1017/S0898030610000308

Fuchs, Ralph F. (1963). "Academic Freedom: Its Basic Philosophy, Function,
and History." *Law and Contemporary Problems* 28 (3): 431–46. http://dx.doi.
org/10.2307/1190640

Ginsberg, Benjamin. (2011). *The Fall of the Faculty: The Rise of the All-
Administrative University and Why It Matters*. New York: Oxford University
Press.

Hamburger, Philip (2004). "New Censorship: Institutional Review Boards."
Supreme Court Review 6: 271–354.

– (2007). "Getting Permission." *Northwestern University Law Review* 101 (2):
405–92.

Hardin, Garrett. (1968). "The Tragedy of the Commons." *Science* 162 (3859):
1243–8. http://dx.doi.org/10.1126/science.162.3859.1243

Harris, John. (2005). "Scientific Research Is a Moral Duty." *Journal of Medical
Ethics* 31 (4): 242–8. http://dx.doi.org/10.1136/jme.2005.011973

Hedgecoe, Adam. (2008). "Research Ethics Review and the Sociological
Research Relationship." *Sociology* 42 (5): 873–86. http://dx.doi.
org/10.1177/0038038508094567

– (2009). "'A Form of Practical Machinery': The Origins of Research Ethics
Committees in the UK, 1967–1972." *Medical History* 53 (3): 331–50. http://
dx.doi.org/10.1017/S0025727300000211

Leland, Hayne E. (1979). "Quacks, Lemons, and Licensing: A Theory of
Minimum Quality Standards." *Journal of Political Economy* 87 (6): 1328–46.
http://dx.doi.org/10.1086/260838

Martin, Randy. (2012). *Under New Management: Universities, Administrative Labor, and the Professional Turn*. Philadelphia: Temple University Press.

McGettigan, Andrew. (2013). *The Great University Gamble: Money, Markets and the Future of Higher Education*. London: Pluto.

Mintzberg, Henry. (1979). *The Structuring of Organizations*. Englewood Cliffs, NJ: Prentice-Hall.

Murphy, Elizabeth, and Robert Dingwall. (2007). "Informed Consent, Anticipatory Regulation and Ethnographic Practice." *Social Science & Medicine* 65 (11): 2223–34. http://dx.doi.org/10.1016/j.socscimed.2007.08.008

Rawls, John. (1971). *A Theory of Justice*. Cambridge, MA: Harvard University Press.

Sauder, Michael, and Wendy Nelson Espeland. (2009). "The Discipline of Rankings: Tight Coupling and Organizational Change." *American Sociological Review* 74 (1): 63–82. http://dx.doi.org/10.1177/000312240907400104

Schrag, Zachary M. (2010). *Ethical Imperialism: Institutional Review Boards and the Social Sciences 1965–2009*. Baltimore, MD: Johns Hopkins University Press.

Stark, Laura. (2012). *Behind Closed Doors: IRBs and the Making of Ethical Research*. Chicago: University of Chicago Press.

Strong, Philip M. (1983). "The Rivals: An Essay on the Sociological Trades." In Robert Dingwall and Philip S.C. Lewis (eds.), *The Sociology of the Professions: Lawyers, Doctors and Others*, 59–77. London: Macmillan.

Tushman, Michael L., and Charles A. O'Reilly, III. (1996). "The Ambidextrous Organizations: Managing Evolutionary and Revolutionary Change." *California Management Review* 38 (4): 8–30. http://dx.doi.org/10.2307/41165852

van den Hoonaard, Will C. (2011). *The Seduction of Ethics: Transforming the Social Sciences*. Toronto: University of Toronto Press.

Waller, Willard. (1936). "Social Problems and the Mores." *American Sociological Review* 1 (6): 922–33. http://dx.doi.org/10.2307/2084617

White, Ronald F. (2007). "Institutional Review Board Mission Creep: The Common Rule, Social Science, and the Nanny State." *Independent Review* 11 (4): 547–64.

Whitney, Simon. N. (2012). "The Python's Embrace: Clinical Research Regulation by Institutional Review Boards." *Pediatrics* 129 (3): 576–8. http://dx.doi.org/10.1542/peds.2011-3455

Zimbardo, Philip. (2008). *The Lucifer Effect: How Good People Turn Evil*. New York: Random House.

2 Fieldwork Double-Bound in Human Research Ethics Reviews: Disciplinary Competence, or Regulatory Compliance and the Muting of Disciplinary Values

RENA LEDERMAN

Ethical presuppositions structure social researchers' expectations about their working relationships not only with colleagues but also with the persons whose behaviour and experience they seek to understand. With respect to the latter, "human-subjects research" regulations in the United States impose a single ethical and methodological standard on an expanding diversity of kinds of research. This chapter explores the implications of such apparent even-handedness with regard to ethnographic fieldwork.

As a research method employed in different ways in sociocultural anthropology and other fields, ethnographic fieldwork (participant observation particularly) is a poor fit with the biomedically rooted assumptions about methodologically competent, ethically responsible research that inform human-subjects research regulations. Especially since the Second World War, biomedical science's epistemological value has depended on the careful delimitation of a specialized relationship between investigators and research subjects and on the quality of investigator control over the conditions necessary for testing theory-driven hypotheses. In contrast, fieldwork's epistemological value depends on the cultivation of multidimensional relationships between investigators and their interlocutors, and on the quality of investigator openness to socially situated contingencies.

In the United States, human-subjects research regulations (Code of Federal Regulations, 2009) and guidance treat the investigative style of biomedicine as what I will call the Standard Model for good research.[1] Consequently, local administrators responsible for institutional compliance are encouraged to treat deviations from this standard as methodologically and ethically suspect. Local ethics boards (termed Institutional Review Boards, or IRBs, in the United States) are often dominated by researchers trained in quantitative biomedical and behavioural sciences and by administrators following biomedically attuned guidance, most of whom find the values of ethnographers unfamiliar and unintelligible. Filtered through the Standard Model, ethnographers' alternatively normed, otherwise-disciplined research practices appear inscrutable or worse: subStandard – unprofessional, ineffective, unreliable and, on those bases at least, unethical.[2]

In this context, researchers who rely on fieldwork face at least two unsavoury choices. Eerily like classic subalterns or "muted groups" (Ardener, 2007), they may shoulder the burden of translation when undergoing formal research ethics reviews. They adopt the language of the Standard Model in an effort to communicate their genuine intentions as responsible researchers. But the resulting translations – for example, using "testing hypotheses" instead of "following informed hunches" or substituting "snowball sampling" for "getting to know a community" – are inadequate and ultimately misrepresent their research philosophies. Alternatively, ethnographers may abandon the foundational methodological and ethical values of their professional competence to comply with those encoded in human-subjects research regulations, a choice that impoverishes our collective understanding (van den Hoonaard, 2011).

This double bind is illustrated with attention, towards the end of this chapter, to recent proposals for overhauling US human-subjects research regulations. The chapter begins with an argument concerning the need to bring together two insights. The first – that disciplinary traditions respectively privilege qualitatively different methodological values – is widely recognized outside of this regulatory discourse but not within it. The second – that practitioners distinguish disciplinary knowledges from one another at least partially in an ethical idiom – is less widely recognized.

Bringing these two insights together is necessary for an adequate response to the regulatory regimes governing human research. This chapter reviews their foundational documents and training materials to establish that US regulators construe researchers' methodological decisions themselves as ethically consequential; in recent years, that otherwise-insightful construal has been applied in a manner that both represses and obscures disciplinary pluralism, prompting responses like those collected in this volume.

Disciplinary Pluralism

Regulatory "regimes" – systems institutionalized and bureaucratically elaborated in the United States, Canada, and elsewhere during the past half century – oversee the ethical conduct of research involving human participants. US regulations are oriented by a representation of research bearing little resemblance to the actual landscape of disciplinary knowledges that have proliferated since the nineteenth century as specializing and distinctive, yet interacting, hybridizing, and fundamentally mutable communities of practice.

On its face, this singular orientation is peculiar. After all, the historically dynamic diversity of disciplinary practices is a given in scholarship on secondary and tertiary education (e.g., Klein, 1996; Boix-Mansilla and Gardner, 1997). Indeed, first-year college writing courses have increasingly acknowledged the value of teaching writing "in the disciplines," with explicit emphasis on the diversity of disciplinary research styles, evidentiary practices (their conventions of imaging, sourcing and citation), and languages for building persuasive arguments (see especially Russell, 2002). Undergraduates fulfilling US liberal arts college distribution requirements learn that, as one moves between departments, what counts as "knowledge" is hardly of a piece. They glean that criteria for competence vary in subtle or dramatic ways even if we restrict our attention to the research practices and products of fields concerned with human behaviour: deconstructing and comparing literary texts, authenticating and interpreting primary historical sources, designing and running subjects in perception experiments, designing and conducting demographic surveys, or inscribing observations, interactions, and other experiences as field journal entries.

Beyond this common knowledge, considerable scholarly attention over the past generation has been devoted to the history and dynamics of disciplinarity (e.g., Klein, 1996). Understanding disciplinary knowledges in terms of their distinctive symbolic forms, materialities, social arrangements, and histories became well established in the field of science studies during the 1980s and 1990s (e.g., Latour and Woolgar, 1979; Knorr-Cetina, 1999) and in similar ways more broadly (e.g., Messer-Davidow et al., 1993; Abbott, 2001). Although arguments about the "Unity of Science" have been renewed in recent years (e.g., Wilson, 1999), historical and sociological studies of science have convincingly called into question the idea of a single "scientific method" (e.g., Creager et al., 2007). They have offered persuasive evidence of epistemological diversity – a "disunity" of knowledges – not just in the social sciences (where it is widely acknowledged) but in the natural sciences as well (e.g., Galison and Stump, 1996; see Kuhn 1970 [1962] for the foundational statement).

A Singular Science: Belmont, CITI, and the Effacement of Difference

In research-ethics regulations in the United States, disciplinary differences are effaced and reconfigured as better or worse versions of a singular way of knowing the world. This is evident in the research ethics training courses developed for administrative staff and investigators. The premier online training site, Collaborative Institutional Training Initiative (CITI), offers a suite of courses covering human-subjects research ethics along with the more general construct of responsible research conduct (also known as RCR, encompassing proscriptions against plagiarism, data fabrication and the like). While course components make reference to particular disciplines and methodological styles, these differences are treated as superficial.

CITI offers separate courses on responsible conduct for biomedicine, physical science, behavioural and social science, and the humanities. Nevertheless, all of these courses rely heavily on scenarios illustrating ethical dilemmas characteristic of lab science – for example, dilemmas faced by graduate students and postdocs whose research and publications are dependent on a laboratory director's government or corporate funding. Unlike in the natural sciences, the political economy and structure of US doctoral and postdoctoral research in the humanities and humanistic (i.e., interpretive) social studies tend not to be organized around senior scholars' funding, let alone corporate sponsorship; nevertheless, CITI treats the latter types of arrangements as paradigmatic.

CITI's tone-deafness concerning disciplinary difference is profound. For example, immediately beneath the heading, *Research Misconduct in the Arts and Humanities*, appears a quotation – "The public will support science only if it can trust the scientists and institutions that conduct research" – attributed to a 2002 Institute of Medicine report on scientific research integrity. Readers are, in effect, invited to transpose the sentiment for arts and humanities ears. Should they have to? Were there no suitable exhortations by arts and humanities scholars? The problem throughout is that the work of transposition is overwhelmingly one-sided: much as references to "mankind" used to stand for all of "humanity," CITI uses "science" and "scientists" as neutral referents despite implying, for humanities readers at least, a load of quite particular content.

CITI offers two human-subjects research ethics training options, biomedical and social-behavioural-educational (SBE). While the 2013 CITI course catalogue asserts that "a close reading of the regulations includes research methods and topics of inquiry relevant for researchers in the social and behavioral sciences and the humanities," this is simply false. Neither the regulations themselves nor conventional guidance and training offered to IRB administrators are designed to address ethical dilemmas characteristic of "oral history," "participant observation," and other forms of interpretive social research (see below).

Not at all neutral, a particular commitment is embedded in the key definition of *research* delimiting the universe of IRB responsibilities: "a systematic investigation, including research development, testing and evaluation, designed to develop or contribute to generalizable knowledge." Within that universe, IRBs specifically oversee research involving "human subjects": a usage alien to the logics of inquiry associated with interpretive methods. *Human subject* is defined as "a living individual about whom an investigator" obtains either "data through intervention or interaction with the individual" or "identifiable private information," the accompanying examples being "venipuncture" and "medical records" (Code of Federal Regulations, 2009: 46.102d, f).

These definitions make sense in light of post–Second World War scandals, particularly those involving biomedical science experimentation.[3] The *Belmont Report* (National Commission for the Protection of Human Subjects of Biomedical and Behavioral Research, 1979) – the foundational rationale and statement of ethical principles on which human-subjects research regulations rest – is explicit about this. The *Belmont Report* begins by mapping "the boundaries between biomedical and behavioral research and the accepted and routine practice of medicine" so as to protect against the kinds of boundary breaches constituting unethical behaviour: "It is important to distinguish between biomedical and behavioral research, on the one hand, and the practice of accepted therapy on the other, in order to know what activities ought to undergo review for the protection of human subjects of research."

In other words, the regulatory concept of *research* is defined specifically in opposition to medical and psychological *therapeutic* practice: "the term 'practice' refers to interventions that are designed solely to enhance the well-being of an individual patient or client and that have a reasonable expectation of success. The purpose of medical or behavioral practice is to provide diagnosis, preventive treatment or therapy to particular individuals" (National Commission, 1979: Part A).

So much for what research is *not*. The *Belmont Report* also specifies in positive terms what research *is*: "the term 'research' designates an activity designed to test an hypothesis, permit conclusions to be drawn, and thereby to develop or contribute to generalizable knowledge (expressed, for example, in theories, principles, and statements of relationships). Research is usually described in a formal protocol that sets forth an objective and a set of procedures designed to reach that objective" (National Commission, 1979: Part A).

The language of this paragraph is echoed in the regulatory definition of research ("designed," "develop or contribute to generalizable knowledge"), albeit without important elements ("to test an hypothesis ... and thereby") that might have kept its original motivating rationale more sharply in view and helped limit the scope of its application.

In sum, the *Belmont Report* locates and buttresses the conceptual wall between two kinds of relationships on ethical grounds: *therapeutic relationships* into which persons enter with a conventional expectation that their individual care is the objective have different ethical entailments from *research relationships* into which persons enter with a conventional expectation that socially beneficial knowledge is the objective. The slippage between individual therapeutic care and social benefits, particularly as it affects participant understanding – the confusion that human-subjects research regulations address – is arguably special to the biomedical and behavioural professions.

The Ethical Value of Methodological Decisions: "Beneficence" at Issue

Medical and behavioural science references continue to pepper regulatory language, official guidance, and IRB forms, but the particularity of those references is persistently downplayed. From the beginning, the scope of human-subjects research regulation has included the social sciences (e.g., anthropology, sociology): fields in which "research" is not conventionally counterposed to therapeutic "practice" and whose ethical dilemmas do not conventionally entail guarding against research/therapy slippages. Over the past 40 years, the scope of regulation has come to encompass still more fields whose typical ethical dilemmas are distant from the historical challenges that the *Belmont Report* addresses (e.g., Gunsalus et al., 2005; Lederman, 2006a, 2006b; Schrag, 2010).

If we are concerned about the future of disciplinary pluralism, then the substantive character of regulatory standards is tremendously consequential. Bureaucratically instituted policy is both coercive and normalizing. Substantively, then, the evaluative assumptions guiding IRB assessments have remained firmly bioethical. Condensed as three philosophical principles – "respect for persons," "beneficence," and "justice" – they are framed as "basic" and "generally accepted" (National Commission, 1979: Part B).

For the future of disciplinary pluralism, the principle of "benefi-cence," which mandates risk/benefit assessments of research projects submitted to IRBs, is especially important. All other things – topical sensitivities, population vulnerabilities, circumstantial complications – being equal, IRBs are charged with evaluating the soundness of research plans. If a plan is unsound, it is presumed that there can be no research-related benefit; if there is no apparent benefit, then both researchers' and participants' time is wasted; and time wasted is harm enough to require revisions or deny approval.

In other words, in practice the principle of beneficence implies that *methodological standards* concerning competent research encode *ethical values*: that is, ethical judgments and assessments of soundness, valid-ity, and the like are internally related (mutually defining), not external to and independent of one another.

These connections are explicit in sources like the *IRB Guidebook* (Penslar and Porter, 1993), which explicates the *Belmont Report*'s bio-medical rationale for IRB professionals.[4] The *Guidebook*'s discussion of assessment – notably chapter IV, "Considerations of Research Design" – links ethical research generally to a particular methodological standard while not marking its particularity:

> One of the ethical justifications for research involving human subjects is the social value of advancing scientific understanding and promoting human welfare by improving health care. But if a research study is so methodologically flawed that little or no reliable information will result, it is unethical to put subjects at risk or even to inconvenience them through participation in such a study. One question that every IRB member asks is "To what degree is it our responsibility to review the underlying science of the proposed research?" Clearly, if it is not good science, it is not ethical.

If we read these references to "research" and to "science" as point-ing specifically to biomedical science (and generally to the history of abuses that prompted human-subjects research regulations), then it makes sense to claim that methodologically flawed research ("bad sci-ence") is unethical. Such work exposes research subjects and the con-sumers of medical treatments based on that research to the possibility of physical harm.

But if we read these references as IRBs have come to interpret them – as applicable to the varied forms of inquiry that IRBs presently oversee – then that claim makes little sense. Readers are offered no useful advice concerning how to think about the ethical challenges of research methods that do not fit the *Guidebook*'s definition of "science" but that IRBs nevertheless evaluate regularly. They are simply left to infer that investigative activities not fitting the official definition of research/science are either incompetent or unethical.

Contemporary online human-subjects ethics training courses (which US investigators must pass as a precondition for IRB approval) echo the 1993 *Guidebook*. As noted above, CITI course modules are the current training benchmark. If one consults the CITI *Arts and Humanities* course module concerning "Research Misconduct," hoping to find guidance concerning ethical standards relevant to the arts and humanities, one reads, "Advances in science, engineering and all fields of research depend on the reliability of the research record."

"Reliability" has self-evident ethico-methodological meaning[5] in the natural sciences, captured, for example, in the following definition offered by the Bioethics Education Project: "When a scientist repeats an experiment with a different group of people or a different batch of the same chemicals and gets very similar results, then those results are said to be reliable. Reliability is measured by a percentage – if you get exactly the same results every time then they are 100% reliable" (http://www.beep.ac.uk/content/573.0.html). To this way of thinking, reliability is a measure of the competent enactment and reporting of hypothesis-testing research designs involving controlled conditions: by conventional expec-tation, scientists' publications should provide colleagues with procedural information sufficient to enable the latter to replicate their results (e.g., National Academy of Sciences, 2009: 9; but see, e.g., Baker, 2015a, 2015b).

Now, social science and humanities researchers also use "reliable" as a praise word (e.g., Howell and Prevenier, 2001). However, their usage has distinctive epistemological and practical connotations not least because "research record" has a different meaning to chemists and

biomedical researchers – whose data tend to be the products of deliberately designed protocols – than it has to historians or anthropologists –
whose data are typically not produced but discovered or "found" –
oftentimes serendipitously – in the uncontrolled conditions of the
archive or of everyday life (Lederman, 2016).

Compare natural science common sense concerning reliability
(above) with reliability rephrased as "integrity," trustworthiness, and
the like and heavily qualified on epistemological grounds in the American Historical Association's *Statement on Standards of Professional Conduct (Updated 2011)*:

> Among the core principles of the historical profession that can seem
> counterintuitive to non-historians is the conviction, very widely if not
> universally shared among historians since the nineteenth century, that
> *practicing history with integrity does not mean being neutral or having no point
> of view* ... For this reason, historians often disagree and argue with each
> other. That historians can sometimes differ quite vehemently not just about
> interpretations but even about the basic facts of what happened in the
> past is sometimes troubling to non-historians, especially if they imagine
> that history consists of a universally agreed-upon accounting of stable
> facts and known certainties. But universal agreement is not a condition to
> which historians typically aspire. Instead, we understand that interpretive
> disagreements are vital to the creative ferment of our profession, and
> can in fact contribute to some of our most original and valuable insights.
> (Original emphasis)

The *Statement* echoes the perspectives of scholars in other humanities
and humanistic social studies, whose theories of knowledge are generally "interpretive" ("reflexive," "contextualizing," and the like) rather
than "positivist" or "objectivist" (the orientation underlying human-
subjects research training courses).[6]

The identification of ethical responsibility with scientific-style
research competence is reinforced as one proceeds through the various sections of the CITI *Arts and Humanities* course. I will mention just
two examples. First, the module, "Data Acquisition and Management
in the Humanities" asserts, "Data are the foundation of research and
scholarship. Accordingly, data integrity is paramount. The first step
in good data management is designing studies that create meaningful
and unbiased data, that will not waste resources, and that will protect
human and animal subjects and preserve their rights."

With regard to the data produced by one's study, it goes on to warn, "If data are not recorded in a fashion that allows others to validate findings, results can be called into question."

No particular fields of study are mentioned, so one surmises that the authors understand the terms "unbiased data" and "validate" to carry no methodological or theoretical biases. The discussion acknowledges that notions of what count as "data" varies across disciplines, but it nevertheless concludes that all disciplines face the same challenge of responsible data management. I ask readers to compare these assertions with the AHA Statement discussed a few paragraphs above.

In this CITI course section all research is reduced to the collection of facts, data, or information: for example, "information" is "collected from historical documents" or in the form of "a filled-out questionnaire." Nowhere is there a hint of recognition that this concept of data as objects collectable and analytically detachable from their sources or contexts reflects a distinctive epistemology. Nowhere is there a suggestion that other theories of knowledge might legitimately inform the investigations of researchers interested in historically and culturally situated meanings (see, e.g., Haraway, 1988; Steinmetz, 2005; Lederman, 2005).[7] In effect, one family of epistemologies and their related ontologies are presumed relevant to all scholars who pursue knowledge by interacting with their fellow humans. Scholars of a contextualizing, interpretive bent – recall, once again, the AHA *Statement* – must study these passages to pass tests in order to earn certificates necessary for IRB approval. Needless to say, this certification process does not earn these scholars' respect.

As a second example, consider again the CITI *Arts and Humanities* module that pretends to be an "arts and humanities"–relevant discussion of "Data Acquisition" while focusing entirely on statistical methodologies. Readers learn that there are choices to be made, although only one kind is offered: "For example, in research that includes a quantitative element, a key component of any protocol design will be the sample size (or 'n'). From a purely methodological perspective, the selection of 'n' hinges on how large an error one is willing to tolerate in estimating population parameters. But statistical explanatory power must be balanced against time, cost and other practical considerations, just like every other element of the protocol. Research designs with too small of an 'n' are unethical because they waste resources and are little more than anecdotal."

The presumption of quantitative analysis and absence of reference (let alone discussion) to non-positivist qualitative methods is obfuscating guidance; the omission of reference to reflexive and interpretive approaches – in an *Arts and Humanities* course no less – is downright incompetent: students and other CITI test-takers (IRB administrators, those students' advisers, etc.) are left to conclude that *not* including "a quantitative element" – that focusing research on a very small 'n': Michael Burawoy's extended cases? Clifford Geertz's thick descriptions? – shows poor methodological, therefore ethical, judgment.

Ethnographic Fieldwork Is Not "Human-Subjects Research"

A case in point, ethnographic fieldwork does not meet the regulatory criteria for science (let alone "good science") informing this influential certification course; but neither does most historical scholarship, journalism, and other knowledge-producing practices that – broadly involving "a systematic investigation" and "interactions with living persons" – have fallen under IRB jurisdiction in recent years.[8] Official resources provided to guide IRB decision-making offer no help in evaluating the methodological competence or ethical soundness of the distinctive features of these activities.

Although it is mostly classified as "social science" by universities, funders, and IRB regulatory guidance, sociocultural anthropology is decidedly anomalous for positioning ethnographic fieldwork (particularly participant observation) as its paradigmatic approach for understanding human experience.[9] For that reason, fieldwork's poor fit with the regulatory definition of "human-subjects research," discussed above, has a major disciplinary impact and reveals, by contrast, the particularity of regulatory assumptions (Lederman, 2007a).

Anthropological fieldwork involves long-term immersive contact with people in their own languages and environments. Compared with neighbouring social and behavioural sciences that rely on interviewing, focus groups, and experimental protocols (whether conducted in labs or in field settings), sociocultural anthropologists do their primary research in "uncontrolled" conditions: that is, in settings neither designed nor manipulated for systematic hypothesis-testing, and in a manner that makes it impossible to remove the investigator's fingerprints from the research record.

"Uncontrolled" is an overly general description: more precisely, among contemporary sociocultural anthropologists, being a fieldworker means putting oneself in social situations controlled by the people whose circumstances one is interested in understanding, who therefore are not so much one's "subjects" (i.e., information sources) as one's hosts, instructors, interlocutors, consultants, or collaborators. Some may become neighbours and friends – relations whose *local* ethical precepts moderate or trump the research relation itself, narrowly defined (a possibility formally acknowledged in the American Anthropological Association's ethics code). Fieldwork cannot to be planned in detail in advance. Engagement in life circumstances controlled by others gives fieldworkers insight into the full complexity of real world conditions not otherwise possible. In effect, fieldworkers trade conventional social science "reliability" for exceptional (albeit imperfect) "realism."

These representations suggest how the conversational, interactive, relationship-building character of fieldwork as a means of knowledge-making poses a distinctive set of ethical challenges.

Relatively "thin" researcher/research participant relationships (defined by the researcher) are a precondition for objectivity in mainstream social and behavioural science. Simulating a targeted slice of social reality under laboratory conditions by means of an experimental design has the advantage of approximating standardized conditions of observation (excising observer idiosyncrasies, controlling reactivity) and makes objectivity claims plausible.

In contrast, over the past hundred years, sociocultural anthropologists have become progressively sceptical about the possibility of factoring observers, their idiosyncracies, and effects out of the scene of research. Relatively "thick" (reciprocally defined) relationships are the enabling conditions for the kinds of intersubjective understanding that many anthropological fieldworkers have, particularly over the past generation, come to value. Although thick relationships are not designed to contribute to the development of statistically testable – in that sense "generalizable" – propositions, they are ideal media for critical intercultural translation. That comparative vantage is a distinctive "value-added" of ethnographic understanding.

These differences suggest why fieldworkers do not find IRB reviews to be a welcoming space for thinking through their actual ethical challenges. Anthropologists typically work in communities or subcultures different from their own; respect for community values and norms is a central precept of their professional ethics. At the same time, communities everywhere are heterogeneous and historically dynamic. Taking all that into account, good fieldwork involves the ongoing working out of acceptable compromises between the necessarily particular leanings of one's primary interlocutors, the shifting mainstream values of those people's communities, and one's own professional and personal ethics.

It follows that field researchers do well to cultivate an attentiveness to emergent conflicts inhering in their complex identities as researchers (designations they work to define) *and* social designations defined for them by their hosts, conflicts that may extend beyond fieldwork.

IRB procedures are simply not designed to address this challenge. The regulatory concept of "informed consent" is a case in point. Regulatory guidance treats "consenting" as an event necessarily occurring before research can properly begin and is attuned to the conditions for enrolling subjects in clinical trials, experiments, or surveys. Consent agreements work like contracts specifying the principle investigator/ participant relationship in terms of sets of socially thin (special purpose) expectations that are defined in advance by an investigator and agreed to by participants. As contract-like agreements, consent forms and oral consent "scripts" are discordant with the emergent character of field relationships; often enough, they are also in conflict with local norms of everyday social practice, which may favour communicative inexplicitness and indirection. Contract-like procedures are especially problematic for student fieldworkers, for whom anxiety about meeting regulatory conditions often takes centre stage, shouldering out their preparation to meet the subtler, unroutinizable ethical demands of fieldwork (see van den Scott, this volume).

Disciplinary Cultures as Distinctive Moral Orders

For all its tone-deafness concerning disciplinary differences, ethics discourse associated with research regulations (described in previous sections) is enlightening for treating research methods and ethics as internally related. Conversely, for all its sensitivity to the diversity of science practices, the literatures on disciplinarity and the academy (noted in an earlier section) pay relatively little focused attention to the ethics of research practice and the moral ordering of academic communities (but see, e.g., Shapin, 1994). Consequently, their representations of cross-disciplinary relationships are not fully adequate for understanding the workings of research ethics regimes, in which differently trained researchers come together to evaluate one another's topics and methods by means of an only nominally neutral, common standard.

These two pieces need to be fitted together.

Acknowledging the actual non-neutrality of that standard means facing the social fact that fields of human study differ in their historically elaborated ethico-methodological values.[10] Doing so opens a window on the difficulties that researchers have with ethics review boards by setting those difficulties in a wider frame. From this vantage, ethics boards are a particularly consequential – therefore particularly fraught – instance of the pervasive challenge of translating across disciplinary cultures.

We have seen how IRB members are encouraged to review applications as better or worse versions of one Standard.Model of research that fits some fields better than others. This works as a version of the not uncommon tendency, *outside* ethics board contexts, for disciplinary practitioners to mistake one another's ethico-methodological conventions as less (occasionally more) adequate versions of their own, instead of as products of partially overlapping but distinctive histories of discovery and argument.

In other words, beneath the placid pluralism evoked in this chapter's first section – the complementarities of college distribution requirements and selective gleaning of cross-disciplinary research – lurks a messier, more contentious reality (e.g., Messer-Davidow et al., 1993; Camic and Xie, 1994; Abbott, 2001; Lederman, 2004, 2016). When scholars are called upon to evaluate one another's work (book reviewing, vetting of research grants and fellowship applications, and the like), their substantive judgments do ethically loaded "boundary-work" (Gieryn, 1999) even when ethics are not overtly on the table.

Historians, for example, appreciate anthropologists' comparatively direct access to contemporary events, whereas they themselves must be content to understand the past through documents and other material traces that have survived into the present (e.g., Darnton, 1984). However, historians tend to look askance at sociocultural anthropologists' standards of evidence. Their resistance to archiving and sharing field notes, and their related habit of substituting pseudonyms for persons and places in their notes and publications, are not just *unconvincing* to many historians – they are ethically *suspect* (e.g., Kuklick, 1997).[11] What is more, from a historiographic perspective, anthropologists' apparent lack of something analogous to (historical) source criticism – their "complicity" with their field communities – likewise undermines their credibility (e.g., Clifford, 1997).

But retaining field notes as a private archive is one way that anthropologists acknowledge their responsibility to keep personal communications with their interlocutors confidential; and a degree of complicity with their hosts enacts the ethical underwriting of their knowledge claims. On their side, anthropologists have reciprocal doubts concerning historiographic practice (e.g., Murphy et al., 2011).

Recognizing that disciplinary practitioners distinguish their modes of knowledge production in an ethical idiom *outside* of the context of research ethics reviews sheds critical light on the difficulties they have *within* those contexts. In IRB deliberations, differences among board members are managed by subsuming them within the ethico-methodological Standard Model: a management strategy barely noticeable to those whose conventional investigative styles converge with that standard, but a distraction and sometime obstacle to competent, ethical research for those whose disciplinary norms diverge from it.

In a word, asserting that disciplinary pluralism takes the form of a diversity of moral orders makes explicit what ethnographers already know in practice, namely, that the regulatory standardization of research ethics promotes the standardization of knowledge production: the two are sides of a coin.

Rationalizing Difference

Bureaucratic logics play an important role in managing a diversity of disciplines as one hierarchy of ethico-methodological values. IRBs regulate research ethics, but their own operations are guided by the distinctive ethics of consistency, means-ends efficiency, and impartiality associated with bureaucratic rationality (Weber, 1992 [1930], 1978; and see e.g. Brenneis, 2005; Bledsoe et al., 2007). The principal of consistency, and the larger project of rationalization, strongly incline regulators towards abstracting research ethics from its diverse contexts of practice and towards adopting one philosophically authoritative ethical framework, presenting its principles as generic, and applying that framework equally across all fields subject to regulation.

Biomedicine is perfectly suited as a template for human "research" (the object of regulation) on account of its widely recognized cultural value. In the United States, that exemplar draws additional legitimacy from a more general privileging of the sciences over the humanities in public discourse. From this vantage, proliferating knowledge styles appear fundamentally as better and worse instances of the biomedical standard.

Ethnographers and others whose styles of investigation diverge more dramatically from the regulatory ideal have a hard time being heard. Their forms of expression do not align with the regulatory language of "recruiting and enrolling subjects" and "sampling": IRBs have terrible trouble understanding ethnographers' references to their community hosts' invitations, their "incorporation into social networks," and the like, all of which appear coy, obscure, or imprecise. The necessarily emergent character of field research – a practice of continual modification responsive to the social and ethical demands of field situations – is inconsistent with a regulatory logic of prior review of research "designs" and their modifications and of formalized consent forms or "scripts." Ethnographers are therefore faced with no-win choices: they can either misrepresent their research plans by expressing them in alien, ultimately misleading terms (an ethical dilemma itself) or they can change their practices to fit regulatory assumptions about what research and its products are or should be.

Taking the second option very seriously, Will van den Hoonaard (2011) and others have argued that research ethics regimes are flattening disciplinary landscapes. As to the first option, considerable anecdotal evidence and at least one recent survey (Wynn, 2011) suggest that many fieldworkers are going along with application checkbox categories (e.g., providing "sample sizes") while neither interpreting those categories as their designers intended nor altering their research practices. Others are flying altogether under the radar (Katz, 2006). Finding the conditions of their professional competence and responsibility precluded by regulatory assumptions, they continue fieldwork without bothering to seek ethics board approval. No matter which path they choose, ethnographers are blocked from describing their actual research plans and therefore rarely receive genuinely useful guidance from their ethics boards (see especially Wynn, 2011).

In short, fieldworkers are double-bound in research ethics reviews. Regulatory compliance entails the muting (distortion, silencing) of disciplinary values and commitments whereas abiding by standards of disciplinary competence entails the violation of regulatory norms. Ethnographers are presumed to be doing human subjects research and expected to submit to IRB reviews; but when they do so in terms that their colleagues deem methodologically competent and ethically thoughtful, they are told they are incongruent with regulatory standards. At every turn within the human-subjects research application process, there is scant space for thinking through the ethical dilemmas of ethnographic fieldwork. This is an especially destructive situation for students and novice fieldworkers.

How We Got Here and Where We May Be Headed

The form and content of research ethics regulations in the United States are products of historically particular circumstances at least as much as of philosophically principled rationales (like those articulated in the *Belmont Report*). Four decades of critical analysis, recent archival research, and publicly available policy documents show that biomedical and behavioural research controversies were and remain central. In 2011, after an extended period of turmoil and critical review, US regulators published proposals for the first general regulatory overhaul since the current system was formalized in the late 1970s/early 1980s. Social scientists were marginal players in the original design of human-subjects research regulations over forty years ago; they remain so today. I offer a sketch of where we have been to preface a discussion of where we may be headed.

By all accounts, the Nuremberg tribunal "cast a shadow" over post Second World War medical research in the United States and elsewhere. The score of controversial medical research cases brought to public attention in a widely read *New England Journal of Medicine* article (Beecher, 1966) reinforced concerns already under study within the National Institutes of Health, which had by 1965 advocated that its grant recipients submit their plans to a prior-review process modelled on one in place since the 1950s at their research hospital in Bethesda, Maryland.

By early 1966, the US surgeon general announced that recipients of Public Health Service (PHS) research grants had to undergo review before receiving funds and indicate the "potential medical benefits" of their investigations; and recipients' institutions had to file "assurances" with the PHS describing their review policies and procedures (Schrag, 2010: 25). So the medical roots of what would become the IRB system were evident well before the news about the PHS's now-notorious Tuskegee syphilis study broke (see endnote 3) and the National Research Act of 1974 was passed, authorizing the widespread establishment of Institutional Review Boards.

The ethical implications of psychological and psychiatric research also troubled members of the US Congress, who were worried about the "invasion of privacy" implications of personality testing, among other things; questions were also raised about survey questionnaire research. But although the executive director of the American Psychological Association was called to testify at Congressional hearings, no social scientists were summoned (Schrag, 2010: 20–7).

This highly selective solicitation of advice became a pattern. The intention to include the social sciences under IRB oversight – explicit at the federal level since the 1960s – has been documented (see especially Schrag, 2010). Nevertheless, social scientists were mostly absent from the panels convened to develop and implement human-subjects research regulations. The key agents were biomedical researchers and practitioners, philosophers (especially bioethicists), and legal scholars, together with a few behavioural scientists: they developed the original NIH policies of the 1950s and 1960s; they advised in the drafting of the original 1974 legislation that still authorizes the administrative elaborations and revisions of IRB regulations; they populated the National Commission responsible for the *Belmont Report*; and they dominated all subsequent panels, commissions, and advisory committees convened to collect information and propose regulatory improvements. This pattern of inclusion and exclusion remained in place during the development of proposals for the first general overhaul of the Common Rule,[12] which were issued for public commentary in preliminary form in 2011 and in near final form in 2015 (as this volume was going to press).

The social sciences and humanities had their own histories of ethical controversy. From the 1950s to the 1970s, the American Anthropological Association, American Political Science Association, American Psychological Association, American Sociological Association, Oral History Association, and other scholarly professional societies either revised or developed formal ethics codes and case material for ethics education. Much of this intensive multidisciplinary thinking about research ethics took place *before* passage of the National Research Act of 1974; nevertheless, it had virtually no impact on the development of human subjects protections, which were adapted ready-made from existing NIH guidance.

Since 1999–2000, for reasons amply described elsewhere, IRBs have experienced what many critics have called "mission creep" (Gunsalus et al., 2005; Lederman, 2006b). The elasticity of the regulatory definitions of "human subject" and "research" has allowed (or propelled)

IRBs to extend their oversight to fields never intended by the authors of the *Belmont Report*: oral historians, journalists, and even creative writing professors have been affected. The expansion of this homogenizing impulse has engendered widespread frustration, anxiety, distrust and disrespect among researchers, with no compensatory ethical benefits for research participants.

Mounting IRB workloads and deepening discontent among researchers of all kinds (including biomedical and behavioral scientists) prompted the formation of commissions and the holding of hearings throughout the 1990s, but especially since 2000. This activity culminated, after a fashion, in July 2011 when the US Department of Health and Human Services and Office of Human Research Protections published an Advance Notice of Proposed Rulemaking (ANPRM).[13] Entitled "Human Subjects Research Protections: Enhancing Protections for Research Subjects and Reducing Burden, Delay, and Ambiguity for Investigators," this ANPRM attributed the expanding workloads of IRBs to an objective increase in the volume and diversity of research.

That increase was part of the problem. However, this diagnosis ignored how the fundamental ambiguity of the regulations *itself* engendered "mission creep," another significant reason for IRBs' mounting workloads. As the American Anthropological Association commentary put it, "The vagueness and generality of the regulatory object invites ever-broadening and variable interpretations by IRBs, which are understandably cautious lest their decisions fail to pass muster with federal auditors."[14]

Instead of directly addressing the ambiguity built into the definitions of "research" and "human subject" that delimit the rule's applicable scope, the ANPRM proposed a new category of "excused" research defined as posing only "informational" risks (i.e., adverse effects attendant on the unintentional release of personally identifiable private information). Research falling into this class would be removed from direct IRB oversight and could commence once investigators file a one-page registration form; however, "data analysis" could not begin until privacy protection measures were taken. Insofar as the ANPRM implied that most social science research procedures (e.g., interviewing, observation) would be eligible for excusal, this proposal appeared to liberate ethnographers and others from administrative burdens entailed in the existing review process.

However, the proposed data privacy protections making excusal thinkable were not devised to accommodate the varieties of work that were likely to meet the new "informational" risk criteria. *True to Common Rule history*, the ANPRM adopted them ready-made from a medical source: in this case, the Health Insurance Portability and Accountability Act (HIPAA). HIPAA privacy standards are designed to protect the confidentiality of health records: they mandate the stripping of personally identifiable private information from medical records before they can be used in research.

Not surprisingly, commentary across the behavioural and social sciences and humanities overwhelmingly opposed this idea. Needless to say, historians – who not infrequently write about living persons – cannot anonymize their narratives and be taken seriously within and outside their profession. For their parts, while anthropologists and other ethnographers have traditionally tried to protect the privacy of their consultants through the use of pseudonyms, ethnographies (like histories) hinge on contextual specificity. De-identifying or anonymizing ethnographic data would render them unusable; in any event, those traditions have been changing with the rising popularity of participatory action research, collaborations between ethnographers and their host communities, and research among scientific and financial elites, among other trends.

Of the host of other problems, I will mention just two. First, the ANPRM presumed a distinction between data collection and data analysis. That distinction makes no sense for ethnographers, for whom "analysis" – that is, the interpretive contextualization of observations, conversations, and the rest – begins during fieldwork in the very process of writing field notes, a point recognized in the American Anthropological Association's website statement on the confidentiality of field materials (http://www.aaanet.org/stmts/fieldnotes.htm). Second, while data anonymization may be feasible in relationship-thin research styles (like surveys and experiments), it is impossible in fieldwork. Genuine anonymization (when investigators themselves cannot re-identify research participants) is impossible when field notes are products of long-term interactions between researchers and their consultants.

As outlined in endnote 13, the 2015 NPRM was more narrowly focused than the preliminary 2011 proposals for regulatory revision and, by some measures, it was less ambitious. For example, unlike the 2011 proposals, the NPRM did not propose a sweeping category of "exclusions" defined in a principled manner around "informational risk" (the overwhelmingly negative response to its related proposal for using HIPAA protocols to manage informational risk precluded that course of action). However, it is also far more deeply and elaborately focused on pressing problems relating to biomedical research: particularly those relating to the ethical management and control of biospecimens – a growing cross-disciplinary research focus – in response to recent revelations of research abuses (see e,g., http://www.nytimes.com/2010/04/22/us/22dna.html?pagewanted=all&_r=0). While this focus is sure to be controversial, it is also well developed; in contrast, references to interpretive social research and the humanities lack anything remotely like a principled rationale.

I cannot do justice to these complex proposals here. My central point in mentioning them in this context is simple: as of this writing, the process of regulatory overhaul has reproduced the very pattern of exclusion that engendered the problems this chapter describes. The social sciences and humanities have remained largely outside the deliberative rethinking of the Common Rule while remaining both implicitly and explicitly subject to them; and the ethico-epistemological framework informing and informed by biomedical practice has continued to be treated as a neutral standard for evaluating all human research.

Conclusion: Solutions?

Fieldworkers and other qualitative social researchers have found themselves double-bound by the present regime of research ethics oversight. Compliance has generally required the muting of disciplinary differences. The situation is eerily similar to the communicative distortions experienced by racial minorities and women, whose experiences and expressive forms are misinterpreted and devalued in majority-cultural contexts: when forced into these contexts, they adopt the dominant communicative code while leading double lives, a costly effort.

The existing hierarchy of values disproportionately stifles fieldwork. Obtaining IRB approval has meant either abandoning the methods and approaches in which one was trained; or holding onto them while filling out applications that misrepresent what one will be doing; or avoiding such misrepresentations by simply not applying.

The point is not that social science and humanities researchers desire freedom from ethical deliberation. On the contrary, this chapter has argued that disciplinary communities are moral orders: individual professional competence and collective professional identities are framed in ethical terms. Over the past 60 years, anthropologists, sociologists, historians, and other human science communities have crafted and revised formal principles and codes of conduct, developed case materials concerning ethical dilemmas, trained novice practitioners, and in various ways, investigated and sanctioned their members' transgressions.

The point instead is that recognition of the ethico-epistemological diversity of human research is an essential basis for any viable ethics policy. Diversity denied, present policy undermines social research training and knowledge production *without* improving ethical practice.

The revised regulatory code will need to articulate a principled recognition of the plurality of answers to the central question of how ethical research is conducted, taught and promoted. For example, the American Anthropological Association's ANPRM commentary noted that "the need for ethical review to be 'multidisciplinary and pluralist' is recognized in Article 19 of the Universal Declaration on Bioethics and Human Rights" and, on that basis, advocated the formation of a new national commission like the one that drafted the *Belmont Report*, only this time composed of social scientists, interpretive social researchers, and humanities scholars.

That plan may neither be realistic nor preferable. In any case, scholarly professional associations and educational organizations ought to take more visible action in supporting, promoting, and publicizing the epistemologically plural character of research ethics. Meanwhile, researchers and administrators ought to make common cause by supporting initiatives like those of the Flexibility Coalition that highlight the leeway in the existing rules.[15] Researchers should also actively "educate their IRBs" (Lederman, 2007b; Wynn, 2011). By joining their boards, getting to know administrative staff, and listening to colleagues' ways of reading one another's applications, they should work towards reciprocal cross-disciplinary translations of ethico-methodological values to improve mutual understanding.

Mutual understanding would serve another end as well. I argued above that whatever solutions or fixes we come up with will be limited if we treat regulatory ethics as an isolated problem. More effective interventions need to take serious account of the wider intellectual landscape of ethical and methodoological value hierarchies within which regulatory regimes are just one part.

NOTES

This chapter is an expanded version of a talk presented at "Ethics Rupture: an Invitational Summit about Alternatives to Research-Ethics Review" convened by Will C. van den Hoonaard, in October 2012, at Fredericton, New Brunswick. I thank Will and the other participants for enlightening exchanges before, during, and after the event. I thank Will in particular for his boundless editorial patience and kindness.

1 A first version of these regulations was adopted directly from guidance developed in the 1960s by the US National Institutes of Health (NIH), and revised in the late 1970s/early 1980s (see generally Schrag 2010). Official US Health and Human Services guidance to IRBs is issued and regularly updated by the Office of Human Research Protections (http://www.hhs.gov/ohrp/index.html).

2 As a non-normative methodology in most social and behavioural science disciplines, fieldwork is not infrequently represented as inherently unethical (e.g., for sociology see Bosk, 2001). In contrast, sociocultural anthropology situates fieldwork as its mainstream mode of understanding human lives. It has a correspondingly robust and complex discourse on the ethical value of fieldwork (e.g., Lederman, 2013; Lambek, 2010; Pels, 1999).

3 In the United States, the Public Health Service's 40 year-long Tuskegee syphilis study stands out because its public exposure in 1972 by the Associated Press was the proximate cause prompting passage of the National Research Act of 1974: the legislative mandate for human-subjects research regulations and for the establishment of ethics review boards at institutions that accept US federal research funding. Briefly, in Tuskegee, Alabama beginning in 1932, the Public Health Service embarked on a study of the long-term course of untreated syphilis, originally recruiting 399 mostly uneducated African-American men with latent syphilis (together with a syphilis-free control group of 201). The experimental character of this study was not revealed to participants, who were led to believe that they were receiving therapeutic treatment for what was locally referred to as "bad blood" (a term covering a wide range of ailments including syphilis: Jones 1993 [1981]). While they were offered free medical exams and general care, meals, and other incentives for remaining in the study, they were never informed of their actual health status. More to the point, the study continued for two and a half decades after the mid-1940s when penicillin became the standard therapy for syphilis. The men were not offered this effective treatment (indeed, they were blocked from

accessing it: ibid.) until the study was made public, by which time many of them and their family members had suffered grievous harm or had died. In this case, research was enabled by an egregious abuse of trust in the form of false promises of personal medical care.

4 The Office of Human Research Protections (OHRP) provides and continually updates many kinds of guidance for IRB administrators; the *IRB Guidebook* is presently available on the OHRP website and still used despite a website warning that some of its advice may be outdated (http://www.hhs.gov/ohrp/archive/irb/irb_guidebook.htm).

5 I apologize for this ugly neologism (and its variant, ethico-epistemological): I mean it to communicate the internal or constitutive relation of ethics and formal ways of knowing also captured by calling disciplines "moral orders" (Lederman, 2004).

6 There are anthropologists, historians, and other humanities scholars who subscribe to positivist epistemologies; there is, however, an undeniably different distribution of interpretive and positivist leanings as one moves between humanistic and natural science scholarship.

7 Much more could be said about the philosophical orientations embedded in CITI training modules and their alternatives. This chapter points emphatically to the existence of those alternatives and suggests why such acknowledgment is important, but does not pretend to provide an adequate discussion.

8 But see below: proposals for a comprehensive revision of the regulations governing IRB activities, published in September 2015 in the *Federal Register* (official journal of the US federal government), would explicitly "exclude" journalism, biography, oral history, and historical scholarship from IRB oversight. Ethnographic fieldwork is nowhere mentioned in these proposed revisions despite its many relevant similarities with journalistic and historiographic activities.

9 As noted in n2 above, other disciplines harbouring ethnographers do not position fieldwork at their methodological cores. For example, sociology's fieldworking traditions in the US and UK are as long-standing as anthropology's. Nevertheless, sociology is dominated by heavily positivist sample survey research. Practicing a non-normative research style in their discipline, ethnographic sociologists are constrained to "warrant" fieldwork relative to that mainstream (e.g., Katz, 1997). In contrast, ethnographers are the norm in sociocultural anthropology, where fieldwork is warranted on its own terms: I present the anthropological view in this section.

10 Attending to the cross-field variability of ethical values appears to conjure the spectral figure of "relativism" exactly where it is most unwelcome (e.g.,

Durkheim, 1982). Unmasking that effect requires extended attention for which there is no room in this chapter.

11 The American Historical Association's *Statement on Standards of Professional Conduct (Updated 2011)* condenses the point this way: "Honoring the historical record also means *leaving a clear trail for subsequent historians to follow*" (original emphasis).

12 IRB regulations (technically 45 CFR 46), in their present form by 1981, have been referred to as the "Common Rule" since 1991 when 17 US federal agencies joined the Department of Health and Human Services in adopting or applying one "policy for the protection of human subjects" (http://www.hhs.gov/ohrp/humansubjects/commonrule/).

13 ANPRMs are an optional stage in the process whereby federal regulations are developed. Generally, federal agencies are obligated to publish Notices of Proposed Rulemaking (NPRMs) in the *Federal Register* so as to solicit public commentary on drafts of new rules before finalizing them (although there is no formula for how agencies must evaluate the comments elicited by their proposals). In this case, the NPRM – with a related but significantly different set of proposals compared with those made public in 2011 – was finally published in the *Federal Register* in September 2015. As this book went to press, the public commentary period was still open and the final rule was not expected for another year or more.

If anything, biomedical concerns (especially in the context of new information-security challenges posed by transformations in communication technologies and by emergent social norms around the sharing of "personal" information in partially "public" virtual spaces) were even more prominent in the 2015 version of the proposed rule than in the 2011 version. For example, partly in response to public ethical controversies relating to the unconsented research uses of biological materials (e.g., blood samples), the proposed rule would expand the definition of "human subject" to include "biospecimen." Language concerning the conditions for storage and future research access to biospecimens originally obtained for non-research purposes (that is, taken in the course of an individual's medical care) was pervasive in the 2015 NPRM.

Nevertheless, in response to objections received during the ANPRM commentary period and afterwards (among others), the 2015 NPRM also opened the possibility of the explicit exclusion of humanities approaches (like oral history, biography, and journalism) from these regulations, although it remains to be seen whether or not this innovation will remain in the final rule. Despite this constructive opening, ethnographic fieldwork

was nowhere named in the 2015 proposals: true to the form, the proposed
rule is entirely unclear concerning how IRB administrators should think
about fieldwork relative either to other interpretive approaches (e.g.,
history, journalism) or to hypothesis-testing bio/behavioral and social
science research (e.g., clinical trials, psychology experiments, sample
surveys).

14 Lise Dobrin (University of Virginia) and I co-authored the American
Anthropological Association commentary on behalf of its Committee
on Ethics and in consultation with colleagues representing different
disciplinary interests (http://www.aaanet.org/issues/policy-advocacy/
Protecting-Human-Subjects.cfm).

15 In the US, many institutions accepting federal funding have declined
to apply the regulations to the non-federally funded research of their
members, an option popularly referred to as "unchecking the box"
(http://www.institutionalreviewblog.com/2009/07/aahrpp-and-
unchecked-box.html). The "Flexibility Coalition," a national coalition
of institutions participating in such initiatives, was formed in 2011 and
currently includes more than 50 research organizations, including the
Association for the Accreditation of Human Research Protection Programs
(AAHRPP).

REFERENCES

Abbott, Andrew. (2001). *The Chaos of Disciplines*. Chicago: University of
Chicago Press.

American Historical Association. *Statement on Standards of Professional Conduct
(Updated 2011)*. http://www.historians.org/about-aha-and-membership/
governance/policies-and-documents/statement-on-standards-of-
professional-conduct.

Ardener, Edwin. (2007). *The Voice of Prophesy and Other Essays*. Oxford:
Berghahn.

Baker, Monya. (2015a). "First Results from Psychology's Largest
Reproducibility Test." *Nature.* http://www.nature.com/news/first-results-
from-psychology-s-largest-reproducibility-test-1.17433

– (2015b). "Irreproducible Biology Research Costs Estimated at $28 Billion
Per Year." *Nature.* http://www.nature.com/news/irreproducible-biology-
research-costs-put-at-28-billion-per-year-1.17711

Beecher, Henry K. (1966). "Ethics and Clinical Research." *New England
Journal of Medicine* 274 (24): 1354–60. http://dx.doi.org/10.1056/
NEJM196606162742405

Bledsoe, Caroline H., Bruce Sherin, Adam G. Gallinsky, Nathalia M. Headley, Carol A. Heimer, Erik Kjeldgaard, James Lindgren, Jon D. Miller, Michael E. Roloff, and David E. Uttal. (2007). "Regulating Creativity: Research and Survival in the IRB Iron Cage." *Northwestern University Law Review* 101 (2): 593–641.

Boix-Mansilla, Veronica, and Howard Gardner. (1997). "Kinds of Disciplines and Kinds of Understanding." *Phi Delta Kappan* (Jan.): 381–6.

Bosk, Charles. (2001). "Irony, Ethnography, and Informed Consent." In Barry Hoffmaster (ed.), *Bioethics in Social Context*, 199–200. Philadelphia: Temple University Press.

Brenneis, Donald. (1994). "Discourse and Discipline at the National Research Council: A Bureaucratic Bildungsroman." *Cultural Anthropology* 9 (1): 23–36. http://dx.doi.org/10.1525/can.1994.9.1.02a00020

– (2005). "Documenting Ethics." In Lynn Meskell and Peter Pels (eds.), *Embedding Ethics: Shifting Boundaries of the Anthropological Profession*, 239–52. Oxford: Berg.

Camic, Charles, and Yu Xie. (1994). "The Statistical Turn in American Social Science: Columbia University, 1890 to 1915." *American Sociological Review* 59 (5): 773–805. http://dx.doi.org/10.2307/2096447

Clifford, James. (1997). "Spatial Practices: Fieldwork, Travel, and the Disciplining of Anthropology." In Akhil Gupta and James Ferguson (eds.), *Anthropological Locations*, 185–222. Berkeley: University of California Press.

Code of Federal Regulations. (2009). Title 45 "Public Welfare, Department of Health and Human Services," Part 46 "Protection of Human Subjects." http://www.hhs.gov/ohrp/humansubjects/guidance/45cfr46.html

Creager, Angela, Elizabeth Lunbeck, and M. Norton Wise (eds.). (2007). *Science without Laws: Model Systems, Cases, Exemplary Narratives.* Durham, NC: Duke University Press. http://dx.doi.org/10.1215/9780822390244

Darnton, Robert. (1984). *The Great Cat Massacre.* New York: Basic Books.

Durkheim, Émile. (1982). *The Rules of the Sociological Method.* Edited by Steven Lukes, translated by W.D. Halls. New York: Free Press.

Galison, Peter, and David J. Stump (eds.). (1996). *The Disunity of Science: Boundaries, Contexts, and Power.* Stanford, CA: Stanford University Press.

Gieryn, Thomas. (1999). *Cultural Boundaries of Science: Credibility on the Line.* Chicago: University of Chicago Press.

Gunsalus, C. Kristina, Edward Bruner, Nicholas C. Burbules, Leon Dash, Matthew Finkin, Joseph P. Goldberg, William T. Greenough, Gregory A. Miller, Michael G. Pratt, and Deb Aronson. (2005). "Improving the System for Protecting Human Subjects: Counteracting IRB 'Mission Creep.'" *The*

Illinois White Paper. University of Illinois at Urbana-Champaign, College of Law.

Haraway, Dona. (1988). "Situated Knowledges: The Science Question in Feminism and the Privilege of Partial Perspective." *Feminist Studies* 14(3): 575–599.

Health and Human Services. (2011). "Human Subjects Research Protections: Enhancing Protections for Research Subjects and Reducing Burden, Delay, and Ambiguity for Investigators." Advance Notification of Proposed Rulemaking. Federal Register 76 (07/26/2011): 44512–44531. http://www.gpo.gov/fdsys/pkg/FR-2011-07-26/pdf/2011-18792.pdf

Howell, Martha C., and Walter Prevenier. (2001). *From Reliable Sources: An Introduction to Historical Methods.* Ithaca, NY: Cornell University Press.

Jones, James H. (1993 [1981]). *Bad Blood: The Tuskegee Syphilis Experiment* (rev. ed.). New York: Free Press.

Katz, Jack. (1997). "Ethnography's Warrants." *Sociological Methods & Research* 25 (4): 391–423. http://dx.doi.org/10.1177/0049124197025004002

– (2006). "Ethical Escape Routes for Underground Ethnographers." *American Ethnologist* 33 (4): 499–506. http://dx.doi.org/10.1525/ae.2006.33.4.499

Klein, Julie Thompson. (1996). *Crossing Boundaries: Knowledge, Disciplinarities, and Interdisciplinarities.* Charlottesville, VA: University of Virginia Press.

Knorr-Cetina, Karin. (1999). *Epistemic Cultures: How the Sciences Make Knowledge.* Cambridge, MA: Harvard University Press.

Kuhn, Thomas. (1970) [1962]). *The Structure of Scientific Revolutions.* 2nd enlarged ed. Chicago: University of Chicago Press.

Kuklick, Henrika. (1997). "After Ishmael: The Fieldwork Tradition and Its Future." In Akhil Gupta and James Ferguson (eds.), *Anthropological Locations*, 47–65 Berkeley: University of California Press.

Lambek, Michael (ed.). (2010). *Ordinary Ethics: Anthropology, Language, and Action.* New York: Fordham University Press.

Latour, Bruno, and Steve Woolgar. (1979). *Laboratory Life: The Construction of Scientific Facts.* Princeton, NJ: Princeton University Press.

Lederman, Rena. (2004). "Towards an Anthropology of Disciplinarity." In David Ball (ed.), *Disciplines and Disciplinarity: Critical Matrix* 15 (Special Issue), 61–75.

– (2005). "Unchosen Ground: Cultivating Cross-Subfield Accents for a Public Voice." In Dan Segal and Sylvia Yanagisako (eds.), *Unwrapping the Sacred Bundle*, 49–77. Durham, NC: Duke University Press. http://dx.doi.org/10.1215/9780822386841-003

– (2006a). "Introduction: Anxious Borders between Work and Life in a Time of Bureaucratic Ethics Regulation." *AE Forum, American Ethnologist* 33 (4): 477–81. http://dx.doi.org/10.1525/ae.2006.33.4.477

– (2006b). "The Perils of Working at Home: IRB 'Mission Creep' as Context and Content for an Ethnography of Disciplinary Knowledges." *AE Forum, American Ethnologist* 33 (4): 482–91. http://dx.doi.org/10.1525/ae.2006.33.4.482

– (2007a). "Comparative 'Research': A Modest Proposal Concerning the Object of Ethics Regulation." *PoLAR: The Political and Legal Anthropology Review* 30 (2): 305–27. http://dx.doi.org/10.1525/pol.2007.30.2.305

– (2007b). "Educate Your IRB: An Experiment in Cross-disciplinary Communication." *Anthropology News* 48 (6): 33–4. http://dx.doi.org/10.1525/an.2007.48.6.33

– (2013). "Ethics: Practices, Principles, and Comparative Perspectives." In James Carrier and Deborah Gewertz (eds.), *Handbook of Social and Cultural Anthropology*, 588–611. London: Bloomsbury

– (2016). "Archiving Fieldnotes? Placing Anthropological Records Among Plural Digital Worlds." In Roger Sanjek and Susan Tratner (eds.). *eFieldnotes: Makings of Anthropology in a Digital World*. Philadelphia: University of Pennsylvania Press.

Messer-Davidow, Ellen, David R. Shumway, and David J. Sylvan (eds.). (1993). *Knowledges: Historical and Critical Studies in Disciplinarity*. Charlottesville, VA: University of Virginia Press.

Murphy, Edward, and David William Cohen. Chandra D Bhimull et al. (eds.). (2011). *Anthrohistory: Unsettling Knowledge, Questioning Discipline*. Ann Arbor: University of Michigan Press.

National Academy of Sciences. (2009). *On Being a Scientist*. 3rd ed. Washington, DC: National Academies Press.

National Commission for the Protection of Human Subjects of Biomedical and Behavioral Research. (1979). *The Belmont Report*. http://www.hhs.gov/ohrp/humansubjects/guidance/belmont.html

Pels, Peter. (1999). "Professions of Duplexity: A Prehistory of Ethics Codes in Anthropology." *Current Anthropology* 40 (2): 101–36. http://dx.doi.org/10.1086/200001

Penslar, Robin Levin, with Joan P. Porter. (1993). *Institutional Review Board Guidebook*. Washington, DC: Office of Human Research Protections, Department of Health and Human Services. http://www.hhs.gov/ohrp/archive/irb/irb_guidebook.htm

Russell, David. (2002). *Writing in the Academic Disciplines: A Curricular History*. 2nd ed. Carbondale: Southern Illinois University Press.

Shapin, Steve. (1994). *A Social History of Truth: Civility and Science in Seventeenth-Century England*. Chicago: University of Chicago Press.

Schrag, Zachary. (2010). *Ethical Imperialism: Institutional Review Boards and the Social Sciences, 1965–2009*. Baltimore: Johns Hopkins University Press.

Steinmetz, George (ed.). (2005). *The Politics of Method in the Human Sciences: Positivism and Its Epistemological Others.* Durham, NC: Duke University Press. http://dx.doi.org/10.1215/9780822386889

van den Hoonaard, Will C. (2011). *The Seduction of Ethics: Transforming the Social Sciences.* Toronto: University of Toronto Press.

Weber, Max. (1992) [1930]. *The Protestant Ethic and the Spirit of Capitalism.* Translated by Talcott Parsons, introduction by Anthony Giddens. New York: Routledge.

– (1978). *Economy and Society: An Outline of Interpretive Sociology.* Translated by Guenther Roth. Berkeley: University of California.

Wilson, E.O. (1999). *Consilience: The Unity of Knowledge.* New York: Vintage.

Wynn, Lisa. (2011). "Ethnographers' Experiences of Institutional Ethics Oversight: Results from a Quantitative and Qualitative Survey." *Journal of Policy History* 23(1): 94–114.

3 IRBan Renewal

PATRICIA A. ADLER AND PETER ADLER

Although regulatory research boards, at one time called Committees for the Regulation of Research or Human Subjects Committees, now called Institutional Review Boards (IRBs) in the United States and Research Ethics Boards (REBs) in Canada, have been around in some form since the 1960s and 1990s, respectively, their scope and power has expanded considerably from their early days. Nearly everyone is familiar with the cases of medical, biological, and psychological research that caused outrage in the public and scholarly communities for which these safeguards were deemed necessary. However, as is often the case, ethics review boards, nestled within academic and governmental bureaucracies, have followed the sociologically well-known tendency to sustain themselves and grow by entrenching and expanding their mission and reach.

There has been a surge of interest in the first decades of the twenty-first century examining the history of research regulation and its transformation from an early focus on the protection of human subjects into an accountability regime of Orwellian oversight, as people have become increasingly concerned about the encroachment of what Zachary Schrag (2010) terms "ethical imperialism" into the social sciences. Scholars have documented the growth and evolution of research regulation from its origins in screening funded medical and psychological research in the US Public Health Service in 1966, to its expansion into the social sciences steered by the US Department of Health, Education, and Welfare following the National Research Act of 1974, being modified and made more "lenient" by a 1978 national commission design to reduce inappropriate IRB oversight, to the beginning of its great period of expansion starting in the late 1990s led by the Office for Protection from Research Risks (see, among others, Dingwall, 2012; Katz, 2007; Schrag, 2010; Swartz, 2007; White, 2007). During this period we have witnessed the rise of the *Belmont Report* and the Common Rule, which have mandated a growing set of checklists designed to promote a zero risk – and therefore impossible – standard for research.

These ethical guidelines, initially developed to assess and to regulate research using experimental design and epistemology, have proved increasingly problematic as they have been extended into the social sciences. Hardest hit by the disjuncture between the vocabulary and framework of these ethical templates and the hypothetico-deductive orientation they are built on has been the domain of field research, or ethnography, with its fundamentally inductive approach. A range of scholars from fields as diverse as anthropology, sociology, education, political science, communication, history, legal studies, urban studies, environmental studies, public health, and others have decried the way ethnographic research has been inappropriately and overly critiqued, misjudged, restricted, and even eliminated by the omniscient claw of these ethics review boards (cf. Annas, 2006; Flicker et al., 2007; Lederman, 2006; McGrath et al., 2009; Swartz, 2007; and Yanow and Schwartz-Shea, 2008).

Because entities such as these Institutional Review Boards have become so powerful and potentially misguided as to impair the acquisition of valuable knowledge about what people do, as opposed to merely what they say, Robert Dingwall (2007) has issued a clarion call for researchers to challenge their legitimacy by exposing their capriciousness, censorship, and ultimately restriction of valuable field research. Malcolm Feeley (2007) urges scholars, particularly those senior in their fields, to take the time to address this issue of central importance, not only to scholars but to the policymakers and public who rely on sound knowledge. In this chapter we add our voices to those of others who care about the importance of first-rate research. We begin by reviewing some of the problems of IRBs, offer some comments on ad hoc evasion techniques, and close with recommendations for more programmatic changes to IRB policies and procedures.

Problems of IRBs

In an earlier collection of essays on research ethics review (van den Hoonaard, 2002) we discussed some of the problems we saw with how research regulation was progressing, becoming more restrictive and capricious in myriad ways (Adler and Adler, 2002). Since that time these problems have intensified in both scope and intensity. Let us summarize some of these, adding our thoughts as we go through them.

One of the most pervasive problems noted in the literature stems from the fact that the ethics review policies continue to be rooted in an experimental design model of research (Feeley, 2007; Flicker at al., 2007; Lederman, 2006; McGrath et al., 2009; Swartz, 2007; van den Hoonaard, 2002; Yanow and Schwartz-Shea, 2008). These policies foster an orientation, and usually a checklist, geared towards a hypothetico-deductive epistemology where the beginnings and ends of research are clearly delineated and known in advance, where research foci and goals are set before data gathering begins, where the costs and benefits can be more easily anticipated, where the location of research can be controlled, and where the literature and the contribution of the research to that literature can be pre-specified. None of these descriptions apply to field research, with its inductive nature, where settings, conceptual concerns, research subjects, location, costs, benefits, and the relationships between researchers and the people they study progressively emerge over the course of a study. This is precisely the beauty of ethnography, and what makes it an invaluable component in the overall research toolkit. It eschews the context of verification, embracing instead the creative context of discovery. Yet these features make filling out an IRB application particularly difficult and make members of IRBs more familiar with the precision of advancing knowledge uncomfortable with ethnography. Based on her experience of sitting on her university's IRB, Rena Lederman (2006) went as far as to allege that her fellow IRB members regarded the practice of ethnography as something "shady" or "disreputable," and tension often filled the room when issues of "cross-disciplinary conflict" arose between the more normative epistemologies and the ethical concerns common to psychological or survey research and ethnographic proposals.

Several people at the 2012 "Ethics Rupture" Summit have discussed the way IRB members have taken it upon themselves to evaluate the strength of a field research design as one component of its review process, making judgments about its epistemological strengths and significance (Denzin and Giardina, 2006; Feeley, 2007; Katz, 2007; Lincoln, 2006; Swartz, 2007; Yanow and Schwartz-Shea, 2008). This is particularly dangerous not only because it over-reaches the ostensible purpose of IRB assessments, but because the people engaged in this exercise are likely unqualified to make these judgments. Scholars lodge the review of research for grants, articles, and books in the hands of experts specially trained in their substantive and methodological fields with proven track records of knowledge. In contrast, IRB members are non-specialists who typically rotate every three years when their terms expire. As such, not only do they lose the institutional knowledge of experience, but also representation on these kinds of ethics boards by qualitative researchers is rare (Lederman, 2006). Lacking adequate expertise or training, these individuals are left to assess proposals according to the indices, standards, or opinions they possess. We and our students are routinely asked to list, for example, the precise questions we will ask research subjects, when participant-observation or an in-depth life history interview more closely resembles a conversation than an interrogation. And our efforts to convince IRB members to accept instead a list of topics with which subjects would be engaged have met with argument from them about proper methodological practices for research.

The IRB policies and procedures are, by design, decentralized; board members are left to "interpret" how rules should be applied at the local level. Although this may offer the flexibility of avoiding a cumbersome array of federal regulations, it leaves a wide leeway among the decisions made between different countries, states, and even schools – and even the same school over (sometimes incredibly short periods of) time. Indeed, as Yanow and Schwartz-Shea (2008), Dingwall (2007), and others have noted, it is not uncommon for multisited research to be approved in one location while the same plan is rejected at another. This problem also occurs with co-authored research, a situation even more common than multisited field research.

Issues of creative interpretation and the solutions that these local ethics review boards manufacture are sometimes resolved in ways that make no sense. For example, over several years of studying self-injury for our recent book, *The Tender Cut: Inside the Hidden World of Self-Injury* (Adler and Adler, 2011), our access to interviewing minors (the largest demographic of the active population) was progressively restricted. What started as a standard requirement that we obtain parental consent and minor assent (a difficulty from the start as many minors hide this behaviour from their parents) was modified over the years to require two parental signatures (even though many in our often Internet-generated population lacked two parents), to requiring our ability somehow to "verify" the parental status of these distant consenting parents, to finally requiring that we state in our consent form that when we found parents who failed to take "appropriate action" following the discovery of their child's self-injury we would have to "report" them.

Aside from the moral issues surrounding threatening people who were trying to help us with punitive action – which might actually endanger our research subjects rather than protect them – this presented us with some serious practical problems of interpretation. For one, it was unclear what "appropriate action" meant. Did we need to ascertain if parents who discovered their children's self-injury checked them into a clinic or hospital, if they sent them to a psychiatrist, if they got them psychiatric medications, or might it be just enough for them to sit down and have a conversation about it with their children? Second, we were mystified by the reporting requirement. To whom should we report this absence of response: the police, some social service agency, the agents of self-injury control? This round of the required yearly revision convinced us formally to abandon our near moribund willingness to accept minors into our study and further alienated us from the concept of research ethics regulation. But even worse, such measures, as Didier Fassin (2006) has noted, are really so far afield from what ethnographers, situated in the field, know are the really important types of protections that research subjects need. Fassin suggests that the current system of research regulation "threatens ethnography by proposing lazy responses to real needs and, thus, avoids the more painful moral and political questions sociologists and anthropologists should deal with" (524).

Perhaps the most problematic and pervasively noted complaint about IRBs is their expansion of their scope (cf. Dingwall, 2007; Feeley, 2007; Katz, 2007; Lederman, 2006; Swartz, 2007), alternately referred to as "mission creep" (Lederman, 2006; White, 2007) or "mission drift" (Swartz, 2007). Philip Hamburger (2004) refers to the vast and expanded "licensing authority" that IRBs seem to have acquired. This is not only clear in its fact, but also ominous in what it portends. These boards have quantitatively and qualitatively absorbed more kinds of inquiry into their domain, they have made standards for researchers tighter while the procedural restraints governing the boards themselves have been relaxed, and they have expanded their authority.

For example, in 2002 we decried the tendency of ongoing research that had been labelled exempt to become expedited while expedited projects were redefined as needing full committee review. But since that time more projects have been defined as simply unresearchable, and IRBs have begun to micro-manage research projects in many more ways. Indeed, whole areas of study, such as oral history, have been incorporated as falling under their jurisdiction. The moral entrepreneurial tendency of such boards was evident when one of our students performing a routine norm violation assignment for a deviance class travelled to another school to stand in their "free speech" circle and talk about sado-masochistic (S and M) sexuality. Somehow the local campus police were summoned, they detained and questioned her, and reported her (not illegal) behaviour to the local ethics review board, who then contacted the IRB at our university, who complained to us that this could not be allowed because the young woman was potentially endangering herself. So much for free speech!

The potential for abuse of power by Institutional Review Boards is high, since their authority is unchecked. While some complain that graduate students and junior faculty bear the brunt of these restrictions (Lederman, 2006; Yanow and Schwartz-Shea, 2008), and they surely command less standing in their universities to resist reasoning with IRB members, senior faculty are far from exempt. At our schools, conducting research without IRB approval carries the potential sanction of tenure revocation and termination. A protocol violation at the medical school at one branch of our state university resulted in the total suspension for months of all research over the entire four-campus system. Another typically egregious incursion occurred to a colleague at a different university working with a graduate student who got the opportunity, at the last minute, to travel to Africa to conduct dissertation research on data and people that were publicly accessible (the legislative chambers of a democratic country and elected officials). Believing that these fell into the exempt category, and lacking the arduous time necessary to go through the ethics review process, she seized the opportunity and gathered the data. Yet, when the IRB found out, it summarily, without communicating with either her or her adviser, imposed what amounted to a "death penalty" on her research, notifying her that she had to destroy all of her data and not use or disseminate any of it for future publications, presentations, or her dissertation.

Even the suspicion of research misconduct may lead IRB members to jump into action. In this last case, the IRB dismissively plunged her adviser and other graduate students with whom he had worked even tangentially (again without communication, inquiry, or due process) into a full "non-compliance audit," assuming that they were similarly negligent. This required suspension of their ongoing research, line-by-line examination of their protocols and data, and immediate mandatory

IRB appearances (despite the fact that they were either abroad gathering data, working with IRB-documented exempt data, not gathering data on human subjects, as yet unengaged in research, or not conducting research under his supervision). Working their way through this process took more than a year. Similarly, with us, the nascent stages of our application (and re-applications) for the self-injury project were met with insistence from an IRB member that self-injury led to suicide and should therefore be treated according to those highly stringent protocols. When Patti disagreed with this (since disproved) assumption to one of the IRB members handling the case, she was encouraged to offer data, in her revised application, to support an alternative view and to offer an epistemological argument for a different ethical response. Yet without contacting us, the head of the review board contacted the chair of her department, informed him that Patti was conducting unethical research in violation of university regulations, and stated that her job was in serious jeopardy. And this was prior to the start of any data gathering! This unwarranted abuse of power labelled her as an ethical violator and, again, required considerable work and time to repair.

Some have suggested that the unexpurgated encroachment of Institutional Review Boards reflects the growth of the surveillance society (White, 2007) or the nanny state (Dingwall, 2007), with a Big Brother panopticon fixing us all with its omniscient gaze. The tension between individual liberty and security is one the world increasingly faces as we are watched by a growing array of cameras and called upon to submit to rising levels of visual, verbal, physical, and documentary registration. Conversations with colleagues in Europe reveal that many of them have no such regulation at all, for which they are grateful daily, although Dingwall (2007) has suggested that the international hegemony of the United States is leading other countries to adopt equally stringent standards. Many scholars view this as a "tool of repression" ushering in a greater "censorship regime" (Feeley, 2007; Katz, 2007). Yet the panopticon of compliance seems to creep increasingly into places where regulation appears unwarranted, as with our journal and book publishers (Dingwall, 2007), subjecting all research to its demands. And as companies move research projects into participant-rich developing countries, these tendencies are not likely to subside. Calls to challenge these developments abound, but are weak against the Goliath of entrenched and encroaching regulation.

The relationship between these codes and the laws of the land seems potentially problematic. Feeley (2007) proposes that IRBs abrogate the "rule of law," while Yanow and Schwartz-Shea (2008) suggest a possible redundancy to existing laws on libel and privacy, noting that the latter may even better protect some research subjects. Yet even without these kinds of formal rules, ethnographic epistemology has long incorporated strong standards for the protection of people in the field, and epistemological treatises stating the importance of ethical commitments of loyalty to research settings and members are canonical (cf. Brenneis, 2005; Douglas, 1976; Klockars, 1979; Polsky, 1969). Field researchers routinely censor their writing to protect those they study (see Adler and Adler, 1993), and the Brajuha (Brajuha and Hallowell, 1986) and Scarce (1994) cases represent fieldworkers who were willing to go to jail to project the confidentiality of their participants.

In fact, as we have previously argued (Adler and Adler, 2002), IRBs seem geared more towards the protections of institutions than human subjects. In our litigious society the university (cf. White, 2007) and governmental (Dingwall, 2012) fears of lawsuits are great, and what Feeley (2007) calls a "risk-aversive hyper-instrumentalism" has come to predominate. We have even been forced to meet with university lawyers to see which research designs they would approve, which begs the question of whether lawyers are the appropriate parties to regulate research. Feeley (2007) cogently argues that the entry of lawyers has led to a rollback of researchers' rights.

Concomitantly, we ask whether the police should be regulating research. Why have the ethics of our professional associations become synonymous with the laws of the land (Adler and Adler, 2002; Yanow and Schwartz-Shea, 2008)? When Mario Brajuha and Rik Scarce were fighting their legal battles the American Sociological Association (ASA) filed *amicus curiae* briefs, supporting withholding their data from the police. Yet shortly thereafter, the ASA revised its code of ethics and, supported by the Consortium of Social Science Associations (COSSA), subjugated their standards to those of the police. We suggest that this was not a wise development, because field researchers and the police have different interests, standards, and values at stake.

Jack Katz (2007) offers a damning critique, documenting ways that Institutional Review Boards have become corrupted by the power of political and business interests in society, with powerful groups suppressing research that might threaten their legitimacy or financial advantage. He charges that subverting independent research to the service of America's rich and powerful has the potential for repressing progressive inquiry and expression. This development should not be surprising to any observer of US politics, governed by money and big business as are many developed and developing countries. We not only bow to the almighty buck, but we worship it with reverence. Yet there is something sad in recognizing that universities, long bastions of free thought, free speech, and independent research, long a foundation of trust, have been so abrogated. Institutional Review Boards, ironically, have become one of the most potent vehicles for the incursion of this type of power and control into the realm of the academy, not only by businesses, but also by the state itself (Ribeiro, 2006). This challenges academic freedom at its the core.

But despite these critiques, let us be entirely clear that we, like others (cf. Dingwall, 2007; Feeley, 2007), are not calling for the complete elimination of research ethics regulation. There are times, places, and domains where it is valuable and necessary. What we advocate, rather is some IRBan Renewal, operating in both formal and informal dimensions.

Informal Management Techniques

The first thing we can do here is to share suggestions with others about ways that we have learned to navigate the complex waters of IRBs with the least damage to ethnographic research studies. Some of these sidestep the problematic nature of the hypothetico-deductive, experimental mindset of these boards by reconstituting the grey areas of field research.

First, we long ago learned that submitting participant-observation research designs was likely to meet with red flags due to committee members' lack of understanding, their resistance, and other issues we might neither foresee nor overcome. We therefore submit, and urge our students to submit, research proposals that are strictly interview studies. We consider any interaction that we have with people in research settings prior or subsequent to these interviews to be merely informal interactions that guide the development and fine-tuning of the interview experience, and falling outside the domain of "real research" (i.e., reviewable).

Second, although our Institutional Review Boards ask for a set of fixed interview questions that participants will be asked as part of the research proposal, we often try to submit a list of research topics that we will investigate. We have had only limited success arguing with IRB members on this point. But we do not belabour it, and are quick to fall back, if necessary, on some fixed interview questions that address the core research interests, as well as these can be anticipated prior to the start of formal research.

A surprising problem we have had with the Institutional Review Boards at our schools involves the size of the research sample. The IRBs require that this be specified in advance. Ethnographers often conduct more interviews than initially estimated. Each time we think about writing a new article we usually return to the field and conduct more interviews. We even discover conceptual and empirical holes when nearing the end of a project, through the creative experience of writing that need to be filled with new data. But an imprecise and inductively expanding sample size has proved especially problematic for many (even in survey research) colleagues in our departments, as the IRBs have prohibited conducting more interviews than originally articulated. Even in-person visits to IRB meetings, where our colleagues have argued passionately that they, as researchers, are the only logical choice when it comes to determining how much data need to be gathered, have met heavy resistance and rejection. Thus, we suggest to students and others to make a very large initial estimate on the desired sample size and approach this limit with care, possibly deflating the actual numbers. As Katz (2006) has noted, this is part of the "outlaw culture" of ethnographic dealings with IRBs.

To make things easy, we recommend calling the local IRB administrator directly (not even the faculty member who's the chair of the committee) to ask what kind of research design would be approvable for a given project. (We informally refer to that person as "god.") We have found that when you get these people on side with research at an early point it has a better chance of success. Talking with such people directly also saves a lot of time because they can point out little nuances of a project that might cause unanticipated problems, enabling design modification prior to submission. Ultimately, however, we and others have had to abandon research designs that are not approvable (yet are not harmful), as Katz (2007) has also noted. But all of this leaves us with the bad feeling that ethnographic research designed to suit the IRB administrator may not be the most epistemologically sound practice. There are near limitless opportunities that scholars have to prostitute themselves, and this represents yet another one.

Programmatic Recommendations

Some have suggested that concerned scholars search for *local* solutions to these problems such as volunteering to serve on their own IRBs, taking the time to educate local IRBs, or inviting researchers to attend

IRB meetings (Stark, 2007, 2012; Swartz, 2007). Although this seems the kind of solution to which the current decentralized system might best respond, we consider this idea problematic for several reasons. These are Band-Aid approaches that tinker with but do not change the severely flawed and dangerous aspects of the current research ethics review process. First, people who enjoy conducting field research are not necessarily the same as those who enjoy doing local administrative service. Second, people who do not believe in the moral legitimacy of IRBs are unlikely, as Dingwall (2007) notes, to invest more time in them. But most critically, local solutions are individual, affecting only one particular review board at one particular school. As sociologists have long recognized, structural reforms trump individualistic reforms. To think about an analogy, it does not do the world much good to send individual rapists to therapy or to anger management classes. The problem of rape can only be solved by structural changes, such as empowering women through education, employment opportunities, reform of marital policies, reform of sexual assault laws, and more stringent enforcement of sentencing policies. Local solutions, moreover, are only temporary in nature, and something more lasting is needed. Therefore, such ideas represent nothing more than cop-outs.

If changes are to be made at a centralized level, it raises the question of what these should be and who should make them. In July 2011 an Advance Notice of Proposed Rulemaking (ANPRM) was launched by the US Department of Health and Human Services with the purported intent of enhancing protections for research subjects while at the same time reducing the onerous burdens, delays, and ambiguities for investigators. Most of these sounded sane (even no-brainers), such as suggestions for making consent forms simpler, eliminating the need for unnecessary annual refiling, moving more projects to departmental and expedited review status, assuming minimal risk unless shown to be otherwise, establishing a centralized site for clearing collaborative research projects, and allowing new methods of data security to replace the need for even expedited review for projects in one of the six exempt categories (including the observation of public behaviour). Others, however, incorporated the risk of potentially invoking stricter standards for the purpose of clarifying boundaries. Yet what has happened to this?

We need, instead, better *real* protection for our human research subjects. Many of these IRB "protections" were deemed necessary because the police have increasingly gained the power to invade and seize researchers' data. We now have to inform our subjects that we are now powerless to protect them. Why don't we have a shield law for research? As Feeley (2007) asks, what does this say about the moral values of our society? How much are the rights of the individual respected versus the needs of society, the values of freedom versus the need for regulation? Societies vacillate back and forth between these sometimes competing drives, and we now appear to be in a period of regulatory embrace, with regulators' capriciousness and power becoming excessive. Who, then, is regulating the regulators and protecting the researchers? Conflicts of interest abound when precisely those who regulate researchers are given the job of protecting them (i.e., the federal government).

Who, then, should set the standards (see White, 2007)? Should these be set across or within countries, states, or schools; across or within the research areas of the natural, medical, and social sciences; across or within disciplines; across or within methodologies/epistemologies? Should these be made by the professional associations of our disciplines (not if you don't like the ASA Code of Ethics) or by the professional associations of our near disciplines (ditto to COSSA)? In the absence of these kinds of guidelines, we have set the default for setting standards to non-specialized IRB members who are stuck with a three-year university service commitment. But might these guidelines be formulated, rather, by trained, senior scholars who specialize in epistemology?

We suggest that explicit standards for ethnographic research be formulated by the Consortium of Social Science Associations. Research is not a one-size-fits-all enterprise, as Lederman (2006) has noted. And we believe that senior scholars could more readily be recruited to serve on a panel making advisory recommendations for national standards for research ethics review than they would for local IRB service.

If such a national panel of senior ethnographers was convened, we suggest that some of the following issues be addressed with a greater and nuanced understanding than current Institutional Review Boards are able to offer.

Membership Research

Membership research is not an uncommon role for researchers to take in the field (see Adler and Adler, 1987) and demands special considerations that current Institutional Review Boards find extremely problematic. Boundaries between the grey area where everyday life ends and ethnographic research begins are vague and hard to delineate. It is often difficult to know when research commences, precisely, with early phases of a research project often drawing on or inspired by retrospective data (Feeley, 2007; Katz, 2006) or autobiographical memory (Katz, 2006). Converting data gathered in a membership role to research is hard to explain to Institutional Review Boards, and yet is a frequent occurrence in this type of research. The boundaries between friendship and research are also difficult to pinpoint precisely (or as Lederman [2006] asked, can a colleague be a human research subject?), leaving scholars who discuss their research with friends and get good ideas unsure about how to treat these. It therefore begs the question of who ethnographers can converse with about their research and what proceeds of those discussions can be used as data. Finally, ethnographers often take on multiple roles in the field (Bradburd, 2006; Lederman, 2006), and these may evolve and/or grow during the course of a project.

Studying Groups

Studying groups may offer difficulties for ethnographers that other methodologies do not face. One of our students, for example, was denied permission to conduct participant-observation research with a support group if a single member of the group objected to her studying them. She said she would gladly exclude anything that objecting members said or did, and would not approach them for interviews, but the IRB rejected this proposal, barring her from studying the group entirely. We suggest that a different policy be adopted for studying groups where not all participants desire to opt in, giving researchers precisely this flexibility specifically to exclude only those who do not want to be studied.

Inductive Research

Guidelines ought to be set to help Institutional Review Boards deal with inductive methods including the issues of emerging (unanticipated) foci, so that researchers can more easily move to drop topics that were thought to be interesting but do not pan out, while adding others that arise during the course of the research project. Inductive methods require a different epistemological mindset from the more familiar hypothetico-deductive research. We need a better way for inductive researchers to handle shifting populations in their studies, with new people being uncovered, others dropped, and new unanticipated lines of inquiry unfolding. The same can be said of hidden populations, such as people often encountered in cyber studies, where some participants lurk without posting and cannot be known. Finally, we have noticed ethnographers having trouble dealing with the nebulous definitions of public versus private spaces (again often found in cyber research) where IRBs are making difficult and sometimes arbitrary delineations between truly public spaces, clearly private spaces, and things in between such as semi-public/private spaces and public spaces where participants have an expectation of privacy. These issues need further clarification at the federal level.

Risk-Benefit Assessments

Risk-benefit assessments often include the caveat that researchers may not include in their calculus of benefits altruistic participant comments about their desire to help the research or to help the research so that others may gain from it. But in conducting our recent study of self-injury we asked numerous participants at the end of the interviews why they came forward and volunteered to be studied and these are precisely the reasons they gave. They wanted our research to help other self-injurers learn, from reading our publications, that they were neither alone nor crazy. So we propose, like White (2007), that this benefit be allowed. Many of our subjects also benefited from the research process itself, as they found it cathartic, or they were able to ask us questions at the end of the interview that enhanced their knowledge and understanding of their own behaviour. Yet this benefit is also banned.

Opt-Out

Opting out as a policy for unfunded research projects has been so widely supported by the ethnographic community as to be nearly universal. Richard Shweder (2006), in fact, effectively clarifies that ethical regulation of unfunded research is not required by the federal government, but is the prerogative of each university. Many have suggested that ethnographic research be exempt (Annas, 2006; Bradburd, 2006; Katz, 2006). This would help defend against the mission creep that IRBs have instituted in their imperialistic over-reach. If such exemptions were legitimately acknowledged, then publishers and other outlets could no longer require blanket IRB approval.

Certificates of Confidentiality

Certificates of confidentiality in the United States should be more widely available from the Department of Health and Human Services, especially for ethnographic research in the areas of deviance and criminality. These used to be available for some drug research, but not only have they become seemingly harder to obtain, they do not offer the protections that they advertise. We looked into this in our study of adolescent cliques (see Adler and Adler, 1998) when participants told us that we needed to talk to them about the way drugs were coming in and breaking apart their cliques. One of our students also looked into the certificate of confidentiality while conducting his study of Mexican-American gangs, to protect his gang members from anything they revealed to him about potentially illegal activities. In both cases we were told that these certificates did not, in fact, offer any protection to research subjects for what they told ethnographers in confidence. Not only, then, were the hoops necessary to get a certificate unbelievably arduous, it was a bait-and-switch proposition – the benefits at the end of the process did not offer what the name suggested. It has become increasingly difficult for ethnographers to study crime and deviance (Ferrell and Hamm, 1998), and research on these topics is vitally important to empirical knowledge, theoretical analysis, and policy formulation. We must find ways to not only enable this research but to promote it – ethnography represents one of the most valuable strategies for gathering information about hidden populations and behaviours of critical importance in our societies.

"Pre-Research Phase"

As a concept, a "pre-research phase" should be introduced into the lexicon of ethnographic research-ethics review. Prior to interacting with setting participants researchers may not be able to negotiate entrée for their studies, ascertain if a setting has the kinds of empirical and conceptual elements that addressing their scholarly interests requires, determine if they will be a good fit into the group so that they can get along with and be accepted by setting members, discover what kinds of topics and issues seem to be relevant and present in such a setting, discern the major groups and key individuals in the setting, determine the extent to which the group is organized or not and who the formal or informal gatekeepers are, find sponsors into the setting, estimate the size of the sample, or to project a research plan. At various periods in our research careers we have found IRB members who have agreed to this concept, allowing up to one year in the field for ethnographers to interact informally with setting members (but then, capriciously and inexplicably, in other periods IRB members have not allowed this). We would recommend that absolutely no interviews be permitted prior to getting formal IRB approval for a project, but a one-year "pre-research phase" would give qualitative researchers the opportunity to learn more about their settings, especially those that do not offer frequent interaction or that may temporarily block research access for any number of reasons, causing extended delays. This is the last, and one of the most critical, of our programmatic suggestions, and we believe it should be universalized.

Programmatic changes such as these would go a long way towards enhancing an appreciation of the ethnographic research model, would remove some of the blockage that has made field research the hardest hit by ethics review regulation and the least understood method undergoing ethics review, and might foster better communication and greater honesty between qualitative researchers and those who monitor them.

REFERENCES

Adler, Patricia A., and Peter Adler. (1987). *Membership Roles in Field Research.* Newbury Park, CA: Sage. http://dx.doi.org/10.4135/9781412984973
– (1993). "Ethical Issues in Self-Censorship: Ethnographic Research on Sensitive Topics." In Claire M. Renzetti and Raymond M. Lee (eds.), *Researching Sensitive Topics*, 249–66. Newbury Park, CA: Sage.
– (1998). *Peer Power: Preadolescent Culture and Identity.* New Brunswick, NJ: Rutgers University Press.
– (2002). "Do University Lawyers and the Police Define Research Values?" In Will C. van den Hoonaard (ed.), *Walking the Tightrope: Ethical Issues for Qualitative Researchers*, 34–42. Toronto: University of Toronto Press.
– (2011). *The Tender Cut: Inside the Hidden World of Self-Injury.* New York: New York University Press.
Annas, George. (2006). "Anthropology, IRBs, and Human Rights." *American Ethnologist* 33 (4): 541–4. http://dx.doi.org/10.1525/ae.2006.33.4.541
Bradburd, Daniel. (2006). "Fuzzy Boundaries and Hard Rules: Unfunded Research and the IRB." *American Ethnologist* 33 (4): 492–8. http://dx.doi.org/10.1525/ae.2006.33.4.492

Brajuha, Mario, and Lyle Hallowell. (1986). "Legal Intrusion and the Politics of Fieldwork: The Impact of the Brajuha Case." *Journal of Contemporary Ethnography* 14 (4): 454–78. http://dx.doi.org/10.1177/0098303986014004005

Brenneis, Donald. (2005). "Documenting Ethics." In Lynn Meskell and Peter Pels (eds.), *Embedding Ethics*, 239–52. Oxford: Berg-Wenner-Gren Foundation.

Denzin, Norman K., and Michael D. Giardina. (2006). *Qualitative Inquiry and the Conservative Challenge*. Walnut Creek, CA: Left Coast Press.

Dingwall, Robert. (2007). "Turn Off the Oxygen...." *Law & Society Review* 41 (4): 787–96. http://dx.doi.org/10.1111/j.1540-5893.2007.00324.x

– (2012). "How Did We Ever Get into This Mess? The Rise of Ethical Regulation in the Social Sciences." *Studies in Qualitative Methodology* 12: 3–26. http://dx.doi.org/10.1108/S1042-3192(2012)0000012004

Douglas, Jack. D. (1976). *Investigative Social Research*. Beverly Hills, CA: Sage.

Fassin, Didier. (2006). "The End of Ethnography as Collateral Damage of Ethical Regulation?" *American Ethnologist* 33 (4): 522–4. http://dx.doi.org/10.1525/ae.2006.33.4.522

Feeley, Malcolm M. (2007). "Legality, Social Research, and the Challenge of Institutional Review Boards." *Law & Society Review* 41 (4): 757–76. http://dx.doi.org/10.1111/j.1540-5893.2007.00322.x

Ferrell, Jeff, and Marc S. Hamm (eds.). (1998). *Ethnography at the Edge*. Boston: Northeastern University Press.

Flicker, Sarah, Robb Travers, Adrian Guta, Sean McDonald, and Aileen Meagher. (2007). "Ethical Dilemmas in Community-Based Participatory Research: Recommendations for Institutional Review Boards." *Journal of Urban Health* 84 (4): 478–93. http://dx.doi.org/10.1007/s11524-007-9165-7

Hamburger, Philip (2004). "New Censorship: Institutional Review Boards." *Supreme Court Review* 6: 271–354.

Katz, Jack. (2006). "Ethical Escape Routes for Underground Ethnographers." *American Ethnologist* 33 (4): 499–506. http://dx.doi.org/10.1525/ae.2006.33.4.499

– (2007). "Toward a Natural History of Ethical Censorship." *Law & Society Review* 41 (4): 797–810. http://dx.doi.org/10.1111/j.1540-5893.2007.00325.x

Klockars, Carl B. (1979). "Dirty Hands and Deviant Subjects." In Carl B. Klockars and Finnbar W. O'Connor (eds.), *Deviance and Decency: The Ethics of Research with Human Subjects*, 261–82. Beverly Hills, CA: Sage.

Lederman, Rena S. (2006). "The Perils of Working at Home: IRB 'Mission Creep' as Context and Content for an Ethnography of Disciplinary Knowledges." *AE Forum, American Ethnologist* 33 (4): 482–91. http://dx.doi.org/10.1525/ae.2006.33.4.482

Lincoln, Yvonna. (2006). "Institutional Review Boards and Mythological Conservatism." In Norman K. Denzin and Yvonna Lincoln (eds.), *The Third Handbook of Qualitative Research*, 165–81. Thousand Oaks, CA: Sage.

McGrath, Moriah McSharry, Robert E. Fullilove, Molly Rose Kaufman, Rodrick Wallace, and Mindy Thompson Fullilove. (2009). "The Limits of Collaboration: A Qualitative Study of Community Ethical Review of Environmental Health Research." *American Journal of Public Health* 99 (8): 1510–14. http://dx.doi.org/10.2105/AJPH.2008.149310

Polsky, Ned. (1969). *Hustlers, Beats, and Others*. Chicago: Aldine.

Ribeiro, Gustavo Lins. (2006). "IRBs Are the Tip of the Iceberg: State Regulation Academic Freedom and Methodological Issues." *American Ethnologist* 33 (4): 529–31. http://dx.doi.org/10.1525/ae.2006.33.4.529

Scarce, Rik. (1994). "(No) Trial (But) Tribulations: When Courts and Ethnography Conflict." *Journal of Contemporary Ethnography* 23 (2): 123–49. http://dx.doi.org/10.1177/089124194023002001

Schrag, Zachary M. (2010). *Ethical Imperialism: Institutional Review Boards and the Social Sciences, 1965–2009*. Baltimore, MD: Johns Hopkins University Press.

Shweder, Richard A. (2006). "Protecting Human Subjects and Preserving Academic Freedom: Prospects at the University of Chicago." *American Ethnologist* 33 (4): 507–18. http://dx.doi.org/10.1525/ae.2006.33.4.507

Stark, Laura. (2007). "Victims in Our Own Minds? IRBs in Myth and Practice." *Law & Society Review* 41 (4): 777–86. http://dx.doi.org/10.1111/j.1540-5893.2007.00323.x

– (2012). *Behind Closed Doors: IRBs and the Making of Research Ethics*. Chicago: University of Chicago Press.

Swartz, James D. (2007). "Where Rigor Becomes Rigor Mortis: Institutional Review Boards and Qualitative Research." *Journal of Ethnographic and Qualitative Research* 2: 1–5.

van den Hoonaard, Will C. (ed.). (2002). *Walking the Tightrope: Ethical Issues for Qualitative Researchers*. Toronto: University of Toronto Press.

White, Ronald F. (2007). "Institutional Review Board Mission Creep: The Common Rule, Social Science, and the Nanny State." *Independent Review* 11 (4): 547–64.

Yanow, Dvora, and Peregrine Schwartz-Shea. (2008). "Reforming Institutional Review Board Policy: Issues in Implementation and Field Research." *PS, Political Science & Politics* 41 (03): 483–94. http://dx.doi.org/10.1017/S1049096508080864

4 The Language of Law: How Research Ethics Review Creates Inequalities for Language Minorities

LAURA STARK

In 1974 the US Congress passed the National Research Act, and during the past 40 years the law has profoundly changed the conduct of research in the humanities, social sciences, and biomedicine. The law requires that scholars and scientists apply to research ethics review committees if they plan to study people (in whole or in part), and get committee approval before they start their work. Researchers' application materials must demonstrate (at least) two things to committee members and research administrators. First, the materials must show that researchers share committee members' sense of the risks and benefits of a given study and, second, that researchers intend to convey this information to the people they want to study through an informed consent process before they start the study. If researchers' formal compliance with the law is any indication, it seems that study participants are better informed and better protected than they were four decades ago.

Yet during these four decades, researchers have also explored a broader span of geopolitical settings, involved a wider range of participants in their studies, and used a greater variety of research methods in their work. At the same time, institutions have enforced regulations for human subjects research (HSR) in a wider array of disciplines (Schrag, 2010; Stark, 2007). As a result, researchers from medicine, the social sciences, and the humanities now commonly work in regions – and with people – using a variety of languages. In biomedical research alone, approximately half of the clinical trials registered with the US government in 2011 took place outside of the United States (Virk, 2011). During the past decade, the number of active investigators under the jurisdiction of the Food and Drug Administration (FDA) conducting research outside of the United States has steadily increased, and over the same period the number of investigators conducting research within the United States has declined (Getz et al., 2009; for one compelling explanation, see Petryna, 2009). It is likely that a growing number of people enrolled in the remaining health research located in North America are non-native speakers of English: the US Census Bureau estimates that 20 per cent of its domestic population speaks a language other than English at home, and the Bureau expects the proportion will grow in the coming years (Shin and Kominski, 2010).

This confluence of dated regulations and expanded research settings has created a number of problems, one of which is a misalignment of languages among members of ethics review boards, researchers, and potential research participants. The intent of this chapter is to illustrate an emerging, systemic bias in research ethics review. The goal is not to be exhaustive or definitive in argument or demonstration, but to document a social and cultural shift that is currently taking shape and to consider some of its causes and consequences.

The legal crux of the problem is that regulations in the United States require *both* that researchers apply for approval by their local Institutional Review Board (IRB) and that researchers accommodate the native languages of the people they hope to study. The working languages are not known for the more than 4,000 IRBs in the United States nor for the 2,000 IRBs registered with the US Office of Human Research Protections (OHRP) that operate outside of the United States.[1] In this chapter, I present evidence and analysis from my long-term ethnographic study of three Institutional Review Boards in the United States, and for these boards English was the dominant language. Researchers who hope to get approval from Institutional Review Boards that use English as the dominant language must manage translation issues to study people who do not primarily or fluently speak English, as well as those who do not speak nor understand English at all. These researchers must either write the consent texts in English and then translate them for participants, or they must translate texts for the ethics review board into English from another language. Adding to the complication, studies often involve people who do not share a single language or dialect.

To analyse the causes and consequences of language mismatch, this chapter develops the concept of *monolingualism*, which is a person's tendency to read, speak, and understand one language dominantly (if not exclusively). I treat monolingualism as a structural barrier in research ethics review – as a formal law, policy, or guideline in place to accomplish an explicit goal that simultaneously and systematically accomplishes other implicit ends with disproportionate and negative affects for some people. This chapter suggests a paradox of the law: the explicit goal of the US National Research Act is to protect research participants equitably, and yet the language of that law – as enacted during IRB meetings – is a structural barrier to the very protection that the law aims to achieve.

Observing IRBs: New Approaches to "Empirical Ethics"

In the past decades, social scientists have shown that ideas about right and wrong are not universal, but instead are the outcome of social processes that are located and generated within specific contexts and are constrained by the local techniques that evaluators conventionally use to make judgments. In short, people's ideas about right and wrong reflect their communities' habits, customs, and hierarchies. Building on this insight, scholars have explored how organizations "make ethical research," including ethics review boards (Stark, 2012; Hedgecoe, 2008), data and safety monitoring boards (Keating and Cambrosio, 2009), and funding review panels (Lamont, 2010). My question is how ethics review boards in the United States do the work of making ethical research.

The premise of sociocultural approaches to studying bioethics is that legal and ethical terms derive their practical meaning and consequences from the way that individuals use and apply them in specific settings, in this case, during the course of IRB meetings. As a result, it is important to study the situations in which individuals enact rules and regulations because it is in these encounters that individuals give abstract rules concrete meaning.

Following this pragmatic approach, I analysed audio transcripts of IRB members' discussions during their full-board meetings for one year (for details on methodology see Stark, 2012). I also observed their meetings and interviewed members of the three Institutional Review Boards between March 2004 and October 2005. To get a broad sense of problems and styles of work in boards reviewing human subjects research, I interviewed 20 IRB chairs at major research universities across the United States in 2003 and 2004 (Table 4.1).

For the interviews with IRB chairs, I drew a random sample of 20 per cent of the 151 universities ($n = 30$) categorized as "doctoral/research universities – extensive" according to the Carnegie Foundation for the

Table 4.1. Institutional Review Boards (IRBs) Observed

	Greenly IRB	Sander IRB	Adams Medical
Duration of observations (months)	12	12	5
Meeting(s) per month (*n*)	1	1	2
New full-board protocols in period (*n*)[a]	40	20	60
IRB members			
Community members (*n*)	2	2	2
Faculty and administration (*n*)	12	11	9

Note: The meetings at Greenly IRB were recorded for 12 months and at Sander State IRB for 7 months. Field notes were taken during all of the board meetings. For a full description of research methods, see the appendix of L. Stark, *Behind Closed Doors: IRBs and the Making of Ethical Research* (Chicago: University of Chicago Press, 2012).

a The number of full-board protocols reviewed is rounded to protect the identities of the institutions. During the meetings, all of the boards also discussed expedited protocols, study amendments, and continuing reviews.

Advancement of Teaching (2001). Colloquially, these institutions are referred to as large research universities. I completed 20 interviews (a response rate of 67%), and used these interviews with this national sample to get a broad view of common issues and modes of operation of Institutional Review Boards in the United States. I also used the contacts I made through these interviews to select the boards that I subsequently observed.

I contacted three of the IRB chairs I had interviewed as part of the national sample to ask whether I could do long-term observations of their full-board meetings. I chose these three IRB chairs because their institutions were within 500 miles of my institution and because they encouraged the project. Thus, one limitation of my data – as indicated by the chairs' willingness to let me, as an outside researcher, analyse the meetings – is that the board members were unusually eager to learn more about their own practices from a sociocultural perspective. Another way to think of this selection bias is to recognize that the boards I observed functioned well and were open to reflection about the way they made decisions; their practices were those of particularly self-aware and self-critical IRB members.

With their members' consent, I attended the monthly full-board meetings of two Institutional Review Boards for one year between 2004 and 2005, and audio recorded most of the meetings. For five months I also observed but did not audio record the twice-monthly meetings of one Institutional Review Board at a medical school. The medical school board was one of several at a university that had additional ethics review boards for non-medical research. This Institutional Review Board, which I call Adams Medical Board, met every other week for three to four hours, during which I took field notes. I also interviewed 10 of the 11 regular members of the board, plus one non-voting administrator. The other two Institutional Review Boards that I observed were the only boards at universities without medical schools (although researchers conducted vaccine trials, physiology studies, and other medical research often in cooperation with local clinics and the schools' infirmaries). At the board that I call Greenly IRB, members gave me permission to audio record their monthly meetings for one year. I supplemented these recordings with handwritten field notes and interviews with 11 of 14 board members. At the third IRB, Sander State IRB, members gave me permission to audio record their monthly meetings after my fifth month with the Board. Thus, I recorded meetings that averaged just under two hours in length for the remainder of the year (seven months) and continued taking field notes. I also interviewed the 12 regular members of the Sander State IRB during the course of the year. In sum, I supplemented my observations of meetings of three Institutional Review Boards with recorded interviews of 34 IRB members. I transcribed the audio recordings of these meetings and interviews, and analysed the transcripts using Atlas.ti, a software program for coding qualitative data that allows a flexible style of open coding without pre-established categories, helping researchers identify emergent phenomena.

Who Is at a Disadvantage in Human Subjects Review?

My study suggests that in North American boards, non-native English speakers – researchers and study participants – tend to be at a disadvantage in the ethics review process.[2] The work of reviewing the ethics of human subjects research is simultaneously a practical and symbolic activity, and IRB members' evaluations in the boards I observed affected both researchers and future research participants.

IRB members tend to concentrate their limited time on a review of researchers' consent materials, perhaps with good reason. Participants, especially those with lower levels of education, find it difficult to understand and remember information about studies, even after a thorough and sensitive consent process (Flory and Emanuel, 2004; Ballard et al., 2011). Part of the explicit task of IRB members is to judge how appropriate content materials are for a given group of participants – whether the materials are intended to be read or heard. To that end, IRB members use standardized tools aimed at improving the readability of consent documents by making the language more colloquial and pithy, while keeping the content legally valid and scientifically accurate.

Yet IRB members' review of consent materials is a challenging task riddled with contradictions. During one IRB meeting, the board's community member counted the syllables in a researcher's consent form and observed that the word "institutional" itself has five syllables. Point taken: a proposed consent procedure that included telling participants that the study had been approved by the "institutional review board" could, in theory, stall IRB approval of the study because of the readability index. Nonetheless, there is a case to be made for simplifying consent materials. In another meeting I observed, board members suggested to the researcher, who was at the meeting, that he could better explain his research to participants, which is a regulatory requirement. The researcher did not see how he could be more clear. "I read through and honestly, I didn't find big words," the researcher explained. "I didn't know what words were too big in the consent form." IRB members offered specific suggestions for edits:

DR MORRIS: When I read these things that have four or more syllables, I get worried.

PRIMARY INVESTIGATOR: Oh, okay.

DR MORRIS: (Quoting an example from the consent form) "Excellerometers measure caloric expenditure."

PI: Right.

DR MORRIS: That's fine if I'm a graduate student in health science, but if I'm somebody else, I'm not sure I can understand what you mean.[3]

PI: I'll have you sit in on one of my classes! (Laughing).

DR MORRIS: But that's what I'm saying. Just make the words so that a person can understand them. (Giving an example) I hate the word "discontinue." That is "stop." I know I harp on people about this, but I really think you can apply simple language for big words and make it a lot easier for people to understand.

PI: Alright.

PROFESSOR HARPER: Another one, is "muscular skeletal." We can put a simple word in instead. I can't even say "musculooo," "muscular skeletal." That's just a bad word. Like "excellerometer." You can put simpler words in there to tell what that means. I'm from the [named department]; we don't have vocabularies either. Little words work.

DR MORRIS: Everyone gets caught in their own technical jargon, but unless you're actually confined to that population of people who can say "Ah, it sounds good," it is hard to see that. Participants might wonder: does an excellerometer, for example, have electrodes stuck into it?

PI: How about "motion detectors"?

DR MORRIS: Yes.

ANOTHER IRB MEMBER: Sure. (Field notes, SG, Nov.)

IRB members have the potential to accomplish practical good for research participants through their review of consent materials. To be sure, they do not always accomplish this goal in part because of the very guidelines they are supposed to follow to ensure participants' protection. Yet in the Institutional Review Boards I studied, the board members' review of materials benefited English-language participants almost exclusively.

IRB members tend to focus on consent forms precisely because the material is consequential for participants, but my research raises questions about the biases and blind spots in the review process. A community member on another board explained that "an important part of my function" is to read consent forms to make sure participants will "understand." She said, "If it's not understandable to me, who's well educated, then I figure somebody with an eighth grade education will not understand it and I will definitely raise that concern" (Field notes, C3). Yet this board member spoke only English. As a result, she could only ensure that participants who shared her language would understand the materials. Likewise, a clinician who also served on this board mentioned the importance of community members, including the volunteer quoted above, in judging the readability of consent documents. However, this IRB member observed that the board had never included a person who spoke Spanish, even though the university ran many community studies in the Spanish-speaking enclaves that surround the hospital setting being studied (Field notes, C6).

During meetings, IRB members discussed language issues on rare occasions. The silence on this topic was all the more apparent because of the large number of researchers who proposed studies with subjects who were not native English speakers. On one of the occasions when IRB members did recognize differences in language they did so by praising one board member's idiosyncratic strength, rather than by reflecting on the board's homogeneity overall and the limits that this homogeneity set. For the study, the researcher had a consent form translated into Spanish for the people she planned to enroll, and she was also in the process of hiring people to conduct Spanish-language interviews in a nearby city. The researcher herself did not speak Spanish. For the consent translation, the researcher depended on a consultant, and she was unable to judge the quality of the translation prior to the IRB review, which she attended. As a result, she could neither confirm nor refute one IRB member's opinion that "the Spanish consent [was] bad." The IRB member claimed, referring to the section on risks, "It says here 'I'm afraid my friends will relax me'" (Field notes, NG, Dec.). Moreover, the researcher was unable to discuss the best way to revise the materials, or to serve as a trustworthy judge of a fresh translation (from a consultant) that IRB members requested before they would approve the study.

These examples suggest that the practical benefits of reviewing human subjects materials privilege participants who share the dominant language of IRB members. In doing so, this disparity perpetuates a pattern in research more broadly. Traditionally, anglophone research, and medical research in particular, has worked to the greater advantage of people with strong English literacy. Similarly, English-speaking research participants would seem more likely to comprehend consent procedures and to get more intelligible consent documents (via researchers) from Institutional Review Boards that share their language.

My interviews with members Institutional Review Boards suggested that the breakdown in language happened in translations, and that the direction of translation might be part of the problem. Because researchers are required to submit both foreign-language and English-language versions of the consent materials, they tend to write in English and have the foreign-language consent materials translated.[4] During one meeting, a board member's idea for how a researcher might improve the foreign-language consent materials pointed to the root of the problem: "Translating English-language consent forms into Spanish is a problem for many IRBs," the board member observed. "There has to be a computer program that can do consent translations" (Field notes, AM, Mar.). Poor-quality translation of consent materials is a pervasive problem in research. Yet IRB members, like many researchers, lack the language skills needed to remedy the problem and – more significantly – to recognize problems with translated materials.

In sum, my empirical study of Institutional Review Boards suggests that the ethics review process creates social disparities based on language, and that these disparities stem from IRB members' tendency to evaluate only those application materials that they can read. IRB meetings were patterned around biases in board members' language skills, and as a result only writing and speech that was conducted in the dominant language of IRB members was open to evaluation. IRB members changed – and one hopes, improved – consent materials most often for future participants who shared the board's dominant language. When consent materials were written in a language other than English, board members tacitly trusted the skill of the translator without requiring information about the qualifications of the translator. Thus any practical benefit of IRB review, such as improved consent materials, may neglect speakers of non-dominant languages.

Monolingualism and Its Implications

Scholars have used two approaches to study language mismatch: *language concordance* and *poststructural monolingualism*. Both approaches acknowledge that language communities map onto regional and cultural communities. Because of this feature of language, people who share a language often share the resonances and implicit meanings of words. They get the joke, so to speak, but also tend to miss the political undergirding of language.

These two approaches build on different assumptions about how language works (including verbal language and symbolic language, e.g., sign language as well as spoken language), and about what languages accomplish unintentionally. As a result, they imply different political and practical responses. First, researchers in health fields have used the term *language concordance* to study accuracy in linguistic translation. Conceptual and evaluative words, such as *fair* and *justice*, are freighted with connotations and histories, and therefore have a range of resonances across language groups. Scholars have shown the special difficulty, even impossibility, of capturing the precise meaning of abstract terms across languages (Tang et al., 2011; Viruell-Fuentes et al., 2011), though language mismatch can also be strategically useful in some circumstances (Ribeiro, 2006). The imperatives of research ethics and regulation, however, require that people communicate and develop a shared understanding of abstract terms, such as *rights* and *respect*.

The implication is that scholars should work harder to make translations as accurate as possible, ideally by involving people from appropriate language communities or by involving members of the actual audience (e.g., research participants) in an ongoing communication process. This latter approach creates a puzzle because regulations concerning human subjects research in many countries require researchers to create texts and scripts before they begin their studies. Still, funders and research institutions have (paradoxically) turned language concordance into a metric of success – a quantitative measure assessing the quality of language, which monitors can track and researchers can compare over time. Scholars who use fieldwork in their research have advocated and developed approaches to work within this communication paradox (Miller et al., 2007).

By contrast, the approach of *structural monolingualism* considers the assumptions that individuals make about people whose language is different from their own. This marks is a niggling but important distinction between the two approaches: whereas language concordance is concerned with *(different) languages* and the process of translation, monolingualism is concerned with *(language) difference* and the production of political inequality. Philosopher Jacques Derrida developed a theory of monolingualism in the 1990s, and took seriously the claim that people think in languages. Because language is verbal and conceptual, one's language organizes both the attributes associated with different social groups and the patterns of chauvinism that result from people's linguistic affinities and familiarities.

Scholars working on structural monolingualism tend to assume that people's thoughts are organized into two categories: what I am and what other people are (Derrida 1998).[5] Some people may be the same as who I am (e.g., Canadian, gay, black, male). People who are not the same as I am are not simply members of any number of alternative, precise categories (e.g., American, straight, white, female). They are "other" than I am; they are different.

Importantly, categories are always formed in relation to each other – as binaries – and they inevitably fall into hierarchies. Categories, according to structural monolingualism, can never be exactly even. One always must be better or worse, superior or inferior, and these relations, Derrida pointed out, map on to people's political intuitions. At the basic level, patterns of discrimination are built into the language communities that frame people's thinking and as a result embed assumptions about what is natural. Similar cases have been made for gender and sexuality (e.g., Schiebinger, 2004), which has fuelled gender studies and queer theory since poststructuralism (Butler, 2006).

Structural monolingualism is not fatalistic about human prejudice, though. The approach acknowledges that inherent human prejudices can be managed and mitigated. The first step is to develop attention to the issue in specific social settings. This chapter holds up IRB meetings as just such an exemplary setting.

These two approaches to the study of language mismatch point to the source of problems in research ethics review and attune observers to solutions. It is common to assume that research review committees strengthen (or at least do not diminish) the comprehensibility of consent materials for research participants. To be sure, many researchers challenge the notion that IRB members' editorial changes to consent materials make substantial improvements, an issue I discuss elsewhere (Stark, 2013). Still some researchers have come to rely on review committees to provide "helpful insight into potentially problematic phrases or words, and to ensure that the documents will be well understood by study participants" (Virk, 2011: 4).

Poor translation of study materials is common in research, and this problem undermines the stated aim of regulating human subjects research: to protect participants. This is a quandary because language barriers are a key contributor to low participation rates of many minority groups in research, including qualitative studies (Gee et al., 2010; Swanson and Ward, 1995). To take an example from health research, the most influential group-specific social factor contributing to the low participation rates of Latinas in breast cancer clinical trials was a lack of English proficiency (Borrayo et al., 2005).

Regulations do not require that individuals who translate materials and lead the consent process share the language or dialect of study participants. Scholars such as Karen Virk (2011) have argued that the consent process in particular is a serious barrier because members of many racial and ethnic minority groups lack strong skills in the language of governance. But there is another way to think about the language mismatch: namely, that many members of ethics review boards and researchers lack skill in the languages spoken by research participants.

Conclusion: The Many Languages of the Law

The increasingly global context of research has enhanced the need to understand how people communicate in research ethics review – how exchanges happen, what they accomplish unintentionally, and how various methods of communication differ (e.g., speaking and writing), especially across language groups. In this chapter, I drew on my long-term observations and audio recordings of the meetings of three Institutional Review Boards, as well as interviews with IRB members and chairs to explore the problem of monolingualism in research ethics review. I considered how language mismatch among participants, researchers, and members of ethics review boards creates disparities in the quality of protection that participants receive – depending on whether IRB members share a language with participants. My research suggests that board members' monolingualism is a structural barrier to the equitable protection of language minorities in research and assessment of research proposals submitted to Institutional Review Boards. The aim of this analysis is to be suggestive rather than definitive, and to encourage scholars, advocates, and policymakers to collect information and focus resources on remedying this issue: the neglected problem of monolingualism.

My work suggests that research participants who have a dominant language that is different from the operating language of their Institutional Review Board are poorly protected when compared with participants who share a review board's primary language. Specifically, the ethics review process results in unequal treatment of research participants who do not share the dominant language of IRB members. As a result, the practical benefits of research ethics review, such as an improved consent process, accrue to people disproportionately. My study documents the ways IRB meetings are patterned around board members' language skills and biases, and how this systematically shapes the boards' decisions. In sum, the practical, human limits of IRB members prevent them from accomplishing the goals of regulating human subjects research when rules and best intentions are directed towards non-dominant languages.

The US Office of Human Research Protections is in the process updating regulations for human subjects research. Policymakers have recognized that high-quality and appropriate consent procedures are essential to protect research participants, and researchers no doubt agree. Although more mundane IRB activities, such as copyediting, are generally an unhappy task for all involved – researchers, their study teams, IRB members, and board staff – such language work (or lack thereof) should be a central focus of efforts to rethink ethics review given the increases in language communities involved in both transnational and domestic studies. As the US OHRP revamps human subjects research regulations, effort could productively be directed towards reforming practices of IRB deliberation and at incorporating language experts or members of a variety of language communities into the review process (Kithinji and Kass, 2010; Miller et al., 2007). The protections put in place for research participants during the 1970s fit awkwardly in the twenty-first century research environment; it is time to broaden the imaginations of researchers and policymakers regarding risks to both researchers and participants who are embedded in multiple language communities.

NOTES

I am grateful to Nathan Pauly and Erin Kelly for indispensable research assistance. I thank Ray De Vries, Jill Fisher, JuLeigh Petty, and the editors of this volume for their feedback on earlier drafts of the chapter. Ethan Kleinberg's advice on Derrida helped immensely, as did Gary Shaw's ideas about theory more generally. I am grateful to Helen Curry, Henry Cowles, Joanna Radin, Lukas Rieppel, and Alistair Sponsel for being a wonderful Sounding Board.

1 Office of Human Research Protections database, accessed 10 Oct. 2012.
2 I discuss language mismatch among ethics board members and researchers elsewhere (Stark, 2013).
3 In general, there is work to be done on the question of whom IRB members imagine when they think of future research participants, a practice that I call "seeing like a subject" (Stark, 2012).
4 For example, the September and March meetings of Sander State involved lengthy discussions of translating consent forms (regarding typos and delays in approval). It was explicit, though it did not seem peculiar to board members that all translations were from English into the non-English language.
5 It is important to note Derrida argued that a person's dominant language also creates alienation of a speaker with herself.

REFERENCES

Ballard, Hubert O., Philip Bernard, Don Hayes, Jr, Joseph Iocono, and Lori A. Shook. (2011). "Parents' Understanding and Recall of Informed Consent Information for Neonatal Research." *IRB: Ethics & Human Research* 33 (3): 12–19.

Borrayo, Evelinn A., Catalina Lawsin, and Carissa Coit. (2005). "Latinas' Appraisal of Participation in Breast Cancer Prevention Clinical Trials." *Cancer Control* (Nov.) Suppl 2: 107–10.

Butler, Judith. (2006). *Gender Trouble: Feminism and the Subversion of Identity.* New York: Routledge.

Carnegie Foundation for the Advancement of Teaching. (2001). *Carnegie Classification of Institutions of Higher Education 2000.* Menlo Park, CA: Carnegie Publications.

Derrida, Jacques. (1998). *Monolingualism of the Other, or, the Prosthesis of Origin.* Stanford, CA: Stanford University Press.

Flory, James, and Ezekiel J. Emanuel. (2004). "Interventions to Improve Research Participants' Understanding in Informed Consent for Research: A Systematic Review." *Journal of the American Medical Association* 292 (13): 1593–601. http://dx.doi.org/10.1001/jama.292.13.1593

Gee, Gilbert C., Katrina M. Walsemann, and David T. Takeuchi. (2010). "English Proficiency and Language Preference: Testing the Equivalence of Two Measures." *American Journal of Public Health* 100 (3): 563–9. http://dx.doi.org/10.2105/AJPH.2008.156976

Getz, Ken S., Rachel Zuckerman, and Stephanie Rochon. (2009). "Landscape Changes Highlight Growing Challenges for Clinical Research Sponsors." https://www.ciscrp.org/patient/facts.html. Accessed 1 October 2013.

Hedgecoe, Adam. (2008). "Research Ethics Review and the Sociological Research Relationship." *Sociology* 42 (5): 873–86. http://dx.doi.org/10.1177/0038038508094567

Keating, Peter, and Alberto Cambrosio. (2009). "Who's Minding the Data? Data Monitoring Committees in Clinical Cancer Trials." *Sociology of Health & Illness* 31 (3): 325–42. http://dx.doi.org/10.1111/j.1467-9566.2008.01136.x

Kithinji, Caroline, and Nancy E. Kass. (2010). "Assessing the Readability of Non-English-Language Consent Forms: The Case of Kiswahili for Research Conducted in Kenya." *IRB: Ethics and Human Research* 32 (4): 10–15.

Lamont, Michèle. (2010). *How Professors Think: Inside the Curious World of Academic Judgment.* Cambridge, MA: Harvard University Press.

Miller, Suellen, Phuoc V. Le, Sienna Craig, Vincanne Adams, Carrie Tudor, Sonam Nyima Droyoung, Mingkyi Tshomo Lhakpen, and Michael Varner. (2007). "How to Make Consent Informed: Possible Lessons from Tibet." *IRB: Ethics and Human Research* 29 (6): 7–14.

Petryna, Adriana. (2009). *When Experiments Travel: Clinical Trials and the Global Search for Human Subjects.* Princeton, NJ: Princeton University Press. http://dx.doi.org/10.1515/9781400830824

Ribeiro, Gustavo Lins. (2006). "IRBs Are the Tip of the Iceberg: State Regulation, Academic Freedom, and Methodological Issues." *American Ethnologist* 33 (4): 529–31. http://dx.doi.org/10.1525/ae.2006.33.4.529

Schiebinger, Londa L. (2004). *Nature's Body: Gender in the Making of Modern Science*. New Brunswick, NJ: Rutgers University Press.

Schrag, Zachary M. (2010). *Ethical Imperialism: Institutional Review Boards and the Social Sciences, 1965–2009*. Baltimore: Johns Hopkins University Press.

Shin, Hyon, and Robert Kominski. (2010). *American Community Survey Report, 2007*. Washington, DC: United States Census Bureau.

Stark, Laura. (2007). "Victims in Our Own Minds? IRBs in Myth and Practice." *Law & Society Review* 41 (4): 777–86. http://dx.doi.org/10.1111/j.1540-5893.2007.00323.x

– (2012). *Behind Closed Doors: IRBs and the Making of Ethical Research*. Chicago: Chicago University Press.

– (2013). "Reading Trust between the Lines: 'Housekeeping Work' and Inequality in Human-Subjects Review." *Cambridge Quarterly of Healthcare Ethics* 22 (4): 391–9. http://dx.doi.org/10.1017/S096318011300025X

Swanson, G.M., and A.J. Ward. (1995). "Recruiting Minorities into Clinical Trials: Toward a Participant-Friendly System." *Journal of the National Cancer Institute* 87 (23): 1747–59. http://dx.doi.org/10.1093/jnci/87.23.1747

Tang, G., O. Lanza, F.M. Rodriguez, and A. Chang. (2011). "The Kaiser Permanente Clinician Cultural and Linguistic Assessment Initiative: Research and Development in Patient-Provider Language Concordance." *American Journal of Public Health* 101 (2): 205–8. http://dx.doi.org/10.2105/AJPH.2009.177055

Virk, Karen P. (2011). "Language Barriers in Global Trials." *Monitor* (Aug.): 1–5.

Viruell-Fuentes, E.A., J.D. Morenoff, D.R. Williams, and J.S. House. (2011). "Language of Interview, Self-Rated Health, and the Other Latino Health Puzzle." *American Journal of Public Health* 101 (7): 1306–13. http://dx.doi.org/10.2105/AJPH.2009.175455

5 Uncomfortable Truths, Ethics, and Qualitative Research: Escaping the Dominance of Informed Consent

MARCO MARZANO

Recent decades have seen striking growth in the tendency to exercise external control over the ethical aspects of social science research: the numbers of research ethics committees have multiplied, and it is now considered compulsory to secure informed consent from the people being studied. Ample documentation exists about the damage this mentality has inflicted on the quality and freedom of social science research in Canada, the United States, the United Kingdom, Australia, and elsewhere (Adler and Adler, 2002; Haggerty, 2004; Tilley and Gormley, 2007; Dingwall, 2008; van den Hoonaard, 2011; Marzano, 2012).

The main victim of the current research ethics climate is the "search for truth" – or perhaps the plural *truths* is more accurate – and especially uncomfortable ones.

The result of this Orwellian climate of obsessive control over the activities of scholars in the field (Katz, 2007) means that the social sciences have too often succumbed to the triumph of rhetoric, to a wave of fine sentiments and hypocrisy. Social science research has produced descriptions of the world that are frequently highly anodyne – visions of reality that are shared by researchers and their subjects but which are often trivial. Generally speaking, this rhetoric has placed great emphasis on compliance. It obscures the presence of social conflict and has discouraged studies of the powerful and the actions of the political and cultural elite. For example, these elites have found a very useful ally in research-ethics review committees and the culture of informed consent in their defence against unwelcome incursions into their territories and uncompromisingly critical descriptions of their activities.

During the 1950s and 1960s, when external controls were less stringent and commonly non-existent, critical social science research, and in particular critical ethnography – "studying up," to use Laura Nader's (1972) celebrated expression – made an extremely significant contribution in providing a detailed and complex picture of modern capitalist society. A well-known example is Donald Roy (1952, 1959) who gave a comprehensive description of the phenomenology of industrial conflict, challenging the notion of the factory as a cooperative place governed by the rules of ascetic Taylorist rationality. The portrait of American corporations painted by Melville Dalton in *Men Who Manage* (1959) was even more pitiless. Firms appeared as theatres of war – a Hobbesian state of nature dominated by internal struggles and cliques, secretive groups dedicated to gaining and maintaining power. In Erving Goffman's ethnographic masterpiece, *Asylum: Essays on the Social Situation of Mental Patients and Other Inmates* (1961), we find a stark description of the organizational mechanisms which, as with any total institution (such as prisons and psychiatric hospitals), are used in attempt to (re) shape the identities and behaviours of those confined in them, as well as the perspectives of those who remain outside.

Roy, Dalton, and Goffman sought no informed consent in carrying out their research; in their day Institutional Review Boards (IRBs) did not exist for the social sciences. Furthermore, all three of these researchers frequently kept their identities secret during their fieldwork. We know little of how Roy and Goffman operated in the field, only that Roy was hired as a factory worker and Goffman was employed as an assistant to a physical education instructor. We do know, however, that Dalton recounted his research environment in an autobiographical article published some years after his book, in 1964, in which he provided a catalogue of the stratagems, ruses, and devices he used to do his research covertly. They included being hired as a clerk and helping a secretary arrange a date with a young man whom she liked, in exchange for access to the organization's personnel files.

It is easy to imagine how the managers of Milo (the name was obviously fictitious) – the company where Dalton collected most of his data – would have stopped the research immediately had they known the methodological and theoretical bases of his work, and if they had understood what Dalton was intending to do when he got himself hired. It is also unlikely that the managers of the St Elizabeths Hospital in Washington, DC, were exactly happy in 1961 when they read the pages of Goffman's *Asylum*, devoted to describing everyday life in the psychiatric institution. These researchers did not name names, of course; they used pseudonyms, made it difficult to recognize the places where the research had been carried out, and then hid the identities of the protagonists. These were not works of fiction, though, and we can be sure that many of the protagonists did recognize themselves in one passage or another. This situation may have been a source of bitterness and anger for those studied, especially because they had placed their trust in someone who betrayed them, who deceived them.

On occasion, people are annoyed or embarrassed when they find their stories reproduced, interpreted, and analysed in a book of sociology. This was the case with Doc, a subject in William F. Whyte's iconic study, *Street Corner Society* (1993 [1955]). Doc's real name was Ernest Pecci, and after experiencing a brief period of fame following the success of the book, Mr Pecci held a deep and lasting grudge against Whyte, his former friend. Pecci said he felt that he had sold out his people, his friends, his compatriots, and possibly even his own identity to this cunning professor of sociology, without having given informed consent, and without knowing what the researcher was going to do with the stories that he had given him (Boelen, 1992).

Having reached this point, some readers of this chapter will have begun to think that Institutional Review Boards and informed consent are innovations that are justified, all things considered, by the risk of harm that qualitative researchers may inflict on the persons they study. This is not the case, however.

In the first place, any harm experienced in the past was not so serious as to excuse the stringent limitations on the freedom to carry out social research. The proportions are wrong. What has been lost by researchers in the social sciences as a consequence of abandoning critical ethnography – essentially the loss of the natural world as a focus of study – is far greater than what has been achieved in terms of protecting the rights of those being studied. The task of those taking the critical approach is to draw attention to power: research strategies that were mostly implicit in the past, methods and strategies that did not disrupt the "natural order" of things in a given social environment. In other words, there is a need to show – to remind ourselves and others, in this case – that it is possible to carry out research in an ethically aware and informed manner without subscribing to the (il)logic of informed consent processes and ethics review board fears induced by university lawyers; doing so in a manner that differs from that employed by the mainstream, but without ignoring the ethics of research. Preserving the natural world for study without inflicting harm on those studied is not difficult. Abundant evidence exists to support this. Yet, for the past

50 years, since the inception of ethics review, few Institutional Review Boards have allowed the covert strategies required in critical ethnographies and similar research.

At least two potential sources of inspiration for critical ethnography exist today. First, we have the proponents of "conflict methodology" (Lehmann and Young, 1974) who have watched with particular concern the rise and spread of the power of corporations as the dominant features of contemporary society. Those who espouse this perspective have responded to the exhortations of C. Wright Mills (1959) and Alvin Gouldner (1970) to study the immoral conduct of the powerful. These and many other authors have pointed out that only very rarely (i.e., nearly never) do overt research and informed consent permit an efficacious study of the behaviour of elites, especially those involved in great public or private organizations. The reason is clear – powerful people typically dislike being observed or obliged to publicly and satisfactorily justify their actions, frequently because they cannot. Further, by virtue of their power, they are too frequently able to prevent being studied by claiming rights to privacy, the need to protect others, citing the need for secrecy, or similar smokescreens. If researchers adhere to conflict methodology when faced with this resistance, they are *morally authorized* by the method to pursue their research aims by drawing on unofficial or unauthorized sources when necessary. For example, conflict methodologists may interview an organization's adversaries, or some of its highly dissatisfied members, or those who have left the organization; they may resort to direct observation, they may lie outright as to the purposes of their research or deny that research is even being conducted.

John Van Maanen's essay "The Smile Factory" (1991) provides an excellent example of the notable analytical results that can be derived by working from a critical and conflict perspective. "The Smile Factory" to which Van Maanen refers is Disneyland, the most famous amusement park in the world, a source of immense profits, and a wildly successful company as acknowledged by business scholars and market success (Peters and Waterman, 2004). Disneyland appears to be a marvellous place when viewed from the outside, in no small part because of "the cheerful demeanour of its employees, the seemingly inexhaustible repeat business it generates from its customers, and the immaculate condition of its grounds" (Van Maanen, 1991: 58) – "the happiest place on earth," according to Disney's own publicity proclamations.

For an employee, however, as Van Maanen himself was for several years in his youth, Disneyland is anything but a paradise. First, to be hired by Disneyland one must have (and maintain) a certain kind of physical appearance. Men cannot have long hair, beards, or moustaches; Walt Disney himself would have had to shave his moustache off to be employable at Disneyland! Men must absolutely not wear earrings, and women "must not tease their hair, wear fancy jewellery, or apply more than a modest dab of makeup" (Van Maanen, 1991: 59). A rigid hierarchical stratification of classes and roles is in place at Disneyland – or better, perhaps, an outright military-style caste system (complete with different uniforms and badges) – within which mobility is practically impossible.

The least idyllic aspect of the life of Disneyland workers, however, is unquestionably the dense network of internal controls over their work and lives. Complex investigation and enforcement systems operated by a fierce, omnipresent, and well-disguised internal police force reports about the private lives and sexual habits of employees, carefully evaluates their personalities – even as they socialize outside working hours – and enthusiastically encourages full and frequent informing on colleagues. This repressive apparatus supervises employees' behaviour and thoughts in relation to even the most trivial of misdemeanours including taking too long a break, not wearing some item of the official uniform (hat, belt, or shoes), excessive fraternizing with a visitor or being impolite to one, or making a ride last for less, or more, than the specified time. The commission of just one of these infringements provided grounds for instant dismissal from Disneyland employment, as Van Maanen himself learned when he was found guilty of having hair deemed too long. The expulsion of "reprobates" from the amusement park, according to Van Maanen's account, follows a very precise, well-entrenched, and highly public degradation ritual, a Goffmanian backstage performance: The soon-to-be dismissed employee is taken to the head office at the end of his or her shift, the employee identification cards are taken away, and a document summarizing the reasons for dismissal is read aloud to the employee by a reified, even deified, supervisor-god. The perpetrator's locker is inspected and publicly emptied. The ritual continues with return of the uniform, and the prominent marking of time cards with "dismissed," so that during the next few days, the employee's colleagues can see the reason for his or her abrupt disappearance as they stamp their cards at the beginning and end of their shifts, and they can be glad it didn't happen to them. Seen by the dismissed employee, we might suppose, this is a penalty, a blot on one's permanent record, rather than a successful jailbreak.

The dismissal ceremony concludes with the removal of the Disneyland parking permit from the miscreant's car.

John Van Maanen reports low pay, arbitrary disciplinary criteria, chaotic working conditions, and very high expectations concerning work performance (unmatched by suitable incentives) in place at Disneyland. Disneyland visitors (from whom the money flows) and Disneyland supervisors (from whom the money does not flow) demand and deserve constantly smiling, if not happy, workers in the park. The situation at Disneyland is not very different from that depicted in the film *The Lives of Others* (2006), an extraordinary portrayal of everyday life in a country – the former East Germany – dominated by espionage. Van Maanen's intention in describing Disneyland is to revalue (à la Marx) the essential role played by its employees in the park's success, and to also reveal lesser known and less evident aspects of life behind the scenes at an iconic company selling happiness. Van Maanen illuminates the skills and talents of the park's management and the people responsible for employee training who, despite everything, still make working at Disneyland highly desirable to many talented people.

It should be stressed that the method employed by Van Maanen – an unauthorized and unsponsored description based mainly on personal experience – did not harm any specific individual; rather the purpose was to describe aspects of organizational life at Disneyland that were little known and important for understanding what happens to people there, for example, what breaches of the official code of conduct were committed more or less regularly, and what strategies were used to keep people believing they are happy in the "happiest place on earth." Society as a whole can be reassured that sociologists like Van Maanen not only seek to satisfy their personal, intellectual, and scientific curiosities, but also want to combine analytical seriousness with civic commitment. This is an important way that qualitative research, specifically critical ethnography, covert research, and auto-ethnography substantially benefit people, improving life in egalitarian societies.

In recent decades, as a consequence of the hegemony of informed consent and regulatory logic, these important studies have become impossible under the ill-fitting rules, leaving investigative journalists and bureaucrats with responsibility but no authority watching those in power (Saviano, 2008; Ehrenreich, 2011). This is not without its consequences, given that analyses by sociologists and anthropologists have different levels of complexity, different perspectives, and different goals when compared with journalists. And, journalists don't have their hands tied behind their backs, that is, they don't have to be concerned with predicting harms or benefit/risk ratios, nor do they have to secure what someone who is not a journalist decides is informed consent. In short, journalists get to use their hands.

Conflict methodology is not the only approach that implicitly, or otherwise, justifies the preparation and publication of critical ethnographies. We can find another extraordinary source of inspiration in the work of Michel Foucault (1983, 1990, 1993, 2009, 2011) and Foucault et al. (2012). The originality of his reflections on ethics lies in their antinormative character – the absence of directive elements. Such an absence is a rather unusual state of affairs in ethics theory, one must admit. For Foucault, ethics do not obey rigid moral precepts; they have their roots in personal experience, in critical reflections on one's existence ensuing from practices such as examining one's conscience, soul-searching, introspection, reflection. Ethics are, in Foucauldian terms, decidedly *not* about following rules. Unlike many traditional moral theorists, Foucault addressed the idea that while concern for others must not be forgotten in our quest for individual freedom, it is crucial that we should not sacrifice our freedom to live fully and authentically while caring for others.

For Foucault, ethical behaviour and the practice of freedom coincide – we are ethical *and* free or neither. They are inextricable; no ethics without freedom, and no freedom without ethics. The development of freedom inherently involves the development of ethics: freedom consists in a concrete opportunity to construct one's identity by freeing oneself from external normative constraints and normalizing pressures, and setting off on a path of true discovery of self and others, of *finding* ways to respect the freedom of Self and Other. And in real time.

Foucault did not concern himself directly with the ethics of social science. But when one reads his work, a number of important treatments of this subject are found. Of special relevance are the final courses Foucault taught at the Collège de France (see Foucault 2009, 2011; Foucault et al., 2012), which were devoted to the philosophy and culture of Ancient Greece and Christianity and to *parrhesia*, which means both "telling the truth" and "freedom of speech."

Parrhesiastes, as Foucault described them, are based on classical philosophy, and are a wonderful source of inspiration for an ethics code more valuable than informed consent processes. For the Ancient Greek philosophers, as cited by Foucault, parrhesia was the practice of "speaking the truth," and doing so not in solitude or in relation to some abstract topic, but face to face with others who are listening (or reading, in our case), and who are directly affected by what is being said, which is the purpose of a parrhesist's discourse. Parrhesiastes sense the moral obligation, an authentic desire, to say (or write) everything they think without pausing, even when faced with the most uncomfortable truths, and without concealing any part of what they have discovered. They do this by using explicit – not cryptic or contorted – language, by using comprehensible and clear words. In doing this, parrhesiastes assume certain risks. The first concerns their personal safety: by telling the truth, they risk being persecuted, imprisoned, killed, but, thankfully, most frequently are stigmatized by those who do not want to hear what they have to say, do not want to confront a discovered truth.

The second risk that parrhesiastes run into is that they will ruin their friendships, and that they will provoke grudges and rancour among those who listen to them. In the case of critical ethnographers, this risk relates to those they meet in the field, people with whom they have lived and had frequently cordial, or even friendly relationships. These people recognize themselves in ethnographic works, where they are described in a manner that is likely different from how they may have wished (or thought was accurate), not unusual in the course of my own ethnographic studies. For example, I witnessed a charismatic healing ritual during which one of the leaders of the group took the opportunity to fondle some of the younger participants. When the prayers finished, I attempted to verify the truth of what I was certain I had seen, and sought confirmation from one of the members of the organization, a woman, with whom I had the closest relationship of trust. "Of course Gianni (a fictitious name) takes advantage of these occasions to touch the girls!" the woman told me: "We know this perfectly well, but we don't really think we should intervene." As I was writing my book (Marzano, 2009), I asked myself what I should do – should I include this episode or not? In the end, I included it because, I concluded, it has a wider significance and it would provide a perception of gender and hierarchical relationships within the organization. Understandably, the protagonist, his wife, and the other leaders of the group were not happy with the decision to include these observations. However, I had witnessed the scene as it happened, and I gave my account of it in a way that, on the one hand, did not allow the people to be identified by those who had not been present, and, on the other hand, told the story of what happened during the ceremony, where the usual conventions regarding physical separation between sexes in social situations were ignored, and how this departure was somewhat openly accepted and acknowledged for what it was by members of the group.

It is not, however – and this must be stated very firmly – the intention of parrhesiastes to cause injury or give offence; it is rather to tell under-represented truths, and so to honour friendships, not to sully them. In the concrete case of social science research, the problem relates to the timing of a revelation, the moment when the truth can be spoken. This is usually the moment when the study is published, at the conclusion of the work. Speaking the truth in advance would seriously compromise the potential benefits of the knowledge gained.

Let us consider, for example, the inhabitants of Ithaca, New York, described in the celebrated work by Arthur Vidich and Joseph Bensman, *Small Town in Mass Society* (1968). The story of the book is well known because it is recounted by the authors themselves: Arthur Vidich had been hired by Cornell University and the Ithaca Town Council to carry out a community study in the small university town. During the course of his research, while he was living in the community, Vidich discovered some not especially edifying aspects of the town's life, which stood in complete contrast to the idealized, harmonious image that the sponsors of the study had wanted to convey. In particular, Vidich realized that notwithstanding the pompous democratic rhetoric, a small group of very powerful people monopolized the most important decisions affecting the life of the town. When Vidich made this discovery, he told his colleague Joseph Bensman, and they decided to write what would become *Small Town in Mass Society*.

Small Town in Mass Society provoked scandal and indignation among many of "Springsdale's" residents. The most striking reaction occurred on the occasion of the traditional Fourth of July parade, when a float carrying a large-scale replica of the cover of the book was followed by a procession of the town's dignitaries who had been described in the book, each wearing a mask bearing the pseudonym given to them by Vidich and Bensman. In this situation, Vidich was the parrhesist, and he preferred to reveal an uncomfortable truth rather that remain silent, and to assume personal liability for the action. Vidich placed his career in jeopardy, and for a long time he was not able to set foot in Ithaca and Cornell University, where he was severely criticized and censured. It is likely that while he was in Ithaca, Vidich had on occasion been reticent, and had hesitated to say everything he thought about the life of the community. But the purpose of his reticence was to be able to state a greater truth, and to do so with the highest degree of sincerity.

For Foucault, parrhesia is the opposite of rhetoric. Rhetoricians do not undertake to speak the truth. They do not say what they think. Rather, they are concerned that their discourse results in certain consequences produced in the minds and/or actions of their listeners, that their words generate desired effects. Good rhetoricians can say the opposite of what they think, know, and believe while stating passionately that they think, know, and believe it. In this sense, rhetoric creates a power constraint between the rhetoricians and their public: they are effective liars who, when successful, manipulate thinking and behaviour. Parrhesiastes, on the other hand, are people of courage who place themselves and their relationships with others at risk in the name of truly believing what they say.

Parrhesiastes also differ from prophets, who speak as representatives of another's voice, and who tell a truth that is not their own. Prophets express themselves cryptically, mysteriously, and through enigmas, revealing a world that would not be accessible without their intermediation. But parrhesiastes do not foretell the future and do not describe imaginary scenarios, rather they help us understand what is already in the life world, who and what we are, and what we do.

Finally, parrhesiastes are different from sages, who speak for themselves and cultivate their wisdom within a space that is secluded and separate from the rest of society. No one forces sages to speak, and they make their pronouncements only in special situations, in emergencies, or when fervently requested to do so, perhaps. For parrhesiastes, speaking is an unavoidable moral duty that they cannot fail to discharge without betraying themselves. To fail would be unethical. They must communicate what they have discovered, and tell people what they have understood about them and their character and behaviour, including defects.

For Foucault, nothing is further from parrhesia than the pastoral power glorified by monotheistic religions, which has been revived in our times in the supervision of researchers' activities by ethics review boards. From a pastoral perspective, what counts is obedience, not freedom. Compliance supplants protection. People are not invited, in fact, not allowed to trust themselves, or each other. Researchers are not trusted to cultivate introspection and examine their consciences, rather these activities are to be turned over to an external power that knows less and cares less about what is happening in the research environment. If this logic is applied, there is no salvation without the intervention of an intermediary (pastoral power, to be precise), who will be the guarantor of a relationship with the divinity. In this way of thinking, we do the right thing when we comply. Authority structures are glorified, and individuals are debased. The courage of a solitary man standing before others who deceive themselves is lost, and the idea takes hold that parrhesia is arrogant presumption, an unanswered faith in oneself, a defect, a danger, or a vice. The risk is that together with the ancient practice of parrhesia, our freedom to criticize the existing order is disappearing.

REFERENCES

Adler, Patricia A., and Peter Adler. (2002). "Do University Lawyers and the Police Define Research Values?" In Will C. van den Hoonaard (ed.), *Walking the Tightrope: Ethical Issues for Qualitative Researchers*, 34–42. Toronto: University of Toronto Press.

Boelen, Marianne W.A. (1992). "*Street Corner Society:* Cornerville Revisited." *Journal of Contemporary Ethnography* 21 (1): 11–51. http://dx.doi.org/10.1177/0891241692021001002

Dalton, Melville. (1959). *Men Who Manage*. New York: Wiley.

– (1964). "Preconceptions and Methods in *Men Who Manage*." In Phillip E. Hammond (ed.), *Sociologists at Work: Essays on the Craft of Social Research*, 50–95. New York: Basic Books.

Dingwall, Robert. (2008). "The Ethical Case against Ethical Regulation in Humanities and Social Science Research." *21st First Century Society* 3 (1): 1–12.

Ehrenreich, Barbara. (2011). *Nickel and Dimed: On (Not) Getting By in America*. New York: Macmillan-Picador.

Foucault, Michel. (1983). *Discourse and Truth: The Problematization of Parrhesia*. Berkeley: University of California Press.

– (1990). *The Use of Pleasure*. New York: Vintage.

– (1993). *Microfisica do poder*. Rio de Janeiro: Graal.

– (2009). *Security, Territory, Population: Lectures at the Collège de France, 1977–1978*. New York: Macmillan-Picador.

– (2011). *The Government of Self and Others: Lectures at the Collège de France, 1982–1983*. Houndmills: Palgrave Macmillan.

Foucault, Michel, Graham Burchell, and Arnold I.I. Davidson. (2012). *The Courage of Truth (The Government of Self and Others II): Lectures at the Collège de France, 1983–1984*. Edited by Frédéric Gros. New York: Macmillan-Picador. C.

Goffman, Erving. (1961). *Asylums: Essays on the Social Situation of Mental Patients and Other Inmates*. Garden City, NJ: Anchor Books.

Gouldner, Alvin. (1970). *The Coming Crisis of Western Sociology*. New York: Basic Books.

Haggerty, Kevin D. (2004). "Ethics Creep: Governing Social Science Research in the Name of Ethics." *Qualitative Sociology* 27 (4): 391–414. http://dx.doi. org/10.1023/B:QUAS.0000049239.15922.a3

Katz, Jack. (2007). "Toward a Natural History of Ethical Censorship." *Law & Society Review* 41 (4): 797–810. http://dx.doi.org/10.1111/j.1540-5893.2007.00325.x

Lehmann, Timothy, and T.R. Young. (1974). "From Conflict Theory to Conflict Methodology: An Emerging Paradigm for Sociology." *Sociological Inquiry* 44 (1): 15–28. http://dx.doi.org/10.1111/j.1475-682X.1974.tb00719.x

The Lives of Others. (2006). Film. *Das Leben der Anderen* (original title). Wiedemann & Berg Filmproduktion, Bayerischer Rundfunk. 137 m.

Mills, C. Wright. (1959). *The Sociological Imagination*. New York: Oxford University Press.

Marzano, Marco. (2009). *Cattolicesimo Magico: Un'Indagine Etnografica*. [Magical Catholicism: An Ethnographic Inquiry]. Milan: Bompiani.

– (2012). "Informed Consent." In Jaber F. Gubrium, James A. Holstein, Amir B. Marvasti, and Karyn D. McKinney (eds.), *The Sage Handbook of Interview Research: The Complexity of the Craft*, 443–56. Thousand Oaks, CA: Sage.

Nader, Laura. (1972). "Up the Anthropologist: Perspectives Gained from Studying." In Dell H. Hymes (ed.), *Reinventing Anthropology*, 284–311. New York: Pantheon.

Peters, Thomas J., and Robert H. Waterman. (2004). *In Search of Excellence: Lessons from America's Best-Run Companies*. New York: HarperCollins.

Roy, Donald F. (1952). "Quota Restriction and Goldbricking in a Machine Shop." *American Journal of Sociology* 57 (5): 427–42. http://dx.doi. org/10.1086/221011

– (1959). "'Banana Time': Job Satisfaction and Informal Interaction." *Human Organization* 18 (4): 158–68. http://dx.doi.org/10.17730/ humo.18.4.07j88hr1p4074605

Saviano, Roberto. (2008). *Gomorrah: A Personal Journey into the Violent International Empire of Naples' Organized Crime System*. New York: Macmillan-Picador.

Tilley, Susan A., and Louise Gormley. (2007). "Canadian University Ethics Review: Cultural Complications Translating Principles into Practice." *Qualitative Inquiry* 13 (3): 368–87. http://dx.doi. org/10.1177/1077800406297654

van den Hoonaard, Will C. (2011). *The Seduction of Ethics: Transforming the Social Sciences*. Toronto: University of Toronto Press.

Van Maanen, John. (1991). "The Smile Factory: Work at Disneyland." In Peter J. Frost, Larry F. Moore, Meryl Reis Louis, Craig C. Lundberg, and Joanne Martin (eds.), *Reframing Organisational Culture*, 58–76. Thousand Oaks, CA: Sage.

Vidich, Arthur J., and Joseph Bensman. (1968). *Small Town in Mass Society: Class, Power, and Religion in a Rural Community*. Princeton, NJ: Princeton University Press.

Whyte, William F. (1993) [1955]. *Street Corner Society: The Social Structure of an Italian Slum*. Chicago: University of Chicago Press. http://dx.doi.org/10.7208/chicago/9780226922669.001.0001

6 Assessing Risk in Psychological Research

PATRICK O'NEILL

One challenge for any system of research ethics regulation is to assess the risk of harm in various disciplines, some of which are somewhat or very unfamiliar to the individuals making ethics decisions. Many researchers who deal with Institutional Review Boards (IRBs) in the United States or Research Ethics Boards (REBs) in Canada complain that ethics review boards do not know what harms are likely, or even possible, in various sorts of research, or how risks are handled in different disciplines. They say that research ethics review boards are often arbitrary in assessing the risk of harm, producing inconsistent decisions. Ethics boards, however, may feel that researchers are too willing to impose risk on participants to further their research agendas.

Disputes between researchers and ethics boards do not necessarily represent ignorance of ethical requirements or ignorance of disciplinary norms. They may represent a principled difference of opinion about the right balance between the risk to research participants and the benefit of gaining valuable knowledge for society.

The Canadian Psychological Association in its 2001 Code of Ethics suggests that ethical psychologists should contribute to society's understanding of itself and human beings generally through free enquiry and the acquisition, transmission, and expression of knowledge. But this academic freedom is not unfettered; the CPA Code also says the psychologist should protect the welfare of participants in research. Some well-known studies in psychology have given us important information about human behaviour and social processes, but they also have been criticized for having posed a risk of harm to participants.

Salient Cases

Three examples from social psychology illustrate the potential divergence between the risk of harm and the benefit of collective valuable data.

Milton Rokeach (1964) wanted to know what happens to people's belief systems when they are confronted by challenges to their core beliefs. He focused on the strongest of beliefs, those concerning personal identity. In the sprawling mental hospital at Ypsilanti, Michigan, he found three mental patients, previously unknown to one another, who each believed he was Jesus Christ. Rokeach arranged to have the three men introduced to each other, have them work together, and even share the same residence room, while his team recorded their attempts to maintain their delusional identities.

The study, which resulted in the social psychological classic *The Three Christs of Ypsilanti*, provided a good deal of information about how people defend entrenched belief systems. The results are relevant to the study of paranoia, of course, and also to phenomena such as racism and sexism. But was the possibility of rehabilitation of these men compromised for the sake of the study? The researchers were not just passive observers. They intervened in various ways that had little to do with advancing therapy. In the subtitle of his book, Rokeach describes the participants as "three lost men." Presumably, if they were already "lost" the question of therapeutic value versus research data would be moot.

My second example is familiar to those interested in research ethics. Stanley Milgram (1974) wanted to know how far ordinary people would go in obeying an authority figure who ordered them to use a procedure that might harm someone. He used a teacher-learner paradigm in which a participant was assigned the role of "teacher," and had to teach something to the "learner" using progressive increases in shock. The learner was a confederate and the shock was simulated. Milgram presented this research as demonstrating that horrendous acts may be committed by ordinary people when obeying authority figures. In popular descriptions of the research, the participants were likened to concentration camp guards (Milgram, 1974).

To the extent that Milgram's research provides information about obedience to authority, it benefits society. But what about the risk of harm to Milgram's participants? In Milgram's film of the experiment, some participants did seem to suffer considerable psychological

distress. Milgram even pointed to that distress to show that the participants were engaging in behaviour that they really believed was causing harm, but he argued that despite the evident stress, participants
suffered no actual breakdowns although former participants were even
less happy about the way they were treated after the experiment (Robert Dingwall, personal communication, 27 Oct. 2012).

Whether they were harmed or not, participants may have suffered
negative consequences if one would give "harm" a broader interpretation. The experiment taught the participants just how far they would
go in shocking someone – knowledge about themselves that was presumably not available before. You cannot "debrief" that information
away. The fact that the "learner" was a confederate does not make any
difference to the knowledge about one's willingness to engage in repre-
hensible behaviour. And, of course, participants were fooled about the
nature of the study; they did not sign up for a voyage of self-discovery.

In my third example, Philip Zimbardo (1971) wanted to know
whether people who were assigned roles in a coercive context would
become so engrossed in those roles that they would do things to other
people that they might not otherwise do. His team created a makeshift
jail. He randomly divided participants, mainly students looking for
summer work, into guards and prisoners for what was intended to be a
two-week prison simulation. "Guards" were soon mistreating "prisoners" to keep them in line, using humiliation, verbal abuse, and some
rough physical treatment. There was a least one breakdown among
those in the role of prisoners. The simulation had to be called off after
just six days.

Zimbardo (1971) has testified before the US Congress and in other
forums, applying his research findings to allow us to understand closed
institutions such as jails. More recently, his findings have been applied
to grasp the abuse that takes place in institutions such as Abu Ghraib
prison and the Guantanamo Detention Centre. The knowledge gained
from the simulation seems to be of benefit to society. Again, as in the
Milgram case, Zimbardo does not believe his participants were harmed,
although he admits they were at risk and he did not know, in advance,
whether they were going to be harmed or not. Obviously justifying a
risky study with a retrospective argument about actual harm in similar
studies is of limited value to ethics boards whose members must assess
prospective risks in new proposals.

The question arises whether ethical misadventures of a few well-known
studies are being inappropriately generalized to an entire field of study,

such as social psychology, anthropology, or ethnography, by research ethics regulators who may not know much about the field. Gestalt psychologist Fritz Heider (1944) coined the famous phrase "behavior engulfs the field" to describe a bias in perception and memory. He argues that some phenomena are particularly salient, and that salience makes it hard to see the rest of the context. Heider's initial observation has been extended to many other subfields of psychology, from causal attribution in interpersonal relations (Heider, 1958) to decision-making in community psychology (O'Neill, 1981). To help regulators get beyond salience effects, it may be useful to think about the sorts of harm that might arise in psychological research and the risk that such harms will occur.

Varieties of Harm

Robert Levine (1988), in his influential book *Ethics and the Regulation of Clinical Research*, divides risks into the following four categories: physical, psychological, social, and economic. With *physical* risks the research participant may suffer bodily harm – minor or serious, temporary or permanent, immediate or delayed – as a result of participating in a study. With *psychological* risks, there may be emotional stress or a threat to the participant's self-esteem. The procedure may cause anxiety or shame, or may induce aberrations in thought or behaviour. With *social* risks, the participant may be exposed to the possibility of discrimination or other forms of stigmatization. With *economic* risks, research participants may directly or indirectly bear financial costs. Any given study may pose more than one type of risk to the research participants.

Charles Weijer (2000) writes about the "ethical analysis of risk," describing studies with non-trivial risks on more than one dimension. He gives the example of a study by Zimbardo et al. (1981) which concerned the relationship between hearing loss and the development of paranoia. In naturalistic studies, there is some evidence that paranoid people in places where elderly people receive care tend to make out better than their more congenial fellow residents. The paranoids think that they are not getting their due, and complain about a lot of things. In neglectful, crowded environments, those who complain are more likely to get what they think they deserve. Zimbardo and his colleagues wanted to know what causes paranoia at a subclinical level. They hypothesized that being hard of hearing contributes to paranoid thinking, especially if the person who is experiencing hearing loss does not know what is happening. If I see but cannot quite hear conversations,

I may think people are talking about me; I may start to develop conspiracy theories.

To test the model, the researchers used hypnotic induction. Under hypnosis, some college students received suggestions that induced partial deafness. One control group had a different induced behaviour (ear scratching), and another experienced hearing loss but knew that hypnotic induction was the cause. After the hypnosis session, participants were given tests that reliably indicated paranoid thinking, and they were asked to do various tasks with two confederates. The conditions were such that participants could misunderstand what the confederates were saying and might interpret a conversation as hostile in nature – specifically as having personal reference when it did not.

The participants who were now partially deaf (without knowledge of where the deafness originated) scored higher on tests of paranoid thinking. They were rated by confederates who interacted with them, and by themselves, as "more irritated, agitated, hostile, and unfriendly" (Zimbardo et al., 1981: 1530) than those in the control groups. Participants were debriefed with and without further hypnosis, and were assessed in a follow-up interview one month later. Charles Weijer (2000) claims that this study posed a variety of risks to participants including the following:

- The distress associated with both paranoia and hearing loss
- The possibility that the participants' paranoia could lead them to harm others or be harmed themselves – even the risk of suicide
- The fact that suspicious people may lose friends and/or their jobs
- There may be harms arising from uncertain side-effects of hypnosis.

These dangers may or may not actually apply to the hypnosis study. Philip Zimbardo and his co-authors do not detail the results of their follow-up (amount of remaining hearing loss, if any; degree of residual paranoid thinking, if any) but they say the changes due to hypnosis were "transitory" (Zimbardo et al., 1981: 1530). Whether or not the actual conditions of this study endangered participants in the ways Charles Weijer suggests, clearly there are a variety of potential harms in research that ethics review boards should be concerned about.

Assessing Risk

In addition to these considerations about harm, it is also necessary to assess the risk that a particular harm or harms will occur as a result of participation in a given study. Does the risk reach or exceed some minimal-risk threshold? The higher the risk, the more carefully an ethics board should look at the details of a research proposal.

The second edition of Canada's *Tri-Council Policy Statement: Ethical Conduct for Research Involving Humans* (*TCPS* 2) defines "a minimal risk situation [as] one in which the nature, probability and magnitude of possible harms implied by participation in the research is no greater" than those encountered by participants in their daily lives (CIHR et al., 2010: 194). A problem with this definition, which the *Tri-Council Policy Statement* recognizes, is that it may discriminate against participants whose lives are particularly risky – especially in ways that relate to the research topic. Consider a study of street prostitutes. They could suffer a variety of harms if they were to participate in an interview study about their working lives. They could be physically harmed – by their pimps, for instance. They might suffer self-esteem problems beyond those inherent in their trade – the researcher's questions may undermine whatever rationalization the prostitutes use to get through the working day. If the research heightens their risk of identification, they may suffer increased social stigma and legal problems.

The fact that an individual's life is filled with risks is hardly a reason to downplay the risks arising from research, however. As the *Tri-Council Policy Statement* states, "REBs have special ethical obligations to individuals or groups who live with relatively high levels of risk on a daily basis. Their inclusion in research should not exacerbate their vulnerability" (CIHR et al., 2010: 24). People in vulnerable situations need more rather than less protection, most would argue. The dichotomy of below or above minimal risk paints research proposals with a rather broad brush. If studies must be below minimal risk in the view of the members of a Research Ethics Board, much potentially valuable research could not be done.

Current practice favours a more refined risk scale, including the category, "a minor increase above minimal risk," which would require more careful scrutiny of a proposal, more questions to be asked of the researcher, and full-board review, among other requirements. Refining categories of risk, however, may not do much to improve the consistency of research ethics review, in large part because decisions are still contingent upon local board interpretations of the rules.

In a study sponsored by the US National Institutes of Health (NIH), Seema Shah and her colleagues (2004) surveyed 188 IRB chairs asking them to categorize risk. They were presented with common research procedures and asked to categorize the proposals as below minimal risk, a minor increase above minimal risk (requiring careful scrutiny), or above moderate risk (and therefore not permissible). The procedures were such things as MRIs, blood draws, allergy skin testing, and testing new drugs on children. The chairs were all from pediatric institutions, and the procedures to be categorized by participants were common in such settings. The major finding of the study was that IRB chairs frequently had very different ideas about risk, no matter what procedure they were assessing.

One stimulus that Shah and colleagues (2004) used, relevant to psychological research, involved "giving a confidential survey of sexual activity to under-age teenagers." When IRB chairs judged this stimulus, 44 per cent said it was "below minimal risk," 29 per cent indicated it was a "minor increase above minimal risk" requiring special scrutiny, and almost 20 per cent said such a survey would be above moderate risk and should be turned down. The question is not which chairs were right or wrong; what matters here is the serious inconsistency among a highly homogeneous group when assessing risk.

Researchers who must have several ethics boards approve a project are often frustrated by the difference of opinion among boards. Some believe that formal accreditation of ethics boards will help to make decisions more consistent – many Institutional Review Boards (IRBs) in the United States are accredited, Research Ethics Boards (REBs) in Canada are not. Nevertheless, it should give us pause to realize that in the study conducted by Shah et al. (2004), all 188 chairs making wildly inconsistent judgments did come from *accredited* IRBs.

Risk of Harm to Whom?

Codes and guidelines typically focus on research participants, but many other people are involved in the research enterprise including researchers, students, assistants, and others. Should the welfare of these individuals be considered by ethics boards? The fact that some boards do consider the risk to non-participants while others do not exacerbates the inconsistency problem.

The *Tri-Council Policy Statement: Ethical Conduct for Research Involving Humans* notes, "Risks in research are not limited to participants. In their conduct of research, researchers themselves may be exposed to risks that may take many forms (e.g., injury, incarceration)" (CIHR et al., 2010: 25).

The following is an example of the sort of research proposal that might worry an ethics board because of the risk to someone other than a participant. A developmental psychologist working for the National Institutes of Health in Washington, DC, had funding to study the interaction in families in which the father was on conditional release after being convicted of physical abuse of children in the family (Penelope Trickett, personal communication, Oct. 1980). The plan called for research assistants to spend time in the family home in the late afternoon and early evening, observing and recording the conflicts that arose in the family and the way they were handled.

This was a potentially valuable study, with results that might help professionals intervene more effectively in at-risk families. But the project was also ethically complex. Among other things, there was risk to those carrying out the research. If abuse occurred, they would be witnesses to the same criminal behaviour that had caused the family to be enrolled in the study. If the abusive father could not control himself in the family setting, what might his reaction be towards a research assistant trying to telephone police about an emergency? And, what might his reaction be to someone taking notes on his angry, abusive behaviour – someone who might be called as a witness against him? In this case, consideration about the risk of harm is extended to individuals working for the principle investigator. Some ethics boards actually censure proposals on the basis of risk to the researcher, even though researchers are overwhelmingly competent adults and, some argue, should be treated as competent, autonomous individuals who should be allowed to take risks if they wish to do so. This case brings to mind another research proposal, one that involved a survey about sex.

Elizabeth Sheff, an assistant professor at Georgia State University, proposed a study of people who identified themselves in a sex survey as "kinky" (Sheff, 2013). She wanted to find out what that meant in contemporary society. However, an IRB prohibited her from visiting respondents in their homes to interview them out of concern for her own safety. The Board not only substituted its assessment of the researcher's welfare for that of the researcher herself, it also apparently came to a conclusion about what "kinky" might mean, which was actually the question the researcher proposed to explore in the study. Sheff, whose scholarly expertise involves studies of sexual behaviour and alternative relationship arrangements (e.g., polyamory), has had a variety of problems getting her work approved by IRBs. Their concerns have made it difficult to follow participants for longitudinal research or to interview teenage children of parents in non-traditional relationships. She speculates that underlying the safety issue is the squeamishness of ethics review boards when considering controversial research topics such as those involving sexuality (Elizabeth Sheff, personal communication, 16 Jan. 2013).

Sometimes it is not clear just who is a participant in a research project. David Rosenhan's (1973) study, "On Being Sane in Insane Places," illustrates the complexity of this issue. He had eight sane people gain secret admission to 12 different psychiatric hospitals. If we think of these pseudopatients as "participants" in the study, then their welfare would be an issue for an ethics review board. There were, in fact, various risks to the eight including possible assault from actual mental patients, side-effects of treatment (pseudopatients were administered 2,100 pills, some of which they had to swallow), and the risks from mistreatment by staff (one pseudopatient saw an actual patient beaten by staff for no reason the observer could discern).

But were the eight actually *participants*? The first was David Rosenhan himself, the principal investigator, who reported, that "The eight pseudopatients were a varied group. One was a psychology graduate student in his 20s. The remaining six included three psychologists, a pediatrician, a psychiatrist, a painter, and a housewife" (Rosenhan, 1973: 521). We might more accurately think of these people as research assistants or confederates. The researcher might well consider any risk to himself, or to his friends and acquaintances who served as pseudopatients, to be outside the mandate of a Research Ethics Board.

The question of "risk to whom" also arises in a follow-up to Rosenhan's first study. Staff at a research and teaching hospital heard about the first results and were publicly sceptical that such an error could occur in their hospital even though Rosenhan informed the staff that at some time during the following three months one or more pseudopatients would attempt to be admitted to their psychiatric hospital. Staff members rated people who came seeking admission as to whether they thought they were pseudopatients. Forty-one of the 193 people who came seeking help were thought to be pseudopatients and, presumably, not admitted for treatment.

Actually, Rosenhan did not send *any* pseudopatients to this hospital. If an ethics review board were assessing the risk of this procedure, who would be the participants to be protected? Perhaps they would be troubled individuals who came to the hospital with a genuine desire for psychiatric help. People who were turned away on the erroneous assumption that they were pseudopatients would not get the treatment they were seeking (and presumably needed). They might suffer from this lack of help, and might even hurt themselves or others. If this happened, it could be considered a result of the experimental arrangement, even though their identities were unknown to the researcher who had no control over what happened to them. And, in some social science work, including some areas of psychology, the people being studied do not know that research is being carried out, or that they are part of any project. They are participants only in a rather euphemistic sense. In community psychology, for instance, research is intended to have ripple effects through a system, making it difficult or impossible to know who the participants are, or what befalls them (O'Neill, 1989).

Benefit to Whom?

Ethics Review Boards are often presented with research proposals in which there is some risk to participants, but which may make a contribution to theory or to social policy. Those assessing the proposal do not necessarily come from the same research domain as the researcher, and may be uncertain about the level of potential risk or potential value of the study. It turns out, for example, that the Milgram obedience study and Zimbardo's prison simulation have sparked many lines of research that were not anticipated at the time of the original studies (DeAngelis, 2013). Despite the difficulty in assessing risk and in knowing what may come of research in another discipline, members of ethics boards find themselves having to balance these aspects of harm and benefit. What principles are appropriate?

Research may be justified by some version of the *utilitarian principle* (John Stuart Mill, 1965), meaning the best course of action is to do what benefits the most people. But as far back as the nineteenth century there has been an argument against risking the welfare of participants for possible good to society. In his influential *Introduction to the Study of Experimental Medicine*, Claude Bernard (1865) argued that one ought not perform an experiment on a human being that might be harmful to any extent, even if the result might be highly advantageous to science and/or society at large. This argument was so entrenched by the twentieth century that it became a key component in the Nuremburg trials. The Nuremburg Code (1964 [1945]) and later restatements such as the 1964 Helsinki Declaration (see World Medical Association, 2008) enshrined the privilege of individual welfare over scientific knowledge or supposed social good.

It is generally acknowledged that participants may consent to risky research if they themselves believe a contribution to knowledge and/ or to society should be privileged over their own welfare. Thus, some patients living with HIV/AIDS may take experimental drugs that present considerable pain and risk with little or no benefit to them personally. It is hard to see how a Research Ethics Board could legitimately refuse to permit such a choice.

Participants who make the choice must, of course, know details about the likely consequences. They must be in a position to give free consent, and the consent must be *informed* about such matters as risk and benefit. Some people are not in a situation in which their consent can be considered freely given, such as prisoners and sick people. Some lack capacity because of age or mental impairment, for instance, to give such consent.

According to the Helsinki Declaration, those who lack the ability to consent (such as children) must not be included in a research study that entails above-minimal risk and that has no likelihood of benefit for them. It may be argued that parents could provide consent for a child to be in such a study. But this is also a controversial area. Parents weigh the risks and benefits for their own child, but what is the moral or legal basis for a parent or guardian to enrol a child in a risky study that has no benefit for the particular child?

Conclusion: The Challenges of Assessing Risk

No one disputes the need to protect participants in research. Nevertheless, scholars from different disciplines are expressing concern about the way in which Ethics Review Boards approach the task of assessing risk, and the apparent lack of consistency among boards (Shah et al., 2004). Many social scientists rue the day that granting agencies decided that ethics should be governed by a single set of rules across disciplines from social psychology to anthropology to medicine. Some argue (e.g., van den Hoonaard, 2011) that the ethics review process, subjecting research to a single set of rules, may deform individual social sciences and methods, including many that involve very low risk to participants.

Scholars who contributed to this book met in Fredericton, New Brunswick, in 2012 to discuss problems with ethics review processes as they affect their disciplines. This chapter is intended to contribute to the knowledge pool by discussing assessment of risk in one particular social science discipline – psychology. I cited several studies, famous both for their ethical challenges and their impact on the discipline. These studies (e.g., Milgram's obedience study, Zimbardo's prison simulation) are so well known that Ethics Review Boards may inflate risks posed by social psychological research.

This chapter includes a discussion about varieties of harm (physical, psychological, economic, and social) that must be considered by Ethics Review Boards, and examples showing how different sorts of harm can occur in a single study. The question is not merely what *sorts of harm* might be relevant in considering a research proposal, but also the *level of risk* of any particular harm. How is minimal risk established? I have noted the definition promulgated by Canada's Inter-Agency Panel on Research Ethics in its *Tri-Council Policy Statement: Ethical Conduct for Research Involving Humans*, namely, that the criterion of risk should be no greater than the risk encountered by participants in daily life. Such a criterion is not without problems. This chapter includes a discussion about situations in which ethics review boards focus on risks of harm to people other than participants, specifically students, research assistants, and even principal investigators. In some cases, boards have actually barred researchers from conducting such research despite general guidance to stick to the task of protecting participants.

Ideas about the need for balance between risks and benefits are offered. In health research such as clinical trials, the risks and benefits frequently apply to the same person. But in the social sciences, the participant may be exposed to risk and the proposed benefit may accrue to scholarship or public policy in general.

Finally, I argue that Ethics Review Boards must be careful that well-known problem studies do not engulf one's judgment. Research from such diverse fields as social cognition (O'Neill, 1981) and international politics (Jervis, 1976) has shown that the decision-making of groups can be deformed by spending too much time and effort on problems that are unlikely to arise.

Those who do research and those who regulate it often come down on different sides of the argument about the value of research versus the need to protect participants. It may be that overvaluing potential knowledge may lead to ignoring some risk factors, while concern about improbable or relatively minor risks may reduce the chance of gaining new knowledge. While I have not advanced one side over the other, I have indicated why the debate will continue, and have argued that the challenge is to balance reasonable concern about risk with the value of knowledge to be gained.

REFERENCES

Bernard, Claude. (1865). *Introduction à l'Étude de la médecine expérimentale*. Paris: Baillère.
Canadian Psychological Association. (2001). *Canadian Code of Ethics for Psychologists*. Ottawa: Canadian Psychological Association.
CIHR et al. (Canadian Institutes of Health Research, Natural Sciences and Engineering Research Council of Canada, and Social Sciences and Humanities Research Council of Canada). (2010). *Tri-Council Policy Statement: Ethical Conduct for Research Involving Humans*. 2nd ed. Ottawa: Interagency Panel on Research Ethics.
DeAngelis, Tori. (2013). "Psychologists Add Caveats to 'Blind Conformity' Research." *Monitor on Psychology* 44 (2): 9.
Heider, Fritz. (1944). "Social Perception and Phenomenal Causality." *Psychological Review* 51 (6): 358–74. http://dx.doi.org/10.1037/h0055425
– (1958). *The Psychology of Interpersonal Relations*. Hillsdale, NJ: Lawrence Erlbaum. http://dx.doi.org/10.1037/10628-000
Jervis, Robert. (1976). *Perception and Misperception in International Politics*. Princeton, NJ: Princeton University Press.
Levine, Robert J. (1988). *Ethics and the Regulation of Clinical Research*. New Haven, CT: Yale University Press.
Milgram, Stanley. (1974). *Obedience to Authority: An Experimental View*. New York: Harper and Row.
Mill, John Stuart. (1965). *Utilitarianism* [1863] (reprinted in *The Utilitarians*. Edited by Jeremy Bentham. Garden City, NY: Doubleday.
Nuremberg Code. (1964) [1945, 1947]. http://en.wikipedia.org/wiki/Nuremberg_Code
O'Neill, Patrick. (1981). "Cognitive Community Psychology." *American Psychologist* 36 (5): 457–69. http://dx.doi.org/10.1037/0003-066X.36.5.457
– (1989). "Responsible to Whom? Responsible for What? Some Ethical Issues In Community Intervention." *American Journal of Community Psychology* 17 (3): 323–41. http://dx.doi.org/10.1007/BF00931040
Rokeach, Milton. (1964). *The Three Christs of Ypsilanti*. New York: Knopf.
Rosenhan, David L. (1973). "On Being Sane in Insane Places." *Santa Clara Lawyer* 13 (3): 250–8.
Shah, Seema, Amy Whittle, Benjamin Wilfond, Gary Gensler, and David Wendler. (2004). "How Do Institutional Review Boards Apply the

Federal Risk and Benefit Standards for Pediatric Research?" *Journal of the American Medical Association* 291 (4): 476–82. http://dx.doi.org/10.1001/jama.291.4.476

Sheff, Elisabeth. (2013). *The Polyamorists Next Door: Inside Multiple-Partner Relationships and Families.* Lanham, MD: Rowman and Littlefield.

van den Hoonaard, Will C. (2011). *The Seduction of Ethics: Transforming the Social Sciences.* Toronto: University of Toronto Press.

Weijer, Charles. (2000). "The Ethical Analysis of Risks and Potential Benefits in Human Subjects Research: History, Theory, and Implications for U.S. Regulation." *The Selected Works of Charles Weijer.* http://works.bepress.com/charlesweijer/124

World Medical Association. (2008). *Declaration of Helsinki: Ethical Principles for Medical Research Involving Human Subjects.* www.wma.net/en/30publications/10policies/b3/index.html

Zimbardo, Philip G. (1971). "The Power and Pathology of Imprisonment." In *Congressional Record. (Serial No. 15, 1971–10–25). Hearings before Subcommittee No. 3, of the Committee on the Judiciary, House of Representatives, 92nd Congress, First Session on Corrections, Part II, Prisons, Prison Reform and Prisoner's Rights: California.* Washington, DC: US Government Printing Office.

Zimbardo, Philip G., Susan M. Andersen, and Loren G. Kabat. (1981). "Induced Hearing Deficit Generates Experimental Paranoia." *Science* 212 (4502): 1529–31. http://dx.doi.org/10.1126/science.7233242

PART II

Outside the Comfort Zone:
New Methodologies

7 The Internet as a Stage: Dramaturgy, Research Ethics Boards, and Privacy as "Performance"

HEATHER KITCHIN DAHRINGER

In this chapter I explore the notion of *privacy* as it may or may not exist on the Internet, posing the question of whether it is at all possible to expect privacy when Internet users reveal facets of themselves through self-disclosures. I examine the blurred borderlands that obfuscate the ostensive privacy of cyber activity as it takes place within the very public domain of the Internet. Through the work of Erving Goffman, my analysis draws on notions of dramaturgy, front and back stages, and impression management, and through Irwin Altman (1977), I deconstruct the notion of privacy and question whether privacy is actually a misnomer when considering many Internet activities. Within my larger discussion, I explore further whether research ethicists in Canada, through allowances provided by the *Tri-Council Policy Statement: Ethical Conduct for Research Involving Humans* (*TCPS* 2), can reframe privacy more appropriately as a form of performance. While some writers (e.g., King, 1996; Warrell and Jacobson, 2014) have expressed concern with the use of textual data drawn through what I conceptualize as "non-intrusive web-based research" (Kitchin, 2007), my discussion here is framed by a specific legislated policy document, and it is situated within the parameters and permissions proffered by that formal policy.

In so pushing the theoretical notion of privacy as a form of performance, we can see that privacy on the Internet is largely mythical; as individuals participate in and engage information technologies they selectively reveal themselves through various levels and means of self-disclosure (see also Chester and Bretherton, 2007). Edgar Gómez et al. (2007: 1) asserted that as a "presentation of the self" online "presentation[s] of personal identity … are often openly exposed and shared," in effect, "telling of the previously unknown so that it becomes shared knowledge" (Joinson and Paine, 2007: 237).

By engaging information technologies through the creation of user-generated content (UGC) (Shade and Landry, 2012: 296), individuals, therefore, selectively reveal information about themselves to a public audience. Contemporary desire for visibility and a "culture of connectivity" in the postmodern world is encouraged and largely generated through computer technologies using social media and networking sites (Deresiewicz, 2009). As posed by Hedges (2009: 23), personal happiness in the postmodern "is bound up in how skillfully we show ourselves to the world," and, indeed, as shown by Chester and Bretherton (2007: 233), online self-presentations are largely "based on socially desirable aspects of offline personality and a desire to present an authentic impression." In Goffmanian fashion, computer technologies yield unprecedented opportunities for persons to present themselves to the world, using cyberspace as the vehicle.

Let us now consider the "paradox of privacy" (Barnes, 2006) through Canada's federally legislated research ethics protocol. The current Canadian research ethics framework consists of the revised *Tri-Council Policy Statement: Ethical Conduct for Research Involving Humans*, known more commonly as the *TCPS 2* (CIHR et al., 2010). The language of the *TCPS 2* around privacy and identification warrants reassessment, or at the very least requires clarification to the extent that researchers are less clouded by nebulous assertions that researchers must somehow maintain privacy when working with many forms of web-based data. Considering the inherently public nature of communication technologies and rapidly advancing methods of technological surveillance, a new ethics of cyberspace requires deeper analysis. In light of such technological advancements and the *TCPS 2*, researchers are entering a new frontier of research ethics laden with ambiguous privacy rules. As a result, Research Ethics Boards (REBs) across Canada will be increasingly challenged to interpret assessments of which forms of Internet research should be exempt from ethics review.

Moving Forward: *TCPS 2*, Internet Research, and Exemptions

As it bade a final farewell to the term *human subject*, the 2010 *Tri-Council Policy Statement: Ethical Conduct for Research Involving Humans* extended a warm welcome to cyber-based research and the virtual "participant." The new language of participant is more accurately aligned with the role or non-role that cyber inhabitants may or may not play in research that is conducted with them or around them. Using the term and/or concept *participant* more closely mirrors particular levels of contact, interaction, and engagement with the researcher (through online activity). The updated *Tri-Council Policy Statement* recognizes that a cyber inhabitant is not engaged in research processes as a research *participant* until the moment at which a researcher makes direct contact. If no direct contact is made with a prospective participant, a researcher is working with virtual communities through a lens of naturalistic observation in a public space, textual documents, public opinions, or some other form of material, all of which are now exempt from REB scrutiny inasmuch as risk remains minimal under *TCPS 2*.

Compared with the earlier version, the second edition of the *Tri-Council Policy Statement* is more in tune with research possibilities posed by information technologies, in that it now overtly recognizes Internet research and attempts to establish ethical parameters for the use of Internet data collection, while still with an eye towards maintaining safety and minimizing harm to those persons who actively participate in online activities. Researchers no longer have to extrapolate from the earlier language around naturalistic observation to determine whether their research enterprise needs to be formally vetted through a Research Ethics Board. The *TCPS 2* provides more clarity around which approaches to Internet research require REB review. As offered by Kitchin (2007), under the larger umbrella of "Internet research," can be derived the embedded rubric of "web-based research" and "online research," with web-based research being either engaged or non-intrusive. Kitchin's typology of identifying particularities of Internet research strategies offers a guideline by which to determine whether a specific Internet research plan requires approval by a Research Ethics Board.

Under the larger rubric of "web-based research" and "online research," collection of data from online activities or through one or more online sites is now mirrored by the *Tri-Council Policy Statement* as either (a) non-intrusive or (b) engaged (Kitchin, 2007). *Non-intrusive* research does not upset or compromise the naturally occurring dynamics of the Internet site or cyber community. Such cases are now exempt from REB review. Conversely, the moment a researcher makes contact with a cyber inhabitant for purposes of research, a human participant becomes constituted. The language of the *TCPS 2* more clearly delineates particular levels of engagement than did the earlier version; *TCPS 1* failed to provide a clear definition of human *subject*. In constituting a human *participant* only through actual contact, the *TCPS 2* assumes the logical and practical view that a human participant does not exist solely because the individual posted materials online. To this point, very importantly, Canada's new research-ethics policy document recognizes the border between text-as-data and research participation. Researchers in Canada may understand, then, that it is only through the *creation* of a human participant that REB review is required. The task now is to ensure an understanding of the point at which a human participant is created.

Figure 7.1 shows that Internet research is now the auspices under which other forms of online and web-based research ethics are guided, mirroring the language of *participant* as a direct result of researcher imposition or contact. The *Tri-Council Policy Statement*, second edition, rightly differentiates between "web-based" research and "online" research. As Costigan (1999: xviii–xix) has observed, "Research on the Internet generally divides into [these] two main categories." The first category represents the ability to search and retrieve data; the second involves *interactive* communications. In the first approach to Internet research, data are collected non-intrusively, wherein the researcher remains invisible and poses no presence within the online site. In the second approach, the researcher interacts at some level with potential participants.

Figure 7.1. Internet research: Ethical obligations.

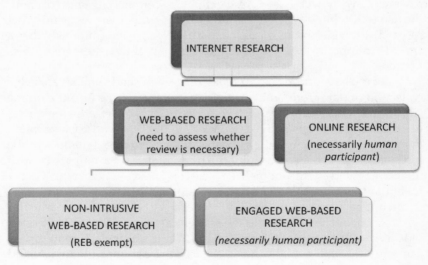

In either approach there may remains some expectation of privacy placed upon the researcher by the *TCPS* 2. When working with Internet materials, however, it may not always be clear as to whether there exists a reasonable expectation of privacy. As observed by Ananda Mitra and Elisa Cohen (1999: 182–3), "overt intertextuality" allows Internet users easy access to view and download pages given that in principle every text is linked to every other. Such interconnectivity and the open nature of the Internet contribute to the assumption that all texts and other forms of materials are created in a public domain. If we agree that the Internet is essentially a public place, we need then to determine what persons, which activities, and/or what topics of discussion can reasonably be delegated as "private."

Berry (2004: 323) observes that the growth of "intranets" and other secure network technology may, indeed, mark a clearer separation between what is public and private online, in that these more private cyber vehicles can securely connect and restrict access to and from the larger Internet system. In so doing, a more viable concept of privacy is offered, given the discontinuity of interconnection. In the event that we can say that there are cases that warrant an expectation of privacy online within the connected and open Internet, we then need consider whether REBs and Institutional Review Boards (IRBs, in the United States) are the best bodies to determine so, given that ethics boards are not legal or judicial authorities. As we move further into such questions, we may find civil law increasingly holding authority over the designation of materials as public or private in cyberspace.

Arguably, commercial violations to the privacy of consumers are not included in this discussion. I am not suggesting that the use of tracking cookies (also known as HTTP cookies, web cookies, or browser cookies) to pull out and exploit otherwise private materials for commercial purposes is an ethical use of the Internet, nor that the information gathered through tracking cookies and a myriad of other methods should fall within what most people would normally consider to be a public realm. Rather, the covert use of tracking cookies collects data that cyber inhabitants do not themselves actively choose to disclose in an informed or even conscientious manner. Nor am I suggesting that researchers not honour a particular site's terms of use. If a site's FAQ states that it is to be considered a private space, then researchers, as a matter of ethics, should respect that position. For example, at the top of the Google Discussion Board "alt.recovery.aa.narkive.com" it is clearly stated "Shared Publicly." Although some persons (including researchers) might assume that recovery in Alcoholics Anonymous is likely a private matter, the board states otherwise.

My primary point of discussion, however, lies instead with those materials that are made available online by individuals themselves, whether in a blog, on a discussion board, or anywhere else on the Internet where texts and photos may appear due to individual or group decisions to make materials available on the Internet. Ultimately, it could be argued that the responsibility of "privacy" begins with the person who is making materials available online, and possibly less with others who tap into the archived online materials. To this point, and bringing responsibility back to the actor, Viseu et al. (2004) add that when we look more closely at the term *privacy* we can see that there are "three organizing "moments" of online privacy: "the moment of sitting in front of the computer, the moment of interaction with it, and the moment after the data has been released" (92).

On the issue of privacy, moreover, Google also underscores the point that its users are operating in a public sphere. Under its "Information You Share" terms, Google (2014; emphasis added) states, "Many of our services let you share information with others. Remember that when you share information *publicly*, it may be indexable by search engines, including Google. Our services provide you with different options on sharing and removing your content."

Importantly, once material is released publicly through Google or similar search engines, the author/contributor no longer owns the material, and if seeking removal must formally apply to parties operating the search engine to request removal.[1] Furthermore, the search engine or webmaster of a particular site is under no obligation to appease one's request to do so. As observed elsewhere by O'Hara and Shadbolt (2010: 1), "Even if you enter the data yourself, for example, onto some Internet service, you do not own it – the service generally does." In signing up, one tacitly gives consent of use to the respective Internet service. Thus, if a poster does not own the text/potential data released to the Internet, the question remains as to whether that poster or blogger (etc.), can rightfully claim misuse.

Clearly, the concept of Internet privacy, while paradoxical, is an important one for those who conduct research through the Internet and the surrounding debates are, indeed, multifarious. In such a "paradoxical world of privacy" (Barnes, 2006: 2), Internet researchers might ask whether REBs are the best entities to determine whether a certain study is exempt under the *Tri-Council Policy Statement*, second edition. If not, we might then ask whether it is possible for researchers themselves to differentiate between online materials warranting privacy protection versus those that do not.

Below we will review some of the emerging issues related to Internet research and researcher responsibility that the *Tri-Council Policy Statement: Ethical Conduct for Research Involving Humans* has yet to consider in its updated document (CIHR et al., 2010). When considering the boundaries between private information and activity involving user-generated content as self-disclosure within cyberspace, REB members may find it challenging to understand (and define) the nature of self-disclosed information found online. REBs may further be challenged to differentiate between a *TCPS 2* legislated right to privacy, and performance, as a desire for visibility, providing an avenue for exemption. Due to "cultural lag" (Ogburn, 1922), however, we are not yet at an intellectual place wherein we fully grasp the interconnectedness of alleged privacy as an online expectation and performance as a presentation of self. I suggest that the notion of privacy online is necessarily belied by the performances acted out on Internet sites. The very real nuances and the relationships between privacy and performance, as they exist together on the Internet, are yet to be reconciled, or even considered, at the level of formal research ethics policy in Canada or elsewhere.

Cultural Lag

The greatest dissonance between formal policy texts and the rapid advancement and proliferation of Internet research is due to "cultural lag" (Ogburn, 1922), or "technology lag" (Convery and Cox, 2002: 51). Cultural lag provides a useful framework for understanding delays between advances in technology and use of the Internet for research purposes and, in turn, the developments in policy that attempt to regulate those technological innovations that motivate a shifting trend towards less traditional approaches to data collection. For Ogburn (1922), cultural lag occurs when non-material culture (ideological, policy-oriented directives) is challenged to stay abreast of the changing material conditions (the Internet, new methods of data collection and analyses, and technologies allowing for more proficient exchanges of knowledge and information). Cultural lag is clearly evident when we explore the gaps between postmodern developments in communications and computer technology and the intellectual and policy-related matters that seek to govern those developments. Even though the *Tri-Council Policy*

Statement first appeared as Canada's official policy document in 1998 now more than 15 years later we still struggle to understand many of the theoretical and interpretative questions around conceptualizing privacy within cyberspace and the related view of performance as it exists there.

Both *TCPS 1* and *TCPS 2*, and the documents on which they are based, attribute a somewhat sacred character to privacy. Indeed, the principles of working with human participants continue to be (a) respect for persons, (b) concern for welfare, and (c) justice (CIHR et al., 2010: 8). These core principles are intended to protect human participants to the extent possible. To this end, obtaining non-coerced informed consent is an integral requirement for researchers, though it is important to keep in mind that in *TCPS 2*, consent tied to Internet research is required only if interaction between researchers and individuals occurs, thereby *creating a participant*.

Textual artefacts found in cyberspace can serve researchers who wish to conduct ethnographies of cyber communities, or "netnographies" (Kozinets, 2002), defined as ethnographies adapted to the study of online communities, that are often less expensive than traditional ethnographies and more naturalistic and unobtrusive than focus groups or interviews. Although Robert Kozinets suggests that marketing researchers should follow four primary rules when conducting netographies, including full disclosure of researcher presence to the online community, the Canadian *Tri-Council Policy Statement: Ethical Conduct for Research Involving Humans*, second edition, holds that "non-intrusive" (Kitchin, 2007; referred to as "unobtrusive" by Kozinets, 202) online ethnographies are currently exempt from ethics review because no direct contact between the researcher and the sources of the textual community takes place. In addition, the *TCPS 2* holds that when researchers capture data through the Internet "non-intrusively" there are no research participants present, given that participants are *created* through direct contact; such non-intrusive approaches to research are now explicitly exempt from ethics review. Paradoxically, however, the *TCPS 2* continues to call for the respect for privacy of persons actively engaged in public online spaces. Importantly, though, it seems contradictory that if a study is deemed exempt from ethics review, a researcher must still conceal particular identifying details of cyber inhabitants already made public by the individuals themselves through an online venue.

Nonetheless, researchers in Canada are expected to pay attention to the environment in which observation takes place, and to monitor whether an expectation of privacy exists within a given online space. Researchers are also expected to consider whether the use of this information in the dissemination of research results (e.g., through publications, photographs, audio recordings, or video footage of groups or particular individuals) will proffer the identification of individuals or the authors of texts they are observing in cyberspace. On the surface, the *TCPS 2* directive may appear unambiguous. However, if we dig more deeply, we can see that *identification* is actually quite problematic; guaranteeing privacy is inappropriately required of a researcher because many individuals engaged in online activities involving user-generated content are breaking their own anonymity. Granted, in some public activities individuals may hope to assume some level of privacy, but how can we make that same argument for those people who, through user-generated content, are self-disclosing information?

Indeed, elsewhere Kitchin (2002), found that even members of Alcoholics Anonymous (AA) publicly displayed their actual surnames, a practice that directly subverts one of the most sacred principles of the AA program – anonymity. In this, and similar cases, is it, then, appropriate to expect a researcher to regard a public discussion board as a private space, and one which necessarily warrants concealing identifiable information of posters? Clearly, the borderlands between private and public spaces online and the aligned research ethics remain blurred, and in fact, the distinctions continue to fall largely upon one's *interpretation* of the *Tri-Council Policy Statement: Ethical Conduct for Research Involving Humans*, second edition.

Privacy as Performance

Given that there remain interpretive spaces within the *Tri-Council Policy Statement* around the question of what constitutes privacy in cyberspace, we can expect that the rules of ethical requirements will continue to be negotiated as they lag behind the material advancements of information and communications technologies. As argued by Convery and Cox (2002), it is "unrealistic to expect that any single set of guidelines can cover all ethical situations" (50) concerning ethics review boards. And as the *TCPS 2* (CIHR et al., 2010: 1) states itself, no document can be designed to cover the ethical conduct of all types of research, and as such the policy document continues to be a work in progress.

Though formalized ethics documents may remain ambiguous and thus interpretive in attempting to differentiate between online public and private spaces, framing one's ethical approach through that of "harm" would help to decipher the moral/ethical parameters of working with materials drawn from cyberspace. Those who conduct research non-obtrusively online may guide themselves by asking whether their research has the potential to pose harm through revealing identifying information. Hence, individuals who provide information about themselves online should similarly consider whether they are making *themselves* available to harm. May we rightly assume that legislated research ethics are designed to protect participants who upon consent are overtly invited into research, in which case participants are supplying data that would not be otherwise available to researchers – either on- or offline? Conversely, when materials are being self-disclosed through user-generated content, the point should be moot as to whether that data collected unobtrusively are known to the discloser. The use of such materials for research purposes does not require informed consent.

Denzin (1999) observed more than 15 years ago that the newly emerging information technologies have ".created a site for the production of new emotional self-stories, stories that might not otherwise be told" (108). To this end, individuals are provided a relatively new public, and global, venue through which to share personal narratives previously unavailable to them in such a public forum. As Denzin (1999) points out, "Self and personality are communicated in written form," and "any reader with a printer can make a perfect copy of an on-screen text" (114). The ease with which Internet materials are made available to consumers shows that what is released electronically into cyberspace quickly becomes digital fodder with enormous viral, commercial, and research potential. Indeed, researchers and journalists are now reporting that images of teenagers' sexts are being appropriated by pornographers and plastered about the Internet (Topping, 2012). Once released into the global matrix of the Internet, material may be virtually impossible to hide or delete. When pieces of our lives are released voluntarily into the public realm of cyberspace, those materials must necessarily be regarded as public, even when Internet users may not be aware that their information can be circulated far beyond their own sites of user-generated content.

Infotainment

Information technologies not only transform human beings into consumers of information (Denzin, 1995: 250), but taken a step further, we can see that they are increasingly offering outlets for amusement, or *infotainment*. Traditionally seen as an artefact of television and journalism, infotainment now may emerge from multidimensional levels of media-based entertainment found on the Internet. Indeed, many websites now identify themselves as sites of infotainment. When a website has a large infotainment appeal it enjoys a large audience, and in so doing concomitantly builds a rich revenue base through advertising. Aside from personal email accounts and programs for which an advertisement-free premium is paid, it is virtually (no pun intended) impossible to find a site online anymore that is not connected to some form of third-party advertising and/or marketing.

Infotainment can also be drawn more subtly from the personal bickering, or "trolling" behaviours found in various online sites, such as CMC discussion boards or social media sites such as Facebook and Twitter. In the same way that audience members attend a public performance to be entertained (whether a busker's performance, street theatre, or even opera), lurkers, audience members, and even researchers attend performances on the Internet. That is, watching the dynamics of personal disputes unfold online feeds the personal amusement of some observers. We are free to sit in our pyjamas at any time of the night or day to be entertained by the interactions and interpersonal conflicts played out online by others. When using media in this way, individuals can frame information and other activities found online as performance.

Use of publicly available material coupled with notions of *performance* may, then, suggest exemption from ethics review. As affirmed in *TCPS 2* Article 2.2, "Research that relies exclusively on publicly available information does not require REB review when: (a) the information is legally accessible to the public and appropriately protected by law; or (b) the information is publicly accessible and there is no reasonable expectation of privacy." In applying this directive, the *TCPS 2* adds that review by a Research Ethics Board is thus exempt in cases where,

> research uses exclusively publicly available information that may contain identifiable information, and for which there is no reasonable expectation of privacy ... Research that is non-intrusive, and does not involve direct interaction between the researcher and individuals through the Internet, also does not require REB review. Cyber-material such as documents, records, *performances* [emphasis added], online archival materials or published third party interviews to which the public is given uncontrolled

access on the Internet for which there is no expectation of privacy is considered to be publicly available information.

Exemption from REB review is based on the information being accessible in the public domain, and that the individuals to whom the information refers have no reasonable expectation of privacy. (15)

In looking more closely at the notion of performance, and the avenues by which researchers might potentially be afforded exemptions from REB reviews, it would seem that the way in which one conceptualizes the research approach informs the ethical implications, and thus obligations, of a given research enterprise. Howard Becker reasoned that he could justify his not seeking ethics approval for his research simply by claiming that "his ethnographic studies [were] a form of conceptual art" (in Shea, 2000: 32). To Becker's point, reframing research itself as "art" and the reference of study as "performance" yields further interpretive possibilities for exemption from ethics review, as provided by the *Tri-Council Policy Statement: Ethical Conduct for Research Involving Humans*, second edition.

Dramaturgy, Impression Management, Front and Back Stages

Through the words of Shakespeare, we are introduced to the notion that:

All the world's a stage
And all the men and women merely players;
They have their exits and their entrances,
And one man in his time plays many parts
                    (*As You Like It*, Act II, scene vii: 1564–67; emphasis added)

If all the world is a "stage," we have never been closer to this truth given the global interconnections proffered by information technologies. Moreover, through Erving Goffman (1959) an interesting paradigm emerges as we work through the concepts of the Internet, privacy, and dramaturgy. Goffman asserts that dramaturgy presupposes the world to be a stage, and that human behaviour is acted out conscientiously through roles; through such performances persons seek to offer an impression of themselves to others. Through Goffman we can understand performance as "the activity of an individual which occurs during a period marked by his continuous presence before a particular set of observers and which has some influence on the observers" (22). Thus, when a person appears in the presence of others on what Goffman names the *front stage*, there is normally a reason to behave in such a way that conveys a particular impression of self to others (4). "Impression management," or "self-presentation," is a process by which individuals attempt to control and influence the impressions that others – or one's audience(s) – form of them. The process of impression management occurs both on- and offline (Chester and Bretherton, 2007: 223).

As individuals move through front stages they necessarily, then, generate impressions of themselves to others. The Internet provides a venue for the performances of millions who now have access to the grandest stage ever known to humankind. In framing this point through Goffman, we can see that the traditional face-to-face front-stage human interaction is increasingly being subsumed through the vast frontiers of the Internet. Metaphorically, one may shape the impressions that others form through front-stage activity, but now, literally, performances are being played out on the Internet in front of audiences in the millions.

For Denzin (1999), information technologies have created spaces for the telling of stories, the revealing of self, and have proffered avenues through which people can now present themselves to others in a global forum. We need to consider, then, that inasmuch as the Internet provides a stage on which millions of people perform every day through revealing pieces of themselves (physically, politically, or intellectually), whether it is plausible to assume that identifiable information related to such performances need be kept private, thus warranting the protection of research ethicists. When we act, or perform, on the public stage of the Internet, we release information about ourselves of our own volition. Bloggers make themselves open to criticism from their audience(s), and "sexters" who send visual images of themselves to an online site similarly enhance the potential of harm to themselves through the usurpation of pornography sites. Conversely, if one remains on the back stage, that place that is concealed from public view, we could rightly assume that privacy is a valid expectation. Indeed, you would not expect an academic researcher to peek in your window and take notes and photos of you as you watched TV in your pyjamas. Those who perform on the "front stage" make themselves available to public review and scrutiny, while those operating on a "back stage" do not. Given the intrinsically public nature of the Internet, only activities conducted within closed, secure sites online could be considered as "back stage."

Irwin Altman (1977) conceptualizes privacy as a dynamic dialectical process wherein individuals "sometimes make themselves open and accessible to others and sometimes close themselves off from others" (67). We can thus understand privacy as a negotiated process in that it is managed through "a process of give and take between and among technical and social entities" (Palen and Dourish, 2003: 129). As a "boundary regulation process" people "optimize their accessibility along a spectrum of openness and closedness" (130). However, when we apply these ideas to Internet activity and related expectations of privacy, we are faced with the reality that once materials are released into cyberspace, it is virtually impossible to rescind them. As Palen and Dourish observe, "Technology's ability to easily distribute information and make ephemeral information persistent affects the [otherwise] temporal nature of disclosure" (133). Those front-stage impressions are normally no longer temporal or open to change or correction. Rather, once released to the Internet, the impressions individuals set of themselves will likely be carved/archived forever in their futures, thereby compromising the ability to manipulate or manage a subsequent image. Given such permanency, privacy may be nothing more than an illusion.

Creative Practice

As discussed, review by a Research Ethics Board is not required if researchers use only publicly available information, even if it contains identifying information and if there is no reasonable expectation of privacy. In addition, "creative practice" activities that do not solicit responses of participants do not require REB review. According to the *TCPS 2* (CIHR et al, 2010: Art. 2.6), "creative practice is a process through which an artist makes or interprets a work or works of art, which can also include a study of the process of how a work of art is generated."

Foucault (1983), within the context of ethics and technologies of the self, states, "We have to create ourselves as a work of art" (237). In drawing on the profundity of Foucault's point, we may conceptualize ourselves, and each other, as sociocultural selves – as created works of art. As such, might we then consider observational activities of others as creative practice? Or for that matter, may we consider our own research as works of art, thus exempting ourselves from REB review? Because we are on the front stage in a public space, to the analytical eye of the researcher individuals are performers, and as such, according to the *TCPS 2*, public performances as forms of entertainment are freely open to analysis without REB review.

The second edition of the *Tri-Council Policy Statement: Ethical Conduct for Research Involving Humans* (CIHR et al., 2010) asserts that privacy refers to "an individual's right to be free from intrusion or interference by others ... and an important aspect of privacy is the right to control information about oneself" (56). When we apply this policy to online activities, it becomes clear that, when posting or proclaiming, in most cases, individuals are controlling information about themselves, and they have enormous potential to present themselves to their publics as they wish. Further, this presentation of self is linked to commercialism and consumerism in that the draw to a particular blog, individual, or website is inextricably intertwined with the potential to generate revenue.

Conclusion

In this chapter, I have considered a number of questions about the nature of online privacy. In exploring conceptual boundaries, it is possible to categorize almost all Internet activities as public interaction and thus exempt from review by a Research Ethics Board. As a public site composed of information provided by individuals themselves as they move through cyberspace, is it reasonable to expect researchers to maintain some level of confidentiality of otherwise identifiable individuals? Moreover, in the event that a research enterprise is clearly exempt from ethics review, should researchers be obligated to maintain anonymity of online actors?

Assessing the ethical parameters and responsibilities of researchers has been simplified by the second edition of the Canadian *Tri-Council Policy Statement: Ethical Conduct for Research Involving Humans* inasmuch as it differentiates between engaged and non-intrusive web-based research. However, the *TCPS 2* has not yet begun to establish the borders separating privacy and performance as mediated by entertainment and infotainment and the roles that commercialization and consumerism play within cyberspace.

Far from being the "end of public space" (Mitchell, 1995), I predict that the Internet will prove to be our new public space, one more enormous and powerful than we might ever have imagined. These will be the spaces where we will continue to see history in the making, spaces in which we will continue to be challenged to negotiate and reconcile the cultural lag between our material worlds and the policy directives that attempt to manage the very real activities that unfold in the very public spaces of the Internet.

NOTE

1 One known exception to this rule is Facebook, which states in its "Terms of Use" that users own their page and the content that they post and share, adding that "when you post, you choose how to share and with whom, and we respect your choice."

REFERENCES

Altman, Irwin. (1977). "Privacy Regulation: Culturally Universal or Culturally Specific?" *Journal of Social Issues* 33 (3): 66–84. http://dx.doi.org/10.1111/j.1540-4560.1977.tb01883.x

Barnes, Susan. (2006). "A Privacy Paradox: Social Networking in the United States." *First Monday* 11 (9). http://dx.doi.org/10.5210/fm.v11i9.1394

Berry, David M. (2004). "Internet Research: Privacy, Ethics and Open Alienation – An Open Source Approach." *Internet Research* 14 (4): 323–32. http://dx.doi.org/10.1108/10662240410555333

Chester, Andrea, and Di Bretherton. (2007). "Impression Management and Identity Online." In Adam Joinson, Katelyn McKenna, Tom Postmes, and Ulf-Dietrich Reips (eds.), *The Oxford Handbook of Internet Psychology*, 223–36. Oxford: Oxford University Press.

CIHR et al. (Canadian Institutes of Health Research, Natural Sciences and Engineering Research Council of Canada, and Social Sciences and Humanities Research Council of Canada). (2010). *Tri-Council Policy Statement: Ethical Conduct for Research Involving Humans.* 2nd ed. Ottawa: Interagency Panel on Research Ethics.

Convery, Ian, and Diane Cox. (2002). "A Review of Research Ethics in Internet-based Research." *Practitioner Research in Higher Education* 6 (1): 50–7.

Costigan, James. (1999). "Forrest, Trees, and Internet Research." In Steve Jones (ed.), *Doing Internet Research: Critical Issues and Methods for Examining the Net*, xvii–xxiv. Thousand Oaks, CA: Sage.

Denzin, Norman. (1995). "Information Technologies, Communicative Acts, and the Audience: Couch's Legacy to Communication Research." *Symbolic Interaction* 18 (3): 247–68. http://dx.doi.org/10.1525/si.1995.18.3.247

– (1999). "Cybertalk and the Method of Instances." In Steve Jones (ed.), *Doing Internet Research: Critical Issues and Methods for Examining the Net*, 107–25. Thousand Oaks, CA: Sage. http://dx.doi.org/10.4135/9781452231471.n5

Deresiewicz, William. (2009). "The End of Solitude." *Chronicle of Higher Education* 55: 21.

Foucault, Michel. (1983). *Michel Foucault: Beyond Structuralism and Hermeneutics*. 2nd ed. Edited by H. Dreyfus and P. Rabinow. Chicago: University of Chicago Press.

Goffman, Erving. (1959). *The Presentation of Self in Everyday Life*. New York: Doubleday.

Gómez, Edgar, Elisenda Ardévol, and Adolfo Estalella. (2007). "Playful Embodiment and Identity Performance on the Internet." Paper presented at Internet Research 8.0: Let's Play, 7–20 Oct., Vancouver.

Google. (2014). *Google Terms of Service, Privacy Terms*, Apr. http://www.google.com/intl/en/policies/terms/

Hedges, Chris. (2009). *Empire of Illusion: The End of Literacy and the Triumph of Spectacle*. Toronto: Vintage Canada.

Joinson, Adam, and Carina Paine. (2007). "Self-Disclosure, Privacy and the Internet." In Adam Joinson, Katelyn McKenna, Tom Postmes, and Ulf-Dietrich Reips (eds.), *The Oxford Handbook of Internet Psychology*, 237–52. Oxford: Oxford University Press.

King, Storm. (1996). "Researching Internet Communities: Proposed Ethical Guidelines for Reporting of Results." *Information Society* 12 (2): 119–28.

Kitchin, Heather A. (2002). "Alcoholics Anonymous Discourse and Members' Resistance in a Virtual Community: Exploring Tensions between Theory and Practice." *Contemporary Drug Problems* 29 (4): 749–78.

– (2007). *Research Ethics and the Internet: Negotiating Canada's Tri-Council Policy Statement*. Halifax: Fernwood.

Kozinets, Robert. (2002). "The Field behind the Screen: Using Netnography for Marketing Research in Online Communities." *JMR, Journal of Marketing Research* 39 (1): 61–72.

Mitchell, D. (1995). "The End of Public Space? People's Park, Definitions of Public and Democracy." *Annals of the Association of American Geographers* 85 (1): 108–33.

Mitra, Ananda, and Elisa Cohen. (1999). "Analysing the Web: Directions and Challenges." In Steve Jones (ed.), *Doing Internet Research: Critical Issues and Methods for Examining the Net*, 179–202.

Ogburn, William F. (1922). *Social Change with Respect to Culture and Original Nature*. New York: B.W. Huebsch.

O'Hara, Kieron, and Nigel Shadbolt. (2010). "Viewpoint, Privacy on the Data Web: Considering the Nebulous Question of Ownership in the Virtual Realm." *Communications of the ACM* 53 (3): 1–3.

Palen, Leysia, and Paul Dourish. (2003). "Unpacking 'Privacy' for a Networked World." *New Horizons* 5 (1): 129–36.

Shade, Leslie, and Normond Landry. (2012). "Social Media and Social Justice Activism." In Les Samuelson and Wayne Antony (eds.), *Power and Resistance: Critically Thinking about Canadian Social Issues*, 5th ed., 296–319. Halifax: Fernwood.

Shakespeare, William. (2001). "All the World's a Stage." In *As You Like It*, act II, scene vii, http://allpoetry.com/poem/8449743

Shea, Christopher. (2000). "Don't Talk to Humans: The Crackdown on Social Science Research." *Lingua Franca* 10 (6): 26–35.

Topping, Alexandra. (2012). "'Parasite' Porn Websites Stealing Images and Videos Posted by Young People." *The Guardian*, 22 Oct.

Viseu, Ana, Andrew Clement, and Jane Aspinall. (2004). "Situating Privacy Online: Complex Perceptions and Everyday Practices." *Information Communication and Society* 7 (1): 92–114.

Warrell, Jacqueline G., and Michele Jacobson. (2014). "Internet Research Ethics and the Policy Gap for Ethical Practice in Online Research." *Canadian Journal of Higher Education* 44 (1): 22–37.

8 Research Ethics Boards: Are They Ready for Auto-Ethnography?

B. LEE MURRAY

> Recognizing how messy writing about intimate others can be, I have wanted to treat all [my] stories with love and care, while at the same time present [my] life as complex and many-sided ... My goal has been to balance my ethical responsibilities to participants with my truth-telling obligations to readers while accepting the risks and taking on the burdens that come with writing intimately about myself and my relationships with others.
>
> Carolyn Ellis (2009)

Auto-ethnography requires a new way of looking at research and our intentions for research. It asks us to examine knowledge from a subjective position, and it asks us to accept human experience as a form of knowing. Auto-ethnography is often about hearing and telling difficult knowledge gained from difficult experiences. It requires thoughtful telling in order to be heard. Sensitive stories require being sensitive – to the writer and the reader. Auto-ethnography is frequently uncomfortable, but comfort seldom promotes change. This chapter explores the nature of informed consent, the treatment of people in protected classes, privacy and confidentiality issues, and other ethics review processes when applied to auto-ethnography.

Anonymity and free and informed consent take on very different meanings in the context of auto-ethnography. Auto-ethnography is my story, so inherently it also includes the stories of my family, friends, and others. Can I hide who we are? How do I protect my family, others, and myself? Does my family feel the need to be protected? This chapter is an inquiry into secrets of mothering and an exploration and analysis of my life situations and the lives of others, our practices, beliefs, values, and feelings. It is an inquiry into secrets and difficult knowledge and how reluctant we are to talk about topics such as developmental disabilities, sexual abuse, divorce, accidents, and illness. This chapter is also the story of the sometimes arduous ethics review process I experienced in gaining approval to do my dissertation research – an auto-ethnographic project.

I am sitting in this familiar room (Room 3058 EDADM), but I am feeling very uncomfortable. I usually enjoy meetings in this room but not today. There is definitely anxiety floating around the room. Pat, one of my co-supervisors for my dissertation project, looks intense, and I am not used to this side of him. Debbie, the other co-supervisor, is intent and thoughtful during the conversation, but I can almost see the hair standing up on the back of her neck. Both Pat and Debbie remain calm, respectful but persistent. At first I cannot believe what I am hearing. A representative from the ethics committee is indicating that there are three main concerns, any one of which could stop the research. Stop the research! What does this mean "stop the research"? Stop is such a strong word. Isn't there any room for understanding and discussion? Will the ethics committee explain each of these concerns and allow room for discussion in context of the methodology?

The first concern is free and informed consent for my children (ages 29, 26, and 21 at the time of the application to the Research Ethics Board [REB]). The concern expressed by the board members is that my children will be unable to give free and informed consent due to the family structure. The committee does not think it is possible for children to be free to refuse consent when the parent is the researcher. They are particularly concerned about Jordan. The board is curious about Jordan's legal status, his ability to give consent and his ability to resist coercion.

I try to explain that my children are quite capable of deciding what they want and/or need to do. I struggle with this. If this were not true my children would never have challenged me, said "No," or made some of the adult decisions they have made. I encouraged Eve to go into nursing; she went into psychology. I knew McLeay was talented, and I was happy when he decided to go into film. I suggested he go to Ryerson because I thought a degree was important; he went to Capilano College because he thought it was a better program, degree or not. There is an assumption that because Jordan has Down's syndrome he is unable to make his own decisions. I thought Jordan might enjoy working in a video store, but he insisted on working in a restaurant. I suggested he begin dating the girl he took to graduation, but he indicated she was too young. All of these are adult decisions. All were made regardless of what I thought or said.

I try to explain that auto-ethnography is "my" story, and I have chosen to be open and transparent about my intentions for the dissertation. I explain that Jordan disclosed the sexual abuse nine years ago and that getting to this place has been a family process. It has been a process of recovery and support. The telling of the story has been a family decision. I'm not sure why the assumption is made that my children are not aware of this decision, and I am quite confused that the assumption would be that I would even think of doing this without discussion and support from my children, in particular Jordan. Ethically and morally, I am responsible to protect my children; I am responsible to protect all children. To meet that social responsibility, this story must be told. I must tell it.

Research has produced statistics and other data related to sexual abuse of people with developmental disabilities. One thousand cases is a statistic: one case is a tragedy, keeps ringing in my head. Statistics do not appear to move people; perhaps this story, and similar ones, will evoke a response and promote action.

The ethics committee member reassures me that the committee concurs that my intentions are proper. I think about this: "Intentions are proper." I have never really thought or considered this before – that a researcher or a student would have improper intentions for a study – but I suppose it might happen.

That all researchers have good intentions is an assumption on my part. I agree with Carolyn Ellis (2007) in that "most people want to do the right thing. As human beings, we long to live meaningful lives that seek the good. As friends, we long to have trusting relationships that care for others. As researchers, we long to do ethical research that makes a difference. To come close to these goals, we constantly have to consider which questions to ask, which secrets to keep, and which truths are worth telling" (26).

The ethics committee member remains concerned about the structural situation of the family. It is not reasonable, from the committee's perspective, to think that my children are free to give consent or not. I try to explain that my children and I are at a place of recovery and that we, as a family, did not come to this decision lightly. It is a difficult story to tell; but we feel an obligation as a family to tell the story.

I continue to question these assumptions surrounding free and informed consent for my adult children, and I keep asking myself why the assumption is not made that as a mother I will not allow any harm that I can prevent to come to my children. Why can't that assumption be made? I finally ask this question of the representative, but I don't remember the answer or if there was a particular answer. However, the discussion begins to revolve around "assuming power in relationship."

Pat indicates, "Many research projects may not go forward if we assume this power." Debbie agrees and makes the point that "if we don't challenge this assumption of power in relationship, important research may be blocked. Parents will not be able to do research with their own families; teachers will not be allowed to do research in their schools, and nurses will not be permitted to do research in their clinical settings."

"Action research, for example, is done in the researcher's own arena. The assumption of power in relationship cannot only be in the context of the home," Debbie adds.

The board members also expressed concern about support for my children and me. The committee is concerned that emotional and psychological support will be needed for me as a researcher and also for me and my children at a more personal level because they believe the writing will involve the reliving of a painful and difficult experience. I have identified support and counselling options in my proposal. However, the committee remains concerned and they indicate that identifying a neutral third party as an emotional support person will compromise the confidentiality of my children. At this point my head is spinning. I have so much I want to say, so much I need to say but the representative from the ethics committee goes on with the last and most problematic concern: confidentiality.

I knew this would be a concern. I had attempted to explain in my proposal that maintaining my confidentiality and my children's was not reasonable in this situation. I had outlined a number of ways to protect the confidentiality and anonymity of others. The REB member indicates that all these concerns are very problematic and indicates again that any one of these concerns alone could stop the research.

Pat looks concerned and troubled. He's very direct but seems to choose his language carefully. He asks, "How do we facilitate this research, not just block it?" He also inquires about whether this is an institutional stance and if this is the road we will continue to go down as a university.

This is an important line of questioning. Can we continue to evaluate qualitative research against the same standards we set for biomedical research? And, as in this case, can we judge auto-ethnography and other forms of narrative, for example, memoir, performance ethnography, and arts-based research, against more traditional qualitative research, such as focus groups, mixed methods, and interviews? And is the role of an ethics review board to regulate or facilitate? How can we work together to make it happen in a thoughtful and considerate manner? The original *Tri-Council Policy Statement: Ethical Conduct for Research Involving Humans* (*TCPS 1*) (CIHR et al., 1998: i) that guided this project and the university ethics committees in Canada until the publication of the second edition of this policy statement, *TCPS 2* (CIHR et al., 2010), encouraged sensitive and thoughtful implementation of the spirit and requirements of the document. The goals of the *TCPS 1* were to address the interdependent duties of researchers, institutional administrators, and members of Research Ethics Boards (REBs) to protect research participants. *TCPS 1* indicated that the benefits and harms of research must be fairly distributed with reasonable flexibility in implementation. The document did not offer definitive rules and answers, but rather it outlined guiding principles and standards, and identified issues and points of debate and consensus (CIHR et al., 1998: i.1–i.3). However, as Carolyn Ellis (2007) states, while these documents offer guidelines, they are typically "grounded on the premise that research is being done *on* strangers with whom we have no prior relationship or plan for future interaction" (5, emphasis added).

The first *Tri-Council Policy Statement* also stated the need for research to "alleviate human suffering; to validate theory; to dispel ignorance; to analyze policy; and to understand human behaviour and the evolving human condition" (CIHR et al., 1998: i.4). *TCPS 1* emphasized respect for human dignity during the research process with morally acceptable ends. It also emphasized morally acceptable means to those ends and a harms-benefits analysis to minimize harm and maximize benefits for participants themselves, for other individuals, or society as a whole, or for the advancement of knowledge. The intent of my research is to accomplish those goals while demonstrating my respect for our family, maintaining our dignity, and perhaps reaffirming our dignity by demonstrating the courage and determination to tell a very difficult story with respect and consideration for the human condition. It is a story that needs to be told – a story that may be unethical *not* to tell. The *Tri-Council Policy Statement* (CIHR et al., 1998: 1.6) supported the telling of difficult stories by indicating that "in evaluating the merit and the scholarly standards of a research proposal, the REB should be concerned with a global assessment of the degree to which the research might further the understanding of a phenomenon, and not be driven by factors such as personal biases or preferences. REBs should not reject research proposals because they are controversial, challenge mainstream thought, or offend powerful or vocal interest groups" (CIHR et al., 2010: 24).

My research challenges mainstream thought, including that of REB members. It is controversial, possibly offending some people. However, the intent is to increase the understanding of secrets of mothering and to challenge the normative discourse related to mothering and difficult knowledge.

"Did the committee have concerns about the methodology?" Pat asks. The ethics committee member replies, "Quite frankly, we did have a discussion about the scientific merit and rigour of auto-ethnography."

Pat is very quick to reply, "Merit and rigour are the responsibility of the student and the supervisors, and not the work of the ethics committee."

The REB member nods and replies reassuringly, but not convincingly, "Their hesitation is not with the methodology. I could offer you some time in front of the ethics committee at their next meeting, which is November 2nd, tomorrow. Also there is an appeal process, which has never been invoked thus far."

I become more unnerved as this conversation continues, and I am happy and relieved when Debbie replies, "We would welcome the opportunity to meet with the committee tomorrow," and with that the REB member leaves, but not before handing Pat a letter dated November 1st. Pat reads the [following] letter.

Ethics Office
MEMORANDUM
To: Dr Pat Renihan, Dr Debbie Pushor, and Ms. Lee Murray
Re: Review of Protocol "A Difficult Story to Tell: A Difficult Story to Hear"

Dear Dr Renihan, Dr Pushor and Ms. Murray:
Thank you for your submission to the Behavioural Research Ethics Board (REB). The full board reviewed the project at its monthly meeting. At that meeting, several very significant concerns were noted that must be

addressed before approval can be considered. I want to alert you to the possibility, that given the seriousness of the concerns raised, this project may not be approved.

Our primary ethical concern centres on the ability of the adult son with Down's Syndrome to give free and informed consent. If his mental capacity is such that he is not considered legally able to give consent on his own, and his mother gives consent on his behalf, then in our opinion there is an irresolvable conflict of interest involved with the researcher's relationship to the participant. If the participant is able to legally give consent, he remains in a highly conflicted situation. In our opinion, it is impossible for him to withhold consent even if he wished to. We are also concerned that the other adult children will feel pressured to give permission for the thesis to be written. Again, this pressure is a function of the family relationships involved rather than of any intentional overt pressure that the researcher might exert. It is a fundamental requirement of any protocol that each participant must be able to give free and informed consent with no possibility of coercion. We do not feel that this requirement can be met, given the present structure of the study.

Another significant concern includes the potential psychological stress that the project might cause both the researcher and the participants. The researcher is attempting to mitigate the possibility of unrecognized and unaddressed distress through the involvement of a relative for support to the participants. Unfortunately, the involvement of the relative raises additional concerns particularly around pressure that the researcher's children might feel to continue offering their support for the project. That is, given the family relationship, the REB is concerned that the researcher's children may feel greater pressure to extend their support for the PhD thesis than perhaps would have been the case with a truly neutral third party. At the same time, the REB also recognizes that involving a neutral third party will potentially compromise any hopes of confidentiality or anonymity for the children.

The issue of confidentiality in general is troubling. As the researcher notes, anyone who reads the thesis who is at all familiar with the family will be able to identify the individuals involved, regardless of the use of pseudonyms. Given the nature of the material, coupled with our perception that children of the researcher will feel pressured to grant permission for their story to be told, the REB sees this potential loss of confidentiality as particularly problematic.

Thank you for taking the time to meet with me. The Board has given this protocol careful consideration, but as the study exists currently, we cannot offer an approval. We would be pleased to discuss this matter further if you require clarification or feel that we have misinterpreted the protocol or overlooked mitigating factors.

The three of us stare at each other for a moment not sure what to say or do. Tomorrow is so soon, and there will definitely be some preparation to do. Maybe it is just as well. If we had to wait until the next monthly meeting of the ethics board, the anxiety would be too much. I will prepare as much as possible but am not sure what else I can do. I am familiar with the ethical guidelines, my purpose, my methodology, and my desire to protect my children, myself, and others involved. I am committed to doing this research as thoughtfully and as diligently as possible and will answer the committee members' questions as thoughtfully and carefully as possible.

Debbie, Pat, and I discussed what we needed to do to prepare, and I thought back to my comprehensive exam and the preparation I did for that. One of the questions was: "Using the *Tri-Council Policy Statement* and other documents on ethics, identify the particular issues that will arise in your research and how you would address these issues. In your response, address the standards for research done on vulnerable populations." I remember the discussion that followed this question and, in particular, issues related to free and informed consent.

According to the *Tri-Council Policy Statement* (CIHR et al., 1998: 2.1), "free and informed consent refers to the dialogue, information sharing and general process through which prospective subjects choose to participate in research," and it is ongoing (e.g., participants are free to withdraw at any time, for any reason). This process included a comprehensive discussion of the research including harms and benefits. We also noted "the requirements for free and informed consent should not disqualify research subjects who were not proficient in the language of the researcher" (2.2), but an intermediary should be used in this case.

The members of the Research Ethics Board may have made the assumption that because my son Jordan has Down's Syndrome he would not be capable of understanding what he was agreeing to do. From my perspective, he understood very well and has supported and encouraged the telling of this story. However, the research proposal also provided for an intermediary (his aunt, a social worker) who would help him understand the implications of his consent. I also understood that this research was above minimal risk.

"Above minimal risk" refers to research that warrants a higher degree of scrutiny and greater provision for the protection of the interests of the prospective participants. This provision, called "proportionate review was intended to reserve most intensive scrutiny to the most challenging research ... it implies different levels of review for different research proposals ... Proportionate review begins with the assessment from the viewpoint of the potential subject" (CIHR et al., 1998: 1.7), and encouraged discussions among researcher(s) and REB members.

> It will be important to inform the committee of Jordan's level of function and competence tomorrow and to help them understand that he is capable of making this decision and understanding the consequences of his decision.

According to the *Tri-Council Policy Statement*, competence "involves the ability to understand the information presented, to appreciate the potential consequences of a decision, and to provide free and informed consent ... It does not require the capacity to make every kind of decision. It requires [the subject] be competent to make informed decisions regarding participation in the research study" (2.9).

Following the *Merriam-Webster's Dictionary of Law* (2011), the legal definition of *incompetence* is the lack of ability, legal qualification, or fitness to manage one's own affairs. Historically, incompetence before the law has been associated with mental illness or mental deficit and an assumption of global incompetence was usually made (Canadian Psychological Association, 2009). Jurisdictions are now less inclined to embrace global incompetence and instead focus on narrow tasks and specific competencies, for example, the ability to care for self, make a will, stand trial, manage personal finances, or give consent. It is important to balance the vulnerability arising from an individual's incompetence with the injustice that would arise from being excluded from the benefits of research (CIHR et al., 1998).

If we restrict research involving people with cognitive challenges, this highly vulnerable population will be denied the possible benefits of research. Strict application of the principles of free and informed consent would deny incompetent individuals many of the benefits of research participation, either directly or indirectly. In a sense, such beneficence-based reasoning and practices intentionally exclude certain groups from research. In attempting to avoid the moral problem of exploiting vulnerable research subjects, such practices may incur the moral problem that individuals in need of the benefits of research may be denied them (CIHR et al., 1998: 5.1). Also "whether intentional or inadvertent, the exclusion of some from the benefits of research violates the commitment to societal justice. Researchers shall not exclude prospective or actual research subjects on the basis of such attributes as culture, religion, race, mental or physical disability, sexual orientation, ethnicity, sex or age, unless there is valid reason for doing so" (1998: 5.2).

The *Tri-Council Policy Statement* indicates groups who have been "disadvantaged in the context of research include women, people of colour or of different ethnicity, the elderly, children and restricted or dependent people" (CIHR et al., 1998: 5.3). It further states, "Although ethical duties to vulnerable people preclude the exploitation of those who are incompetent to consent ... there is an obligation to conduct research involving such people because it is unjust to exclude them from the benefits that can be expected from research" (5.4). There is a need for research that involves people who are not able to consent for themselves precisely because they are "unique individuals who command respect, justice, and inclusiveness that are accorded competent individuals" (5.4).

I believe that Jordan is competent to make this decision, but this belief does not preclude safety measures from being in place. The question remains, however, that even if he were deemed incompetent, should the research be prevented from going forward? Would this designation have prevented the discussion of issues – difficult issues – experienced by people with disabilities and other vulnerable populations? Would it have denied Jordan and others the benefits of research?

We would have to be prepared to discuss confidentiality, anonymity, and privacy concerns for our meeting with the REB the following day. Privacy and confidentiality are constitutional rights protected by federal and provincial statutes that indicate that private information must be treated in a respectful and confidential manner. The *Tri-Council Policy Statement* also states that, when we are considering who can be included in research, we must ask if "the overall benefits and burdens of research are distributed fairly and [if] disadvantaged individuals and groups will receive a fair share of the benefits of research" (CIHR et al., 1998: 5.1). Distributive justice means that individuals and groups should neither bear unfair burdens of participating in research nor be unfairly excluded from the potential benefits of inclusion.

I am prepared, as prepared as I can be, but sitting here in front of the ethics committee, I wonder who they see when they look at me. Do they see a researcher? Do they see a student? Do they see a colleague, a fellow faculty member? Do they see a nurse? And most importantly, do they see a mother? A mother whose son has been sexually abused. A mother who has taken many risks to tell this story, and a mother who will take many more risks before the story is told in a public realm. Do they understand that I am multiple selves? When they talk to me as a researcher, they also talk to me as a mother. Their objective and detached questions do not fit in my mother ears. I come to this meeting in ways they do not understand. And they come in ways that I do not understand. Do they see themselves as only committee members at this moment or as fellow researchers, colleagues, and perhaps parents? The meeting is a blur, and I recall discussing the three main concerns and I hope I have been convincing.

The next day Debbie is in touch, and she indicates a representative of the ethics committee has just called her. She tells me, "The representative began the telephone conversation by stating that the board members asked themselves if they would ever be comfortable with auto-ethnography and with someone who had experienced a traumatic encounter. But the REB member also indicated that they did not want to stop this type of research." Debbie continues, "The committee is still concerned about the consent/assent and wondered if I would be willing, and if I thought it appropriate, to be the agent to talk to your adult children and get consent from them. What do you think, Lee? The committee also thought it was important for me to make it clear that consent was completely voluntary, and I was encouraged to explicitly tell them that their not wanting to participate would not imperil your ability to get a PhD."

I am happy to have Debbie as the agent to obtain consent. I don't understand it, but it is workable. I am happy to name a backup therapist for my children and me. I am happy to provide more clarity. I wonder if the board will ever be comfortable with auto-ethnography and research that addresses someone who has experienced a traumatic encounter. I don't know if that comfort will come to the board. I don't think we should feel comfortable with pain and suffering, but I don't believe that avoidance will heal the suffering or address the issues. Perhaps comfort never comes with trauma, but perhaps hope and understanding may come from sharing. I then work with Debbie and Pat to develop a new proposal. I am happy with the result. The proposal now reflects the intent of my research without taking away from what I want to accomplish, and I am hopeful it will also meet the requirements of the REB. It has been more than a month now – a month of uncertainty, a month of re-thinking, negotiating, and struggling – struggling to open a door, struggling to remain positive, and struggling to see a clear path to completing the dissertation. I look at the revised proposal and wonder what the response will be. The revised proposal is sent before the deadline, and now we wait. Again.

The response from the REB arrives December 10th. It is a one-page form letter. Simple and to the point is the certificate of approval. One simple page that means so much to me, but also to auto-ethnography, other forms of narrative research, and to future researchers "of like mind" who may have a smoother journey.

Debbie, Pat, and I are able, now, to step back from our experience with the research-ethics review process and reflect with less emotion, but there is still a sense that we would not want to make the journey again. And our experience is valuable for others. How then do we begin to reposition REBs differently within the research community and the university setting? What ethical considerations need to be made in projects involving evocative research methodologies such as auto-ethnography? And, what is the role and purpose of REBs when considering this and similar methodologies? Methodology is the concern of the researcher but it also impacts the ethical decisions that must be made.

There is currently a palpable sense that the REB is a gatekeeper for what research will be allowed. How can we reposition REBs, instead, to assume a role as supportive facilitators of research, particularly research that involves sensitive stories and vulnerable populations?

How do we invite REB members to make visible the (often unconscious) assumptions they bring to reviewing research proposals? We must explore these assumptions and their relevance to narrative methods, and challenge those that are not helpful. In my auto-ethnography, *Secrets of Mothering* (Murray, 2010), I had multiple roles; not only was I a researcher, but also a mother, daughter, partner, nurse, and student. When I sat in the room with the REB members, answering questions about the sexual abuse of my son, about my son's capabilities as an individual with Down's Syndrome, I was first a mother.

We recognize that not all ethical considerations apply in the same way in all methods. Perhaps notions of free and informed consent, anonymity, confidentiality, and what constitutes data must be reconsidered in the face of methodologies that are situated within the personal realm. How do we ensure that both procedural and relational ethics will be addressed? How do REBs take into consideration the moral responsibilities for this work in addition to the ethical issues? Is it the responsibility of the REB to protect the researcher as well as the participants in the story? Is it their responsibility to protect the perpetrators of abuse as well as the victims of abuse? What if the victims want to tell their story? How can a REB facilitate the telling of those very difficult stories when *not* telling perpetuates secrecy and shame surrounding the experience? In the name of protecting the marginalized and vulnerable, why do we too often exclude them from research? And when we protect the perpetrator, we protect him or her from exposure – exposure that could benefit potential victims.

As I reflect I wonder how my journey may have been different if I had started it much earlier. What if I had met with the REB when I was first considering this approach, knowing that vulnerability would be an issue for me as well as my children and other family members? What if Debbie, Pat, and I worked together with the REB to consider both the ethical considerations *and* the support needed to tell such a difficult but very significant and valuable story? What if we met on occasion as the auto-ethnography progressed to address issues that arose along the way? And what if we worked together to solve these challenges? The assumptions of and the approach by the REB would have to shift, and perhaps the perception of REB as gatekeepers would no longer persist.

ACKNOWLEDGMENT

This chapter is based on an excerpt of my dissertation *Secrets of Mothering* (Murray, 2010) also from Murray et al. (2012).

REFERENCES

Canadian Psychological Association. (2009). *Ethical Guidelines for Supervision in Psychology: Teaching, Research, Practice and Administration.* Ottawa: Canadian Psychological Association.
CIHR et al. (Canadian Institutes of Health Research, Natural Sciences and Engineering Research Council of Canada, and Social Sciences and Humanities Research Council of Canada). (1998 , with 2000, 2002, 2005 amendments). *Tri-Council Policy Statement: Ethical Conduct for Research Involving Humans.* Ottawa: Interagency Panel on Research Ethics.
– (2010). *Tri-Council Policy Statement: Ethical Conduct for Research Involving Humans.* 2nd ed. Ottawa: Interagency Panel on Research Ethics.
Ellis, Carolyn. (2007). "Telling Secrets, Revealing Lives: Relational Ethics in Research with Intimate Others." *Qualitative Inquiry* 13 (1): 3–29.

– (2009). *Revision: Autoethnographic Reflections of Life and Work*. Walnut Creek, CA: Left Coast Press.

Merriam-Webster's Dictionary of Law. (2011). "Competence." *Merriam-Webster's Dictionary of Law*. Springfield, MA: Merriam Co.

Murray, B. Lee. (2010). "Secrets of Mothering." Doctoral dissertation, University of Saskatchewan.

Murray, B. Lee, Debbie Pushor, and Patrick Renihan. (2012). "Reflections on the Ethics-Approval Process." *Qualitative Inquiry* 18 (1): 43–54.

9 A Two-Eyed Seeing Approach to Research Ethics Review: An Indigenous Perspective

JULIE BULL

The landscape for research ethics review in Canada is a challenging one that is constantly changing. With the development and implementation of various policies and guidelines, especially in research involving Aboriginal peoples,[1] there appears to be no end to the ethics review process. To complicate things further, the Province of Newfoundland and Labrador has recently passed legislation requiring that all health research studies conducted in that province undergo provincial research-ethics review, above and beyond any review requirements already in place. These multiple layers and stages of review are likely to leave researchers confused regarding what they need to do in order to fully meet requirements at all levels.

This chapter provides a brief history of the development of guidelines and policies for research involving Aboriginal people, as well as the circumstances that necessitated those changes. This includes a review of Aboriginal and non-Aboriginal ethics review and a discussion about the complexities of community consent and research resistance within Aboriginal communities themselves. Following that review, I argue that using a two-eyed seeing model,[2] which incorporates both Aboriginal and Western principles of research ethics, for research involving Aboriginal people will yield better outcomes both for the researchers and for the communities being studied. Given that Canada is one of the leading countries in this area of study, it is of great value to determine the best possible way to conduct research ethics review. This is especially true considering that the Province of Newfoundland and Labrador is currently undergoing major policy and legislative changes[3] that are designed to contribute to a greater understanding of ways to streamline the cumbersome process for researchers conducting research involving Aboriginal people, while still assuring adequate protection for the participants.

Research Involving Aboriginal Peoples in Canada

Context

This section provides a brief history of research involving Aboriginal people in Canada by highlighting some of the key assumptions that underpin policies in this country. This is followed by a chronological account of the development of research ethics policies and guidelines in Canada for research involving Aboriginal people. This section will introduce the problematic assumptions that underlie how research involving Aboriginal peoples has typically been conducted, and then provide an overview of recent efforts within Canada to recognize and address these issues.

The history of research with Aboriginal people in Canada mirrors that of Indigenous people worldwide: research has traditionally been done *on* the population due to governmental and cultural assimilation or segregation policies, exoticization of Aboriginal ways of life, and misappropriation of their cultures (Smith, 1999; Battiste and Henderson, 2000). With scant attention having been paid to the role of Aboriginal people themselves, policymakers have only recently developed guidelines for the ethical conduct of research that actually regards Aboriginal perspectives and goals for research as central concerns.

During the past two decades, the ethical governance of research involving Aboriginal peoples has garnered international, national, provincial, and local attention (Kaufert et al., 2004), with a particular focus on Aboriginal ethics and the effects of health research on these social groups. This type of interest in health research originally grew primarily from genetic research with collectivities (groups of people who share a genetic similarity). Together, concerns regarding health research involving collectivities and Aboriginal people have fuelled much debate regarding the importance of research involving Aboriginal peoples and the ethical concerns associated with doing so.

Historically, four key assumptions contributed to the questionable treatment of Aboriginal peoples in research, and each of these remains evident in government policies. The first assumption is that Aboriginal peoples are inferior and are not capable of self-governing. The second is that treaties are merely "a form of bureaucratic memorandum of understanding, to be acknowledged frequently, but ignored often," according to the Royal Commission on Aboriginal Peoples (RCAP; Indian and Northern Affairs, 1996: 4). Third, policies have assumed that actions deemed to be of potential benefit to Aboriginal communities do not require consent or consultation by these communities. The fourth assumption is that non-Aboriginal values are sufficient in driving individual or community development, without the presence of Aboriginal values. Many scholars have described these false assumptions in detail (e.g., Smith, 1999; Battiste and Henderson, 2000; Gegeo and Watson-Gegeo, 2001; Ermine, 1995), and the Royal Commission on Aboriginal Peoples itself summarizes these assumptions in Part II of its 1996 report (Indian and Northern Affairs, 1996). While these assumptions have gradually become less explicit through the evolution of policies, they do continue to "significantly underpin the institutions that drive and constrain the federal Aboriginal policy process" (4).

Criticism of these assumptions within the literature on Indigenous ethics and policy has significantly shaped the formation of new guidelines for health research involving Aboriginal peoples in Canada, primarily through the work of the Royal Commission on Aboriginal Peoples. These efforts resulted in the creation of the Institute for Aboriginal Peoples Health(IAPH), as one of the arms of the Canadian Institutes of Health Research (CIHR), and its Aboriginal Capacity and Development Research Environments (ACADRE)[4] centres, and culminated in the CIHR Guidelines for Health Research Involving Aboriginal Peoples (2007). More than 350 research projects were commissioned through the Royal Commission on Aboriginal Peoples, including research on the ethics of research involving Aboriginal peoples, and research on respecting the culture, language, knowledge, and values of Aboriginal peoples. According to the Royal Commission on Aboriginal Peoples, this renewed attention reflected the view that "Aboriginal peoples have distinctive perspectives and understandings deriving from their cultures and histories and embodied in Aboriginal languages [and therefore] research that has Aboriginal experience as its subject matter must reflect these perspectives and understandings"[5] (Indian and Northern Affairs, 1996: 2). The important contribution of the Royal Commission on Aboriginal Peoples with respect to research involving Aboriginal peoples, then, was the assertion that a blanket approach to research ethics and health services is insufficient – that the particular needs and cultural qualities of different peoples necessitate the formulation of specific and unique guidelines for research involving Aboriginal peoples.

In 2001, Canada's prime minister established the Commission on the Future of Health Care in Canada. The mandate was to review Medicare (Canada's publicly funded universal health insurance system) and consult with Canadians about the future of health and the health care system. Led by Roy Romanow (a former premier of Saskatchewan), the Commission released *Building on Values: The Future of Health Care in Canada* in 2002 – the *Romanov Report* (Commission on the Future of Health Care in Canada and Roy J. Romanow, 2002). As the Royal Commission on Aboriginal Peoples did in 1996, the *Romanow Report* identified the need for restructuring health research involving Aboriginal peoples. Importantly, the *Romanow Report* stressed the need for community input and collaboration through holistic approaches as the means to accurately reflect the needs of the community.

Policies

The recommendations of the Commission on the Future of Health Care in Canada coincided with the movement towards self-determination by Aboriginal peoples in Canada and elsewhere, which, along with the subsequent rise in research on community health in Aboriginal contexts, led many Aboriginal communities to develop their own ethics review processes and procedures. According to Iara Guerriero (personal communication with W.C. van den Hoonaard, Oct. 2011), Canada has some 33 ethics guidelines that outline the nature of ethical research involving Aboriginal peoples. One of the most significant developments was produced by the Steering Committee of the First Nations Regional Longitudinal Health Survey, which, in conjunction with the First Nations Centre at the National Aboriginal Health Organization (NAHO), developed principles of Ownership, Control, Access, and Possession (OCAP) of data[6] as "an expression of self-determination in research" (Schnarch, 2004: 81). These principles, which incorporate themes advocated by First Nations in Canada regarding research,[7] were very clearly "a political response to tenacious colonial approaches to research and information management" (80). Identifying the principles as "a way out of the muddle of contemporary Aboriginal research and the ethical dilemmas that characterize it" (80), Schnarch argued that researchers should become aware of these new principles and integrate them into their research

Canada's *Tri-Council Policy Statement: Ethical Conduct for Research Involving Humans (TCPS 1)*, developed by the Tri-Council Working

Group, included a section about research involving collectivities, but the final 1998 policy statement did not (CIHR et al., 1998). In its place was section 6, a temporary "place holder" for guidelines for research involving Aboriginal peoples. The preface noted that section 6 had undergone insufficient consultation at the time of publication, such that it was premature to establish policy for ethics involving Aboriginal peoples. Section 6 was to be developed through discussions and consultations with Aboriginal peoples.

In 2003, the Interagency Panel on Research Ethics (PRE), as the trustee of Canada's *Tri-Council Policy Statement: Ethical Conduct for Research Involving Humans*, was committed to revising the *Statement*, including section 6.[8] Meanwhile, drawing on the OCAP principles, the ACADRE Centres, in collaboration with researchers and Aboriginal communities, the Canadian Institutes of Health Research ethics office, and the CIHR Institute of Aboriginal Peoples' Health, conducted background research with the goal of creating a set of guidelines for research involving Aboriginal peoples (PRE, 2002).[9] From that process, the Canadian Institutes of Health Research created an external advisory body called the Aboriginal Ethics Working Group in 2004 (CIHR et al., 1998). That group then collaborated with the ACADRE Centres, Aboriginal communities, and scholars in Indigenous studies, anthropology, ethics, law, medicine, public health, and the natural and social sciences (CIHR et al., 1998), resulting in the development of the 2007 *CIHR Guidelines for Health Research Involving Aboriginal People*. These *Guidelines* were officially implemented by the Canadian Institutes of Health Research in 2009.

Less than a year later, in 2010, the three federal research agencies (Canadian Institutes for Health Research, the Natural Sciences and Engineering Research Council of Canada, and the Social Sciences and Humanities Research Council of Canada, collectively known as the "Tri-Council") released its new draft of the second edition of the *Tri-Council Policy Statement: Ethical Conduct for Research Involving Humans* (*TCPS 2*). This document replaced the placeholder in the original *TCPS* with a full chapter about research involving First Nations, Inuit, and Métis people and communities.[10]

Principles of Aboriginal and Non-Aboriginal Ethics

There are many ways in which Aboriginal and non-Aboriginal perspectives differ with regard not only to how research is conducted but also how proposed research is assessed, and how these differences lead to issues that must be addressed in order for research in Aboriginal communities to be done in an appropriate manner. Combining all Aboriginal and non-Aboriginal principles together is ill-advised, especially considering the obvious variations, deviations, and overlaps that exist within each group. However, to get a clear idea of the fundamental differences between these groups with respect to how they understand ethics in research, it is necessary to juxtapose the basis of these principles.

Non-Aboriginal notions of ethics, as developed within the biomedical framework, focus primarily on the individual (Beauchamp and Childress, 1994). The cornerstone principles of bioethics are autonomy (self-determination), non-maleficence (no harm), beneficence (obligation to do good), and justice (fair treatment and privacy). The biomedical framework sees the individual "self" in a way that is spatially and temporally different from conceptualizations of the self that exist within Aboriginal frameworks. In traditional Aboriginal ways, the self is not bound by the individual. Rather, it includes past and future generations in the community. The Aboriginal notion of the "self" constitutes a sacred space, with interconnected relationships among living humans and other spiritual entities, the land, ancestors, and animals; there is no separation of the individual from these other elements (Ellerby et al., 2000). Non-Aboriginal concepts of "self" give little or no regard to such relationships.

The focus on "individual ethics" is therefore culturally inappropriate in most Aboriginal contexts. Consequently, it is necessary "to view contemporary ethical standards for Aboriginal health research within a broader historical context and through both Aboriginal and western scientific perspectives" (CIHR, 2007: 10). Such integration of two world views (or more, considering the possible existence of differences *within* the two categories) is reflected in Marshall's understanding of two-eyed seeing (Bartlett and Marshall, 2010), and supports the notion that considering these two world views yields greater understanding of and outcomes for those involved. With these issues in mind, researchers must alter their methodologies to reflect a holistic undertaking that reflects Aboriginal perspectives – rather than the typical individual-centred approach – and they may also have to re-evaluate their understanding of concepts like *ownership* and *sharing*. Even the ethics review itself must be altered in order to accommodate how this process is understood and perceived by Aboriginal peoples.

Formulating research ethics that suit a particular group (e.g., Aboriginal peoples) involves establishing research methodologies that reflect (or at least do not contradict) local cultural norms and community values, obviating the norms and values held by the researcher, regulator, research institution, or participant (Weaver, 1997). This approach does not necessarily require complete changes to research methods – it can be as simple as engaging in an interview instead of survey research. As Renee Louis (2007) states, "Indigenous methodologies can invigorate and stimulate geographical theories and scholarship while strengthening Indigenous people's identities and supporting their efforts to achieve intellectual self-determination" (137). Thus, a holistic research approach is more favourable in Aboriginal methodologies (Ermine, 1995; Smith, 1999; Battiste and Henderson, 2000; Atleo, 2004; Porsanger, 1999), in contrast to many Western methodologies that have the "tendency to compartmentalize experience and thus assume that some parts have no relationship to other parts" (Atleo, 2004: xi).

In addition to addressing how research is conducted, researchers must also consider how Aboriginal cultural values and concerns apply to the ownership and sharing of data, and how this differs from the traditional ways in which data are conceptualized and handled. The importance of protecting traditional knowledge stems from issues of fundamental justice and of protecting and preserving culture (Smith, 1999). Protection of Aboriginal people is necessary in part because of the misuse and misappropriation of traditional knowledge by mainstream interests (Smith, 1999). To address critical issues of colonialism and to avoid both misrepresentation and marginalization of Aboriginal ways of knowing, Aboriginal communities have developed Indigenous knowledge frameworks (Battiste and Henderson, 2000; Smith, 1999). The language of ethics coming from Aboriginal peoples, scholars working in the field, and from Aboriginal communities, indicates the existence of conflicting interpretations of ethics that are based in different world views (Smith, 1999; Battiste and Henderson, 2000; Bull, 2010).

There is a general mistrust of research and researchers in Aboriginal communities, which can be especially problematic considering that trust is a key element of research. A researcher entering an Aboriginal community for the first time can expect trust to be absent and hard to earn, thanks mostly to a long history of political oppression. To rebuild this trust, researchers need to create relationships on a foundation of respect, relevance, responsibility, and reciprocity (Bull, 2010). While these fundamental notions of respect are not unique to Aboriginal value systems, all of them have been seriously lacking in mainstream research practices and are particularly important in the case of Aboriginal peoples. Indeed, values of respect, relevance, responsibility, reciprocity, and protection do not contradict the applied principles in conventional non-Aboriginal ethical frameworks, but this framework undergoes a shift when applied to research in Aboriginal communities.

In terms of developing trust, researchers must remember that political and economic oppression cannot be separated from issues of research. As Joseph Kaufert et al. (2004) remind us, "Research should focus on locally relevant problems, or ensure that there be a commitment to community-based capacity building and the generation of local knowledge" (25).

The lack of understanding by researchers (and by non-Aboriginal ethics review committees) of the historical processes of oppression and injustice "represent[s] a fundamental shift in the philosophical basis influencing the guidelines" in the *Tri-Council Policy Statement: Ethical Conduct for Research Involving Humans* (Kaufert et al., 2004: 44).

Research Resistance

This section highlights the necessity for decolonization in research involving Aboriginal people and research resistance from within Aboriginal communities themselves.

To address the numerous issues that arise from differences in perspectives and values, Gillam and Pyett (2003) propose a complementary process where multifocused frameworks and documents are used to express key points of convergence and disconnection between Aboriginal communities and non-Aboriginal ethics review committees, including Research Ethics Boards (REBs). However, resistance to non-Aboriginal research approaches and their ethical suppositions began much earlier, in the 1970s, when Aboriginal scholars and writers began to criticize the imposition of research on Aboriginal peoples (Deloria, 1991). Aboriginal scholars provided important critiques, highlighting the problem that Western research conducted on Aboriginal communities invalidated Aboriginal knowledge, leading to a disconnect in "traditional teachings, spirituality, land, family, community, spiritual leaders [and] medicine people" (Absolon and Willett, 2004: 9). The process of decolonization does not merely include the rejection of Western scientism – it is also about "centering our concerns and world views and coming to know and understand theory and research from our own perspectives and for our own purposes" (Smith, 1999: 39). The concept of *pluralism* is an essential dimension in Aboriginal ethics wherein the diversity among and within Aboriginal communities makes it difficult to develop widely applicable ethical decision-making processes. As Jonathan Ellerby et al. (2000) aver, "Despite some shared beliefs, each cultural group must be treated with respect and an understanding of inherent diversity" (70).

Scrutinizing the purpose of the research itself is a significant aspect of the movement to decolonize research involving Aboriginal peoples. Westerners, particularly anthropologists, have primarily conducted research that is of an exotic (and essentializing) nature, at the expense of research that might have improved the well-being of Aboriginal people. Much of the research conducted in Aboriginal communities historically has had little or no positive impact on the health or social well-being of those communities, and even tends to paint Aboriginal people as inferior by focusing more on perceived deficits rather than on the strengths of people or communities. Aboriginal communities are now understandably cautious, and are challenging the research community to be cognizant of research practices that are based on exploitation, racism, ethnocentricity, and harmfulness (Smith, 1999; Battiste and Henderson, 2000): "Homogenisation, exoticisation, and misrepresentation are an interrelated cluster of historical contexts that shape the meaning of 'ethical' research and define contemporary strategies for ownership, control, access, and protection" (Brunger and Bull, 2011: 133). As the CIHR Guidelines for Health Research Involving Aboriginal People remind us, "[All] parties should understand that all research involving Indigenous knowledge, even when not commercially motivated, has the potential to be commercialized and possibly misappropriated when publication occurs" (CIHR, 2007: 23).

Political climates in and among Aboriginal communities cannot be separated from ethical and epistemological perspectives. Ethical frameworks that are meant to function in Aboriginal contexts must incorporate Aboriginal values and must disallow the forced Western imposition that has characterized past practice (Scott and Receveur, 1995; Brant-Castellano, 2004). To accomplish this, researchers must take cultural norms and values into account in research design and methodology. Yet, making predictions based on general tendencies can be problematic, as well, due to the variability that exists not only between groups but also within them. The importance of attending to cultural values and beliefs is not for predictive value, but rather to offer a critique of the degree of generalizability of established cultural norms (e.g., the importance of individualism in non-Aboriginal bioethics systems) to all contexts.

Some of the concerns expressed by Aboriginal people are rooted in their own values and ethics systems, which in some cases differ greatly from Western views. Nonetheless, many Aboriginal values, ethics, and epistemologies are parallel to those of the Western world, such that the goals of Western approaches to research ethics are not necessarily incompatible with Aboriginal understandings of ethical research. The disconnection that arises relates more to the ideologies and theories about *how* to conduct ethical research and the actual *processes* of conducting ethical research. The most notable example of this is informed consent. In theory, informed consent is an ongoing process, rather than the single act of signing a consent form. However, it is not uncommon for researchers to reduce the process of informed consent to the one-time signing of a consent form. This problem, rooted in the discrepancy between what consent is intended to represent and how it is actually handled within research, is not unique to research with Aboriginal people.

Community-Driven Ethics Review

As a natural extension of self-determination, Aboriginal communities are (re)claiming control over programs and services; as a result, research ethics and governance have become priorities in Aboriginal communities. This section explains the complexities of community consent and highlights the importance of community relevance in research involving Aboriginal people. Aboriginal communities have developed highly effective community consent contracts and ethics review systems and procedures. The Code of Ethics of the Kahnawáke Schools Diabetes Prevention Project (1996) and the *Manitoulin Island Guidelines for Ethical Research* (2001) provide two of the best examples. By controlling their own research agendas, Aboriginal people are able to use their spiritual and philosophical foundations to guide how research is done (Smith, 1999). This does not mean that only Aboriginal people can conduct Aboriginal research, but that they are intent on playing a greater role in how that research is conducted. Communities that are actively engaged in developing research priorities have a greater sense of involvement, ownership, and accomplishment overall.[11]

Community Consent

These community-driven research agreements have both shaped and been shaped by academic writings on the very issue of collective consent to research. Where an entire community is at risk, even if only a few people from the community participate, individual consent is necessary but not sufficient (Greely, 1997; Weijer et al., 1999; Burgess and Brunger, 2000; Kaufert et al., 2004). According to Henry Greely (1997), "It is the group's collective autonomy that is challenged if researchers, with informed consent of only a few individuals in the group, can probe for information about the whole group" (1431). Likewise, health research can present genuine risks for socially identifiable populations, further indicating that individual informed consent is not sufficient for ethical research involving Aboriginal peoples (Brunger and Weijer, 2007; Weijer et al., 1999; Kaufert et al., 1999).

The approach to gaining community consent in Aboriginal communities is similar to the process of conducting research in a school environment. Researchers are frequently required to get approval from the school board, principal, teacher(s) of class(es), parents of children participating, and finally the children themselves. Likewise, consent within an Aboriginal community may involve getting different forms of consent that go beyond just the consent of the study participants. Yet, the kind of approach described above does not always articulate the complex realities of authority structures within Aboriginal communities. The lines of accountability are not obvious, especially if no group of elders or a politically appointed council exists. At the same time, one must consider how the individual interests of those who might be in a position to offer consent for the community may conflict with research beneficial to that community. Consider the scenario of a researcher examining Aboriginal chiefs' perspectives on, and their treatment of women. Community members may be eager to participate in such a study, but how would "community consent" be obtained? It is unlikely that chiefs would agree to this proposed research given that they likely perceive they are being targeted by it. For this reason, Aboriginal communities are implementing research governance structures that are independent of political governance.

A common issue raised in relation to community consent is finding the appropriate authority. Organizations in every province are in place to provide assistance, as is recognized in the CIHR Guidelines for Health Research Involving Aboriginal People: "The determination of a

community's best interests regarding knowledge may be the responsibility of the family, the band (several families combined), the tribe
(several bands combined), or the confederacy (several tribes together)"
(CIHR, 2007: 15). This discourse is specific to First Nations, but similar
structures can exist in other Aboriginal communities, many of which
have multiple structures of authority, meaning that discussion and
negotiation is necessary in order to identify the most appropriate body
for any given project. Researchers should not "assume that one political body has complete authority" (16), as is typical in non-Aboriginal
systems. Negotiating these political relations is necessary but difficult:
such relationships and structures differ not only from community to
community, but also over time.

When an appointed authority and a cohesive community are in
place, researchers must collaborate with that community to ensure that
the research goals are appropriate, that they explain and justify potential harms and benefits, and that methods are congruent with the community needs and expectations (Greely, 1997; Bull, 2010; Weijer et al.,
1999; Burgess and Brunger, 2000). Brunger and Bull (2011) make the
point that "speaking on behalf of a group raises problems of representation and authority given intra-group politics and power differentials,
even within a relatively cohesive community" (136). Individual consent should be obtained only after this community-level consultation
begins. The importance of community consent and collective decision-
making in general does not erode individual autonomy or the requirement for individual informed consent in these situations.

Conceptual and operational problems plague attempts to define *community* and *community consent*, but, according to Joseph Kaufert and his
colleagues (2004), "this debate also reflects a general and continuing
lack of consensus over their meaning" (13). In the context of Aboriginal
research, community "constitutes a structure of support mechanisms
that includes an individual's personal responsibility for the collective, and reciprocally, the collective's concern for individual existence"
(CIHR, 2007: 15). It is also important to recognize that many Aboriginal
communities have "distinct political, legal, and cultural governance
structures that have political legitimacy and that support their jurisdic-
tional and decision-making authority on a broad spectrum of issues"
(16). Community guidelines, according to Kaufert et al. (2004), "tend to
emphasize the uniqueness of each community and hence, the need for
approval of research studies that could have implications for the community as a whole" (16). Thus, researchers have an "obligation to learn

about the local customs of an Aboriginal community" (CIHR, 2007: 24) and abide by these customs every time.

Community Relevance

Community relevance in Aboriginal research is part of the ethics review process from the community perspective. REBs should not be responsible for connecting the researcher with the community. Instead, the onus is on the researcher to establish this relationship. Communities have for many years been giving research information and data to researchers who have used that information *only* for the researcher's benefit, sometimes only in pursuit of academic degrees. Consider a small Aboriginal community with increasing rates of suicide. Such a community would not likely be open to researchers interested in the prevalence of suicide, but will welcome those who will be exploring the issue of access to mental health services and care for those suffering from suicidal ideation.

Though it may be the case that some community members have a misconception of what research can and cannot do, they ought to realize that the concept of *benefit* should not be taken to mean benefits in specific health outcomes. Some research will prioritize social or economic benefits as being valuable. These types of benefits range from discussing intervention- or program-based conclusions to offering to assist in building local capacity. Community members generally understand that not all research will have direct or immediate benefits. Although researchers cannot promise such things, indirect benefits may come to the community being studied; these may include "financial or other direct remuneration to participants or to community cause; clinical outcomes for individuals; evidence to support a local initiative to secure program funds; employment for research assistants; and workshops or trainings sessions in the community for capacity building" (Brunger and Bull, 2011: 132).

Ethical Space and Two-Eyed Seeing

Ethical space refers to understanding the strengths and challenges of bringing together different ways of knowing and applying it to practice. The concept, originally coined by Roger Poole (1972), was further developed by Willie Ermine (1995) into a theoretical framework with Western and Aboriginal knowledge relative to research. Ethical space essentially represents a complicated and abstract realm in which two entities with different intentions can meet. It is unlikely that the community (one of the two entities) will have one united set of intentions and perspectives, so any ethical space will inevitably be complicated at the community level due to conflicting views within and among bands, chiefs, elders, community members, and organizations. Ermine's notion of ethical space helps illuminate the complexities of the researcher–research community relationship.

Part of understanding an Aboriginal ethical space is to understand the role of traditional knowledge and sacred space in research. This is especially pertinent with research specifically examining a sphere of traditional or sacred knowledge; however, it should be applied to all research involving Aboriginal people. As the *CIHR Guidelines for Health Research Involving Aboriginal People* asserts, "Any research involving Aboriginal people will involve the sharing of some cultural knowledge, practices, and/or traditions even when these are not the subject of the study, as they provide necessary context" (CIHR, 2007: 22).

If we consider this abstract space as the meeting point of two world views, it is in that space that the model of two-eyed seeing is evident and valuable. Mik'maq Elder, Albert Marshall (see (Bartlett and Marshall, 2010) submits that seeing the world from Indigenous and Western perspectives yields a more holistic understanding of any given phenomenon. In this case, bringing together principles and practices from Western and Indigenous ethics and ethics review gives a greater understanding of how to implement policies such as the *Tri-Council Policy Statement: Ethical Conduct for Research Involving Humans.*

From Principles to Practice

Research with Aboriginal peoples does not require a complete dismissal of traditional academic research processes. Rather, researchers and communities should work together on the basis of respect for the ethical spaces of all parties, asking continuously, "Is this ethical?" (CIHR, 2007: 17). Achieving this goal requires discussions of the "intentions, values, and assumptions" (17) throughout the duration of the project.

The NunatuKavut (formally the Labrador Métis Nation) is introducing a rigorous community-based research review process. Brunger and Bull (2011) conducted a study in Labrador to find out what should be included in community research ethics review and identify "whether and how community review should be distinct from the centralized 'institutional' research ethics review that would be the mandate of the Newfoundland and Labrador's ... provincial research authority" (127).

The research relationship between Brunger, Bull, and the NunatuKavut community began in 2006 after a workshop about community health research, called "Learning, Listening and Working Together," that was sponsored by the Atlantic Aboriginal Health Research Program. This workshop brought together health workers, community members, and university-based researchers to identify priorities for health research. Two overarching themes emerged: (1) research ethics and (2) the governance of health research involving Aboriginal people. A key outcome of the workshop was the development of the Labrador Aboriginal Health Research Committee (LAHRC).[12] The LAHRC assumed the role of advisory committee for Brunger and Bull's (2011) project and identified key people in the community to be interviewed. These interviews identified several concerns related to benefit sharing,[13] dissemination, and community autonomy: "This cluster of interrelated concerns was understood and discussed as being inextricably connected to the context of ongoing colonization, assimilation, and exoticism" (131).

The issues raised by community members in Labrador echo the concerns mentioned throughout this chapter. By having a community ethics review system in place, the interests of the local group can be recognized and considered. The policy set out in Newfoundland and Labrador clearly defines the role of ethics review and community review, and serves as a good example of how to streamline the review process for research involving Aboriginal people. There must be clear evidence of acceptable community review before the Health Research Ethics Board (HREB) will approve any research involving Aboriginal people. It is recognized that Aboriginal communities are at different stages of developing research review committees, and not all communities have the capacity to review projects. For this reason, if there is a community authority, there is a requirement to have a community-researcher agreement. If no clear authority structure exists, a community consultation and a letter of support are necessary prior to obtaining HREB approval.

Conclusion

This chapter addresses many of the issues and challenges raised in chapter 9 of the 2010 *Tri-Council Policy Statement: Ethical Conduct for Research Involving Humans* (*TCPS 2*). However, it is not evident in this policy statement how to actually enact its principles. Because the focus of the *TCPS 2* has shifted to participant involvement and community engagement, it is imperative to determine a way to operationalize these concepts and enact the principles. A common challenge, of course, lies in the fact that any principle-based approach is open to interpretation, may be understood differently by different people, and may be criticized for being unscientific. What is evident is the need to incorporate non-Aboriginal and Aboriginal frameworks using a two-eyed seeing model. The work being done by Brunger et al.[14] in Newfoundland and Labrador will continue to contribute to the body of knowledge about ways to streamline the research-ethics review process and develop a theoretical framework for implementing the principles of the *Tri-Council Policy Statement: Ethical Conduct for Research Involving Humans* in Aboriginal settings.

NOTES

1 The term *Aboriginal* is used to refer to Canada's Indigenous peoples – First Nations, Inuit, and Métis. These three groups are recognized by the Constitution Act of Canada, section 35.

2 The Two-Eyed Seeing Model was developed by Mik'maq Elder Albert Marshall (Bartlett and Marshall, 2010). Marshall's development of "Two-Eyed Seeing" teaches us to use the best of both Aboriginal and non-Aboriginal world views to make positive strides forward. He recognizes the substantial value that multiple perspectives give and it is by using multiple perspectives that a better and more holistic understanding is achieved.

3 Since the proclamation of the Health Research Ethics Authority in 2011, all research conducted in the province of Newfoundland and Labrador must undergo two levels of review: one by the provincial Health Research Ethics Board (HREB) and a second by Aboriginal communities themselves. The HREB requires researchers to adhere to both the *TCPS 2* and the *CIHR Guidelines for Health Research Involving Aboriginal People* (CIHR, 2007) and will not approve projects until community acceptance has been obtained and proved through submission of a community-researcher agreement (where a research authority exists) or a support letter through consultation (where no research authority exists).

4 Revamped and renamed Network Environments for Aboriginal Health Research (NEAHR).

5 This is not to say that every research project is required to incorporate spiritual or cultural components. For example, a study designed to

identify the prevalence of a chronic disease may not explicitly refer to the spirit world. However, Aboriginal peoples may appeal to these views, and it will become part of the research whether the researcher anticipates it or not.

6 The National Aboriginal Health Organization (NAHO) was incorporated in 2000. It is designed and controlled by Aboriginal peoples while advocating for the health and well-being of all Aboriginal peoples. NAHO has three centres – First Nations Centre, Ajunnginiq (Inuit) Centre, and Métis Centre. Each centre focuses on the distinct needs of their respective populations while promoting culturally relevant approaches to health care service and delivery. Available from http://www.naho.ca/jah/english/jah01_01/journal_p80-95.pdf

7 OCAP principles were developed by First Nations for use in First Nations communities; however, some Inuit and Métis communities also apply notions of OCAP in their governance of health research.

8 The Interagency Panel on Research Ethics (PRE) was established in 2001 by the three national funding agencies – CIHR, NSERC, and SSHRC – as a joint effort to support the development of the *Tri-Council Policy Statement: Ethical Conduct for Research Involving Humans*.

9 Established by CIHR's Institute of Aboriginal Peoples Health, the ACADRE Centres were implemented in 2001. These centres were developed to encourage networking and the development of Aboriginal capacity in health research. Now called the Network Environments for Aboriginal Health Research. ACADRE funding ended in 2007; funding started in November 2007 for NEAHR.

10 The *CIHR Guidelines* specifically state that researchers who do not comply will lose funding from that source. Because no such prescriptive measure is in place in the *TCPS 2*, there is some controversy about the policy within Aboriginal communities.

11 This community-driven approach generally elicits practical outcomes that yield direct benefits to the community (Sinclair, 2007). This is not to say that only community-based research among Aboriginal people is ethical or that all research must provide explicit benefit to a particular community.

12 Comprised of representation from Nunatsiavut Government, NunatuKavut, Shshatshui and Mushuau Innu Health Commissions, Health Canada, Labrador-Grenfell Regional Health Authority, Rural Secretariat Provincial Department, Atlantic Aboriginal Health Research Program, and the Labrador Institute-MUN Extension.

184   Julie Bull

13 Especially in terms of applicability to community well-being rather than individual health.
14 F. Brunger (PI), J. Bull, J. Graham, D. Pullman, D. Wall, C. Weijer (Co-Investigators), The Labrador Inuit-Métis Research Ethics Project: An Experiment in Aboriginal Governance of Health Research in Complex Communities, CIHR Operating Grant, 2010–13 ($180,000).

REFERENCES

Absolon, Kathy, and Cam Willett. (2004). "Putting Ourselves Forward: Location in Aboriginal Research." In Leslie Brown and Susan Straga (eds.), *Research as Resistance: Innovative, Critical and Anti-oppressive Approaches to Knowledge Creation*, 97–126. Toronto: Canadian Scholars Press.

Atleo, E. Richard. (2004). *Tsawalk: A Nuu-Chah-Nulth worldview*. Vancouver: UBC Press.

Bartlett, Cheryl, and Albert Marshall. (2010). "Two-Eyed Seeing Science Curricula." Paper presented at the Community Education Strategic / Operational Planning Symposium for "Language and Culture" of Mi'kmaw Kina'matnewey, 11 Mar., Dartmouth, NS,.

Battiste, Marie, and J. Youngblood Henderson. (2000). *Protecting Indigenous Knowledge and Heritage*. Saskatoon: Purich.

Beauchamp, Tom L., and James F. Childress. (1994). *Principles of Biomedical Ethics*. New York: Oxford University Press.

Brant-Castellano, Marlene. (2004). "Ethics of Aboriginal Research." *Journal of Aboriginal Health* (Jan.): 98–114.

Brunger, Fern, and Julie Bull (2011). "Whose Agenda Is It? Regulating Health Research Ethics in Labrador." *Études/Inuit/Studies*. 35 (1–2): 127–42. http://dx.doi.org/10.7202/1012838ar

Brunger, Fern, and Charles Weijer. (2007). "Politics, Risk, and Community in the Maya-ICBG Case." In J.V. Lavery, E. Wahl, C. Grady, and E.J. Emanuel (eds.), *Ethical Issues in International Biomedical Research: A Case Book*, 35–42. New York: Oxford University Press.

Bull, Julie R. (2010). "Research with Aboriginal Peoples: Authentic Relationships as a Precursor to Ethical Research." *Journal of Empirical Research on Human Research Ethics* 5 (4): 13–22. http://dx.doi.org/10.1525/jer.2010.5.4.13

Burgess, Michael M., and Fern Brunger. (2000). "Collective Effects of Medical Research." In Michael McDonald (ed.), *The Governance of Health Research Involving Human Subjects*, 117–52. Ottawa: Law Commission of Canada.

CIHR (Canadian Institutes of Health Research). (2007). *CIHR Guidelines for Health Research Involving Aboriginal Peoples: Draft for Consultation.* http://www.cihr-irsc.gc.ca/e/29134.html

CIHR et al. (Canadian Institutes of Health Research, Natural Sciences and Engineering Research Council of Canada, and Social Sciences and Humanities Research Council of Canada). (1998, with 2000, 2002, 2005 amendments). *Tri-Council Policy Statement: Ethical Conduct for Research Involving Humans.* Ottawa, ON: Interagency Secretariat on Research Ethics.

– (2010). *Tri-Council Policy Statement: Ethical Conduct for Research Involving Humans.* 2nd ed. Ottawa: Interagency Panel on Research Ethics.

Commission on the Future of Health Care in Canada and Roy J. Romanow. (2002). *Building on Values: The Future of Health Care in Canada.* (Romanov Report). Saskatoon: Commission on the Future of Health Care in Canada. http://publications.gc.ca/collections/Collection/CP32-85-2002E.pdf

Deloria, Vine. (1991). "Commentary: Research, Redskins, and Reality." *American Indian Quarterly* 15 (4): 457–68. http://dx.doi.org/10.2307/1185364

Ellerby, Jonathan H., John McKenzie, Stanley McKay, Gilbert J. Gariépy, and Joseph M. Kaufert. (2000). "Bioethics for Clinicians: Aboriginal Cultures." *Canadian Medical Association Journal* 163: 845–50.

Ermine, Willie J. (1995). "Aboriginal Epistemology." In M. Battiste and J. Barman (eds.), *First Nations Education in Canada: The Circle Unfolds,* 101–112. Vancouver: UBC Press.

Gegeo, David W., and Karen A. Watson-Gegeo. (2001). "How We know: Kwara'ae Rural Villagers Doing Indigenous Epistemology." *Contemporary Pacific* 13 (1): 55–88. http://dx.doi.org/10.1353/cp.2001.0004

Gillam, Lynn, and Priscilla Pyett. (2003). "A Commentary on the NH and MRC Draft Values and Ethics in Aboriginal and Torres Strait Islander Health Research." *Monash Bioethics Review* 22 (4): 8–19. http://dx.doi.org/10.1007/BF03351399

Greely, Henry T. (1997). "The Control of Genetic Research: Involving the 'Groups Between.'" *Houston Law Review* 33 (5): 1397–430.

Indian and Northern Affairs. (1996). "Royal Commission on Aboriginal Peoples." http://www.ainc-inac.gc.ca/ch/rcap/sg/sgmm_e.html http://www.collectionscanada.gc.ca/webarchives/20071115053257/

Kahnawáke Schools Diabetes Prevention Project. (1996). *KSDPP Code of Research Ethics.* http://www.ksdpp.org/media/ksdpp_code_of_research_ethics2007.pdf.

Kaufert, Joseph M., Laura Commanda, Brenda Eilias, Rhoda Grey, Kue Young, and Barney Masazumi. (1999). "Evolving Participation of Aboriginal

Communities in Health Research Ethics Review: The Impact of the Inuvik Workshop." *International Journal of Circumpolar Health* 58 (2): 134–44.

Kaufert, Joseph M., Kathleen C. Glass, William L. Freeman, and Lisa LaBine. (2004). *Background Paper on Issues of Group, Community or First Nation Consent in Health Research.* Working Paper commissioned by the Aboriginal Ethics Policy Development Project and Canadian Institutes of Health Research-Ethics Office and Institute for Aboriginal Peoples Health, 110:26.

Louis, Renee P. (2007). "'Can You Hear Us Now?' Voices from the Margin: Using Indigenous Methodologies in Geographic Research." *Geographical Research* 45 (2): 130–9. http://dx.doi.org/10.1111/j.1745-5871.2007.00443.x

Poole, Roger. (1972). *Towards Deep Subjectivity.* New York: Harper Torch Books.

Porsanger, Jessica. (1999). "An Essay about Indigenous Methodology." http://munin.uit.no/bitstream/handle/10037/906/article.pdf

PRE (Interagency Advisory Panel on Research Ethics). (2002). *Process and Principles for Developing a Canadian Governance System for the Ethical Conduct of Research Involving Humans.*

Schnarch, Brian. (2004). "Ownership, Control, Access, and Possession (OCAP) or Self-Determination Applied to Research: A Critical Analysis of Contemporary First Nations Research and Some Options for First Nations Communities." *Journal of Aboriginal Health* 14 (16): 80–95.

Scott, Kim, and Olivier Receveur. (1995). "Ethics for Working with Communities of Indigenous Peoples." *Canadian Journal of Physiology and Pharmacology* 73 (6): 751–3. http://dx.doi.org/10.1139/y95-099

Sinclair, Raven. (2007). "Participatory Action Research and Aboriginal Epistemology." *Teaching and Learning* 4 (2). http://www.aboriginalsocialwork.ca/special_topics/par/epistemology.htm

Smith, Linda. (1999). *Decolonizing Methodologies: Research and Indigenous Peoples.* New York: Zed Books.

Weaver, Hilary N. (1997). "The Challenges of Research in Native American Communities: Incorporating Principles of Cultural Competence." *Journal of Social Service Research* 23 (2): 1–15. http://dx.doi.org/10.1300/J079v23n02_01

Weijer, Charles, Gary Goldsand, and Ezekiel Emanuel. (1999). "Protecting Communities in Research: Current Guidelines and Limits of Extrapolation." *Nature Genetics* 23 (3): 275–80. http://dx.doi.org/10.1038/15455

PART III

Analysis of Change: When Superficiality Displaces Substance

10 The More Things Change, the More They Stay the Same: The *TCPS 2* and the Institutional Ethical Oversight of Social Science Research in Canada

KIRSTEN BELL

The current system of research ethics oversight in Canada and elsewhere is not working. Variously characterized as "broken," "in crisis," and "using a sledgehammer to crack a nut" (Gunsalus et al., 2007; McCullough, 2010), it is clear that the research ethics juggernaut has taken on a life far beyond what was initially anticipated by its creators. No one is more cognizant of this than social scientists, who have observed that the ethics review system was designed for biomedical research, there is no evidence that it makes social science research more ethical (and some evidence to suggest precisely the opposite), and that it is leading to an insidious and unnecessary impoverishment of social science research (e.g., Haggerty, 2004; Bledsoe et al., 2007; Schrag, 2010; van den Hoonaard, 2011).

In light of the limitations of prevailing models, efforts have been recently made to improve systems of research ethics oversight in several countries. In the United States, the Department of Health and Human Services, the institution that oversees the Office of Human Research Protections (OHRP), has proposed sweeping changes to the national framework that would exempt several types of social science research from institutional ethics review. It would also create allowances for self-exemptions and remove continuing review requirements for minimal-risk research, among other changes (DHHS, 2011). However, whether the proposed changes will ultimately be implemented, and in what form, remains an open question. Other countries have tried to improve the process of research ethics review by refining their existing guidelines and frameworks. In the case of Canada, the national human research ethics guidelines are the *Tri-Council Policy Statement: Ethical Conduct for Research Involving Humans* (*TCPS*), which underwent a major overhaul in 2010.

Five years into the second edition of the *Tri-Council Policy Statement*, the changes to Canadian human research ethics guidelines have done little to curb the excesses of institutional research ethics oversight. Indeed, in some respects they have inadvertently served to make the situation worse. In providing an overview of the limitations of the revised *Tri-Council Policy Statement* (*TCPS 2*), I aim to demonstrate that nothing short of a radical overhaul of the current system of research ethics review will resolve the underlying issues. Finally, I provide some suggestions as to the form this new structure might take.

Overview of the *TCPS* and the Governance of Research Ethics in Canada

The Canadian system of research ethics oversight bears a number of similarities to, but also some important differences from, the systems in place in other countries. Until the 1990s, different universities had their own systems for reviewing the ethical implications of research, although they were guided by the individual guidelines disseminated by the three federal granting agencies (known as the Tri-Council): the Medical Research Council (now the Canadian Institutes of Health Research), the National Sciences and Engineering Research Council, and the Social Sciences and Humanities Research Council. In 1994, the Tri-Council began a process to develop a shared set of policies and guidelines regarding human research ethics; the resulting 1998 *Tri-Council Policy Statement: Ethical Conduct for Research Involving Humans* (CIHR et al., 1998) was more encompassing, standardized, and prescriptive than the guidelines that preceded it (Dehli and Taylor, 2006).

Unlike the system in the United States, the Canadian framework was not a regulatory one: the *Tri-Council Policy Statement* was framed as a policy document rather than a legal one (van den Hoonaard, 2011). However, any institution that wished to be eligible to receive funding from the Tri-Council agencies had to sign a memorandum of understanding agreeing to abide by the *Tri-Council Policy Statement*, which mandated the establishment of a Research Ethics Board (REB) to subject all research with human subjects to up-front review. Importantly, the *Tri-Council Policy Statement* required that *all* research pass ethical muster in order for universities to continue to receive funding from the Tri-Council, regardless of whether any given study was federally funded (van den Hoonaard, 2011). Thus, unlike the United States, which gave academic institutions the choice of whether to extend oversight beyond federally funded research (see Plattner, 2006; Shweder, 2006),[1] Canadian institutions wanting federal funds have no say in the matter of ethics review.[2]

From its inception, many social scientists were critical of the underlying biomedical orientation of the *Tri-Council Policy Statement*, while others argued that it was more inclusive of social science research than generally presented (e.g., Ells and Gutfreund, 2006). In 2001, the Tri-Council created the Interagency Advisory Panel on Research Ethics (PRE), and improving the *Tri-Council Policy Statement* became its major focus for the next decade (van den Hoonaard, 2011). This period saw the creation of numerous working groups tasked with tackling the major areas of the document requiring revision, and culminated in the publication of a draft version of the *TCPS 2* in 2008, and the publication of a revised draft in 2009, both of which were circulated for public comment. Responses to the public consultation were incorporated into the final guidelines that came into effect in December 2010 (CIHR et al., 2010).

Framing Research

The first chapter of the second edition of the *Tri-Council Policy Statement: Ethical Conduct for Research Involving Humans* sets up the conceptual framework for the guidelines and has several features worth highlighting. First, while acknowledging the existence of different types of research in the social sciences, humanities, natural sciences, engineering, and health sciences, the framework treats research as a singular phenomenon with an instrumental purpose, stating, "There can be no doubt that research has greatly enriched and improved our lives ... A fundamental premise of this Policy is that research can benefit human society" (CIHR et al., 2010: 7). As the Society for Academic Freedom and Scholarship (SAFS, 2010) notes, central to this conception of research is the assumption that good research produces certain concrete positive outcomes.

This instrumental approach to research aligns with the objectives of the Tri-Council agencies themselves, including the Social Sciences and Humanities Research Council, which is increasingly committed to funding studies directed towards solving "economic, social and cultural challenges and problems" (Dehli and Taylor, 2006: 105). However, as Richard Shweder (2006) notes, "Although federal funding agencies may define their funding mission and justify it to Congress and the public on that basis (and although that standard may be appropriate for certain kinds of biomedical research), it is a misguided norm for a research university" (515). Especially in the social sciences and humanities, scholars often engage in research because they are intellectually curious about a topic; moreover, they may be interested in topics that the public finds upsetting, or thinks are not particularly beneficial for society (Shweder, 2006). It thus seems problematic that federal granting agencies get to determine the scope of what constitutes legitimate research. As Gustavo Lins Ribeiro (2006) asks, "Should the state be the keeper of supposedly universal ethical standards of knowledge production? No, most scholars would agree" (530).

As Ribeiro (2006) points out, however, institutional ethics review processes are merely the "tip of the iceberg." Therefore, it is important to situate these developments within larger transformations in the academy, especially the rise of the "managed university," which has seen institutional autonomy and academic freedom fundamentally reworked (Marginson, 1997).[3] In this environment, academics are increasingly being refashioned as entrepreneurial subjects, encouraged to direct their efforts towards social and economic issues; the master frame is that of "knowledge mobilisation" and "knowledge transfer" (Dehli and Taylor, 2006). Thus, academics pursue a kind of regulated freedom, with most forms of knowledge "produced on terrain which – though it is not directly administered by governments – is ordered and sanctioned by them" (Marginson, 1997: 361).

Risky Business

Another key feature of the framing of research in the second edition of the *Tri-Council Policy Statement* is its characterization of research as an intrinsically risky enterprise: "Research is a step into the unknown. Because it seeks to understand something not yet revealed, research often entails risks to participants and others. These risks can be trivial or profound, physical or psychological, individual or social. History offers unfortunate examples where research participants have been needlessly, and at times profoundly, harmed by research, sometimes even dying as a result" (CIHR et al., 2010: 7).

As Kari Dehli and Alison Taylor (2006) point out, it is noteworthy that the *Tri-Council Policy Statement* fails to include a category of "no risk" research, although various types of social science research conceivably fall into this category. Moreover, these statements present research risks as differing in *degree* rather than in *kind*; psychological and social risks are mentioned in the same breath as physical risks, and trivial risks are mentioned in the same breath as profound ones.

Beyond framing research as a harm that is only justified if it is conducted for the good of society, this also sets up an intrinsic tension between the interests of researchers and participants – an "adversarial culture" as Mark Israel et al. (chapter 15 in this volume) describe. The *Tri-Council Policy Statement* states, "The importance of research and the need to ensure the ethical conduct of research requires both researchers and REB members to navigate a sometimes difficult course between the two main goals of providing the necessary protection of participants and serving the legitimate requirements of research" (CIHR et al., 2010: 11).

In this conceptualization, the interests of researchers are fundamentally in opposition to the interests of research participants. Therefore, research subjects must be "protected" from researchers. As Will van den Hoonaard (2011) points out, this framing undercuts the notion of the moral agency of researchers. Thus, while these framing statements assert a series of truth claims in which "culturally specific notions of 'the subject' are naturalised and instrumentalised" (Dehli and Taylor, 2006: 112), with human subjects appearing to possess conditional reason, they *also* assert a series of truth claims about researchers. In this framing, researchers, too, possess conditional reason. Ostensibly driven by our own lust for knowledge, career advancement, and other personal gain, we are seen as being incapable of recognizing the ethical issues that our own research poses to participants.

Paved with Good Intentions

Although the second edition of the *Tri-Council Policy Statement: Ethical Conduct for Research Involving Humans* suggests a unitary framework for all research, various accommodations for social science and humanities research have been made throughout the document. Some of these changes are superficial and largely symbolic, serving to demonstrate an inclusive attitude towards social science research. The shift from "human subject" to "human participant" is one such change (see Gontcharov, chapter 13 in this volume). Thus, the *TCPS 2* states, "This Policy prefers the term 'participant' because it better reflects the spirit behind the core principles: that individuals who choose to participate in research play a more active role than the term 'subject' conveys. As well, it reflects the range of research covered by this Policy" (CIHR et al., 2010: 16). However, it is worth noting that the switch in terminology has come under fire, as commentators point out that there are numerous studies where human participants are indeed the subjects of research rather than active participants in it (e.g., Leslie and Leahy, 2010).

A second more substantive change is the definition of *research* outlined in the *TCPS 2*. According to the original *Tri-Council Policy Statement*, "Research involves a systematic investigation to establish facts, principles or generalizable knowledge," and social scientists saw this as yet further evidence of the clinical and quantitative bias of the document. These problems were explicitly acknowledged and addressed by the working group set up to revise the definition of research, which observed that "these terms may not be sufficiently flexible when transferred to a broader context that includes humanities and social sciences activities in which research does not necessarily rely on hypothesis testing" (ProGroup, 2008: 2). Consequently, the revised definition of research outlined in the *TCPS 2* states, "Research is an undertaking intended to extend knowledge through a disciplined inquiry or systematic investigation" (CIHR et al., 2010: 15). As should be evident, the term "generalizable knowledge" has been removed and the concept of research now hinges on the notion of intent.

Although many social scientists initially applauded this change, I have come to the conclusion that in the absence of a more meaningful restructuring of ethics review processes, it is doing more harm than good. The problem is that the definition of research is now so broad and encompassing that virtually everything is included in its scope. In Jack Katz's (2006) view, the older definition of research provided ethnographers and other qualitative researchers with ethical escape routes: "Read as limited to investigations that are systematically designed, as that concept is understood within the traditional rhetoric of science, the 'research' governed by IRBs [institutional review boards] would not cover the unsystematic, constantly changing, informally devised methods of ethnographic fieldwork" (503). However, the revised *Tri-Council Policy Statement* has effectively blocked this interpretation of the rules.

An atmosphere of uncertainty about which studies require institutional ethics review has become even more acute in the *TCPS 2* era. Although the revised *Tri-Council Policy Statement* does list some research exemptions, these exemptions are very conservative, including only research with publicly available data, naturalistic observation in public places, and secondary use of anonymously collected data. Thus, the breadth of the new definition of research, combined with the well-documented conservatism of research ethics administrations (Shweder, 2006; Bledsoe et al., 2007; van den Hoonaard, 2011), promotes ethics creep, serving to justify the colonization of new groups and practices (Haggerty, 2004: 394). For example, Canadian research ethics administrators and boards are now grappling with the question of whether researchers who wish to draw on autobiographical anecdotes in publications are required to undergo institutional research ethics review.

Another major change is that the second edition of the *Tri-Council Policy Statement* includes a new chapter on qualitative research, addressing studies with an emergent design, obtaining consent in qualitative research, consent for naturalistic observation, disclosing participant identities, and obtaining ethics approval for data collection. This chapter does pose some important caveats regarding the review of qualitative research; however, when read in the context of the larger document there seems to be limited scope in which to shift the standard requirements around informed consent, up-front review, etc. that contribute to the mismatch between the level of specificity typically required in the ethics review process and the information that qualitative researchers can legitimately provide.

For example, Article 10.5 of the *TCPS 2* states, "In studies using emergent design in data collection, researchers shall provide the REB with all the available information to assist in the review and approval of the general procedure for data collection" (CIHR et al., 2010: 144), and the application section recognizes that elements of the study may evolve as the project progresses. However, although stating that researchers should not be forced to provide Research Ethics Boards with final versions of interview guides, etc. in the initial review, the reader is informed that "final versions should be submitted as soon as they become available" (ibid.). Beyond the question of whether an interview guide is ever really final in many types of qualitative research, the ability to provide *any* documentation at all of interview content is a fundamentally artificial exercise in the context of the unstructured conversations that characterize forms of qualitative research such as long-term anthropological fieldwork (*IRB Advisor*, 2006).

One Step Forward, Two Steps Back

There is a clear reluctance within the revised *Tri-Council Policy Statement: Ethical Conduct for Research Involving Humans* to fully commit to changes in policy regarding issues with particular pertinence for social science research. Thus, whenever appearing to take a stance on such issues, the *TCPS 2* immediately goes on to undermine it. Consider, for example, the concept of proportionate review. Article 2.9 of the *TCPS 2* states, "The REB shall adopt a proportionate approach to research ethics review such that, as a preliminary step, the level of review is determined by the level of risk presented by the research: the lower the level of risk, the lower the level of scrutiny (delegated review); the higher the level of risk, the higher the level of scrutiny (full board review)" (CIHR et al., 2010: 24).

This emphasis on proportionate review is reiterated in Article 6.12 of the chapter on research ethics governance. However, the application section of Article 6.12 goes on to state, "Research ethics review by the full REB should be the default requirement for research involving humans" (CIHR et al., 2010: 77). Establishing full-board review as the standard inhibits precisely the sort of "proportionate approach" the *TCPS 2* advocates, because delegated review is implicitly treated as an exception to the norm.

This is a consistent pattern throughout the current *Tri-Council Policy Statement*, where processes affecting the review of social science research are set up as exceptions that require justification. For example, a topic that often poses particular challenges for social scientists is informed consent. At several points, the *TCPS 2* states that a variety of ways of obtaining informed consent exist that do not boil down to a signed consent form (see Articles 3.2 and 10.2). For example, Article 10.2 states, "Under a variety of circumstances, signed written consent is not appropriate in qualitative research." But the application section immediately goes on to note, "However, where there are *valid reasons* for not recording consent through a signed written consent form, the procedures used to seek and confirm consent must be documented" (CIHR et al., 2010: 140, emphasis added).[4] This clause sets up signed consent forms as the norm, and suggests that exceptions to written consent must be justified. Moreover, the vagueness of the terms "valid reasons" and "justified" leaves it up to the individual board to determine whether the researcher's reasons are, in fact, valid and adequately justified. The end result is a position virtually indistinguishable from *TCPS 1*, which allowed for exceptions to signed consent when "there are good reasons for not recording consent in writing" (CIHR et al., 1998: 2.1).

A similar issue plagues the discussion of the elements of informed consent in Article 3.2, where it states, "Researchers shall provide to prospective participants, or authorized third parties, full disclosure of all information necessary for making an informed decision to participate in a research project" (CIHR et al., 2010: 30). This suggests that the information provided to participants should be tailored to the specifics of the project, a position affirmed in the application section, which states that not all the standard disclosure elements are required for all research. Theoretically, this helps resolve the issue of lengthy consent documents containing numerous clauses about wholly irrelevant and inappropriate study risks. However, this stance is immediately undermined in the following sentence: "If a researcher does not include some of the listed disclosure requirements, they should explain to the REB why these requirements do not apply to that particular project" (30). Once again, alternatives are set up as deviations from the default process and require justification.

Policy versus Practice

Even if the second edition of the *Tri-Council Policy Statement* were a gutsier document, this would still not resolve the underlying issues that have long plagued research ethics oversight. The fundamental problem relates to the ways the guidelines are *interpreted* by administrators and Research Ethics Boards (van den Hoonaard, 2011). Carolyn Ells and Shawna Gutfreund (2006) argue that the original *Tri-Council Policy Statement* was not as conservative as social scientists often have assumed, and they point out that the document did allow for alternative modes of consent, exceptions to anonymity rules, etc. In their view, the problems lay in its "interpretation and application" (361). Joan Sieber et al. (2002) have made similar points regarding the regulations in the United States, noting that local review boards "interpret the requirements of the Common Rule in a manner more appropriate to high risk biomedical research, ignoring the flexibility available to them in the Common Rule" (2).

Nevertheless, while these national frameworks do theoretically accommodate difference, such flexibility is fundamentally counter to the nature of review boards themselves. First, boards are bureaucratic entities, with a tendency towards the proliferation of rules and processes (Haggerty, 2004; van den Hoonaard, 2011). As Bruce Kapferer (1995) has noted, central to the taxonomic schemes that characterize bureaucracy is an attention to surface features that subdue and subsume difference, a process he defines as "bureaucratic erasure." Second, the fundamentally conservative nature of Research Ethics Boards themselves also hinders flexibility. In the words of Caroline Bledsoe et al. (2007), "Terrified at the specter of their institutions losing all federal funds, [IRBs] opted overwhelmingly for conservatism ... They began to convert choice to requirement, treating the guidelines as rules" (612). Indeed, Research Ethics Boards have a tendency to treat the available guidelines as a minimum standard, often placing additional requirements on top of those outlined in formal policies (van den Hoonaard, 2011; Israel and Hay, 2006) and viewing these stiffer rules as "virtuous" (Hamilton, 2002). As ethnographic research has also shown (e.g., Stark, 2006; Israel et al., chapter 15), Research Ethics Boards tend to place considerable emphasis on the need to make locally consistent decisions over time (whether they actually succeed in this is an open question). There is thus a strong concern with local precedents among Research Ethics Boards that shape REB members' remedies to ethical concerns and also guide the problems that they read into proposals in the first place (see Stark, 2006: 227). There is no reason to believe that Research Ethics Boards will function any differently in the *TCPS 2* era.

Finally, it is important to note that developing guidelines that accommodate social science research does not actually resolve the issue of the lack of methodological expertise on Research Ethics Boards, which is a persistent problem. As Ted Palys and John Lowman (2010) ask, "Will creating a chapter on qualitative methods make the experimentalist from computing science or psychology an authority on qualitative method ethics issues?" Simply adding more social scientists to, or creating separate social science and behavioural REBs, is not necessarily the answer. Social science is a vast field including an array of theoretical and methodological approaches. According to Rena Lederman (2004),[5] "Part of the problem is that disciplines have diverse research cultures: distinct, sometimes contradictory ethical practices underwrite knowledge claims in the humanities, social sciences and biomedicine (with important differences even within those categories)" (8). Different disciplinary traditions mean that approaches to qualitative research, even named approaches such as "ethnography" and "phenomenology," look rather different depending on the background of the researcher. There is a real danger that certain styles of ethnography (or phenomenology, etc.), especially those more amenable to established procedural guidelines, will become the standard against which other forms of ethnographic fieldwork are measured (van den Hoonaard and Connolly, 2006; van den Hoonaard, 2011).

Where to from Here?

If we accept that the revised *Tri-Council Policy Statement: Ethical Conduct for Research Involving Humans* has not resolved the fundamental problems connected with institutional oversight of research ethics in Canada, it is important to acknowledge that improving the present environment requires some changes in our own mindset as well. Although the problems with research ethics governance are sometimes portrayed as a conflict between administrators and academics, Bruce Kapferer (1995) argues that it is important to avoid simple oppositions that separate the thinking and practice of administrators from those of the people to whom they attend. Although many research ethics administrators remain committed to the prevailing system, and unquestioningly parrot the party line (Fitzgerald, 2004), a number are also well aware of the system's limitations (see Bledsoe et al., 2007; van den Hoonaard, 2011). In the words of Caroline Bledsoe et al. (2007), "IRB staff have sometimes had to step in diplomatically to rescue a project from a zealous social-science faculty panelist threatening to dismember it altogether" (616–17). As they observe, the critical impulse among academics, bred into us through endless rounds of reviewing research proposals, journal articles, and student papers, tends to make for fastidious REB members prone to find fault with the submissions they receive.

Empirical studies with academic anthropologists and sociologists (e.g., Taylor and Patterson, 2010; Wynn, 2011) have also shown that many social scientists see ethics oversight as a necessary evil, despite considerable concerns about the overarching system. For example, several years ago I had a conversation with a psychologist colleague about some of the problems with research ethics oversight. At the end of our discussion, he said something along the lines of "Yes, but look at Tuskegee," as if this conclusively settled the matter. In this framing, research ethics oversight is necessary, not for ourselves, but rather for some vaguely defined, dangerous Other who would be out there committing rampant abuses if not held in check through a formalized review process.

A related problem is that of academic passivity and our tendency to accept systems of audit and accountability that are a poor fit with our research, and I speak here not only of systems of institutional ethics oversight but of growing moves to quantify research output based on positivistic models and a variety of other initiatives with noticeably corrosive effects on social science scholarship. Although many social scientists have perfected the art of "principled dodging" (Bledsoe et al., 2007), it is questionable whether these tactics ultimately serve our interests. As Rena Lederman (2007) notes of anthropologists who simulate compliance with the regulatory ideal, "It doesn't help IRBs [Institutional Review Boards] really understand what ethnographers actually do" (33) and contributes to misinformation about ethnographic fieldwork (cited in *IRB Advisor*, 2006: 103). According to Gustavo Lins Ribeiro (2006), if researchers want to guarantee academic freedom, they need to "do politics" within and beyond their institutions: "If they do not, other people will, and sooner or later researchers will see themselves caught within other people's webs of stereotypes and regulations" (530).

Potential Models

Many possible models could be adopted for social science research in Canada. One model would be an exemption system along the lines of what is currently being proposed by the Office of Human Research Protections (OHRP) in the United States, where various types of social science research would be exempt from institutional ethics oversight altogether. Following the proposed OHRP model, the current Canadian exemptions could be expanded to include all surveys, interviews, and similar procedures done with competent adults, along with other specified categories of social science research (e.g., oral histories). However, as the American Anthropological Association (AAA, 2011) cautions in its response to the proposed model, one of the limitations of the exemption system is that such "list-making results in a welter of qualifications and addenda that engender freshly conflicting interpretations and further caution-motivated full board reviews" (3).

Similar to the model advocated by the American Anthropological Association, the definition of research could be dramatically reined in to focus specifically on biomedical research and other procedures involving risks of physical harm to participants and/or experiments or other methodologies where results depend on limiting or controlling information available to research subjects (AAA, 2011). There is some precedent for this framework in Canada. A 2004 report for the Interagency Panel on Research Ethics by the Social Sciences and Humanities Research Ethics Special Working Committee advised, "PRE should consider exemptions from review for social science and humanities research that involves standard practice in the discipline involved, particularly in these situations: where the research participant is not a 'human subject,' where there is no identifiable harm, and where the provisions of confidentiality ensure that participants cannot be identified" (SSHWC, 2004: 6–7). Social scientists would still be expected to follow the *TCPS 2* guidelines, and their own disciplinary codes of ethics, but they would not be required to submit any documentation to their ethics board in order to proceed with their research.

This is not to suggest that some formal discussion of and reflection about research ethics is unwarranted. Such conversations are clearly important and necessary, although evidence suggests that they can occur most effectively when removed from the context of bureaucratized institutional oversight. As numerous scholars have noted, discussions of research ethics invariably focus on getting *through* the ethics *process*, which tends to crowd out "real" conversations about ethics (Lederman, 2007; van den Hoonaard, 2011; see also van den Scott, chapter 12 in this volume). Disciplines should provide appropriate education in research ethics by incorporating it into key courses. Graduate students in the social sciences should be required to explicitly consider ethical issues when developing research proposals and be asked to reflect on such issues as they undergo their thesis defence. After all, it is often in the writing period that ethical issues become apparent in social science research.

Conclusion

At this stage, it is clear that the problems with ethics review of social science research go beyond isolated incidents. According to Zachary Schrag (2010: 9), the malfunctions result not just from operator error but also from design flaws inherent in the machine. While the second edition of the *Tri-Council Policy Statement: Ethical Conduct for Research Involving Humans* has softened the sharp edges, this has not resolved the fundamental mismatch between the ethics review process and social science methods and epistemologies.

Scaling back research ethics oversight will not be easy. At this stage, it has become enmeshed with institutional policies, funding frameworks, and publication requirements.[6] Thus, rethinking systems of oversight will require coordination and cooperation at all levels. This will necessitate collective effort on the part of social scientists, as well as a willingness on the part of federal bodies and local institutions to rethink the current framework. However, we appear to have reached an important historical moment in which such change has become *thinkable* in a way that was not the case a decade ago, and we should not let this opportunity pass us by.

NOTES

1 As Richard Shweder (2006) points out, the situation in the United States was more complicated than this because although the federal government gave universities the option of limiting IRB oversight to federally funded studies, most administrators extended IRB oversight because they presumed this is what federal regulators wanted. It is also worth noting that the proposed changes to the Common Rule would remove the possibility of exempting unfunded studies from IRB oversight.
2 Although the Canadian Society for Academic Freedom and Scholarship (SAFS, 2010) has challenged the legal basis of this blanket fiat, they have not to date received a satisfactory response from the PRE about its mandate concerning unfunded research.
3 It is also related to the emergence of audit culture, and the rise of rituals of verification that, rather ironically, perpetuate the very mistrust they are designed to dispel (Strathern, 2000; see also Robert Dingwall, chapter 1 in this volume).
4 Interestingly, the first draft version of the *TCPS 2* did not contain this clause, suggesting a trend toward greater conservatism with each subsequent iteration.
5 See also Rena Lederman (chapter 2 in this volume), for further discussion of issues of cross-disciplinary translation.
6 See Will C. van den Hoonaard (2011) for a discussion of the ways that regimes of institutional ethics oversight have become tied up with publication requirements.

REFERENCES

AAA (American Anthropological Association). (2011). "Comments on Proposed Changes to the Common Rule (76 FR 44512)." http://www.aaanet.org/issues/policy-advocacy/upload/Human-Subjects-Research.pdf
Bledsoe, Caroline H., Bruce Sherin, Adam G. Gallinsky, Nathalia M. Headley, Carol A. Heimer, Erik Kjeldgaard, James Lindgren, Jon D. Miller, Michael E. Roloff, and David E. Uttal. (2007). "Regulating Creativity: Research and Survival in the IRB Iron Cage." *Northwestern University Law Review* 101 (2): 593–641.

CIHR et al. (Canadian Institutes of Health Research, Natural Sciences
    and Engineering Research Council of Canada, and Social Sciences and
    Humanities Research Council of Canada). (1998, with 2000, 2002, 2005
    amendments). *Tri-Council Policy Statement: Ethical Conduct for Research
    Involving Humans.* Ottawa: Interagency Panel on Research Ethics.
– (2010). *Tri-Council Policy Statement: Ethical Conduct for Research Involving
    Humans.* 2nd ed. Ottawa: Interagency Panel on Research Ethics.
Dehli, Kari, and Alison Taylor. (2006). "Toward New Government of
    Education Research: Refashioning Researchers as Entrepreneurial and
    Ethical Subjects." In Jenny Ozga, Terri Seddon, and Thomas S. Popkewitz
    (eds.), *World Yearbook of Education 2006: Education Research and Policy –
    Steering the Knowledge-Based Economy*, 105–18. London: Routledge.
DHHS (US Department of Health and Human Services). (2011). "Human
    Subjects Research Protections: Enhancing Protections for Research Subjects
    and Reducing Burden, Delay, and Ambiguity for Investigators." *Federal
    Register* 76 (143): 44512–31.
Ells, Carolyn, and Shawna Gutfreund. (2006). "Myths about Qualitative
    Research and the Tri-Council Policy Statement." *Canadian Journal of Sociology*
    31 (3): 361–73. http://dx.doi.org/10.2307/20058715
Fitzgerald, Maureen H. (2004). "Big Basket or Mission Creep?" *Professional
    Ethics Report* 17 (2): 1–3.
Gunsalus, C. Kristina, Edward M. Bruner, Nicholas C. Burbules, Leon Dash,
    Matthew Finkin, Joseph P. Goldberg, et al. (2007). "The Illinois White Paper:
    Improving the System for Protecting Human Subjects: Counteracting
    IRB 'Mission Creep.'" *Qualitative Inquiry* 13 (5): 617–49. http://dx.doi.
    org/10.1177/1077800407300785
Haggerty, Kevin D. (2004). "Ethics Creep: Governing Social Science Research
    in the Name of Ethics." *Qualitative Sociology* 27 (4): 391–414. http://dx.doi.
    org/10.1023/B:QUAS.0000049239.15922.a3
Hamilton, Ann. (2002). *Institutional Review Boards: Politics, Power, Purpose and
    Process in a Regulatory Organization.* Doctoral dissertation, University of
    Oklahoma.
IRB Advisor. (2006). "Ethnography Proposals Pose Problems for IRBs." *IRB
    Advisor* (Sept.): 102–4.
Israel, Mark, and Iain Hay. (2006). *Research Ethics for Social Scientists: Between
    Ethical Conduct and Regulatory Compliance.* London: Sage.
Kapferer, Bruce. (1995). "Bureaucratic Erasure: Identity, Resistance and
    Violence – Aborigines and Discourse of Autonomy in a North Queensland
    Town." In Daniel Miller (ed.), *Worlds Apart: Modernity through the Prism of
    the Local*, 69–108. London: Routledge.

Katz, Jack. (2006). "Ethical Escape Routes for Underground Ethnographers." *American Ethnologist* 33 (4): 499–506. http://dx.doi.org/10.1525/ae.2006.33.4.499

Lederman, Rena S. (2004). "Commentary: Bureaucratic Oversight of Human Research and Disciplinary Diversity: IRB Review of Oral History and Anthropology." *Anthropology News* 45 (5): 8. http://dx.doi.org/10.1111/an.2004.45.5.8

– (2007). "Educate your IRB: An Experiment in Cross-Disciplinary Communication." *Anthropology News* 48 (6): 33–4. http://dx.doi.org/10.1525/an.2007.48.6.33

Leslie, Josh, and Aaron Leahy. (2010). "*TCPS2* Response." Comments 2009/123_ Josh%20Leslie%20and%20Aaron%20Leahy.pdf.

Marginson, Simon. (1997). "How Free Is Academic Freedom?" *Higher Education Research & Development* 16 (3): 359–69. http://dx.doi.org/10.1080/0729436970160309

McCullough, Melissa. (2010). "One Size Does Not Fit All: The Ethical Imperative to Limit the Concept of Research Exceptionalism." *American Journal of Bioethics* 10 (8): 60–1. http://dx.doi.org/10.1080/15265161.2010.482643

Palys, Ted, and John Lowman. (2010). "*TCPS*-2's Enduring Challenge: How to Provide Ethics Governance While Respecting Academic Freedom." Comment2009/63_Lowman%20John%20and%20Palys%20Ted.pdf.

Plattner, Stuart. (2006). "Comment on IRB Regulation of Ethnographic Research." *American Ethnologist* 33 (4): 525–8. http://dx.doi.org/10.1525/ae.2006.33.4.525

ProGroup: Subgroup on Procedural Issues for the *TCPS*. (2008). *Proportionate Approach to Research Ethics Review in the TCPS: Towards a Revised Definition of Research in the TCPS*. Ottawa: Interagency Advisory Panel and Secretariat on Research Ethics.

Ribeiro, Gustavo Lins. (2006). "IRBs Are the Tip of the Iceberg: State Regulation, Academic Freedom, and Methodological Issues." *American Ethnologist* 33 (4): 529–31. http://dx.doi.org/10.1525/ae.2006.33.4.529

SAFS (Society for Academic Freedom and Scholarship). (2010). *Comments on TCPS Revised Draft Second Edition (2009)*. http://www.pre.ethics.gc.ca/pdf/eng/Comments2009/60_Society%20for%20Academic%20Freedom%20and%20Scholarship.pdf

Schrag, Zachary M. (2010). *Ethical Imperialism: Institutional Review Boards and the Social Sciences, 1965–2009*. Baltimore: Johns Hopkins University Press.

Shweder, Richard A. (2006). "Protecting Human Subjects and Preserving Academic Freedom: Prospects at the University of Chicago." *American Ethnologist* 33 (4): 507–18. http://dx.doi.org/10.1525/ae.2006.33.4.507

Sieber, Joan E., Stuart Plattner, and Philip Rubin. (2002). "How (Not) to Regulate Social and Behavioral Research." *Professional Ethics Report* 15 (2): 1–4.

SSHWC (Social Sciences and Humanities Research Ethics Special Working Group). (2004). *Giving Voice to the Spectrum*. Ottawa: Interagency Advisory Panel on Research Ethics.

Stark, Laura. (2006). *Morality in Science: How Research Is Evaluated in the Age of Human Subjects Regulation*. Doctoral dissertation, Princeton University.

Strathern, Marilyn (ed.). (2000). *Audit Cultures: Anthropological Studies in Accountability, Ethics and the Academy*. London: Routledge. http://dx.doi.org/10.4324/9780203449721

Taylor, Judith, and Matthew Patterson. (2010). "Autonomy and Compliance: How Qualitative Sociologists Respond to Institutional Ethical Oversight." *Qualitative Sociology* 33 (2): 161–83. http://dx.doi.org/10.1007/s11133-010-9148-y

van den Hoonaard, Will C. (2011). *The Seduction of Ethics: Transforming the Social Sciences*. Toronto: University of Toronto Press.

van den Hoonaard, Will C., and Anita Connolly. (2006). "Anthropological Research in Light of Research-Ethics Review: Canadian Master's Theses, 1995–2004." *Journal of Empirical Research on Human Research Ethics* 1 (2): 59–69. http://dx.doi.org/10.1525/jer.2006.1.2.59

Wynn, Lisa L. (2011). "'Ethnographers' Experiences of Institutional Ethics Oversight: Results from a Quantitative and Qualitative Survey." *Journal of Policy History* 23 (1): 94–114. http://dx.doi.org/10.1017/S0898030610000333

11 Should Data Sharing Be Regulated?

NATASHA S. MAUTHNER

Over the past two decades, the United Kingdom has seen the introduction and institutionalization of research data-management and -sharing requirements as part of growing research ethics and governance regimes. Funding agencies, universities, and scientific journals are increasingly requiring researchers to make their data more widely available through archiving in digital repositories. The introduction in 2000 of the Freedom of Information Act (see http://www.legislation.gov.uk/ukpga/2000/36/contents) has moreover made it possible to legally enforce such data-sharing mandates. Policymakers make the case for regulating data sharing on several grounds. They see sharing research data as critical to the ethic and practice of open scientific inquiry, and to the promotion of scientific accountability, innovation, and progress. They consider that proper data storage reduces the information security risks associated with maintaining duplicated data sets in more than one location. They suggest that data reuse is a cost-efficient use of public funds and reduces the burden on participants and communities who are part of multiple data-collection efforts. Data depositories are also seen to provide an important resource for training in research. With data now viewed as a significant scientific and economic resource, the scope of researchers' professional and moral responsibilities is being expanded to include data management and sharing, which in turn is being incorporated into research ethics and governance requirements, regulatory and funding frameworks, and publishing mechanisms.

The case for promoting data management and sharing is compelling. It is hard to argue against the development of more systematic and transparent ways of labelling, storing, and organizing research data, practices that could safeguard against data loss and ensure long-term preservation of data. Furthermore, some disciplines already enjoy a long-established data-sharing ethic and tradition because of its perceived scientific, social, and historical benefits (e.g., ecology, oral history, genomics). In areas such as qualitative sociological research, data sharing is opening up new research opportunities particularly for longitudinal research (Neale et al., 2012; Thomson and McLeod, 2015). And in the medical field, powerful arguments exist for releasing all, rather than selective, medical trial data so that doctors and patients can make more fully informed decisions about the effectiveness and side-effects of particular drugs (Goldacre, 2012).

The question here is whether these potential benefits warrant the *regulation* of data sharing, and the institutionalization of one-size-fits-all policies deemed applicable to *all* disciplines, scholarly traditions, and research projects. Evidence across the social and natural sciences suggests that data-sharing perspectives and practices are diverse, contested, and context-specific (Mauthner, 2012; Mauthner and Parry, 2009, 2013). In the case of human subjects research, scholars working across fields as varied as genomics and sociology argue that data sharing can expose participants to potential harm and violate relationships of trust with researchers. In the United Kingdom, the most frequent reasons given by researchers funded by the Economic and Social Research Council (ESRC) requesting exemption from archiving are ethics-related, for reasons of lack of consent and the difficulty of maintaining confidentiality.[1] These concerns affect up to 25 per cent of qualitative collections offered for data archiving (Bishop, 2009; see also Perry, 2008). In the natural sciences, researchers who support the principle of data sharing and engage in its practice may nevertheless be reluctant to deposit data within large-scale centralized repositories. Some favor instead informal and personal data-sharing activities through research networks, based on relationships of trust, respect, and reciprocity, and guided by a common interest (Research Information Network, 2009; Zimmerman, 2007). Indeed, the complexities of putting data-sharing imperatives into practice are such that Borgman (2012) has suggested that still relatively few research data are being released and circulated beyond the research teams that produce them, which is leading to the problem of "empty archives" (Nelson, 2009). This limited compliance with data-sharing mandates is seen to stem from particular problems that can be solved by improving ethical, legal, governance, scientific and technical infrastructures, guidelines, and regulation. While these technical issues are critical, equally important is the question of whether regulatory and normative policies, and the enforcement of rigid rules, are effective ways of encouraging changes in data-sharing cultures and practices.

These are the issues to be addressed here. The chapter begins with a discussion of the means through which policies regulate data sharing, the moral grounds on which policymakers justify the regulation of data sharing, and the increasingly prescriptive ethical guidelines that researchers must follow with respect to data sharing. Next is a discussion of unintended consequences of regulating data sharing, including potential ethical and moral risks and violations. In the last section, alternatives to the regulatory model of data sharing are presented, with an argument made for flexible, collaborative, case-by-case, project- and context-specific data-sharing practices.

Two final introductory remarks are worth highlighting. First, social science and humanities scholars object to the regulation of research ethics and current formal ethics-review processes on the grounds that they are rooted in biomedical research, and they fail to adequately address the nature and ethical requirements of non-medical, low-risk research (e.g., van den Hoonaard, 2002). In the case of data sharing, however, regulatory and rule-bound approaches are being challenged by social and biomedical researchers alike due to the implications for the treatment of human subjects and personal information. For this reason, it is useful to turn to the biomedical sciences and the growing unease being felt there with regards to the normative ethical frameworks informing the sharing of genetic and genomic information. Second, this chapter focuses specifically on developments within the United Kingdom. The arguments being made, however, have relevance in broader contexts, partly because many other countries are in the process of establishing data-sharing policies and infrastructures, and partly because understanding country-specific regulatory frameworks is important in a context where data are viewed as a global resource and barriers to international data sharing are being minimized (Noble et al., 2011).

Regulation Creep: The Regulation of Data Sharing

The practices of archiving, sharing, and reusing data are not new: they can be traced back decades, have largely been self-regulated and shaped by disciplinary and community norms and traditions, and can be found across the arts and humanities, social sciences, and natural sciences (Mauthner, 2015; Mauthner and Parry, 2013). More formal institutionalized approaches to sharing data emerged in the 1950s when World Data

Centres were created, particularly in the geophysical sciences, designed to minimize the risk of data loss and maximize data access (Shapley and Hart, 1982). The 1980s witnessed more widespread application of this idea in the natural sciences. In particular, GenBank was one of the earliest bioinformatics community projects on the Internet, promoting open access communications and data sharing among bioscientists (Benson et al., 2008). The early 1990s saw the emergence of a more concerted and orchestrated international move towards treating research data as an open, globally shared resource in the natural sciences (e.g., OECD, 1994). The formal regulation of data sharing emerged a decade later, largely in response to the publication in 2007 of *Principles and Guidelines for Access to Research Data from Public Funding* by the Organization for Economic Cooperation and Development (OECD, 2007; see also Arzberger et al., 2004). This document has been influential in shaping policy developments in this area. The principle of open access is central to the document and specifies that "publicly funded research data should be openly available to the maximum extent possible" (Arzberger et al., 2004: 136). Peter Arzberger and his co-authors argue that the principle of openness to research data should apply "to *all* science communities" (144, original emphasis), and they urge that this imperative be backed with "formal policy frameworks and regulations" (146). This set the scene for the introduction of formal, regulatory, and bureaucratic data-management policies and systems, along with a set of normative expectations and requirements promoting open access to publicly funded research data as a gold standard by the OECD.

Research Funders' Data-Sharing Policies

This has led grant agencies increasingly to expect that research grant applicants specify data storage, access, and management plans, and these agencies are instituting measures to motivate researchers to share their data such as "conditions being attached to funding schemes" (Ruusalepp, 2008: 3). Overall, funding agencies are encouraging or mandating their grant holders to share their data, with as few restrictions as possible, usually within a specified time frame after completion of the research (see SHERPA; Digital Curation Centre). In the United Kingdom, making research data available to other users is now a core part of the Research Councils' (RC) remit, as articulated in RCUK's *Common Principles on Data Policy* (2015a) and in their *Concordat on Open Research Data* (2015b; undergoing consultation at the time of writing).

The United Kingdom's Economic and Social Research Council, for example, requires its grant holders to make their data available for reuse (unless there are convincing reasons for not doing so), usually within three months of a grant ending (ESRC, 2015a: 4).

University Data-Sharing Policies

Universities in the UK have been under pressure to develop data management policies and practices, and institutional data repositories, in order to align their processes with RCUK's *Common Principles on Data Policy*. In particular, they have had to ensure that they are compliant with the Engineering and Physical Sciences Research Council's (EPSRC) *Policy Framework on Research Data* and its expectation that EPSRC-funded research data be archived, and in principle accessible, by 1 May 2015 (EPSRC, 2014). As well as developing institutional data management policies, and the necessary technological infrastructures to support these, universities are incorporating data management and sharing requirements into ethics and research governance regulations and procedures.

Journal Data-Sharing Policies

A further trend is the implementation of data-archiving policies by scientific journals that require authors to publicly archive supporting data sets as a condition of publication. This is a well-established tradition in fields such as crystallography (Arzberger et al., 2004) and molecular biology (Benson et al., 2008), and has recently been introduced by several key journals in the fields of evolution and ecology (Bruna, 2010; Whitlock et al., 2010). Some journals in the social sciences are also now requiring or encouraging data sharing (e.g., *British Journal of Political Science, Journal of Peace Research, International Studies Quarterly, Economic and Social Review, Canadian Journal of Economics*).

Information-Sharing Legislation

The introduction of freedom of information legislation in the United Kingdom (Freedom of Information Act, 2000; Freedom of Information (Scotland) Act, 2002; Environmental Information Regulations, 2004; Environmental Information (Scotland) Regulations, 2004) has been a further driver for the development of data-sharing policies, as well as a means of enforcing data releases into the public domain. Authorities have designed these Acts, which came into force in 2005, to provide the public with a right to access information held by public authorities in the United Kingdom (including universities) and to ensure accountability and good governance in public agencies (Rusbridge and Charlesworth, 2010). The requested information can include research data and must be provided unless an exemption or exception allows an institution not to disclose them. The exemptions, which may be absolute or qualified, generally relate to considerations such as national security, law enforcement, commercial interests, and data protection. Exemptions in Scotland differ in certain important aspects from those in the remainder of the United Kingdom. This legislation means that researchers can now be legally forced to release their data.

The Ethics Creep: The Moral and Ethical Case for Regulating Data Sharing

The notion of "regulation creep" (Dingwall, 2006; see also Rena Lederman, this volume) derives its legitimacy from "ethics creep" (Haggerty, 2004) whereby regulators now define data sharing as a moral duty and ethical responsibility, and thereby incorporate it into research ethics regulation in the United Kingdom. Of special interest is the central participant-protection process of informed consent.

Data Sharing as a Moral Duty

The moral case for data sharing draws in part on the notion that, as public sector workers undertaking publicly funded research, researchers are accountable to the public and have a moral duty, obligation, and responsibility to make their research data available to the public. The Medical Research Council (2015) policy on data sharing, for example, explains that "publicly-funded research data are a public good, produced in the public interest, and ... they should be openly available to the maximum extent possible." A moral mandate to share research data has not traditionally featured within ethical codes of conduct. Rather, the expectation has been that researchers undertake and disseminate research that is ethically and scientifically sound (e.g., Social Research Association (SRA), 2003: 13), with an emphasis on data protection. Until relatively recently, data policies tended to encourage the destruction of human data within a specified time period (Willinson,

1998). Indeed, some social scientists still make the assumption that they should destroy research data (particularly personal data) once they have analysed them and written up their findings (Cheshire, 2009). For decades, destroying data after a specified time period was seen as good practice in sociology; and data protection policies adopted by funding agencies, professional associations, and universities reflected this practice (Carusi and Jirotka, 2009).

Shifts in policy, however, in favour of open over restricted access to research data are changing normative ethical regulations, guidelines, and practices. The ESRC's (2015b) *Framework for Research Ethics* illustrates this change. The *Framework for Research Ethics* sets out ESRC ethics approval requirements, and its views on good practice for all social science research. Compliance with the *Framework for Research Ethics* is mandatory for research funded by the Economic and Social Research Council, and is becoming a condition of funding by other research councils and agencies that fund social research (Jennings, 2012). The ESRC *Framework for Research Ethics* specifies that "researchers who initially collect the data should be aware that the ESRC expects that others will also re-use the data. The original researcher should take into account the long- term use, including the potential for data linkage and preservation of data, when obtaining consent" (25). Seeking informed consent to data sharing is becoming recommended, if not mandatory, practice, over and above obtaining consent for participation in the study and for using data in publications (see also Van den Eynden et al., 2011: 23). Although the Economic and Social Research Council recognizes that in some cases it may not be possible to make the data sufficiently anonymous to make them available in a data archive, the Council reminds researchers that they nevertheless have a responsibility and obligation to seek informed consent for data sharing from their research participants regardless of whether and how the data are later archived or shared. On this approach, researchers' *primary* responsibility is framed in terms of following the ESRC *Framework for Research Ethics* guidelines and now-normative default expectation and practice of seeking informed consent to data sharing, rather than considering whether such guidelines are ethically appropriate in a specific research context.

In practice this means that social scientists should ensure that research participants are aware of and consent to arrangements made with regard to the management and security of data, the preservation of anonymity, and any risk that might arise during or beyond the project itself, and how these might be minimized or avoided (ESRC, 2015b). This is despite the fact that elsewhere in the *Framework for Research Ethics* document, the Economic and Social Research Council recognizes that digital data sharing and reuse is a form of research that involves "more than minimal risk" because (1) it has the potential to breach confidentiality agreements, making it more likely that personal data will be disclosed; (2) it increases the possibility of identifying participants; and (3) it can lead to the use of data for purposes not anticipated in the initial consent to deposit.

Data Sharing as Ethical Responsibility

The moral case for data sharing is built on the assumption and expectation that following the recommended and prescribed ethical guidelines will ensure that sharing data is both ethical and legal. The Economic and Social Research Council refers researchers to the United Kingdom Data Archive (UKDA) for advice on securing consent for secondary use. The UK Data Archive houses the United Kingdom's largest collection of digital research data in the social sciences and humanities. It provides best practice guidelines (see Van den Eynden et al., 2011), and funding agencies refer researchers to the UK Data Archive for advice and protocols for dealing with ethical issues in digital data sharing. The UKDA *Principles of Research Ethics* identifies the following set of key principles related to sharing or archiving confidential research data: (1) a duty of confidentiality towards informants and participants; (2) a duty to protect participants from harm by not disclosing sensitive or identifying information; (3) a duty to treat participants as autonomous, intelligent beings, able to make their own decisions about how the information they provide can be used, shared, and made public (through the informed consent process); (4) a duty to inform participants about how information and data they provide will be used, processed, shared, and disposed of; and (5) a duty to wider society to make resources produced by researchers with public funds available for use by other researchers or anyone who requests the data (http://www.data-archive.ac.uk/create-manage/consent-ethics/legal).

The UK Data Archive recognizes that ethical and legal uncertainty about what is permissible to share is inhibiting data sharing by researchers. The guidelines are aimed towards alleviating these concerns and reassuring researchers that they can share their data ethically and legally if the recommended guidelines are followed: "A combination of gaining consent for data sharing, anonymizing data to protect people's identities and controlling access to data will enable sharing people-related research data – even sensitive ones – ethically and legally." In cases where anonymization would result in too much loss of data content, they advise regulating access to the data. This can be done in a number of ways: secondary users may need specific authorization from the data owner to access data; confidential data can be embargoed for a given period of time; access can be restricted to approved researchers only; and restrictions can be placed on data downloading. There is a reminder to researchers, however, that "restricting access to data should never be seen as the only way to protect confidentiality. Obtaining appropriate informed consent and anonymising data enable most data to be shared."

There is a tension, however, between the prescriptive nature of ESRC and UKDA guidelines and more flexible approaches advocated by professional associations such as the Social Research Association (2003), British Sociological Association (2002), and Association of Social Anthropologists of the United Kingdom and Commonwealth (2011). In particular, the professional associations emphasize that guidelines cannot resolve ethical dilemmas in a vacuum; that the reputations of the disciplines in question and their researchers depend less on the ethical norms issued by professional bodies and more on the conduct of individual researchers; that social researchers' individual ethical judgments and decisions need to be informed by shared values and experience, rather than imposed by the profession; and that researchers must take ethical responsibility for their own practices. In sum, they privilege the use of context-specific ethical practices and sound professional judgment over abstract and universal ethical principles.

The professional associations highlight researchers' multiple obligations towards different constituencies including research participants, sponsors, funders, employers, co-investigators, colleagues, the discipline, and wider society. The guidelines emphasize that researchers are faced with competing duties, obligations, and conflicts of interest; and stress that they do not seek to privilege one set of principles or interests over another. The Social Research Association (2003), for example, notes, "Concern for individual rights needs to be balanced against the benefits to society that may accrue from research activity. Such ethical conflicts are inevitable. Above all, however, researchers should not automatically assume that their priorities are shared by society in general" (15). And the Association of Social Anthropologists of the United

Kingdom and Commonwealth (2011) notes that anthropologists have a responsibility to resolve ethical problems, insofar as it is possible, without harming the research participants or the scholarly community. The Association urges anthropologists to do their utmost to ensure they leave the field in a state that permits future access and use by other researchers. Again, these guidelines contrast with those issued by the Economic and Social Research Council and the UK Data Archive, which implicitly prioritize the interests of "the public" and the agencies that fund social research, interests that are further reinforced by freedom of information legislation, its presumption in favour of data release, and its privileging of the "public interest." Data-sharing mandates mean that researchers are entering the field a priori privileging specific principles and interests. This position has significant ethical, moral, ontological, and political consequences, as illustrated in the next section.

The Regulation of Data Sharing and Its Unintended Consequences

The Ethics of "Broad Consent"

Regulatory regimes regard the practice of seeking informed consent as one of the main strategies for protecting the rights of research participants. Traditionally, informed consent has been sought in relation to a particular research project. This approach, however, restricts how data can be used as it requires researchers to contact participants and seek their consent for every new research project. This has prompted a move towards "broad consent," or "open consent," which is being proposed as best practice for biobanks and others types of data repositories (Cambon-Thomsen et al., 2007). Some medical and health science researchers support this move (Kozlakidis et al., 2012); opponents, however, view broad consent as a dilution of ethics that could destroy public trust (Caulfield et al., 2008). Henry Greely (2007) criticizes informed consent as inadequate for addressing ethical concerns because in practice it is satisfied by "largely ignorant blanket permission" (361). Achieving the required level of understanding for truly informed consent in the data-sharing context is difficult. Researchers can provide only limited information and reassurances about potential future uses and users of shared data (Greely, 2007). Placing data within a public digital archive means that both researchers and participants lose control over how the data are or will be used. Indeed, retrospective discovery by research participants of unknown applications of their data, and uses they did not consent to, has led to legal disputes (O'Brien, 2009). Furthermore, broad consent requires proxy decision-making by secondary data users and/or research ethics committees and transfers ethical decision-making to third parties who may lack relevant and context-specific knowledge or expertise. A further issue concerns national variations in ethical norms, guidelines, and practices that may render data reuse across national borders unethical and illegal. For example, the Western tradition of informed consent operates according to the principle that the most specific consent is the best consent. When data are exchanged internationally, there is little ability to regulate whether data sharing conforms to the specific purposes that participants consented to (Cambon-Thomsen et al., 2007).

In the context of social research, the Economic and Social Research Council mandates researchers to seek their participants' informed consent for data preservation and sharing. The same question arises as to how ethical it is to seek participants' "informed" consent for future unknown uses of their data by unknown third parties (Richardson and Godfrey, 2003; Mauthner, 2012), particularly within the context of international research where informed consent and data archiving and sharing may have culturally specific meanings (Morrow, 2009; Morrow et al., 2014). The UK Data Archive guidelines (http://ukdataservice.ac.uk/), however, argue that participants are protected from any potential harm caused by data reuse by virtue of the End Use Licence that data reusers are required to sign, which has contractual force in law, in which they agree to certain conditions, such as not to disseminate any identifying or confidential information on individuals, households, or organizations; and not to use the data to attempt to obtain information relating specifically to an identifiable individual. While this might protect participants from possible identification, it does not protect them from potentially morally harmful effects of seeing their data used for different purposes and in different contexts, which, some authors argue, can cause significant moral harms to research participants (e.g., Oakes, 2002; Jacobson et al., 2007; van den Hoonaard, 2002). As Tim Bond (2012) explains, the excessive fixation on harm avoidance overshadows other, more likely and subtle forms of harm such as damage to "intangible social assets such as identity, relationships or reputation, which derive their significance from the social context and are contingent on the perceptions of the people affected" (101). This challenges the assumption that uninvolved third parties, who are far removed from the data-gathering contexts, can or should make ethical and moral judgments about potential harms to participants (Mauthner, 2012).

In social research, the UK Data Archive (http://www.data-archive.ac.uk/home) advises researchers to anonymize the data they will lodge in a digital archive in line with agreements made with participants during the informed consent process. However, given that the protective power of anonymization is weakened within a digital context where data linkage heightens the risk of identification (see Zimmer, 2010; ESRC, 2015b: 5), the ethics of following the recommended guidelines by anonymizing narratives and telling participants that this will protect their identity are questionable. Furthermore, in some cases participants feel they lose ownership of their stories when data are anonymized, and they want to be named and acknowledged in research outputs. As Anne Grinyer (2002) explains, participants will have different preferences and these issues can only be decided on a case-by-case basis.

The recommended guidelines and procedures do not, therefore, universally guarantee that data sharing is ethical and legal because of the impossibility of making promises and assurances when working in a digital data-sharing context where there is less control over the data and how they are used. A further risk is that researchers will seek to comply with these guidelines and procedures, even if they do not agree with them, in an effort to secure future funding. These ill-fitting rules in turn may lead researchers to subtly coerce their participants into agreements to allow their data to be shared. In short, guidelines can become more coercive than ethical (see Haggerty, 2004).

Reconciling the Public's with Research Participants' Interests

The official presumption of releasing data tends to privilege the public's over research participants' interests. In some cases, researchers may view this as a violation of the trust-based relationships and moral responsibilities they have developed towards their participants. As Jane Kaye and her co-authors explain (2009), "The obligation to share genomic data may be perceived as an imposition on the relationships that have been built between researchers and participants" (333). Additional concerns were expressed by researchers in a recent freedom of information request in Scotland. In September 2011, tobacco company Philip Morris International submitted a series of freedom of information requests to the University of Stirling to gain access to research data gathered during a 10-year period that explored attitudes towards smoking among 6,000 teenagers and young adults. The researchers feared that releasing confidentially shared data to the tobacco industry would breach the trust established with the young participants (Christie, 2011). Another example comes from the United States where Boston College is fighting an ongoing legal battle with the British, US, and Irish governments over the release of oral history interviews conducted with former IRA paramilitaries in 2001 who were assured by the researchers that the interviews would not be made public until after their deaths (http://bostoncollege subpoena.wordpress.com). Such cases underscore the ethical risks posed by data-sharing mandates: risks of breaching not only existing but also potential future relationships with participants through the erosion of the perceived trustworthiness of researchers which may in turn deter the public from participation in research. This is especially true of attempts to apply these data-sharing mandates retroactively. These risks to participants (and researchers), however, tend not to be seen by regulators as legitimate concerns with data sharing because the normative ethics framework informing data-sharing practices is focused on "harm." But as Sean Jennings (2012) points out, perhaps the greatest risk of social science research lies not so much in its potential to inflict *harm* but rather in its capacity to *wrong* research participants: "The key risks involved are of breaching the trust, exploiting or taking advantage of subjects. When you start researching people directly by accessing data about them, talking to them, and finding out about their lives, you enter into a relationship with them. That relationship engenders responsibilities just as other professional relationships do. To fail to meet those responsibilities is to wrong your research subjects even if it does not harm them in any physical sense and even if they never find out about it" (90).

Data-Sharing Mandates and the Nature of Data

Data-sharing mandates change both the relationships of trust that researchers establish with participants and the moral conditions of possibility for participants' storytelling. Seeking informed consent from participants to share their stories, for example, changes the very nature of these stories in the same way that having other people in the room when telling a story shapes the story that is narrated. Similarly, data-sharing mandates reconfigure a researcher's interviewing style. For example, knowing that the interview will be shared with a broader audience may shape the interviewer's willingness to disclose personal experiences as part of building relationships of trust with participants.

These effects are particularly significant in the context of studies that focus on research topics that are personally or politically sensitive.

Another example of the ontological effects of data-sharing mandates on the nature of data is the normative practice of anonymizing archived data. To avoid the lengthy and resource-intensive process of anonymizing data after they have been collected, the UK Data Archive (http://www.data-archive.ac.uk/home) recommends that researchers keep some personal names and issues out of the interview conversation from the outset: "Pre-planning and agreeing with participants during the consent process, on what may and may not be recorded or transcribed, can be a much more effective way of creating data that accurately represent the research process and the contribution of participants. For example, if an employer's name cannot be disclosed, it should be agreed in advance that it will not be mentioned during an interview. This is easier than spending time later removing it from a recording or transcript."

The UK Data Archive suggests that researchers might extend this policy to other personal identifiers: names of friends, relatives, places, institutions, etc. As with informed consent, however, asking informants to refrain from using personal identifiers in their narratives has ontological effects on the resulting conversation. Expressing interest in the personal details and specificities of research participants' lives and experiences, and remembering and using this information to generate further questions and stories, are practices that play a part in making the narratives that are told. These practices build particular kinds of relationships between researchers and participants that in turn help constitute the very nature of research participants' stories.

As seen through these examples, the regulation of research, data sharing, and research ethics is not neutral in its effects. It changes not only research methods and practices, but the researchers' relationships with participants and the stories that participants tell about their lives. This regulatory approach makes a material difference not only to what researchers discover about the social world, but perhaps more importantly, to what will be systematically and constitutively excluded from and by their investigative practices (see also Stanley and Wise, 2010; Haggerty, 2004; van den Hoonaard, 2001).

Reconfiguration of Researchers' Intellectual Property Rights

Data-sharing mandates and legislation are reconfiguring researchers' intellectual property rights and raising associated ethical and political issues. Prima facie ownership of intellectual property is vested in the creator. However, when an employee creates in the course of employment, ownership frequently belongs to the employer. This applies to intellectual property such as literary works, musical works, computer programs, and databases. In a research context, this means that universities, as employers of researchers, have long had legal ownership of the research data that researchers produce. In practice, however, they have rarely exercised these rights, and researchers have enjoyed moral ownership rights and control over their data. The introduction of freedom of information legislation, however, is eroding these informal moral ownership practices while strengthening legal and institutional ownership rights. Today universities are much more likely to, and can now more easily, exercise ownership rights. This was illustrated in the high-profile case of Mike Baillie, a dendrochronologist from Queen's University Belfast, who was forced to release tree-ring data under the Freedom of Information Act in April 2010. The Information Commissioner's Office ruled that the university must release the data to the public because Baillie did all the work while employed at a public university. Baillie unsuccessfully contested this directive by claiming that the tree-ring data he had collected during a 40-year career were his own personal intellectual property (Baillie, 2010). Freedom of information legislation stipulates that these intellectual property rights will not be infringed where an act is authorized by an Act of Parliament. Responding to a freedom of information request is an act authorized by Parliament and so disclosures under freedom of information provisions do not infringe intellectual property rights. In other words, freedom of information legislation can effectively override intellectual property rights. The recent regulatory, policy, and legislative changes therefore represent a significant moral and political shift in relation to the ownership and control of data.

The case of Mike Baillie illustrates how data-sharing mandates and legislation are changing relationships between universities and their employees. Relationships among co-investigators, and between supervisors and their doctoral students, are similarly undergoing transformation. Junior researchers, PhD students, and/or technicians tend to be the key producers of research data. These researchers may lack the time and resources available to senior researchers to make full and timely use of the data they generate. Their data-collection efforts are typically, though not necessarily, recognized and rewarded (e.g., joint publications); however, recognition of their labour is less likely within the context of open data sharing as currently constituted. Power and status differentials among team members risk leaving junior researchers open to exploitation as principal investigators have responsibility for making decisions about data sharing. Even where senior colleagues consult junior team members, by dint of their power and status they may privilege their own objectives. Within the context of international projects, there is a further risk that data sharing becomes a form of scientific neo-colonialism.

Although turning data into a shared resource has the potential to provide post-colonial contexts with easy and cheap access to data generated elsewhere, they may lack the necessary scientific, technical, digital, or cultural capital and resources to make full and speedy use of the data (see Luo and Olson, 2008). In practice, it may be primarily well-resourced researchers and nations who stand to gain from data sharing, by reaping scientific and economic benefits and rewards from data generated by researchers and nations with fewer resources. From this perspective, a global data-sharing project risks reproducing exploitative relations among nations, and among data users and data producers.

Should Data Sharing Be Regulated?

From Regulation to Collaboration

The grounds for regulating data sharing imply that it constitutes an unconditional good (Mauthner, 2014). Yet, as the Royal Society report on *Science as an Open Enterprise* (2012: 9) suggests, "Opening up scientific data is not an unqualified good. There are legitimate boundaries of openness which must be maintained in order to protect commercial value, privacy, safety and security." Data sharing is not necessarily appropriate for all types of data or all types of research. Nor are the interests of the public, research participants, researchers, and research funders universally and necessarily best served by the imposition of data-sharing mandates. In light of this, regulators need to recognize that different data-sharing models are appropriate for different projects and that top-down, one-size-fits-all approaches need to be reconsidered. Potential benefits and harms of data sharing are individual-, project-, and context-specific. Researchers cannot necessarily predict, at the outset of a project, whether and how data sharing will be feasible or beneficial, or what its potential impacts on and acceptability to research participants are likely to be. Those directly involved in data gathering (the researchers and the participating individuals and/or organizations) are best placed to understand the potential harms and benefits of data sharing and make specific and contextual, that is, meaningful judgments about it. Institutional mechanisms must find ways of recognizing researchers' and participants' rights and judgments in relation to data sharing. The complexities of data sharing demand more flexible, inclusive, and collaborative approaches in which researchers, research participants, research funders, universities, and publishers work together to devise context-specific data-sharing practices on a case-by-case basis.

Technological and legislative changes have weakened researchers' control over data security, data protection, data privacy, data access, data integrity, data use, and data ownership. These changes in the research landscape are reconfiguring research practices and relationships, raising new questions: What kinds of reassurances, if any, can researchers provide to participants in the data-sharing environment? Should researchers be reconsidering their promise-making practices, and with what effects? And how is this new environment challenging and changing the trust-based relationships that have characterized social research over previous decades?

The critical point is that data-sharing regulation further increases the risks of research by putting participants at greater risk of being identified and having their data used in ways they do not consent to. Yet the research environment itself – and specifically its digital nature – may demand a move away from precisely this kind of regulation towards ways of working with participants that are based on collaboration and a partnership approach in which researchers and participants acknowledge risks and share responsibilities. Monitoring and negotiating risks in dynamic, ongoing and collaborative ways is important in this new research landscape, yet this is an approach that runs counter to the "anticipatory regulatory regimes" (Murphy and Dingwall, 2007) characterizing the current system.

From the "Right to Require" and the "Duty to Comply"
to the "Right to Request" and the "Duty to Consider"

The potential benefits of data sharing have been established. The question is whether there is scope to move away from a regulatory and normative framework through the introduction of data-sharing policies that provide the right to *request* (on the part of regulators and research funders) and the duty to (carefully) *consider* (on the part of researchers) data sharing in replacement of "the right to *require* and the duty to *comply*" approach of current policies. Funding agencies like the Australian Research Council (ARC, 2015) adopt such an approach: "The ARC considers data management planning an important part of the responsible conduct of research and strongly encourages the depositing of data arising from a Project in an appropriate publically accessible subject and/or institutional repository" (19). Indeed, the RCUK draft *Concordat on Open Research Data* currently undergoing consultation, and the Royal Society report on *Science as an Open Enterprise* (2012), recognize and take into account the ethical and moral challenges of sharing research data and signal a potential shift away from a rigid regulatory and normative framework in UK data-sharing policy and practice.

Recognizing the Moral Ownership Rights of Research Participants

Normative ethical frameworks are paternalistic in nature and can overlook the right-of-say of research participants. Promotive frameworks work with a more sophisticated notion of what it means to be a research participant. They seek to enhance the autonomy of participants, involve them as active contributors in research, and allow them some say in how their data are used (see Budin-Ljosne, 2012, for a biomedical example). In this approach to data sharing, research participants have greater rights, including the right to withdraw their data from a database at a later date if they wish to do so.

Taking Responsibility for Our Ethical Practices

Regulators see ethical responsibility as the uncritical implementation of prescribed, normative, abstract, and seemingly universal, ready-made ethical principles. Yet, as illustrated here, these rule-following approaches can contribute to a range of practices that, when implemented, can turn out to be unethical. In particular, regulation represents a low level of ethical commitment and can lead to an abrogation of ethical responsibilities towards participants (Mauthner, 2012; see also Bond, 2012). As others have pointed out, one of the paradoxes of implementing formal and regulated ethics systems is the rupture they create between following the rules and conducting ethical research (Haggerty, 2004; Miller et al., 2012).

   If researchers are to be encouraged to consider data management and sharing as an inherent part of research practice, ethics, and governance, they will benefit from working within a framework that is designed to stimulate critical engagement with, rather than compliance with, data-sharing programs. As Jennings (2012) points out, "When ethics committees are set up to be venues for ethical reflection, and researchers own them as such, [only then] will we reap the full potential benefits of ethics review" (92). In this way, researchers will be better able to take responsibility for their data-sharing practices and for their specific ethical, moral, legal, and ontological consequences and effects.

NOTE

An earlier version of this chapter was first presented at "The Ethics Rupture: An Invitational Summit on Finding Alternatives to Formal Ethics Review," Fredericton, October 2012. I thank Will van den Hoonaard, and the organizing committee, for inviting me to take part in the Summit. Thanks also to Will and Ann Hamilton for their comments on an earlier version, and for their careful editing of my chapter. I am also grateful to the other conference attendees for their helpful comments and feedback during the Summit. Final thanks go to the Society for Research into Higher Education for funding my research on digital-data sharing.

1 The Economic and Social Research Council is the UK's leading research and training agency addressing economic and social concerns.

REFERENCES

Arzberger, Peter, Peter Schroeder, Anne Beaulieu, Geoffrey Bowker, Karen Casey, Leif Laaksonen, David Moorman, Paul Uhlir, and Paul Wouters. (2004). "Promoting Access to Public Research Data for Scientific, Economic, and Social Development." *Data Science Journal* 3: 135–52. http://dx.doi.org/10.2481/dsj.3.135

Association of Social Anthropologists of the United Kingdom and the Commonwealth. (2011). *Ethical Guidelines for Good Research Practice* www.theasa.org

Australian Research Council. (2015). *Funding Rules for Schemes under the Discovery Program (2015 edition).* http://www.arc.gov.au/sites/default/files/filedepot/Public/NCGP/DP17/Discovery_Programme_Funding_Rules_2015.pdf

Baillie, Mike. (2010). "Tree-Ring Patterns Are Intellectual Property, Not Climate Data." *The Guardian*, 11 May.

Benson, Dennis A., Ilene Karsch-Mizrachi, David J. Lipman, James Ostell, and David L. Wheeler. (2008). "GenBank." *Nucleic Acids Research* 36: Database issue D25–D30.

Bishop, Libby. (2009). "Ethical Sharing and Reuse of Qualitative Data." *Australian Journal of Social Issues* 44: 255–72.

Bond, Tim. (2012). "Ethical Imperialism or Ethical Mindfulness? Rethinking Ethical Review for Social Sciences." *Research Ethics* 8 (2): 97–112. http://dx.doi.org/10.1177/1747016112445419

Borgman, Christine L. (2012). "The Conundrum of Sharing Research Data." *Journal of the American Society for Information Science and Technology* 63 (6): 1059–78. http://dx.doi.org/10.1002/asi.22634

British Sociological Association. (2002). *Statement of Ethical Practice 2002.* http://www.britsoc.co.uk/media/27107/StatementofEthicalPractice.pdf

Bruna, Emilio M. (2010). "Scientific Journals Can Advance Tropical Biology and Conservation by Requiring Data Archiving." *Biotropica* 42 (4): 399–401. http://dx.doi.org/10.1111/j.1744-7429.2010.00652.x

Budin-Ljosne, Isabelle. (2012). "A Review of Ethical Frameworks for the Disclosure of Individual Research Results in Population-Based Genetic and Genomic Research." *Research Ethics* 8 (1): 25–42. http://dx.doi.org/10.1177/1747016111435576

Cambon-Thomsen, Anne, Emmanuelle Rial-Sebbag, and Bartha M. Knoppers. (2007). "Trends in Ethical and Legal Frameworks for the Use of Human Biobanks." *European Respiratory Journal* 30 (2): 373–82. http://dx.doi.org/10.1183/09031936.00165006

Carusi, Annamaria, and Marina Jirotka. (2009). "From Data Archive to Ethical Labyrinth." *Qualitative Research* 9 (3): 285–98. http://dx.doi.org/10.1177/1468794109105032

Caulfield, Timothy, A.L. McGuire, M. Cho, J.A. Buchanan, M.M. Burgess, Ursula Danilczyk, Christina M. Diaz, Kelly Fryer-Edwards, Shane K. Green, Marc A. Hodosh, et al. (2008). "Research Ethics Recommendations for Whole-Genome Research: Consensus Statement." *PLoS Biology* 6 (3): e73–5. http://dx.doi.org/10.1371/journal.pbio.0060073

Cheshire, Lynda. (2009). "Archiving Qualitative Data: Prospects and Challenges of Data Preservation and Sharing among Australian Qualitative Researchers – Discussion Paper." Canberra: Australian Social Science Data Archive.

Christie, Bryan. (2011). "Tobacco Company Makes Freedom of Information Request for University's Research." *British Medical Journal* 343 (sep05 2): d5655. http://dx.doi.org/10.1136/bmj.d5655

Dingwall, Robert. (2006). "Confronting the Anti-Democrats: The Unethical Nature of Ethical Regulation in Social Science." *Medical Sociology Online* 1: 51–8.

EPSRC (Engineering and Physical Sciences Research Counil). (2014) Clarifications of EPSRC expectations on research data management https://www.epsrc.ac.uk/files/aboutus/standards/clarificationsofexpectationsresearchdatamanagement/

ESRC (Economic and Social Research Council). (2015a). *ESRC Research Data Policy.* http://www.esrc.ac.uk/files/about-us/policies-and-standards/esrc-research-data-policy/

– (2015b). *Framework for Research Ethics.* http://www.esrc.ac.uk/files/funding/guidance-for-applicants/esrc-framework-for-research-ethics-2015/

Goldacre, Ben. (2012). *Bad Pharma.* London: Fourth Estate.

Greely, Henry T. (2007). "The Uneasy Ethical and Legal Underpinnings of Large-scale Genomic Bio-Banks." *Annual Review of Genomics and Human Genetics* 8 (1): 343–64. http://dx.doi.org/10.1146/annurev.genom.7.080505.115721

Grinyer, Anne. (2002). "The Anonymity of Research Participants: Assumptions, Ethics, and Practicalities." *Social Research Update* (36): 1–4.

Haggerty, Kevin D. (2004). "Ethics Creep: Governing Social Science Research in the Name of Ethics." *Qualitative Sociology* 27 (4): 391–414. http://dx.doi.org/10.1023/B:QUAS.0000049239.15922.a3

Jacobson, Nora, Rebecca Gewurtz, and Emma Haydon. (2007). "Ethical Review of Interpretive Research: Problems and Solutions." *IRB Ethics and Human Research* 29 (5): 1–8.

Jennings, Sean. (2012). "Response to Schrag: What Are Ethics Committees for Anyway? A Defence of Social Science Research Ethics Review." *Research Ethics* 8 (2): 87–96. http://dx.doi.org/10.1177/1747016112445423

Kaye, Jane, Catherine Heeney, Naomi Hawkins, Jantina de Vries, and Paula Boddington. (2009). "Data Sharing in Genomics: Re-shaping Scientific Practice." *Nature Reviews. Genetics* 10 (5): 331–5. http://dx.doi.org/10.1038/nrg2573

Kozlakidis, Zisis, Robert J.S. Cason, Christine Mant, and John Cason. (2012). "Human Tissue Biobanks: The Balance between Consent and the Common Good." *Research Ethics* 8 (2): 113–23. http://dx.doi.org/10.1177/1747016112442031

Luo, Airong, and Judith S. Olson. (2008). "How Collaboratories Affect Scientists from Developing Countries." In Gary Olson, Ann Zimmerman, and Nathan Bos (eds.), *Scientific Collaboration on the Internet,* 365–76. Cambridge, MA: MIT Press. http://dx.doi.org/10.7551/mitpress/9780262151207.003.0021.

Mauthner, Natasha S. (2012). "'Accounting for Our Part of the Entangled Webs We Weave': Ethical and Moral Issues in Digital Data Sharing." In Tina

Miller, Maxine Birch, Melanie Mauthner, and Julie Jessop (eds.), *Ethics in Qualitative Research*, 157–75. London: Sage.

– (2014). "Digital Data Sharing: A Genealogical and Performative Perspective." *Studia Socjologiczne* 3 (214): 177–86.

Mauthner, Natasha S., and Odette Parry. (2009). "Qualitative Data Preservation and Sharing in the Social Sciences: On Whose Philosophical Terms?" *Australian Journal of Social Issues* 44 (3): 289–305.

– (2013). "Open Access Digital Data Sharing: Principles, Policies, and Practices." *Social Epistemology* 27 (1): 47–67. http://dx.doi.org/10.1080/02691728.2012.760663

Mauthner, Natasha S. (2015). "'The Past Was Never Simply There to Begin with and the Future Is Not Simply What Will Unfold': A Posthumanist Performative Approach to Qualitative Longitudinal Research." *International Journal of Social Research Methodology* 18 (3): 321–336. http://www.tandfonline.com/eprint/MWQYRS6CazSgCrqcr7Sm/full

Medical Research Council. (2015). *MRC Policy on Data Sharing and Preservation*. http://www.mrc.ac.uk/research/research-policy-ethics/data-sharing/policy/

Miller, Tina, Maxine Birch, Melanie Mauthner, and Julie Jessop (eds.). (2012). *Ethics in Qualitative Research*. 2nd ed. London: Sage. http://dx.doi.org/10.4135/9781473913912

Morrow, Virginia. (2009). *The Ethics of Social Research with Children and Families in Young Lives: Practical Experiences*. Working Paper No. 53. Oxford: Department of International Development, University of Oxford.

Morrow, Virginia, Janet Boddy, and Rowena Lamb. (2014). *The Ethics of Secondary Data Analysis: Learning from the Experience of Sharing Qualitative Data from Young People and Their Families in an International Study of Childhood Poverty*. Novella Working Paper. http://www.younglives.org.uk/publications/WP/ethics-secondary-data-analysis-novella

Murphy, Elizabeth, and Robert Dingwall. (2007). "Informed Consent: Anticipatory Regulation and Ethnographic Practice." *Social Science & Medicine* 65 (11): 2223–34. http://dx.doi.org/10.1016/j.socscimed.2007.08.008

Neale, Bren, Karen Henwood, and Janet Holland. (2012). "Researching Lives through Time: An Introduction to the Timescapes Approach." *Qualitative Research* 12 (1): 4–15. http://dx.doi.org/10.1177/1468794111426229

Nelson, Bryn. (2009). "Data Sharing: Empty Archives." *Nature* 461 (7261): 160–3. http://dx.doi.org/10.1038/461160a

Noble, Susan, Celia Russell, and Richard Wiseman. (2011). "Mind the Gap: Global Data Sharing." *IASSIST Quarterly* 6 (35).

Oakes, Michael J. (2002). "Risks and Wrongs in Social Science Research: An Evaluator's Guide to the IRB." *Evaluation Review* 26: 443–79.

O'Brien, Stephen J. (2009). "Stewardship of Human Biospecimens, DNA, Genotype, and Clinical Data in the GWAS Era." *Annual Review of Genomics and Human Genetics* 10 (1): 193–209. http://dx.doi.org/10.1146/annurev-genom-082908-150133

OECD (Organisation for Economic Co-operation and Development). (1994). *Global Change of Planet Earth.* Paris: OECD.

– (2007). *Principles and Guidelines for Access to Research Data from Public Funding.* Paris: OECD.

Perry, Carol M. (2008). "Archiving of Publicly Funded Research Data: A Survey of Canadian Researchers." *Government Information Quarterly* 25 (1): 133–48. http://dx.doi.org/10.1016/j.giq.2007.04.008

Research Councils UK. (2015a). Common Principles on Data Policy. http://www.rcuk.ac.uk/RCUK-prod/assets/documents/documents/RCUKCommonPrinciplesonDataPolicy.pdf

– (2015b). Concordat on Open Research Data. http://www.rcuk.ac.uk/RCUK-prod/assets/documents/documents/ConcordatOpenResearchData.pdf

Research Information Network. (2009). *Patterns of Information Use and Exchange: Case Studies of Researchers in the Life Sciences.* London: Research Information Network.

Richardson, Jane C., and Barry S. Godfrey. (2003). "Towards Ethical Practice in the Use of Archived Transcripted Interviews." *International Journal of Social Research Methodology* 6 (4): 347–55. http://dx.doi.org/10.1080/13645570210142874

Royal Society. (2012). *Science as an Open Enterprise.* https://royalsociety.org/~/media/policy/projects/sape/2012-06-20-saoe.pdf

Rusbridge, Chris, and Andrew Charlesworth. (2010). *Freedom of Information and Research Data: Questions and Answers.* London: JISC.

Ruusalepp, R. (2008). JISC. "Comparative Study of International Approaches to Enabling the Sharing of Research Data: Summary and Main Findings." London: JISC. https://www.era.lib.ed.ac. Accessed 28 November 2015.

Shapley, Alan H., and Pembroke J. Hart. (1982). "World Data Centres." *Eos, Transactions, American Geophysical Union* 63 (30): 585. http://dx.doi.org/10.1029/EO063i030p00585-01

SRA (Social Research Association). (2003). *Ethical Guidelines, 2003.* http://the-sra.org.uk/wp-content/uploads/ethics03.pdf

Stanley, Liz, and Sue Wise. (2010). "The ESRC's 2010 Framework for Research Ethics: Fit for Research Purpose?" *Sociological Research Online* 15 (4). http://eprints.lancs.ac.uk/55430/

Thomson, Rachel, and Julie McLeod. (2015). "New Frontiers in Qualitative Longitudinal Research: An Agenda for Research." *International Journal of Social Research Methodology* 18 (3): 243–250. http://www.tandfonline.com/doi/pdf/10.1080/13645579.2015.1017900

Van den Eynden, Veerle, Louise Corti, Matthew Woollard, Libby Bishop, and Horton Laurence. (2011). *Managing and Sharing Data: Best Practice for Researchers*. Colchester: UK Data Archive, University of Essex.

van den Hoonaard, Will. (2001). "Is Research-Ethics Review a Moral Panic?" *Canadian Review of Sociology/Revue canadienne de sociologie* 38 (1): 19–36. http://dx.doi.org/10.1111/j.1755-618X.2001.tb00601.x

– (ed.). (2002). *Walking the Tightrope: Ethical Issues for Qualitative Researchers*. Toronto: University of Toronto Press.

Whitlock, Michael C., Mark A. McPeek, Mark D. Rausher, Loren Rieseberg, and Allen J. Moore. (2010). "Data Archiving." *American Naturalist* 175 (2): 145–6. http://dx.doi.org/10.1086/650340

Willinson, Donald J. (1998). "Health Services Research and Personal Health Information: Privacy Concerns, New Legislation and Beyond." *Canadian Medical Association Journal* 159 (11): 1378–80.

Zimmer, Michael. (2010). "'But the Data Is Already Public': On the Ethics of Research in Facebook." *Ethics and Information Technology* 12 (4): 313–25. http://dx.doi.org/10.1007/s10676-010-9227-5

Zimmerman, Ann S. (2007). "Not by Metadata Alone: The Use of Diverse Forms of Knowledge to Locate Data for Reuse." *International Journal on Digital Libraries* 7 (1–2): 5–16. http://dx.doi.org/10.1007/s00799-007-0015-8

12 The Socialization of Contemporary Students by Ethics Boards: Malaise and Ethics for Graduate Students

LISA-JO KESTIN VAN DEN SCOTT

The increase in power of Institutional Review Boards (IRBs, in the United States) and Research Ethics Boards (REBs, in Canada) has serious implications for research by graduate students. I explore these implications by considering the experiences of graduate students as symptoms of the malaise, the prevailing social context, and the direct impact of research ethics review on research. Finally, I also call for solutions to this malaise.

Writing from the perspective of an American graduate student, I draw on informal conversations with other graduate students at conferences and workshops in both the United States and Canada, as well as conversations within my own university. I emphasize that I am making broad points, rather than offering complaints about specific ethics boards (fortunately, I have no complaints about my university ethics board and I have not individually suffered from many of the broader systemic problems I address in this chapter). I am an inside informer, that is, I participate in the community of graduate students. These conversations occur when graduate students meet after-hours at conferences and other formal and informal gatherings discussing their experiences. I share the single-minded fascination and frustrations that dominate graduate student interactions when they discuss their own research and experiences with ethics review committees. I also draw on a growing body of literature pointing to some deep concerns about the current malaise about research ethics review.

Symptoms of Malaise

My conversations with graduate students indicate fear as one of the pervasive themes of contemporary graduate-student life facing research ethics review (Katz, 2007; Loftus, 2008). They fear the impact of ethics boards on their future careers, their reputations, and their performance within a publish-or-perish framework. Many graduate students express deep (and justified) concerns about their careers being threatened if they step out of line. When the topic turns to ethics review in a room full of graduate students, students display exasperation and a sense of helplessness. They carefully craft proposals, consuming months of work. This step in the research process becomes the all-encompassing focus in the life of anxiety-driven students, a central life-interest (Dubin, 1956). Failing to get "ethics approval" means changing a project, possibly adding a year or more to the degree program. Getting past formal ethics review is, for many students, the name of the game. After the REB/IRB grants its approval, the rest of the research process is peanuts. However, if a planned and approved interview runs over by 10 minutes, categories of potential participants expands, or questions must be revised in situ, fears resurface.

Reframing or rewording interview questions provokes a troublesome problem: What constitutes "substantial changes" that require the researcher to go back to the research ethics committee? Graduate students often silently grapple with these issues, but in the end they feel bound by their "protocol documents" and are aware that formally adding a question to this document could substantially slow down their research, including the possibility of another full-board review. Some researchers are inclined, however slightly, to disobedience (and do not report changes they consider reasonable), still other student-colleagues have remarked to me that although a particular new line of thought in their research seemed more interesting or important, that line of thought fell outside of their approved research. They decided to abandon that line because it might jeopardize the research timeline. As explained above, the thought process revolves around the interaction between the student and the review board, rather than the field site and the participants, for whom the entire system ostensibly exists.

Conversations about research ethics, from what I have observed, are almost entirely narrowed to research ethics *review* rather than about ethical *research* in the broader sense (Lynch, 2000). One evening, for example, sitting among a half-dozen graduate students and one invited faculty member at an informal gathering of a reading group, I noted the conversation had turned to ethics. The faculty guest began to speak about how he tried to find the balance between revealing (or not revealing) all the information he had obtained in the field. I was eager to hear how he negotiated his own ethical decisions in the field, but he spoke only briefly before other students brought the discussion back to the ethics *review* process. Ethics review boards consume graduate student thoughts and drive conversations that have become so routine that it is hard for students to have a different kind of conversation outside the context of the demands of the review boards. Graduate students stand unsteadily in the stream of ethics review processes and protocols, frequently, it seems, frozen with fear.

I have spent more leisure hours discussing proposals, applications, protocols, rules, norms, regulations, and tricks for getting through ethics review boards with my fellow graduate students than we have spent discussing our work, interests, or, for that matter, what might constitute an actual ethical approach to research in our field. Some students resort to superstition, not wanting to talk about the review boards so as not to jinx proposals. Folklore abounds about the application rejected for its "low N," or severe consequences for a 10-minute overrun of interviews (as mentioned above). Many share IRB/REB applications forms in attempts to demystify the process. They carefully craft proposals, requiring months of work and attention.

In many respects, it was graduate students themselves who led me on their journey of the specific impacts of ethics review boards on student research. When the topic of ethics arose, they frequently launched into discussions about the technicalities demanded by the ethics boards, and the ever-present fear and frustration were palpable (Bond, 2012). How can they get their application through? Who is the best person to talk to at their own university? When should they start applying? Whose application was recently approved? How did he or she do that? Whenever I attempted to expand the conversation, directly asking about their fears, they were too focused on these technicalities and injustices to be derailed now from such a narrow preoccupation. Those who insisted they were not afraid of undergoing the ethics review process would, instead, provide advice by telling me who was the easiest to approach on their ethics board and how to write section X or paragraph Y.

Through my interactions with graduate students, I became aware that they exhibit a deeply cynical anger and claim (in sufficiently informal contexts so as to feel safe venting) that research ethics review boards are only concerned with protecting the university from liability, to the detriment of protecting the researcher or the research participant. The legal process and legalistic language also feeds this deep resentment. They go as far as to claim that ethics boards are not about research ethics, yet they give the ethics boards priority over ethics in their research practices. The genuine belief that students may have that ethics review boards are about ethics is quickly countered by their rancour over the legalistic approach that, in the end, undermines that belief as much as their fear will allow. I would assert that research ethics review boards will likely face fewer and fewer challenges as incoming cohorts of students are schooled to accept the appropriate levels of fear as par for the course in their future.

The Prevailing Social Context of Research Ethics Review

To understand the social context of research ethics review, it is useful to consider Becker's hierarchy of credibility (1967) – the idea that institutional hierarchies exist that privilege higher status groups' interpretations over the interpretations and experiences of marginalized groups. Experts, such as prison wardens are more readily believed about their understanding of prison settings than what prisoners themselves say about prisons.

In the context of research ethics review, ethics boards are placed higher in the hierarchy of credibility than students. Researchers, too, occupy a lower stratum of credibility than ethics boards. However, research participants believe they occupy a yet lower place in the hierarchy of credibility than researchers. I shall now turn to each of these groups.

Students

Research ethics boards socialize graduate students into thinking about ethical research in terms of the framework created by the ethics boards, creating a docile acceptance of the solidification and permanency of ethics review boards in, by now, generations of researchers (Cohen, 2007; Derbyshire, 2006; Dougherty and Kramer, 2005; Epstein, 2007).

As we know, filling out forms has little to do with ethics (Iphofen, 2011), yet ethics review boards impress upon students that it *constitutes* ethical research. One can easily see how this kind of bureaucratic pressure *turns researchers' thoughts inward, onto themselves, rather than outward, onto their participants.* Rather than preparing for research by contemplating potential participants, graduate students contemplate their own careers, their own potential for publication, and how the approval of research ethics review boards is necessary to achieve those ends. They wonder how *they* can get through the process, rather than how to more ethically engage with their participants.

Researchers

These elements relate to Becker's (1967) hierarchies of credibility. He states, "In any system of ranked groups, participants take it as given that members of the highest group have the right to define the way things really are. And since ... matters of rank and status are contained in the mores, this belief has a moral quality ... Thus, credibility and the right to be heard are differently distributed through the ranks of the system" (241). Becker emphasized the need for researchers to upend that hierarchy, giving credibility and legitimacy to those less powerful.

The definitions and decisions rendered by ethics review boards solidify existing hierarchies of credibility that many social researchers seek to overcome. The process of ethics review, through the use of risk management and legal discourse, forces the researcher to take a position within the upper echelons of the hierarchy of credibility rather than facilitating the upending of these hierarchies.

Researchers not only believe they are unable to challenge institutional hierarchies, but also lack the skills to approach their work with a revolutionary mindset aimed at overturning long-existing hierarchies of credibility in the field site, in publishing, and in teaching.

Reflecting the biomedical paradigm that underlies ethics codes (Block, 2008; van den Hoonaard, 2011), the point of view of the ethics board places members of ethics review boards at the pinnacle in the board-to-researcher relationship, and the researcher at the pinnacle of the hierarchy of credibility in his or her research arena. The ethics review boards define what ethical behaviour is for the researcher, and the researcher defines ethical behaviour for participants, as we shall see.

Research Participants

Interestingly, the ethics review board establishes its hierarchical purview of research participants on the basis of written text, without any direct, or face-to-face contact with participants – just as there is typically no face-to-face interaction between the ethics board and the researcher (Scott, 2005; Hemmings, 2006).

Not only must researchers make assumptions on behalf of participants about what constitutes ethical conduct, but also they must determine the questions for interviews in advance or risk rejection of the proposal because, in large part, of the bias towards biomedical, positivistic harm/benefit analyses and other requirements inappropriate for social scientists (Becker-Blease and Freyd, 2006). Providing research proposals to the ethics review board also frames the researcher as the expert in the lives of unknown others, the expert at knowing what the important questions are, or what he or she can get away with asking, at least officially. By forcing the researcher to assume a position superior to that of the participants and higher in the hierarchy of credibility, the ethics boards slam shut the doors of the possibility, even the need, to accommodate issues that participants themselves may find important or problematic (Azar, 2002; Barrera and Simpson, 2012). This interaction between the ethics board and the researcher quiets the voice of the participant in specific ways, namely, silencing the participants' own expertise in their own lives, stripping away their autonomy – the pinnacle of disrespect – by privileging the researcher's understanding of the participants' world. However, when researchers learn, once they are in the field, that more interview questions may be needed, questions concerning different issues that arose inductively may need to be added or removed, and the predicted duration of interviews may need to be changed, etc. They know that they cannot presume to make these adjustments in advance. Still, the privileged position accorded to researchers removes the possibility of dismantling the hierarchy of credibility. It can be argued then that this system diminishes substantially the likelihood that the hierarchy is even *seen*.

In many ways, the graduate student stands alone. Many chapters in this volume, *The Ethics Rupture*, express familiarity with how research-ethics review boards are changing the ways social scientists perform their research, as well as how students "perform." From the graduate-student perspective, much of this performance relates to the separation of supervisors from decisions made by ethics review boards. Many supervisors no longer initiate conversations about ethics, relegating that responsibility to the ethics board. Supervisors may check to assure themselves that a student has obtained or is in the process of obtaining approval from a board. If so, the job is finished. There is, often, little mentoring to help students conceptualize ethics on their own and to guide them in the field.

Graduate students lament a lack of help from supervisors about how to actually engage with the ethics review boards in terms of the mechanics and/or the process of the application. Students learn to navigate on their own or through what they can glean from departmental ethics workshops (Newman, 2004), but it is rare that a supervisor gives advice, or even talks about the ethics review board with students. The

236 Lisa-Jo Kestin van den Scott

supervisor may have his or her own problems with the board and may not want to hurt their own (or their student's) chances for approval. The quandary for the student, then, becomes how to make both the ethics board and the supervisor happy. How should the student go about complying with the mandates of ethics review boards, while at the same time meeting the expectations of a supervisor and other committee members? One solution is to fall back into doing interviews as the only form of collecting qualitative data.

Given the formal concern that the student may lack any foundational knowledge related to research ethics review, the research ethics regime in the United States now mandates the student take the Collaborative Institutional Training Initiative, an online test (CITI, 2013), and pass several modules individually. Each module consists of a page of text about a given area, such as the history of the Milgram experiment (Milgram, 1974; Srivastava, 2011), or the intricacies of issues such as vulnerable populations, consent, or conflicts of interest. The test is a form of ethics instruction that graduate students must complete prior to applying to the ethics review boards. The Collaborative Institutional Training Initiative also tests the students on history that, from the perspective of social scientists, seems largely irrelevant to their field and studies. Many graduate students see the process of CITI testing, along with the entire process, as a charade. Sometimes the CITI pages have links to other pages with more information. When a student has read the page, he or she clicks the next button and answers four or five multiple-choice questions based on the reading. The student can take each module as often as he or she wants to.

Although students are warned in strict terms that their tests will be timed and any tomfooleries will be investigated, students find creative ways to circumvent the intentions of the course. One can open the questions in a new tab and have both pages open simultaneously, for example.

The true legal role of the boards is framed as the promotion of ethics in research (primarily to protect research participants); however, the popular student discourse interprets that role as one that concerns itself with liability. The existence of both perceptions produces comments from students about how their intelligence has been insulted. The rampant cheating on the CITI tests is simply an expression of a cynical approach towards them.

Nevertheless, this does not negate the preoccupation students have with ethics review boards, nor their fear of them, nor does it prompt students to think independently about ethics on the ground.

Implications for Research, Now and Later

Following through on the above, one wonders whether students are now depending on research ethics review boards to denote the ethical aspects of their research rather than sustaining a path of self-reflection on ethics in research. Self-reflection is an absolute need: research is messy (Boman and Jevne, 2000; Punch, 1994). Researchers can and should expect ethical surprises in the field. Ethical behaviour looks different on the ground than from the vantage point of ethics board members' conceptualizations of it. When students finally get the seat of their pants dirty, à la the Chicago School tradition in sociology, they witness the mismatch between research reality and research fantasy. Now what? To whom can they turn? In part because of the justifiable fear of the power of the ethics review boards over their careers, in part because they have gained little, if any, perspective from conversations with academics, supervisors, and other faculty, students in this situation often seem paralysed. On the one hand, a seasoned researcher knows that an interview may take an hour and a half, it may take 2 hours and 10 minutes, or it may take even longer. The length of time is of no consequence. A graduate student, on the other hand, may conduct an interview that goes for 2 hours and 10 minutes and then realize he or she got approval for only a one-hour interview. How is the student to know whether this is a serious violation of protocol or not? She or he cannot ask anyone without disclosing what happened, and that would leave the student entirely vulnerable. Panic sets in. What if the ethics board finds out? What if the resulting paper cannot be published? What if one graduates without publications? What then? And, what if a *real* question of ethics arises?

Student researchers no longer have to think too deeply about ethics in research. They merely have to fill out the appropriate forms, submit them at the right time, and their "tick-box" ethics journey, along with any mandated ethical considerations, is virtually complete. One might indeed aver that thinking about ethics from the perspective of one's disciplinary practice might conflict with the formal mandated ethics promulgated by the research ethics review boards. It is best to wage that battle later in one's research career!

Within the current framework, students are losing the skills, or are not getting the skills in the first place, to use their own discretion and to have confidence in their own ethical judgments. Graduate students see that their faculty members are not trusted as professionals and, as a result, they themselves are not deemed trustworthy either (Tinker and Coomber, 2004; Wiles et al., 2006). Students are not educated about how ethics works in the research setting – which, in any case, may run counter to what ethics boards believe about ethics in research. They get generic guidance from the boards about how to get a review passed. They learn how to avoid rocking their own boat.

The process to educate graduate students about ethics in research seems disconnected, and it can even eclipse coursework. Departmental ethics workshops highlight this separation; they are often conducted by ethics board staff (presenting themselves as experts) and focused on "protocols" and procedures of the application process. Graduate students learn how to make it *look* like they are taking the process seriously. They learn terms like "minimal risk" and "protocol document," perpetually reinforcing the paperwork components of the process. And, alarmingly, ethics boards are becoming a source of methodological advice, sidestepping supervisors in the process, and too frequently not allowing unfamiliar forms of research (Lincoln, 2006).

Research ethics review boards mandate the student to believe that the use of consent forms equals permission or consent (Bell, 2014; Miller and Bell, (2002). Attempts by ethics boards to standardize values and ethics across a broad range of academic disciplines (Bhattacharya, 2007) is no more logical than assuming that the social/cultural world is homogeneous. As Bruner (2004) points out, the "meaning of risk and harm are symbolically constructed and culturally defined" (10). My own work with Indigenous populations in Nunavut, and the work of others, such as Hannah Bradshaw in Columbia and Venezuela, would be completely unethical if we were to follow unquestioningly the guidelines of the ethics review boards. Each of these groups is unique, with particular historical contingencies that must be considered, as well as differing cultural practices that require showing respect in differing ways.

Historical relations with Western culture make it difficult for many populations to say "No" when asked to sign a document. Risk is understood differently across cultures (Bruner, 2004). Inuit culture, for example, places value on people making their own mistakes. So, some would sign the form simply to allow the researcher to make the mistake of having asked, and to learn from that encounter. Another example involves researching Indigenous communities in the Guajira region of Colombia and Venezuela, where ethical researchers cannot use consent forms and standardized explanations because of both the social and historical contexts of the region (Hannah Bradshaw, personal communication,

2012). Other members of marginalized groups may feel intimidated by the presence of the researcher and sign only to manage their presentation of self in front of the researcher, or they may feel pressure to sign because of the power imbalance (that is also presumed by the researcher, who plays the part of The Superior One). Regardless, asking people to sign documents that they may not be able to read is hardly a civilized way of asking consent. It may not be a simple case of literacy, but rather the intersection of an oral culture and an inscriptive culture, with the attending power dynamics. But literacy alone is enough for Bruner (2004) to call the request to sign a "horror story."

Presenting a written document for signature is (at least sometimes) a demonstration of total disregard and lack of respect for an oral culture. In oral cultures, trust is a key component of the research process, as is made abundantly clear in ethics boards guidelines such as Canada's *Tri-Council Policy Statement: Ethical Conduct for Research Involving Humans,* or *TCPS 2* (CIHR et al., 2010; Bell, herein, Chapter 10) and the Nunavut Research Institute (see ITK and NRI, 2006), as well as among scholars who engage in community research (Brugge and Missaghian, 2006; Silka et al., 2008; van den Scott, 2012). The researcher must develop real relationships with the participants, enough of a relationship for mutual trust to develop. If the researcher then asks the participant to sign a form that protects *the researcher* or the *university* from getting sued by the participant later on, this is a breach of trust. The participant's word, namely, the oral acknowledgment that he or she consents to be studied should be trusted (and for those who think litigiously, verbal consent can be captured in a recording, though this can be as intimidating for some as signing a form would be – again, context matters). Trust-based commitments to the participant extend indefinitely, far beyond the time when research ethics review boards are satisfied that the commitment is fulfilled (Bergum, 1991). The point is not to argue for a blanket rule about specific populations, rather that there can be no specific, universal rules about marginalized groups.

Consent forms equal neither permission nor consent. Power imbalances impact the willingness of participants to sign when permission can only be obtained through forming a trust-based relationship, one in which participants feel safe saying "No." For example, when a participant openly told me she did not want her picture taken, it was both a sign of a successful trust-based relationship and a sign that the participant was comfortable declining to allow pictures, and that the informed consent process was successful.

One should consider how a consent form may be presented. It would be easy, in a position of power, to present the consent form in particular ways, even though the body language could undermine the purpose of the consent form. Other examples abound. When a social researcher asked medical surgeons to sign a consent form during her participant-observation study, they refused, despite consenting to the study. As members of an elite group, they believed it was inappropriate for them to be asked to do this by someone who was clearly not in their league (Conn, 2008).

Decisions by ethics review boards also affect the student's choice of subject matter. Fewer and fewer graduate students are encouraged to study protected or vulnerable populations despite the importance of researching them. These populations particularly need to be studied. Sometimes the only time that the ethics board is mentioned by a supervisor or faculty member to a graduate student is when a graduate student has an idea concerning a protected (vulnerable) population, and the faculty member wishes them luck in getting it through the ethics review (Bradley, 2007). Students do change their projects to avoid the ethics boards and do choose more amenable topics to make the ethics-approval process easier and faster. Oddly enough, by finding out more about the settings and conditions of marginal groups, research enhances the protection of such groups. Many benefits to qualitative research exist (Childress, 2006), both long term and immediate. Many groups are capable of protecting themselves. How can researchers claim to be striving towards an understanding of the social world if we study only mainstream groups? Many graduate students avoid studying these groups because of the "REB/IRB challenge." I have heard countless graduate students say, "I really wanted to study X, but it would be too hard to get it approved by the boards."

The "REB/IRB challenge" scares students away from pursuing critical, timely, relevant, and necessary research (Adler and Adler, 1993). The ethics review board should help students with their application, but the board dispenses advice on methodology. At my university, ethics review boards appear quite comfortable telling us when we can and cannot take notes. And many graduate students neither question them nor fully understand that the boards may have an imagined understanding of the field that lacks the complexities of real fieldwork (Bosk and De Vries, 2004; Berreman, 2003) and the complexities of that student's particular site. What is more, when graduate students across the board adopt only REB/IRB-prescribed research methods, they are not taught nor encouraged about evolving or innovative forms of research, nor are they then likely (Bledsoe et al., 2007), I hypothesize, to engage in other forms of research at a later point in their career. Often universities encourage students to do a simple survey, quantitative study so that they can finish quickly, never learning more than the most basic interview techniques, particularly when doing an MA. Students learn avoidance rather than revolution. Covert research is condemned or highly restricted and all but lost (Spicker, 2011).

Such considerations lead one to imagine the fuller impact of research ethics review on research in the social sciences. We see the homogenization of research that Will C. van den Hoonaard (2011) warns us about. We see the marginalization of certain empirical areas of research, such as sexualities research (Irvine, 2012). The diversity of the social sciences is, as a consequence, pauperized.

We do not want the shape of research to continue along this path, impoverishing and homogenizing methodologies. Graduate students are accepting this system as a given, even if they speak of unfairness and lack of logic in the system. With the next generation of students, even fewer will feel they have the time to think critically, or be encouraged to take on institutions like research ethics review boards which, we hope, will become anachronistic.

Having strictly mandated ideas about ethics can also have a detrimental effect on how graduate students do research before they have direct contact with research participants. Generic ethics review boards across disciplines often do not take into consideration individual or cultural settings. Following the conventions of some ethics boards, the protection of Aboriginal populations requires the researcher to use consent forms. Such conventions are, however, not ethical, culturally appropriate, or sensitive.

Referring to research participants as "subjects," as is the case with many ethics review boards, impacts how graduate students write about participants. "Subject" reifies certain notions of research and works against participatory research in any of its many forms (Boser, 2007). This distinction can impact how graduate students form their understandings about what research means. It is not surprising to see researchers centring on themselves. The researcher is the expert in this system, rather than the participant. People, when they become part of a study, are no longer considered autonomous experts in their own lives.

Conclusion

Three themes stand out from our above discussion. First, the graduate student is likely to accept the perspective of the research ethics review board as normal; second, there is a crying need for supervisors to stand up for students as they work their way through the research ethics regime; third, one must ethically question the practice of ethics review boards of intimidating students.

A graduate student who has not done previous research may even come to share the REB/IRB's *imagined* perspective about what ethics looks like in the field, and how science is supposed to work (McGinn and Bosacki, 2004). The impact of ethics boards on graduate students affects not only their work, but also how they *think* about their work. This is the most concerning issue. By virtue of their silence and compliance, ethics review boards, department chairs, supervisors, and other faculty members engage in the socialization of graduate students, creating a docile acceptance of the sedimentation of the review boards.

Many reading this volume were students before this era. Graduate students today, along with their younger supervisors, have only experienced the near-absolute reign of research ethics review boards. It is, therefore, harder for today's students to engage in disobedience and resistance – ethics review is a system that has always been part of their relevant life experience. It is harder to cognitively distance oneself from the reality that is the current ethics regime. Socialization is virtually complete. Graduate students do not know what it is like to conduct research without ethics review boards. They cannot imagine wrestling with ethical dimensions on their own; they do not see the opportunities as readily as they might with a less-entrenched system. Faculty members now present the existence of these boards as a necessary evil, a headache to be endured, and most of all, as inevitable (Coe, 2007). I recently said this to a fellow graduate student who paused, looked confused, and then asked, "If there were no ethics boards, what would there be?"

So why consider the graduate student experience? We must explore the impacts of ethics boards on graduate students and how the system of research ethics review boards system is changing the shape of academia as the students of today mature and eventually take on their own graduate students. As Robert Dingwall explains in this volume (chapter 1), there are social costs, but graduate students are not in a position to recognize these costs as they have no experience outside the current regime. The costs become invisible and too frequently forgotten.

I add my voice to the growing call for a mediating body at the departmental level to work with ethics review boards to both guide and mediate on behalf of graduate students. I call for defenders. I call for mentors who not only can support forms of research that make ethics review boards twitch, but also can engage the boards on our behalf so that our first experiences in the field are not solely "tick-box ethics" (Carter, 2009; West et al., 2010), and do not involve major battles. Students must issue and sustain a call for mentors to discuss ethical challenges, to have a hand in student engagement with the ethics review board, and to guide thinking about ethics – rather than the ethics review boards doing the guiding. Graduate students need defenders. They need heroes.

Graduate students have many times wished for supervisors to engage in the ethics review process, and for a review body to be established at the departmental level to both educate and to defend methodologies and participating populations to ethics review boards. The graduate students in my department, at conferences, and workshops have varied experiences with ethics boards. However, the intricacies and nuances of each system hide the same problems. This is not a fight that graduate students are equipped to take on. Nor would it be wise for untenured faculty to stage a revolution. Senior faculty must use their rich intellect, status, and experience on behalf of social scientists, themselves included, particularly when defending methodologies.

Finally, we may ask ourselves whether it is ethical for research-ethics review boards to instil trepidation within the hearts and minds of students? To what end? To create and sustain a power imbalance – a hierarchy of credibility – with students? Or do the ethics boards' legal responsibilities obscure their relationships with and responsibilities to students? In short, is it ethical to impose a system on graduate students that incurs harm?

REFERENCES

Adler, Patricia A., and Peter Adler. (1993). "Ethical Issues in Self-Censorship: Ethnographic Research on Sensitive Topics." In Claire M. Renzetti and Raymond M. Lee (eds.), *Researching Sensitive Topics*, 249–66. Newbury Park, CA: Sage.
Azar, Beth. (2002). "Ethics at the Cost of Research." *Monitor on Psychology* 33 (2): 38–40.
Barrera, Davide, and Brent Simpson. (2012). "Much Ado about Deception: Consequences of Deceiving Research Participants in the Social

Sciences." *Sociological Methods & Research* 41 (3): 383–413. http://dx.doi.
org/10.1177/0049124112452526

Becker, Howard S. (1967). "Whose Side Are We On?" *Social Problems* 14 (3):
239–47. http://dx.doi.org/10.2307/799147

Becker-Blease, Kathryn A., and Jennifer J. Freyd. (2006). "Research Participants
Telling the Truth about Their Lives: The Ethics of Asking and Not Asking
about Abuse." *American Psychologist* 61 (3): 218–26. http://dx.doi.
org/10.1037/0003-066X.61.3.218

Bell, Kirsten. (2014). "Resisting Commensurability: Against Informed Consent
as an Anthropological Virtue." *American Anthropologist* 116 (3): 1–12.

Bergum, Vangie. (1991). "Being a Phenomenological Researcher." In Janice
Morse (ed.), *Qualitative Nursing Research: A Contemporary Dialogue*, 55–71.
London: Sage. http://dx.doi.org/10.4135/9781483349015.n8

Berreman, Gerald D. (2003). "Ethics Versus 'Realism' in Anthropology:
Redux." In Carolyn Fluehr-Lobban (ed.), *Ethics and the Profession of
Anthropology: Dialogue for Ethically Conscious Practice*, 2nd ed., 51–84. Walnut
Creek, CA: AltaMira Press.

Bhattacharya, Kakali. (2007). "Consenting to the Consent Form: What
Are the Fixed and Fluid Understandings between the Researcher and
the Researched?" *Qualitative Inquiry* 13 (8): 1095–115. http://dx.doi.
org/10.1177/1077800407304421

Bledsoe, Caroline H., Bruce Sherin, Adam G. Gallinsky, Nathalia M. Headley,
Carol A. Heimer, Erik Kjeldgaard, James Lindgren, Jon D. Miller, Michael
E. Roloff, and David E. Uttal. (2007). "Regulating Creativity: Research and
Survival in the IRB Iron Cage." *Northwestern University Law Review* 101 (2):
593–641.

Block, Jeremy N. (2008). "Research on Disabled Populations: IRB Membership
Considerations." Blog, *Science Policy Development*. http://sciencepolicydev.
blogspot.ca/2008/02/research-on-disabled-populations-irb.html

Boman, Jeanette, and Ronna Jevne. (2000). "Ethical Evaluation in Qualitative
Research." *Qualitative Health Research* 10 (4): 547–54. http://dx.doi.
org/10.1177/104973200129118633

Bond, Tim. (2012). "Ethical Imperialism or Ethical Mindfulness? Rethinking
Ethical Review for Social Sciences." *Research Ethics.* 8 (2): 97–112. http://
dx.doi.org/10.1177/1747016112445419

Boser, Susan. (2007). "Power, Ethics, and the IRB: Dissonance over Human
Participant Review of Participatory Research." *Qualitative Inquiry* 13 (8):
1060–74. http://dx.doi.org/10.1177/1077800407308220

Bosk, Charles L., and Raymond G. De Vries. (2004). "Bureaucracies of Mass
Deception: Institutional Review Boards and the Ethics of Ethnographic

Research." *Annals of the American Academy of Political and Social Science* 595 (1): 249–63. http://dx.doi.org/10.1177/0002716204266913

Bradley, Matt. (2007). "Silenced for Their Own Protection: How the IRB Marginalizes Those It Feigns to Protect." *ACME: An International E-Journal for Critical Geographies* 6: 339–49.

Brugge, Doug, and Mariam Missaghian. (2006). "Protecting the Navajo People through Tribal Regulation of Research." *Science and Engineering Ethics* 12 (3): 491–507. http://dx.doi.org/10.1007/s11948-006-0047-2

Bruner, Edward. (2004). "Ethnographic Practice and Human Subjects Review." *Anthropology News* 45 (1): 10. http://dx.doi.org/10.1111/an.2004.45.1.10.1

Carter, Bernie. (2009). "Tick Box for Child? The Ethical Positioning of Children as Vulnerable, Researchers as Barbarians and Reviewers as Overly Cautious." *International Journal of Nursing Studies* 46 (6): 858–64. http://dx.doi.org/10.1016/j.ijnurstu.2009.01.003

Childress, Herb. (2006). "The Anthropologist and the Crayons: Changing Our Focus from Avoiding Harm to Doing Good." *Journal of Empirical Research on Human Research Ethics* 1 (2): 79–88. http://dx.doi.org/10.1525/jer.2006.1.2.79

CIHR et al. (Canadian Institutes of Health Research, Natural Sciences and Engineering Research Council of Canada, and Social Sciences and Humanities Research Council of Canada). (2010). *Tri-Council Policy Statement: Ethical Conduct for Research Involving Humans.* 2nd ed. Ottawa: Interagency Panel on Research Ethics.

CITI (Collaborative Institutional Training Initiative). (2013). https://www.citiprogram.org/index.cfm?pageID=88

Coe, F.L. (2007). "The Costs and Benefits of a Well-Intended Parasite: A Witness and Reporter on the IRB Phenomenon." *Northwestern University Law Review* 101 (2): 723–33.

Cohen, Patricia. (2007). "As Ethics Panels Expand Grip, No Field Is Off Limits." *New York Times*, 28 Feb.

Conn, Lesley Gotlib. (2008). "Ethics Policy as Audit in Canadian Clinical Settings: Exiling the Ethnographic Method." *Qualitative Research* 8 (4): 499–514. http://dx.doi.org/10.1177/1468794108093897

Derbyshire, Stuart W.G. (2006). "The Rise of the Ethics Committee: Regulation by Another Name?" In James Panton and Oliver Marc Hartwich (eds.), *Science vs Superstition: The Case for a New Scientific Enlightenment*, 35–50. London: Policy Exchange Ltd and University of Buckingham Press.

Dougherty, D.S., and M.W. Kramer. (2005). "Organizational Power and the Institutional Review Board." *Journal of Applied Communication Research* 33 (3): 277–84. http://dx.doi.org/10.1080/00909880500149494

Dubin, Robert. (1956). "Industrial Workers' Worlds: A Study of the 'Central Life Interests' of Industrial Workers." *Social Problems* 3 (3): 131–42. http://dx.doi.org/10.2307/799133

Epstein, R.A. (2007). "Defanging IRBs: Replacing Coercion with Information." *Northwestern University Law Review* 101 (2): 735–47.

Hemmings, Annette. (2006). "Great Ethical Divides: Bridging the Gap between Institutional Review Boards and Researchers." *Educational Researcher* 35 (4): 12–18. http://dx.doi.org/10.3102/0013189X035004012

Iphofen, Ron. (2011). "Ethical Decision Making in Qualitative Research." *Qualitative Research* 11 (4): 443–6. http://dx.doi.org/10.1177/1468794111404330

Irvine, Janice M. (2012). "'Can't Ask, Can't Tell': How Institutional Review Boards Keep Sex in the Closet." *Contexts* 11 (2): 28–33. http://dx.doi.org/10.1177/1536504212446457

ITK and NRI. (2006). *Negotiating Research Relationships with Inuit Communities: A Guide for Researchers*. Scot Nickels, Jamal Shirley, and Gita Laidler (eds.). Ottawa and Iqaluit: Inuit Tapiriit Kanatami and Nunavut Research Institute.

Katz, Jack. (2007). "Toward a Natural History of Ethical Censorship." *Law & Society Review* 41 (4): 797–810. http://dx.doi.org/10.1111/j.1540-5893.2007.00325.x

Lincoln, Yvonna. (2006). "Institutional Review Boards and Mythological Conservatism." In Norman K. Denzin and Yvonna Lincoln (eds.), *The Third Handbook of Qualitative Research*, 165–81. Thousand Oaks, CA: Sage.

Loftus, Elizabeth F. (2008). "Perils of Provocative Scholarship." *APS Observer* 21 (5).

Lynch, Michael. (2000). "Against Reflexivity as an Academic Virtue and Source of Privileged Knowledge." *Theory, Culture & Society* 17 (3): 26–54. http://dx.doi.org/10.1177/02632760022051202

McGinn, Michelle K., and Sandra L. Bosacki. (2004). "Research Ethics and Practitioners: Concerns and Strategies for Novice Researchers Engaged in Graduate Education." *Forum: Qualitative Social Research* 5 (2): Art6.

Milgram, Stanley. (1974). *Obedience to Authority: An Experimental View*. New York: Harper and Row.

Miller, Tina, and Linda Bell. (2002). "Consenting to What? Issues of Access, Gate-keeping and 'Informed' Consent." In Tina Miller, Maxine Birch, Melanie Mauthner, and Julie Jessop (eds.), *Ethics in Qualitative Research*, 53–69. London: Sage. http://dx.doi.org/10.4135/9781849209090.n3

Newman, Colin D. (2004). "Analyzing Research Ethics: I Wish I didn't Know Now What I Didn't Know Then." B.Sc. thesis, Acadia University, Wolfville, NS.

Punch, Maurice. (1994). "Politics and Ethics in Qualitative Research." In
    Norman K. Denzin and Yvonna S. Lincoln (eds.), *Handbook of Qualitative
    Research*, 83–96. Thousand Oaks, CA: Sage.
Scott, Craig R. (2005). "Anonymity in Applied Communication Research:
    Tensions between IRBs, Researchers, and Human Subjects." *Journal
    of Applied Communication Research* 33 (3): 242–57. http://dx.doi.org/
    10.1080/00909880500149445
Silka, Linda, G. Dean Cleghorn, Milagro Grullon, and Trinidad Tellez.
    (2008). "Creating Community-Based Participatory Research in a Diverse
    Community: A Case Study." *Journal of Empirical Research on Human Research
    Ethics* 3 (2): 5–16. http://dx.doi.org/10.1525/jer.2008.3.2.5
Spicker, Paul. (2011). "Ethical Covert Research." *Sociology* 45 (1): 118–33.
    http://dx.doi.org/10.1177/0038038510387195
Srivastava, Sanjay. (2011). "CITI Is Still Misrepresenting Milgram's Obedience
    Research." *The Hardest Science: A Psychology Blog*. (6 July).
Tinker, Anthea, and Vera Coomber. (2004). *University Research Ethics
    Committees: Their Role, Remit and Conduct*. London: King's College.
van den Hoonaard, Will C. (2011). *The Seduction of Ethics: Transforming the
    Social Sciences*. Toronto: University of Toronto Press.
van den Scott, Lisa-Jo K. (2012). "Science, Politics, and Identity in Northern
    Research Ethics Licensing." *Journal of Empirical Research on Human Research
    Ethics* 7 (1): 28–36. http://dx.doi.org/10.1525/jer.2012.7.1.28
West, Julia, Karen Bill, and Louise Martin. (2010). "What Constitutes Research
    Ethics in Sport and Exercise Science?" *Research Ethics Review* 6 (4): 147–53.
    http://dx.doi.org/10.1177/174701611000600407
Wiles, Rose, Vikki Charles, Graham Crow, and Sue Heath. (2006).
    "Researching Researchers: Lessons for Research Ethics." *Qualitative Research*
    6 (3): 283–99. http://dx.doi.org/10.1177/1468794106065004

13 The Eclipse of "Human Subjects" and the Rise of "Human Participants" in Research Involving Humans

IGOR GONTCHAROV

Until recently the concept of human research subjects[1] was central to the conceptual framework of the system of research ethics review in Canada.[2] The purpose of ethics review was to protect human subjects from the risks of harm associated with their involvement in research. In December 2010 the three major research agencies in Canada – the Canadian Institutes for Health Research, the Natural Sciences and Engineering Research Council, and the Social Sciences and Humanities Research Council (the Agencies) – adopted the second edition of the *Tri-Council Policy Statement: Ethical Conduct for Research Involving Humans (TCPS 2)* (CIHR et al., 2010). The first *Tri-Council Policy Statement (TCPS 1)* was adopted in 1998 and established the biomedical model of ethics review as a standard of ethical governance in all research involving humans (CIHR et al., 1998).

In agreement with the accepted biomedical terminology, the first *Tri-Council Policy Statement* used the concept of human *subjects* to refer to those humans who bear the risks of the research. The second *Tri-Council Policy Statement* features human *participants* as its new central concept. Given the potential impact of this subtle terminological change, which can be viewed as necessitating a profound revision of ethics review and the entire approach to the governance in research involving humans, this chapter identifies reasons for the change in terminology, and proceeds as follows: After considering policy definitions and providing background on the human subjects approach to research governance, I discuss possible reasons for adopting the new language. In particular, I consider whether the new language (1) is a result of an attempt to better accommodate the social sciences and the humanities; (2) is an outcome of the responsive elements in the current regulatory framework;

or (3) is a response to the performativity of *subjects* and *participants*, when the use of the concepts comes along with a corresponding philosophy and approaches to governance that are reflected in the name itself; or (4) is a combination of these options.

Policy Definitions of Subjects and Participants

The first *Tri-Council Policy Statement* preserved in an endnote an interesting fragment of the conceptual history of human subjects. It provides in it a rationale for preferring *subjects* to *participants*. This endnote is evidence that the development of a "harmonized"[3] approach to research governance posed a specific set of regulatory challenges that policymakers tried to address by locating an "optimal term":

> During preparation of this Policy Statement, there was extensive discussion of the optimal term to describe those on, or about whom, the research is carried out. This discussion focused on the terms "participant" and "subject." Though research subjects may participate actively in research, so also do many others, including the researchers and their staff, administrators in the institutions, and funding sponsors and members of research ethics boards (REBs). Research subjects are unique among the many participants because it is they who bear the risks of the research. The Agencies have therefore chosen to retain the word "subject" because of its relative unambiguity in this context, and because the prime focus of the Policy Statement is on those who bear the risks of research. (CIHR et al., 1998: i.3, n2)

Twelve years later, the revised *Tri-Council Policy Statement* introduces the shift from *subjects* to *participants*:

> Human participants are unique among the many parties involved in research, because they bear the primary risks of the research. These individuals are often referred to as "research subjects." This Policy prefers the term "participant" because it better reflects the spirit behind the core principles: that individuals who choose to participate in research play a more active role than the term "subject" conveys. As well, it reflects the range of research covered by this Policy, and the varied degree of involvement by participants – including the use of their data or human biological materials – that different types of research offer. The core principles of this Policy – Respect for Persons,

Concern for Welfare, and Justice – help to shape the relationship between researchers and participants. (CIHR et al., 2010: 16)

In 1998 (the year *TCPS 1* was published) *research subjects* was considered a relatively unambiguous term that described those individuals who bear the risk of research. Research subjects belonged to a broader category of research participants. In the 2010 *Tri-Council Policy Statement 2*, the term *subjects* disappears in the body of the document, being only present in the references and in the quotation above. In place of *subjects* the policy uses *participants*, who are seen as those who bear the "primary risks" of the research. If previously research subjects were unique among research participants, now research participants are considered to be unique among "the many parties involved in research." Importantly, and a bit ironically, the second *Tri-Council Policy Statement* indicates that we are still speaking about the same individuals, only using juxtaposed labels.

The second *Tri-Council Policy Statement* offers human *participants* as a term that "better reflects the *spirit* behind the core principles" (emphasis added). While the first *Tri-Council Policy Statement* justified the choice of human *subjects* by referring to the context, the second *Tri-Council Policy Statement* refers to the *spirit* behind the core principles. The context of the first *Tri-Council Policy Statement* was largely biomedical, and it became normative for all research involving humans, thus introducing tensions in the system of ethical governance of the social sciences and humanities. A question arises: Is the "spirit" of the second *Tri-Council Policy Statement* not of the same biomedical quality? Does the concept of *participants* change and challenge in any way the vision of the second *Tri-Council Policy Statement* in relation to the actual governance of research involving humans? Or is it merely a linguistic transplant, likely to be subsumed by the unshaken normative underpinnings of the first *Tri-Council Policy Statement* so that nothing changes except the term?

The first *Tri-Council Policy Statement* puts forth human *subjects* as the "optimal term" (and we might notice that *optimal* is originally a word in biology).[4] Language in the second *Tri-Council Policy Statement* is less optimistic about locating an optimal term, demonstrating a preference for human *participants* as described above. The rationale for replacing *subjects* with *participants* is not clearly spelled out in the Policy and not directly intelligible. Instead, authors of the second *Tri-Council Policy Statement* invoke the *spirit* of the core principles provoking the need for a séance to clarify the meaning of human *participants*. Irony aside, the absence of a meaningful explanation for the transition to *participants* does not mean that there is a lack of explanations for the ongoing conceptual overhaul of the *Tri-Council Policy Statement*. Was the replacement of *subjects* with *participants* motivated by the participatory mindset of policymakers? Was the change an outcome of the tensions produced by the subsuming of social research into an ethical governance framework designed for biomedical research?

The Human Subjects Approach to Research Governance

From the viewpoint of governance, the adoption of *participants* may serve as a focus for profound changes in the regulatory approach. In order to understand how this shift in terminology may transform ethics review, it is necessary to clarify why this change is taking place at all. Consider three aspects of this question – factual, comparative, and programmatic. First, it is important to determine what happened that made the term *human subjects* problematic. Did the concept itself become a conceptual and practical hurdle to be overcome? Second, why is the concept of *participants* used to replace *subjects*? Were alternatives considered? Finally, what are the limitations and implications of the old and new language for the ethics of human research? What has *happened* as a result of this change? What might happen?

Prior to the second *Tri-Council Policy Statement*, the very experience of being a research subject was a problem for policymakers. This problem emerged as a result of a growing awareness that some biomedical and behavioural experiments in Canada are conducted unethically – under pressure, without consent and without disclosing information about foreseeable risks, and involving vulnerable populations including prisoners and psychiatric patients. Accordingly, the task was to develop a regulatory approach that would effectively limit such activities; the result was the protectionist mindset of the first *Tri-Council Policy Statement*, incorporating a risk-management approach based on free and informed consent and concerned with special protections for vulnerable populations.

In human subjects research, researchers are viewed as possessing certain "power over" (Boser, 2007) their research subjects, who are seen as vulnerable and defenceless. The relationship between the two parties is hierarchical, and accordingly, there is a possibility for abuse, given the fact that biomedical researchers are prone to conflicts of interest. In this situation the state is expected to intervene and protect vulnerable subjects by developing, implementing, and maintaining a system to oversee research institutions and researchers. Importantly, the first *Tri-Council Policy Statement* implied that the experience of research subjects is a universal trans-disciplinary phenomenon, requiring an omni-disciplinary (i.e., to include all academic disciplines, research methodologies, or research situations) application of protectionist measures. Because the biomedical approach was used as a normative basis for the integrated system of ethics review, it mandated the mechanism of risk management for all research involving humans.

The Challenge of *Participants*

The adoption of human *participants* demarcates a conceptual end of the human *subjects* approach to risk management. The new approach corresponds to the participatory philosophy of the concept of *participants*. While overcoming the *subjects* in human *participants* remains a problem, the focus now falls on ensuring that human *participants* are indeed participants and not merely humans involved in research.

The task can no longer be reduced to protectionism, to acting on behalf of human *subjects*. It must go beyond determining the degree of risk to participants, checking for conflicts of interest among researchers, and ensuring that researchers seek free and informed consent. The task now is to empower human *participants*, to awaken their agency, and to engage them in the research process as partners. In other words, the new concept emerges as a direct challenge to the "nanny state" (White, 2007) and the patriarchal modes of conceptualizing the research process.

Such items in the regulatory agenda emerge if we deal primarily with the semantics of the concept of participants, which is not sufficient, given the complexity of the context and specific trajectory of ethical governance in research involving humans in the past decades. This included the problems that emerged in the process of adopting a common standard of ethics review as a universal approach to the governance of research involving humans. Accordingly, the semantics of *participants* and the participatory philosophy rendered by the concept and embedded within the overall conceptual framework of the second *Tri-Council Policy Statement: Ethical Conduct for Research Involving*

Humans should be considered in the context of the ongoing efforts to standardize ethics review.

If we focus on the semantics alone, the change in language may appear as a progressive step, an institutional achievement, but in practice, the new language has encountered the limitations similar to those that prompted the dismissal of its predecessor. When ethics review expanded to the social sciences, human *subjects* was used as a universal cross-disciplinary concept, but it did not fare well in this capacity; it poorly reflected how research is approached in the social sciences and the ways of human involvement in it. The concept of *participants* is no more likely to succeed as a universal concept. Indeed, it may be able to relieve some of the tensions (including those stemming from the weak integration of the social science perspectives), but unavoidably, it will engender new ones. The concept of *participants* is not applicable in some biomedical research situations. For example, a person in a coma can hardly give consent. Moreover, a universal application of human *participants* may harm a number of research fields and methodologies in the social sciences, including critical policy and public health research, or criminological research, for example, in observational studies or research on corruption in public offices, when it is crucial that "participants" do not act as co-researchers, but continue to engage in their routine activities.

As long as the problem of integrating the social sciences into the existing model of ethics oversight is approached superficially, rather than through a substantial revision of the foundation of the system, it will be challenging to locate a single satisfactory term. In a revised approach to research governance, the task of locating a suitable universal term may no longer be on the agenda. Further, any presumably universal social science research concept, such as human *participants*, or *research projects*, changes meaning when transplanted to the biomedical conceptual framework of the *Tri-Council Policy Statement*. Accordingly, the problem of the "optimal term" can hardly be addressed until the *Tri-Council Policy Statement* embraces an ethical/legal pluralist framework (Moore, 1973; Griffiths, 1986; Galanter, 1981; Merry, 1988) and welcomes social disciplines individually, rather than treating social research as a homogeneous entity.

Research *Participants* as a Way of Responsive Regulation?

The regulatory framework of the *Tri-Council Policy Statement: Ethical Conduct for Research Involving Humans* conforms in its basic design to the principles advocated by reflexive law, responsive regulation, and new governance scholars (Burris, 2008). "New governance" puts an emphasis on gaining input of the regulated, broad participation in decision-making, and mobilization of situated knowledge and capacity, thus engaging in the process of governance the expertise, technologies, and resources of those who work on the ground and calls for the use of hybrid forms of governance designed to be responsive, to transcend the limitations of regulatory and deregulatory approaches.[5]

Indeed, the regulatory framework of the *Tri-Council Policy Statement,* both its first and second versions, has a number of elements consistent with new governance. For example, ethics review is decentralized – local boards review research projects in close proximity to the sites of everyday decision-making in human research, interpreting general ethical guidelines to applying them to specific research situations.[6] However, the system of ethics oversight features a strong central element – "common" and "shared" fundamental ethical principles.[7] These principles are articulated by the three major Canadian research councils, without input from a representative spectrum of research participants and researchers. It should be noted, though, that contrary to the position expressed in the *Tri-Council Policy Statement* universal ethical principles are universal in a declarative sense only – they are not shared by all research disciplines, and they reflect the values of a particular research paradigm. Because the articulation of ethical principles in research involving humans is centralized, the governance model implemented in the *Tri-Council Policy Statement* can be best understood as a hybrid. It does incorporate a number of responsive regulatory mechanisms, such as self-governance, or use of situated knowledge and capacity, since Research Ethics Boards (unless research institutions appoint an external REB) generally consist of local researchers and community members who review the projects of their peers. But, again, a deeper discussion is necessary to determine whether and how a localized ethics review benefits from situated knowledge and capacity. Does it allow, for example, the engagement of various research disciplines and systems of knowledge in the governance of research involving humans?

If the *Tri-Council Policy Statement* is an example of responsive governance, then the adoption of the concept of *participants* can be considered a step towards further responsiveness, an example of a responsive governance framework in action. However, this explanation presents at least two problems: (1) Research Ethics Boards are, in fact, constrained in their reflexive capacity and unable to take advantage of their regulatory autonomy, and (2) the *Tri-Council Policy Statement* has not been sufficiently attuned to the diverse interests of various actors involved in research and its governance.

REBs and the Challenges of Decentralized Governance

Presumably, the degree of freedom given to Research Ethics Boards, as well as their advantageous position in close proximity to many research sites, should promote flexibility, adaptability, and promptness in REB decision-making. In practice, however, this has not happened. The benefits of regulatory decentralization are restrained by a number of factors, including challenges in creating an ethics review environment that acknowledges and accommodates diverse methods of research. For example, a disproportionate number of REB chairs represent clinical psychology, which generally follows the biomedical model (van den Hoonaard, 2011). However, this is not just a problem of expertise on the board and/or adequate representation of the disciplinary spectrum in the board membership. The dominance of positivism at the REB level stems from the fact that the presumably existent "common" and "shared" ethical principles are not as common and shared as assumed in the *Tri-Council Policy Statement*. Thus, the principles of "free and informed consent" and "respect for privacy and confidentiality" are not universally shared, for example, by criminologists,[8] ethnographers (Bosk, 2007; Tolich and Fitzgerald, 2006; Lederman, 2007), policy researchers, biographers, journalists, and others. Some of the principles in the first *Tri-Council Policy Statement* can be understood as being antagonistic, for example, "respect for human dignity" and "balancing harms and benefits," which belong to deontology and utilitarianism, respectively, and policymakers do not offer an effective strategy of reconciling them.[9]

The first *Tri-Council Policy Statement* also postulates a principle of "respect for vulnerable persons" that introduces a category of "vulnerable persons/populations": "Children, institutionalized persons or others who are vulnerable are entitled, on grounds of human dignity, caring, solidarity and fairness, to special protection against abuse, exploitation or discrimination" (CIHR et al., 1998: i.5).

It is unsettling to see policymakers who view research through the lenses of "abuse, exploitation or discrimination." It is one of the perspectives that reinscribes *vulnerable persons* in the new regulatory framework and imposes double standards through the language of special protection. The second edition of the *Tri-Council Policy Statement* makes an effort to resolve some of these tensions – it offers a simplified ethical framework, based on the concept of human dignity, expressed through three core principles – *respect for persons, concern for welfare,* and *justice.* Thus, the priority is now clearly given to the deontological approach. However the second *Tri-Council Policy Statement* retains the harm-benefit analysis and the two major categories of human participants, even if revising its language – human participants and human participants in vulnerable circumstances. Accordingly, the lack of an updated conceptual framework for the second edition of the *Tri-Council Policy Statement* continues to be a source of significant tension, affecting the decision-making of Research Ethics Boards, reducing the methodological options for researchers, and ignoring the autonomy of competent adults. The decentralized governance model also poses challenges to multisite studies – not only is it often necessary to get permission from multiple Research Ethics Boards that may require numerous incompatible changes, it also puts additional logistical and financial burdens on researchers that delay the production of new knowledge (potentially useful to people in general). This situation sometimes forces research sponsors to transfer research to countries with a more favourable research environment.[10]

REBs and the Challenges of Responsive Governance

The regulatory design implemented in the *Tri-Council Policy Statement* suggests that policymakers and regulators at the institutional level must be interested in collaborating with the interest groups who are subject to the Policy. With respect to researchers, REB members are recruited from among the researchers of a particular institution, and these Research Ethics Boards are situated in the same institution, thus allowing for unmediated communication between REB members and researchers. With the degree of freedom in interpreting and applying the *TCPS* principles, this may appear from afar as a model of self-governance. However, this has not been the case in practice, because Research Ethics Boards remain cautious in exercising their liberty of interpreting the *Tri-Council Policy Statement*, preferring to act conservatively and redirect the questions to the Interagency Advisory Panel on Research Ethics (PRE).

Speaking in terms of policymaking, the drafting of the second *Tri-Council Policy Statement* was also a fairly open multistage process, involving working groups,[11] *TCPS* consultations, and written comments. Thus, it is stated on the *TCPS* website that following the release of the first draft of the second edition of the *Tri-Council Policy Statement*, in December 2008, "Panel members participated in 58 events attended by approximately 1,800 people in 17 cities." The second draft was released in December 2009, and written comments were accepted until March 2010. In this very short period of time, for which the Panel was justly criticized (see Onyemelukwe and Downie, 2011; Downie, 2009), it received written comments from over 123 institutions, Research Ethics Boards, and individuals.[12] This reflects a high degree of interest and (academic) public participation in developing the policy, and allows characterizing the process of drafting the second *Tri-Council Policy Statement* as an open one. However, taking into account that the *Tri-Council Policy Statement* is envisioned as a "living document," and gets its first major update in 12 years, it is difficult to explain such a limited consultation period and the rush to adopt a new edition.

Nevertheless, one should note that while the Panel takes initiative in engaging researchers in developing the Policy, Research Ethics Boards remain passive in this regard. For example, Research Ethics Boards could not establish themselves as institutions that seek dialogue on ethical issues with researchers – by far the social group most affected by the *Tri-Council Policy Statement*. By and large, Research Ethics Boards do not demonstrate interest in researchers' feedback, and even less in how they conduct research or understand research ethics. Instead of engaging researchers in the governance process, Research Ethics Boards invest resources in educating researchers about the ethics review process. It is common to offer REB 101 sessions and "Best-Practices" workshops (Mueller, 2006). These workshops are designed to provide researchers with useful tips about gaining ethics approval. Below is a typical workshop agenda, this one from a leading US research university in 2012. Notice the language of human *subjects* is still current in the United States, where ethics review is done by Institutional Review Boards (IRBs):

- A history of human subjects protection and the ethical principles that guide human subjects research

- An overview of the federal regulations for the protection of human subjects in research
- Criteria for IRB review
- Tips for submitting complete and understandable new protocols, modifications, renewals, and adverse event reports
- Tips for obtaining IRB approval more quickly
- The RASCAL system [a web-based research management and compliance tool]
- The IRB review process.[13]

"Best-Practices" workshops are hardly a reflexive moment in the system of research ethics oversight. The goal is not to learn from researchers, but rather to ensure compliance through REB indoctrination, the imposition of a biomedical understanding of research, and a process of prospective review as the only way of ensuring research safety. Contrary to its own expectations, the first *Tri-Council Policy Statement: Ethical Conduct for Research Involving Humans* has not been particularly effective in "encourag[ing] continued reflection and thoughtful consensus around more contentious ethical issues" (CIHR et al., 1998). Consensus is *sought*, not imposed: If the *Tri-Council Policy Statement* is to be seen as a platform conducive to a multilateral dialogue about research governance, then it is important to make progress by embracing a pluralist framework in acts rather than only in words.

Meanwhile, the input of those the first *Tri-Council Policy Statement* refers to as research *subjects*, as yet another interested group, has also been rather limited. A community representative on the REB panel may speak for some research subjects but it is a question of whether this person is able to represent the interests of a wide range of research subjects. In practice, community representatives represent the REB community – they are appointed by REB administrators. They are neither delegates, nor trustees. They are not elected nor selected by participants. Community representatives do not report back to any community. Moreover, if *community* refers to a geographic community, rather than a community of research participants, as it is implied in the second edition of the *Tri-Council Policy Statement*, then for many research projects geography is not an important factor. It is also questionable if community representatives can represent the diversity of communities and perspectives within them.

Furthermore, it is not even clear whether all research subjects require representation. In critical research, representation may lead to censorship and may even pose harm to researchers, for example, in critical policy research when the studied community may perceive the researchers as a threat to its cultural practices. None of this, of course, explains a general lack of interest in incorporating the views of research subjects. Members of the Interagency Advisory Panel on Research Ethics assume, as they did in relation to researchers, that research subjects are a homogeneous group, and therefore do not need broad interdisciplinary representation.[14] The paternalistic mentality of the institutions of ethical governance prescribes them to speak for research subjects, determining, without consultation, their vulnerability status, questions of proper compensation, and informed consent issues. The first *Tri-Council Policy Statement* did not accept research subjects as autonomous agents capable of contributing to the governance of research involving humans, and accordingly the change to research *participants* at the end of the life cycle of the first *Tri-Council Policy Statement* has also occurred without the input of research subjects. Accordingly, the regulatory emancipation of research *subjects* who have acquired the label of *participants*, if not the rights of participants, in the second edition of the *Tri-Council Policy Statement* was neither a revolution nor a gift.

It is difficult to maintain the initial presupposition that the adoption of human *participants* is an outcome of the reflexive governance framework; there is limited evidence that the elements of new governance have yielded an institution interested in engaging researchers and research subjects in the governance process. Accordingly, it is difficult to see the adoption of *participants* as a response to the criticisms of research ethics oversight from the side of social scientists.

What Is in a Name?

If there is little evidence that the transition to the new term was prompted by the new governance framework, then one might assume that policymakers were motivated by an aspiration to eschew the factual or potential performativity of the term *subject*, just as they hoped to engage the performativity of *participants*. This assumption involves the following two points: (1) The language of the Policy is indeed performative enough (or at least potentially performative) to produce passive, disinterested, and defenceless research subjects, and (2) the Interagency Advisory Panel on Research Ethics takes this performativity seriously. This is something more than merely omitting research subjects from the list of policy actors in whose feedback Research Ethics Boards should be interested as a site of responsive ethical governance.

This explanation is not easy to rule out altogether. Names and/or labels are performative and things can be made with words (Austin, 1962). It has also been suggested that powerful institutions rely on the acceptance of a submissive designation by their subjects, for example, religious followers accept the authority of their churches, when they accept their "rottenness" (De Certeau, 1988). In a similar fashion, humans involved in research accept that they are merely subjects of research interests, a datum for scientists. Indeed, with 40 years of using the language of *subjects* in the system of research oversight, it may have taken root in public consciousness. Especially when the public has learned that it was the subject of harmful government-sponsored experiments, such as the infamous Tuskegee syphilis study, radiation studies, and LSD experiments in the military. The main message was that various population groups (some more than others) were used as guinea pigs for government experiments, or in other words, as research *subjects*. The concept of research *subjects* has never been neutral. It has never been divorced from the institutional history of state-sponsored (and highly unethical) research and remains integral in maintaining the hierarchical structures of modern social and political institutions. In light of this institutional history, one can explain the adoption of the concept of *participants* as an attempt to disrupt the political economy of *subjects*-based state-sponsored research disasters.

Some objections to this explanation have emerged. First, human subjects themselves may not be universally aware that they are research *subjects* and that this is how the first *Tri-Council Policy Statement: Ethical Conduct for Research Involving Humans* identified them in their relationship to research and researchers. Second, researchers may not use this designation either, and therefore, if research *subjects* accept the designation it is not because they are referred to in this way. If they accept it at all, then this is because for them the distinction between research *subjects* and research *participants* (or any other possible label) is a difference that does not *make* a difference.

When I fill out a questionnaire I do not necessarily think of myself as a research *subject*, even if I am addressed in this way on a consent form, which is unlikely. Neither do I think the research benefits me directly. And, if I am a *subject* of an observational study I may not even be aware of the research or my place in it. The concept of *subjects* is not meaningful in all research situations. Being a *subject* implies obedience or compliance; neither is present in observational research. Only in a very limited sense one could say that a person who unknowingly participates in an observational study somehow complies. An individual being observed is likely conforming to numerous situational norms, and the researcher is likely doing the same thing when observing, and when characterizing the observations and writing about them. How is it the case that these people, researchers and the people observed, need protections from going about their daily lives?

If the problem that the second edition of the *Tri-Council Policy Statement* tried to address is not the autonomy of research subjects, then it is likely the case that it wishes to somehow *correct* the mindset of researchers. Namely, researchers are set up as masters, as royalty, because they have subjects. The testimony to this is the very language of human *subjects*, which is widely used in biomedical and behavioural sciences, but not common in the social sciences. The mindset of royalty/subjects, masters/slaves is not universal in scientific research. In policy research, for example, a researcher may be under the influence of (i.e., subjugated to) a more powerful organization or person. Therefore, by adopting the concept of human *participants*, authors of the second edition of the *Tri-Council Policy Statement* are addressing a problem that rarely if ever exists in social science.

Conclusion

The search for "optimal" language can be productive for the system of ethics oversight in research involving humans, but only if policymakers are successful in adopting a more nuanced understanding of the ethical concerns present in social science research. Such understanding can best be achieved by engaging a large number of interested parties in all stages of the governance process. At present, however, significant barriers hamper Research Ethics Boards from becoming sites of responsive governance. It is not possible to resolve the continuing methodological crisis (Gontcharov, 2013) in the social sciences through conceptual means alone, without also challenging the biomedical standard underpinning research ethics review.

The adoption of research *participant* speaks to the following phenomena. First, it is the continuing expansion of ethics oversight and the corresponding erosion of its original biomedical conceptual framework. Ethics creep continues,[15] and the concept of human *subjects* is no longer adequate to address this ever-broadening field of research involving humans. In an attempt to embrace social science scholarship, policymakers have adopted a new major concept. Research *participants* may relieve some tensions in the current conceptual framework, but it will be a source of new ones, because the concept is not at home in either social or biomedical research. Moreover, in the social sciences the concept of human *participants* continues to impose the biomedical understanding of research ethics by insisting on informed consent forms, especially standardized ones, and thus obstructing social science scholarship, especially participant observation, covert research, and the use of confederates, for example.

Second, the term research *subject* is politically obsolete. The concept is historically conditioned and possesses negative connotations. In this respect, the task of the word *participant* is to change the mindset of both researchers and the researched, and to empower humans involved in research. It is questionable, however, that such a task can be accomplished through locating a new term. Moreover, there is no guarantee that the participatory aspect will make its way into the actual practice of research involving humans. For this reason the adoption of *participant* may be seen as an attempt to evade existing problems, to serve as a distraction (much like the near endless editing of consent documents) rather than resolving problems in an open process involving all stakeholders. This situation can be described as a euphemistic spiral: when a word becomes offensive, a taboo, it is necessary to substitute it with a new one in order to be able to continue referring to the same thing. And of central importance here, no data exist that demonstrate the *Tri-Council Policy Statement* makes any positive contribution to research safety. The term human *subject* has become an obscene term, and policymakers are happy to introduce *participant* to continue the business of regulating research and research *subjects*. This situation cannot last very long; the new term will soon meet the same fate because the change changes nothing.

In psychoanalysis, *patient* is no longer deemed an acceptable term because it speaks of illness, and *client* is not acceptable – it speaks of money. So, the (same) person on the couch is referred to as *analysand*. Nevertheless, this *analysand* neither annuls nor subsumes the patient and the client. This parallel may sound ironic, but the way researchers and participants see each other is necessarily plural. Researchers may (or may not) see research participants as participants, colleagues, interviewees, patients, clients, nameless individuals, and someone known or unknown, and even as *subjects*. Social researchers study social situations, whereas the *Tri-Council Policy Statement* requires them to reduce the richness of a research situation to consenting individuals involved in research. To become myopic about specific terms is to continue missing the point of research ethics.

NOTES

An earlier version of this chapter was published in the Osgoode CLPE Research Paper Series (Gontcharov, 2012).

1 I use "human subjects," "research subjects," and "subjects" interchangeably throughout the chapter.
2 While I focus on the Canadian approach to ethics oversight, the discussion is relevant to other jurisdictions, and, in particular, to the United States. The system of oversight in the United States also exhibits similar tensions that emerged after the expansion of the system of ethics review beyond the field of biomedical research, but at the moment the research ethics approach in the United States remains loyal to the term *human subjects*. It is important to note that US federal regulations have been and continue to be more consistent in following the language of human subjects, while the *TCPS 1* was speaking already in 1998 in terms of humans rather than human subjects. Consider, e.g., the full title of the *Belmont Report: Ethical Principles and Guidelines for the Protection of Human Subjects of Research* (National Commission, 1979), and its successor, the *Federal Policy for the Protection of Human Research Subjects* (1991), whereas the subtitle of the *TCPS* (CIHR et al., 1998, 2010) is *Ethical Conduct for Research Involving Humans*. The omission of "subjects" in the *TCPS 1* can be understood as a transition point to the new language, and a point of conceptual divergence from the perspective in the United States.
3 *TCPS 1* uses the term *harmonization* rather than *integration. Harmonization* implies that the perspectives of the social sciences will be reflected in developing a common approach to research ethics: "The Policy seeks to harmonize the ethics review process. The Agencies expect that REBs will benefit from common procedures within a shared ethical framework. This will also benefit those projects involving researchers from different disciplines or institutions. The Agencies hope that the Policy will serve as an educational resource" (CIHR et al., 1998: i.2)
4 E.g., http://www.etymonline.com/index.php?term=optimal
5 See Lobel (2004), Teubner (1983, 1992), Ayres and Braithwaite (1992), and Trubek and Trubek (2005).
6 After the adoption of the *TCPS 2*, the Interagency Advisory Panel on Research Ethics is taking a more active role in interpreting the policy,

thus limiting the deregulatory elements of the original *TCPS*, in part also responding to the demand of REBs for such interpretations. The PRE website has a new dedicated section on the interpretation of the policy. See http://www.pre.ethics.gc.ca/eng/policy-politique/interpretations/Default/

7 The *TCPS 1* also speaks in the same way about values and interests in research involving humans.

8 See, e.g., multiple contributions by Ted Palys and John Lowman, available at http://www.sfu.ca/~palys/articles.htm

9 Hence, in actual REB deliberations, a utilitarian approach is often dropped, and the harm-benefit analysis, which is offered as a main decision-making mechanism, is reduced to an often nonsensical analysis of harm.

10 It has been suggested that decentralized ethics review is behind Canada's dwindling share of the global market of clinical trials. See, e.g., Senate of Canada (2012).

11 See http://www.ethics.gc.ca/eng/archives/policy-politique/reports-rapports/reports-rapports/

12 The number is probably higher. I included only those individuals and institutions whose comments were published on the *TCPS* website. http://www.ethics.gc.ca/eng/archives/participation/comments-commentaires2009/

13 Agenda for 24 July 2012 IRB 101 Seminar, offered by the Columbia University IRB.

14 Community representatives on REBs for the most part are retired scientists or biomedical participants and patients. Among PRE members currently there is no community member who would represent participants in social research.

15 On "ethics creep" see Kevin D. Haggerty (2004), Ronald F. White (2007), and C.K. Gunsalus et al. (2007).

REFERENCES

Austin, J.L. (1962). *How to Do Things with Words*. Oxford: Clarendon.

Ayres, Ian, and John Braithwaite. (1992). *Responsive Regulation: Transcending the Deregulation Debate*. New York: Oxford University Press.

Boser, Susan. (2007). "Power, Ethics, and the IRB: Dissonance over Human Participant Review of Participatory Research." *Qualitative Inquiry* 13 (8): 1060–74.

Bosk, Charles L. (2007). "The New Bureaucracies of Virtue or When Form Fails to Follow Function." *PoLAR: Political and Legal Anthropology Review* 30 (2): 192–209.

Burris, Scott. (2008). "Regulatory Innovation in the Governance of Human Subjects Research: A Cautionary Tale and Some Modest Proposals." *Regulation and Governance* 2 (1): 65–84.

CIHR et al. (Canadian Institutes of Health Research, Natural Sciences and Engineering Research Council of Canada, and Social Sciences and Humanities Research Council of Canada). (1998, with 2000, 2002, 2005 amendments). *Tri-Council Policy Statement: Ethical Conduct for Research Involving Humans*. Ottawa: Interagency Panel on Research Ethics.

– (2010). *Tri-Council Policy Statement: Ethical Conduct for Research Involving Humans*. 2nd ed. Ottawa: Interagency Panel on Research Ethics.

De Certeau, Michel. (1988). "The Institution of Rot." In D.B. Allison (ed.), *Psychosis and Sexual Identity: Toward a Post-Analytic View of the Schreber Case*, 35–46. Albany: SUNY Press.

Downie, Jocelyn. (2009). "Letter to PRE Members Regarding the Proposed Revised Draft Second Edition of the TCPS." http://www.pre.ethics.gc.ca/pdf/eng/Comments2009/114_%20Downie,%20Jocelyn.pdf

Galanter, Marc. (1981). "Justice in Many Rooms: Courts, Private Ordering and Indigenous Law." *Journal of Legal Pluralism* 19 (1): 1–47.

Gontcharov, Igor. (2012). "The Eclipse of 'Human Subjects' and the Rise of 'Human Participants' in Research Involving Humans." Osgoode CLPE Research Paper No. 5/2012, http://dx.doi.org/10.2139/ssrn.1896464

– (2013). "Methodological Crisis in the Social Sciences: The New Brunswick Declaration as a New Paradigm in Research Ethics Governance?" *Transnational Legal Theory* 4 (1): 146–56.

Griffiths, John. (1986). "What Is Legal Pluralism?" *Journal of Legal Pluralism and Unofficial Law* 24 (1): 1–55.

Gunsalus, C.K., Edward M. Bruner, Nicholas C. Burbules, Leon Dash, Matthew Finkin, Joseph P. Goldberg, and William T. Greenough. (2007). "The Illinois White Paper – Improving the System for Protecting Human Subjects: Counteracting IB 'Mission Creep.'" *Qualitative Inquiry* 13 (5): 617–49.

Haggerty, Kevin D. (2004). "Ethics Creep: Governing Social Science Research in the Name of Ethics." *Qualitative Sociology* 27 (4): 391–414.

Lederman, Rena. (2007). "Research: A Modest Proposal Concerning the Object of Ethics Regulation." *PoLAR: Political and Legal Anthropology Review* 30 (2): 305–27. http://dx.doi.org/10.1525/pol.2007.30.2.305

Lobel, Orly. (2004). "The Renew Deal: The Fall of Regulation and the Rise of Governance in Contemporary Legal Thought." *Minnesota Law Review* 89 (Nov.).

Merry, Sally Engle. (1988). "Legal Pluralism." *Law & Society Review* 22 (5): 869–96. http://dx.doi.org/10.2307/3053638

Moore, Sally Falk. (1973). "Law and Social Change: The Semi-Autonomous Social Field as an Appropriate Subject of Study." *Law & Society Review* 7 (4): 719–46. http://dx.doi.org/10.2307/3052967

Mueller, John H. (2006). "Best Practices: What Perspective, What Evidence?" *Journal of Social Distress and the Homeless* 15 (1): 13–22. http://dx.doi.org/10.1179/sdh.2006.15.1.13

National Commission (National Commission for the Protection of Human Subjects of Biomedical and Behavioral Research). (1979). *The Belmont Report: Ethical Principles and Guidelines for the Protection of Human Subjects of Research*. DHEW Publication No. (OS) 78–0012. Washington, DC: US Government Printing Office. (First published 1978).

Onyemelukwe, Cheluchi, and Jocelyn Downie. (2011). "The Tunnel at the End of the Light? A Critical Analysis of the Development of the Tri-Council Policy Statement." *Canadian Journal of Law and Society* 26 (1): 159–76. http://dx.doi.org/10.3138/cjls.26.1.159

Senate of Canada. (2012). *Canada's Clinical Trial Infrastructure: A Prescription for Improved Access to New Medicines*. Ottawa: Standing Senate Committee on Social Affairs, Science and Technology.

Teubner, Gunther. (1983). "Substantive and Reflexive Elements in Modern Law." *Law & Society Review* 17 (2): 239–86. http://dx.doi.org/10.2307/3053348

– (1992). "Regulatory Law: Chronicle of a Death Foretold." *Social & Legal Studies* 1 (4): 451–75. http://dx.doi.org/10.1177/096466399200100401

Tolich, M., and M.H. Fitzgerald. (2006). "If Ethics Committees Were Designed for Ethnography." *Journal of Empirical Research on Human Research Ethics* 1 (2): 71–8. http://dx.doi.org/10.1525/jer.2006.1.2.71

Trubek, David M., and Louise G. Trubek. (2005). "Hard and Soft Law in the Construction of Social Europe: The Role of the Open Method of Co-Ordination." *European Law Journal* 11 (3): 343–64. http://dx.doi.org/10.1111/j.1468-0386.2005.00263.x

van den Hoonaard, Will C. (2011). *The Seduction of Ethics: Transforming the Social Sciences*. Toronto: University of Toronto Press.

White, Ronald F. (2007). "Institutional Review Board Mission Creep: The Common Rule, Social Science, and the Nanny State." *Independent Review* 11 (4): 547–64.

14 Ethics in Social Science and Humanities Research: Brazilian Strategies to Improve Guidelines

IARA COELHO ZITO GUERRIERO

This chapter describes a specific way of understanding research traditions, highlighting the idea that each tradition of research faces its own ethical dilemmas. In many countries, guidelines for research ethics are based on a biomedical model. The Brazilian guidelines on ethics in human research were under revision in 2011 and 2012. During the process of public consultation, the national associations of social sciences and humanities researchers organized themselves. This was fundamental to the development of specific ethics guidelines for social sciences and humanities research. First, I will briefly describe the Brazilian system of research ethics, followed by a discussion of underlying values in social science and humanities research, the fit of research ethics systems for them – especially the biomedical hegemony in the current system – and will conclude with a summary of actions for change in Brazil.

Brazil's System of Research Ethics

In Brazil, the National Commission on Ethics in Research (Comissão Nacional de Ética em Pesquisa, CONEP) and approximately 700 research ethics committees (comitês de ética em pesquisa, CEPs) constitute the ethics review system. They work together, each entity having specific roles. Each local research ethics committee reviews its institution's research and promotes ethics in research. The National Commission on Ethics in Research is responsible for keeping the national guidelines updated, registering and supervising research ethics committees, reviewing research protocols from special areas, promoting ethics in research, and is the body for hearing appeals. The National

Commission on Ethics in Research is one of the commissions of the National Health Council, which in turn is part of the Ministry of Health. Nowadays Brazil's guidelines include 11 resolutions, written by the National Commission on Ethics in Research, and approved by the National Health Council.

Researchers' Basic Belief Systems

Researchers in the social sciences and humanities assume different basic belief systems, adopt diverse theoretical and methodological references, and research a huge variety of themes. For this chapter, I assume the definition of *paradigm* proposed by Yvonna Lincoln and Egon Guba (1994): "the basic belief system or worldview that guides the investigator, not only in choices of methods but in ontologically and epistemologically fundamental ways" (105).

I will exemplify a basic belief system that can be shared by some qualitative researchers. My intention is to use this exemplum to contrast with the positivist paradigm, which is hegemonic in biomedical research.

It is important to understand the basic belief systems underlying decisions and actions (or no actions) of researchers, especially because often researchers are not aware of these belief systems, and frequently it is difficult to explain them concisely. The constant practice of reflexivity allows us to recognize these belief systems and act in a way that is coherent. Ethical research is an ongoing process, always under revision, continually adapting to the specific research situation. The following is a brief description of positions held by researchers and other stakeholders, including members of ethics review boards and funding agencies that must be considered when developing research ethics guidelines.

First, there is no single truth to be discovered, nor is there a single knowledge. Michel Foucault (2012) posits that truth "is to be understood as a system of ordered procedures for the production, regulation, distribution, circulation and operation of statements" (54). Foucault submits that truth "is linked in a circular relationship with systems of power which produce and sustain it, and to effects of power which induce and extend it" (54). Therefore, truth is built through a process of intersubjective agreement, and truth should be used in the plural to help researchers and regulators reflect, and realize that truth and rules are, as Ann Hamilton (2002: 81) says "liquid and local" phenomena.

Knowledge is built the same way – through intersubjective agreement about what something is or what it means.

Second, reality is shaped by "social, political, cultural, economic, ethnic, and gender values crystallized over time" (Lincoln et al., 2000: 168), and each person articulates these aspects, constructing narratives through dialogue with others in a specific context and moment, so reality is co-created (i.e., socially constructed).

Third, researchers are not neutral. Individuals are shaped by the specific context and historical moment in which they exist. We are shaped by our context, and we transform that context through our actions. Researchers are (or become) part of the context they study.

Fourth, the knower is present in the knowledge produced. Researchers see the world from a specific position, which includes a specific scientific community and particular methods. This point of view affects not only the methods of research, but also findings are interpreted based on researchers' specific scientific approaches, beliefs, perceptions, histories, and frames of reference.

Fifth, ethics, as a set of beliefs, and informed consent, as a set of rules, are not (or should not be) limited to a specific moment. Obtaining informed consent should be a process constructed through dialogue, and the consent process should continue during the entire research process.

Sixth, results must make sense to researchers, participants, and consumers of research. And, the *first* judgment about the validity of the research should be made by the participants themselves, and only then by the scientific community (see Lincoln, 1995; Lincoln et al., 2000; Sarti, 2008).

Seventh, as co-producers of knowledge (and reality and truths), participants should benefit from research.

The ideas that no single truth exists to be discovered, and that reality is created through dialogue with others in specific contexts and moments become the basic underlying structure on which research and other social accomplishments are built. Over time, this structure becomes invisible to people operating within the particular context (such as a specific social science discipline) and moment. This underlying structure is a form of local knowledge; it is constituted around themes adopted by a particular social group (Santos, 2004).

Understanding a specific process in depth helps us understand other contexts. In this way, knowledge is both local and global simultaneously (Santos, 2004). Ethics, as well as knowledge and truth, are intersubjective processes rather than specific events. Decisions about what is right or wrong (ethically, scientifically, or factually) are taken through dialogue, throughout the research process. It is through dialogue that data are co-produced among researchers and research participants, and the validity of the data is evaluated in the same space, that is, intersubjectively. Validity is related to appropriate representations of participants and their communities. Validity points to the question: "Are these findings sufficiently authentic that I may trust myself in acting on their implications?" (Lincoln et al., 2000: 178). Researchers (and publishers) should ensure that the voices of participants are included and treated fairly and with balance, in the eyes of the participants themselves. Even though it is important to consider that the researcher has a central role to analyse and contextualize the data, and the very complex discussion about first and second order constructs (Schutz 1970), participants should see what they perceive to be an accurate view of themselves and of their communities when they read the narratives that constitute research results. Inclusive narratives, the ones that include the research participants in the process of preparing them, are not only more fair and accurate in the view of the participants, they also better acknowledge the complexity of the life world.

Researchers' Responsibilities

During the research process, through the practice of reflexivity, we must keep in mind that, as researchers, we receive many benefits from conducting research including degrees, promotions, respectability, prestige, and sometimes money. What does the participant receive?

The knowledge that research produces is itself an important benefit, however ethics cannot be reduced to issues surrounding scientific merit. In positivist and post-positivist paradigms, ethics are considered extrinsic to the research process, and action is not considered a researcher's responsibility. In fact, in these paradigms, action is viewed as "'advocacy' or subjectivity, and therefore a threat to validity and objectivity" (Lincoln et al., 2000: 172). When we move to critical theories (frequently found in social science and humanities research), ethics are *intrinsic* to the research process, and action is "found especially in the form of empowerment; emancipation anticipated and hoped for; social transformation, particularly toward more equity and justice" (ibid.). In addition, constructivism and participatory research, in which ethics are also intrinsic, go further in affirming: "Action is intertwined with validity, inquiry often incomplete without action on the part of participants; constructivist formulation mandates training in political action if participants do not understand political systems" (ibid.). The researcher works actively to transform the world – to recognize the intersubjectivity of research, and how it exists and affects actions in the context of a specific life world.

Researchers use their skills and methodologies to "prepare a reality for a transformed presentation ... we contextualize events in a social system, within a web of meaning, and provide a nameable causation. We transform them into meaningful patterns, and in so doing, we exclude other patterns, meanings, or causes" (Fine, 1993: 290).

It is through narratives that individuals make sense of their lives, narratives they build according to available collective stories. A new story may focus on participants' vulnerability, or their potential. A new story may exclude vulnerabilities or potentialities. When researchers write narratives, they promote the meanings constructed during the research process. It is the researcher's point of view, a specific way of understanding the research process in a specific context, which can benefit or be prejudicial to participants and their communities. Research is most beneficial (and more valid, as mentioned) when researchers share those narratives with participants and their communities. Too often, though, research is discussed at length only with other researchers in highly specialized academic communities.

Narratives can reproduce and reinforce systems of domination based on gender, ethnicity, scientific tradition, geographic regions, and in nearly every context. The central point is to expose social, economic, political, and cultural hegemony (Foucault, 2012). New narratives must challenge hegemony, offering new meanings, new truths, and new ways to establish and maintain relationships. Collective stories (i.e., those written *with* participants) give voice to those who have been voiceless; researchers "convert private problems into public issues, thereby making collective identity and collective solutions possible" (Richardson, 1990: 28). Social science and humanities researchers, through self-reflection, must continually rethink methods and ethics, and ways to benefit the essential collaborators – the research participants. As authors of new narratives, researchers must accept and meet strong ethical responsibilities. Social science and humanities research is not innocuous; it has the possibility to produce harm as well as benefits to participants.

Frequently, researchers and publishers agree that a given research text is very good, but when considering the participants, the text is viewed differently. Who would like to have one's home described as poor or dirty? In a special issue of the *Journal of Contemporary Ethnography* (1992), Laurel Richardson wrote about William Foote Whyte's iconic ethnographic study, *Street Corner Society* (1993 [1955]). Whyte wrote in a very precise way about how power relations were established and maintained in a gang that was supposed to be without hierarchies. Whyte's work contributed substantially to the leader of the gang losing his power. So the publication of these results negatively affected the leader's life, from the leader's point of view, while it elevated Whyte's standing in his community. The research participant lost his position as a leader; his reputation was irrevocably damaged because the gang thought he had shared their secrets with Whyte. As Laurel Richardson (1992) highlights, "The social skills that we use to do ethnographies attach us to real human beings. They connect us to people in deeply human ways. And then, we become (solo) authors of 'true' texts ... When we bring real humans into our stories, our ethnographic writings might be 'right,' but what we do to those who host us might be very 'wrong' ... we will have to seriously and self-reflexively 'deconstruct' our practices so that we can 'reconstruct' them with fewer negative consequences" (118).

If a researcher's basic beliefs about research participants include the idea that the participants are the first judges of the validity of research results, that researcher will include participants in the process to ensure they are well represented in the text. If the narrative is not adequate in the opinion of the research participants, it is likely the researcher is not able to understand the participants adequately, their attitudes, beliefs, values, emotions, and actions. It is easy to judge, but much more challenging to understand.

It is important to remember that every statement made by a researcher is affected by the researcher's gender, social position, belief system, and the specific scientific community to which the researcher belongs. As Maria Cecília Minayo (2010) points out, "There [are] no (research) findings, everything is built and built by someone who is a subject, who has interest and ideology" (88). Therefore it is important that the researcher make clear the position from which she or he talks and the context in which his or her study is being conducted.

When deciding about whether to publish or not, especially analyses that are not attractive to research participants, we must keep in mind that our research should not be restricted to scientific goals, but should also focus on the dignity of the research participants. Returning to the example about describing participants' houses as dirty, if we consider the research context, the house may be described as a normal one. The words we choose to present our analysis make a meaningful difference, because the text creates meanings that can represent our research participants in a proper way within the context, or meanings that can be damaging. Social research conducted with Aboriginal people too frequently has exemplified ways researchers can represent a participant community in a negative – and inaccurate – light. So, when researchers consider research participants as the first judges of the analysis, harms can be minimized and understanding improved. And an added benefit of listening to the participants exists: the diversity within the groups studied will also be much better understood.

Researchers can make many decisions with participants. During the research process researchers discuss the methodology and ethical aspects of the study with participants. Ethical treatment should be intrinsic to the research process. The various traditions in social research have their own ethical dilemmas. Many social scientists and humanities researchers must decide how to represent research participants. Making such decisions puts the researcher in a methodological and ethical bind. Ethics in research is so broad and complex that it is a field of study itself.

In addition to the consideration of ethics as a process, developed between the researcher and the participants throughout the research process, there is also the discussion about ethics in research occurring in external contexts. Specific scientific disciplines often promote guidelines – the American Psychology Association (APA), the American Anthropology Association (AAA), and the Brazilian Anthropological Association (Associação Brasileira de Antropologia, ABA) are some examples, among many others. Further, there are guidelines established outside specific research contexts and even outside the academic community. These include the numerous national, regional, and local political bodies that develop both laws and guidelines that are supposed to be applied to all research. Even though there is agreement about the importance of respecting the dignity of research participants and their culture, the way it will become practice can be very different according to the researcher's affiliation and the characteristics of research participants. Therefore, the greater the distance between the actual research activities and where the research ethics guidelines were produced, the greater the possibility that the procedures the guidelines involve will not be adequate in specific contexts. I now turn to the last point: the fit of rules based on biomedical models when applied to the social sciences and humanities.

National Guidelines on Ethics in Research: Do They Fit Everybody?

One of the hottest points at the Ethics Summit was the hegemony of the biomedical model over social science and humanities research. Many guidelines on research ethics, including those of Australia, Brazil, Canada, New Zealand, and the United States, have adopted – universalized – key features of the biomedical model. In Brazil, Resolution 196/96 (enacted in June 1996), the same definition of research is found that was originally offered more than 20 years ago in the *International Ethical Guidelines for Biomedical Research Involving Human Subjects*, written by the Council for International Organizations of Medical Sciences (CIOMS) in collaboration with the World Health Organization (WHO), and published in 1993. The CIOMS guidelines were written by physicians to regulate ethics in biomedical and behavioural research. However, Resolution 196/96 was applied to research in all fields. Unfortunately, the newest guidelines, Resolution 466/12 (enacted in June 2013), revoked Resolution 196/96 but kept the same logic. Resolution 466/12 offers a different definition of research, but the new definition is no major philosophical or procedural transformation. The biomedical hegemony persists. Rena Lederman, in her presentation at the Ethics Summit, stated that biomedical hegemony continues to operate in research ethics regimes also, and that research ethics regimes in fact maintain and reinforce this hegemony, often unconsciously.

With respect to this hegemony, we are talking about power that exists in relationships among fields of knowledge and among people. Power is difficult to find within some contexts; the holders of power do not typically wish to call attention to themselves. Powerful people work to maintain the status quo from behind the scenes because they recognize that hidden power, invisible power, is superior. Foucault (2012) wrote that "this thing so enigmatic, at the same time visible and invisible, present and hidden, invested everywhere, which is called power" (138). We can ask, who exercises power? When? At which level? Over whom? About what? Usually power has capillarity; it is present in each situation in daily life. Power does not come from a specific point, but rather from numerous points in society. Foucault (1988) calls this "polymorphous techniques of power." One of these techniques is the incitement to speak about ethics, as if it were necessary to reduce ethics to the level of language, to control ethical behaviour through discourse. In the case of research ethics, a combination of public dialogue and rigorous prohibition exists. Power struggles develop around a particular focus of power, and talking about it publicly is an improvement because it confiscates, even if momentarily, the power from those in control. The Ethics Summit serves as an example: this event was especially important because it established a place and time for open discussion of the hegemonic system, to denounce the hegemony of the biomedical model in research ethics for social science and humanities, and to offer relevant solutions to the difficulties in the current system. In Brazil in 2007, the Health Department of the City of Sao Paulo, in collaboration with the Special Program for Research and Training in Tropical Disease Research, hosted at the World Health Organization (TDR/WHO), organized a meeting designed to produce suggestions for improving Brazil's guidelines on research ethics. Thirty top scholars participated. A report written by the participants (Health Department of the City of Sao Paulo, 2007) was sent to the Brazilian National Commission on Ethics in Research (CONEP) – unfortunately, the Commission did not respond or even acknowledge the report.

If we do not know who exercises power in the research ethics review system, we do know very well who does *not* exercise it. And we know that power is available to different people in different positions, and nearly always in the same direction. The biomedical hegemony, which can be identified in this situation as the positivist hegemony, is well known in many countries, and is therefore easily recognized – it has become comfortable. This hegemony is entrenched by funding agencies: consider the percentage of funding that goes to biomedical research compared with funds supporting the social sciences and humanities. These ratios are similar among most countries. Ultimately, as with most complex social processes, multiple causes for this ill-fitting system exist. Individuals in power interact to keep everything the way it is, until it becomes natural for everybody, entrenching a poorly adapted system. This is where real power lives. The ethics regime is part of a mostly invisible web of power that perpetuates the biomedical, positivist hegemony.

Those Able to Ask a Question Are Able to Answer It

I question whether we understand the research ethics review system. It seems we should by now be able to understand this situation; we have studied it, discussed it in depth for a long time. We have organized meetings, we think, discuss, and write some more. How is it that things do not change?

What is the power system that blocks, silences, and invalidates our discourse? Our research? Our knowledge and autonomy? In which ways is it formed? Most of all, how does it stay in place in the face of so much evidence that it doesn't fit where it is lodged?

We have not yet found the tip of the wire to unravel this web. Working to understand and to change this situation for decades has not produced the changes required; small reforms have not substantially improved the situation for social science and humanities researchers. A major revolution is needed – one that should be done by social scientists and humanities researchers, as Foucault (2012) wrote, "Reform claimed, demanded by those who it concerns, and there is no longer a reform, it is a revolutionary action that by its partial character is determined to put in question the totality of power and its hierarchy" (133)

The following activities are needed to change the research ethics review system. Social scientists and humanities researchers must:

1 Work together using a multinational and a multidisciplinary approach.
2 State positions in living documents.
3 Review those documents at regular meetings.
4 Sign our individual names and our affiliation to these documents.
5 Inform our countries, institutions, and research ethics committees about these documents and ideas.
6 Promote these ideas in our own countries, universities, research ethics committees, and among our students.

Just one researcher talking with students or a research ethics committee will not generate change; however, without individual actions, the changes will not happen either.

To Be the Change We Want in the World: Actions for Change in Brazil

Years ago, social researchers chatted about their problems with research ethics committees. However, nearly no one wrote or published information about these problems. As a member of Brazil's National Commission on Ethics in Research from 2003 to 2007, I served as a representative of the social science and humanities areas, and I was the only psychologist. When I was in this position, many researchers talked with me, explaining in detail the difficulties they were facing with their research ethics committees. I frequently tried to help in these specific situations, and I strongly suggested these researchers write about their experiences and submit these narratives for publication. Being a member of Brazil's National Commission on Ethics in Research was difficult. As a PhD student among full professors, it was difficult to have my voice heard. If, during this time, I had had publications available to me about problems with research ethics committees, they would have been very helpful in explaining why the rules don't fit social science and humanities research, and in demonstrating the scope of the problem. During my time on the Commission, I experienced first-hand how powerful the hegemony of the biomedical model is. I realized it was not my relative position as a member of the Commission that was the problem; I realized that even if I were more qualified, my ideas would still be rejected because the central question is not about my qualifications, it is about hegemony, resistance to change, and the preservation of power. After my term on the National Commission on Ethics in Research concluded, I attended an event where I saw a doctor, a CONEP member who held a high position in a public university, being disqualified as I had been, by people from the pharmaceutical industry. In this case, even though she is a doctor, and was defending a research participant's rights against the abuses of Big Pharma, she was ignored because she was not accommodating the biomedicine-is-king perspective. The disqualification process was the same. In some sense, it doesn't matter who you are, you will be disqualified if you argue against the interests of those in power.

We know people pay attention to a message based on the source of that message. The more qualified a person is perceived to be (i.e., in this case, the more you conform to the dominant ideology), the greater the possibility that the person's message will be heard. In terms of ethics review, it is clearly more important to conform than to be qualified.

Problems with research ethics committees have grown. Many national associations of graduate studies and researchers in the social sciences and humanities increased their actions to change the guidelines and to address ways that research ethics committees have been revising research projects. Some associations have their ethics commissions working on research issues. In addition to events and publications produced by these associations, researchers have begun to

278 Iara Coelho Zito Guerriero

publish their problems with research ethics committees and Brazil's National Commission on Ethics in Research (Victora et al., 2004; Guerriero, 2006; Guerriero and Dallari, 2008; Diniz, 2008, 2010; Diniz and Guerriero, 2008; Guerriero et al., 2008; Fleischer and Shuch, 2010; Guerriero and Minayo, 2013; Sarti and Duarte, 2013; Minayo and Guerriero, 2014'; Guerriero and Bosi, 2015, among others).

The stated aim of the Brazilian guidelines is to protect research participants; however, it does not mean that the hegemony of the positivist paradigm should be confirmed. It is naive to argue that ethics rules must be the same for everybody, and that the social sciences and humanities must follow the same procedures as those designed for biomedical research. To do this is oversimplifying both ethics and science.

Resolution 196/96 was under revision in 2011 and 2012. When the National Commission on Ethics in Research posted the new text for public consultation, the version was seen as being as bad as the old, because the biomedical model persisted. After discussion, academic associations talked about the best way to react. Many of these groups decided that no individual commentaries or suggestions would be posted. Rather the National Association of Graduate Studies and Research in Psychology and the National Association of Occupational Therapists signed a letter stating that this new text was not appropriate and asked for a specific resolution for social sciences and humanities. The Brazilian Anthropological Association, along with the National Association of Graduate Studies and Research in Social Sciences, the Brazilian Society of Sociologists, and the Brazilian Association of Political Sciences signed another letter, stating that the new version was not appropriate to them and asking that the system on ethics in research should move to the Ministry of Science, Technology, and Innovation, rather than being in the Ministry of Health. After all, why should researchers who don't study health issues follow guidelines approved by the National Health Council? However, the minister of science, technology and innovation did not approve the proposal, and the ethics regime in Brazil continues to be linked to the National Health Council, for all research involving human beings.

As a result of the work done by national associations on social sciences and humanities, and by members of CONEP (with backgrounds in social science and humanities), Resolution 466/12 states that Brazil will have a specific resolution for research in the social sciences and humanities – a big step forward.

In July 2013 the National Commission on Ethics in Research established a working group to develop guidelines for social science and humanities research, and I was nominated its chair. This working group includes 18 national associations of social sciences and humanities researchers and representatives of the Ministry of Health and the National Health Council. It was challenging to develop a document that could be agreed to by those in the social sciences and humanities. This working group has been working for two years to write the text of the new resolution, which was under public consultation between July and September 2015 and received 394 contributions. Those in the working group of social sciences and humanities analyse very carefully all suggestions and updated the text. Now, the text of the new resolution for research ethics in social sciences and humanities is ready, and it is waiting the approval by the National Health Council. After this approval, a new stage of our work will begin: the modification of Plataforma Brasil (a system through which all protocols are submitted, reviewed, and receive the final letter) according to the new resolution and the capacitation of all members of the system made up by committees on research ethics and the National Commission on Research Ethics.

NOTES

It was a wonderful invitation from Will van den Hoonaard to attend and subsequently present a paper at the Ethics Summit: Alternatives on Research-Ethics Review, held in Fredericton, New Brunswick, Canada, in October 2012. The Ethics Summit brought together top scholars who have been publishing about research ethics around the world. This chapter was inspired by that meeting.

I thank the Canadian Department of Foreign Affairs and International Trade (DFAIT) for funding part of my bibliographical research, and Deborah van den Hoonaard for having welcomed me at St Thomas University in Fredericton during this Post-doctoral Fellowship, as my supervisor, and for her careful review of this chapter, which helped me to strengthen it; all mistakes are my own.

REFERENCES

Diniz, Debora. (2008). "Ética na pesquisa em ciências humanas – novos desafios." *Ciencia & Saude Coletiva* 13 (2): 417–26. http://dx.doi.org/10.1590/S1413-81232008000200017
Diniz, Debora. (2010). "A pesquisa social e os comitês de ética no Brasil." In Soroya Fleischer and Patricia Shuch (eds.), *Ética e regulamentação na pesquisa antropológica*, 183–92. Brasília: Letras Vivas.

Diniz, Debora, and Iara Coelho Zito Guerriero. (2008). "Ética na pesquisa social: Desafios ao modelo biomédico." *RECIIS* 2 (1): 78–90. http://dx.doi.org/10.3395/reciis.v2.Sup1.211pt

Fine, Gary A. (1993). "Ten Lies of Ethnography: Moral Dilemmas of Field Research." *Journal of Contemporary Ethnography* 22 (3): 267–94. http://dx.doi.org/10.1177/089124193022003001

Fleischer, Soraya, and Patricia Shuch (eds.). (2010). *Ética e regulamentação na pesquisa antropológica*. Brasília: Letras Vivas.

Foucault, Michel. (1988). *História da sexualidade I: A vontade de saber*. Rio de Janeiro: Graal.

– (2012). *Microfísica do poder.25*. Rio de Janeiro: Graal.

Guerriero, Iara Coelho Zito. (2006). *Aspectos éticos das pesquisas qualitativas em saúde* [Ethical Aspects of Qualitative Health Research]. Doctoral dissertation, São Paulo University.

Guerriero, Iara Coelho Zito, and Sueli Gandolfi Dallari. (2008). "The Need for Adequate Ethical Guidelines for Qualitative Health Research." *Ciencia & Saude Coletiva* 13 (2): 303–11. http://dx.doi.org/10.1590/S1413-81232008000200002

Guerriero, Iara Coelho Zito, S. Schmidt Maria Luiza, and Fabio Zicker (eds.). (2008). *Ética nas pesquisas em ciências humanas e sociais na saúde*. São Paulo: HUCITEC.

Guerriero, Iara Coelho Zito, and Maria Cecília de Souza Minayo. (2013). "O desafio de revisar aspectos éticos das pesquisas em ciências sociais e humanas: A necessidade de diretrizes específicas." *Physis (Rio de Janeiro, Brazil)* 23 (3): 763–82. http://dx.doi.org/10.1590/S0103-73312013000300006

Guerriero, Iara Coelho Zito, and Maria Lucia Magalhães Bosi. (2015). "Research Ethics in the Dynamic of the Scientific Field: Challenges in the Building of Guidelines for Social Science and Humanities." *Ciencia & Saude Coletiva* 20 (9): 2615–24.

Hamilton, Ann. (2002). *Institutional Review Boards: Politics, Power, Purpose, and Process in a Regulatory Organization*. Doctoral dissertation, University of Oklahoma.

Health Department of the City of Sao Paulo. (2007). *Meeting on Ethics in Qualitative Health Research: Report*. Sao Paulo: Coordination Iara Coelho Zito Guerriero.

Lincoln, Yvonna S. (1995). "Emerging Criteria for Quality in Qualitative and Interpretive Research." *Qualitative Inquiry* 1 (3): 275–89. http://dx.doi.org/10.1177/107780049500100301

Lincoln, Yvonna S., and Egon G. Guba. (1994). "Competing paradigms in qualitative research." In Norman K. Denzin and Yvonna S. Lincoln (eds.), *Handbook of Qualitative Research*, 105–17. Thousand Oaks, CA: Sage.

Lincoln, Yvonna S., Susan A. Lynham, and Egon G. Guba. (2000). "Paradigmatic Controversies, Contradictions, and Emerging Confluences." In Norman K. Denzin and Yvonna S. Lincoln (eds.), *Handbook of Qualitative Research*, 163–88. Thousand Oaks, CA: Sage.

Minayo, Maria Cecilia de Souza. (2010). *O desafio do conhecimento: Pesquisa qualitativa .em saúde* [The Challenge of Knowledge: Qualitative Health Research]. São Paulo: HUCITEC.

Minayo, Maria Cecilia de Souza, and Iara Coelho Zito Guerriero. (2014). "Reflexividade como éthos da pesquisa qualitativa." *Ciencia & Saude Coletiva* 19 (4): 1103–12. http://dx.doi.org/10.1590/1413-81232014194.18912013

Richardson, Laurel. (1990). *Writing Strategies: Reaching Diverse Audiences*. Newbury Park, CA: Sage.

– (1992). "Trash on the Corner: Ethics and Technography." *Journal of Contemporary Ethnography* 21 (1): 103–19. http://dx.doi.org/10.1177/0891241692021001006

Santos, Boaventura S. (2004). *Um discurso sobre as ciências* [A Discourse about Sciences]. São Paulo: Cortez.

Sarti, Cynthia Andersen. (2008). "A Difficult Dialogue." *Ciencia & Saude Coletiva* 13 (2): 315–8. http://dx.doi.org/10.1590/S1413-81232008000200004

Sarti, Cynthia Andersen, and Luiz Fernando Duarte (eds.). (2013). *Antropologia e ética: Desafios para a regulamentação*. Brasília: ABA.

Schutz, Alfred. (1970). *Reflections on the Problem of Relevance*. New Haven: Yale University Press.

Victora, Ceres, Oliven Ruben George, Maria Eunice Maciel, and Pedro Oro Ari (eds.). (2004). *Antropologia e ética: O debate atual no Brasil*. Niterói: Editora da Universidade Federal Fluminense.

Whyte, William F. (1993) [1955]. *Street Corner Society: The Social Structure of an Italian Slum*. Chicago: University of Chicago Press. http://dx.doi.org/10.7208/chicago/9780226922669.001.0001

PART IV

Solutions: Renewal, Reform, or Dismemberment?

15 Australian Research Ethics Governance: Plotting the Demise of the Adversarial Culture

MARK ISRAEL, GARY ALLEN, AND COLIN THOMSON

During the past few years, researchers have expressed serious concerns about the impact of the requirements for research ethics review on the nature of social science research in general and qualitative research in particular. Such fears have been raised repeatedly in countries with relatively lengthy histories of research ethics regulation, including Australia, the United States, and Canada. Discontent has also surfaced in the United Kingdom and Brazil as they have moved towards a more centralized response to research ethics and integrity. Social scientists complain that neither the writers of the codes that govern research nor the local ethics board members who review research projects understand their roles (Israel, 2015). As a result, researchers believe that important work, work that is both ethically and methodologically sound, is being blocked and even stigmatized by the research ethics bureaucracy. In some places, the end result is a system where regulators and regulated view each other as responsible for an increasingly antagonistic relationship. In short, we have seen the growth of elements of an adversarial culture in the regulation of research ethics.

The problems social scientists have faced in Australia should come as little surprise. Not only were they predictable, they were actually predicted (or, at least, identified) early on. In 1998, Donald Chalmers and Philip Pettit warned against the path that Australian research ethics was taking: "the controversy machine has left us with a system of ethical review that is in danger of becoming extremely adversarial ... Researchers are regarded as the source of ethical problems: they are cast in the role of potential offenders. And reviewers are regarded as those with the unique responsibility, and the unique power, to prevent those problems arising: they are cast in the role of protectors and police" (Chalmers and Pettit, 1998: 81).

The identity of the authors is startling. Donald Chalmers and Philip Pettit were, respectively, chair and member of the Australian Health Ethics Committee (AHEC), a principal committee of the National Health and Medical Research Council (NHMRC). The Council has a statutory obligation to issue ethical guidelines for the conduct of medical research. Further, Philip Pettit was appointed in 1984 as the inaugural chair of the Institutional Ethics Committee of the Australian National University. Their paper "represented the consensual view" of the Australian Health Ethics Committee and was "approved for publication" by that body. However, such formal and insightful recognition by key regulators that all was not well also helps point to the common ground that may exist among some researchers, managers, and regulators – one that we have explored in attempting to negotiate the establishment of better practices and outcomes in governance in Australian universities, research organizations, and government agencies.

In this chapter, we discuss the extension of research ethics governance over the social sciences in Australia; identify the points at which as researchers, managers, and regulators we began wrestling with the consequences of poor governance; and discuss some of the work we have undertaken together as consultants in response to the adversarial culture.

Research Ethics Governance in Australia

Unlike in the United States, regulations governing research ethics in Australia did not grow amid public scandal. Although Australian medical researchers and scientists had participated in experimentation for the military that exposed servicemen to serious risks and failed to obtain informed consent (McNeill, 1993), these experiments did not come to public attention. Neither did the vaccine research conducted with babies and children in orphanages in the 1940s and 1950s (Senate Community Affairs References Committee, 2004), the physiological research conducted with Aboriginal men in the 1930s (Thomas, 2004), nor the strontium-90 studies of bones supplied by Australian pathologists for two decades from the mid-1950s (Australian Health Ethics Committee, 2002). Although some Australian institutions operated ethics committees in the 1960s, the growth of the system of regulating research ethics appears to have been the initiative of Australia's medical research body, the National Health and Medical Research Council.

The NHMRC first issued a *Statement of Human Experimentation* in 1966, revising it in 1973 and again in 1976. The revisions meant the end of self-regulation by researchers and left implementation of review processes to their institutions. Don Chalmers (2001) notes that these changes were "contemporaneous with demands for open government and greater public accountability, demands for expanded civil liberties, and demands for consumer rights" (A8); nevertheless, it seems likely that the timing was related to the 1964 *Declaration of Helsinki: Ethical Principles for Ethical Research Involving Human Subjects* issued by the World Medical Association, as the content of the NHMRC *Statement* closely followed that of the *Declaration*. It is equally probable that Australian medical researchers were keen to secure access to research funds from the United States, especially the US National Institutes of Health.

One reason for the 1973 revision was the need for an NHMRC subcommittee to assess the ethical propriety of research that sought to test the effects of marijuana on healthy volunteers. As part of its deliberations, the subcommittee resolved there should be "peer group assessment of experiments involving human subjects" (NHMRC Ethics in Clinical Research Subcommittee Minutes, 27 March 1973, cited in McNeill, 1993). The 1976 revision extended the remit of the NHMRC's *Statement* beyond medical research, incorporating other experiments engaged in "investigations on human behaviour," though without much discussion of what this might entail in terms of the kind of research that might be included and the groups of researchers who would be needed to undertake peer review of non-medical research. As a result, Paul McNeill (1993: 72) concluded the *Statement* remained "obviously designed for medical research" as neither "the extension of the jurisdictions" of the university-based research ethics committees "nor their use by institutions was accompanied by a reconsideration of their membership or procedures" (Dodds et al., 1994: 21). If Australia diverged from the United States in avoiding scandal, it followed a remarkably similar path in extending a medical model of research ethics to non-medical research without considering what such a system might really need, without consultation with researchers, and with little commitment to negotiation. Like the United States, this established a pattern in Australia that has continued to dog the research ethics review system.

In 1982, an NHMRC Working Party report revealingly entitled, "Ethics in Medical Research," prompted a change in name for local research-ethics committees. Previously they had been known as "Medical Ethics Research Committees." Now they were to be called "Institutional

Ethics Committees" (IECs), reflecting the incorporation of psychological research. However, the NHMRC did not change the name of its own standing committee, the Medical Research Ethics Committee.

In 1984, the National Health and Medical Research Council was able to insist that universities – or indeed any institution that chose to apply for and receive NHMRC research funds – establish local institutional ethics committees and review all human research whether medical or not and whether funded by the National Health and Medical Research Council or not. There appears to have been little reaction to the imposition of a condition that, in retrospect, far exceeded the scope of the NHMRC's responsibility for health and medical research. Social science projects were increasingly subjected to the NHMRC's ethics review structures, and by 1988–89, behavioural and social science projects made up 20 per cent of the load reviewed by Institutional Ethics Committees (McNeill et al., 1990; see also Ann Hamilton, herein, chapter 17). Despite this, research experience on these committees continued to be provided by medical graduates with research experience who also played the key role in decision-making (McNeill et al., 1994). Social scientists complained to the NHMRC's relevant body at IEC Workshops in 1991, 1993, and again in 1995 (NHMRC, 1996; Parker et al., 2003), but without result.

In 1991, the Australian Commonwealth government combined the NHMRC's Medical Research Ethics Committee with the National Bioethics Consultative Committee to form the Australian Health Ethics Committee. The functions of the Australian Health Ethics Committee were set out in Section 35 of the National Health and Medical Research Council Act 1992 and included the mandate "to develop and give the Council guidelines for the conduct of medical research involving humans." The composition of the Australian Health Ethics Committee, as stipulated under Section 36(1) of the Act, was suitable for the NHMRC's statutory functions confined as they were to ethics in health and in medical research. The Australian Health Ethics Committee was to include members with knowledge of the ethics of medical research, and of the regulation of the medical profession; experience in medical research, public health research, clinical medical practice, nursing, or allied health practices; understanding of health consumer issues, and of the concerns of people with a disability. In short, eight positions were designated for people with a stake in health research. In contrast, just one position each was assigned to someone with expertise in law, philosophy, and religion. A further position was reserved for an expert in social science research. In practice, many of these positions have also been filled by members whose primary area of interest was health.

In 1992, the National Health and Medical Research Council reissued the *Statement on Human Experimentation* accompanied by Supplementary Notes that provided additional guidance for the functions of Institutional Ethics Committees, research with children and others with limited capacity, clinical trials, in vitro fertilization, fetal tissue, somatic cell therapy, and for epidemiological research. The *Statement* was entrenched in the language and practices of medical research many of which were "simply inapplicable to social and behavioural research" (Dodds et al., 1994: 23). Worse still, some of the provisions might have been partly applicable to social research but it was difficult to tell when or how as they were coupled with references to matters such as experimentation, clinical procedures, and patients.

Not surprisingly, following the 1992 *Statement*, Susan Dodds (2000) noted that different institutions dealt with social science research in various ways: "Some IECs did not review research involving humans which was not health research, others reviewed social science and qualitative research, but evaluated the 'science' and merit of the research based on criteria which are appropriate to clinical trials, perhaps, but very poorly suited to many well-established methodologies in the social and behavioural sciences. Some university ethics committees established sub-committees for the review of 'non-health' research involving human participants; others expanded the membership of their IECs/HRECs to include members with an understanding of research methodologies outside of health and medical sciences" (11).

As a result, social science researchers in some institutions were excluded from review, while others had to deal with committees with little or no experience of non-medical research but who insisted that research conform to the medical research paradigm (Bouma and Diemer, 1996). Only in some institutions were social scientists able to seek review from peers with appropriate expertise (Parker et al., 2003). This lack of consistency was a feature of submissions to a 1996 Review of the Role and Functioning of Institutional Ethics Committees (NHMRC, 1996). Susan Dodds et al. (1994) also found researchers were concerned that the process of research ethics review would be used as a form of gatekeeping, masking the true reasons members of a committee may have for blocking research that might involve personal distaste for the topic, lack of sympathy or ignorance of the proposed methodology, or even protection of vested interests. The 1996 Review also found that "there was widespread concern expressed by social and behavioural researchers about the suitability of expertise of IECs, as presently constituted, for the review of social research. The medical model of a research practice and problems was seen as inadequate. Many expressed the need for changed membership to reflect suitably the expertise employed in social research and for extensive information and education of IECs about social research methodology and the frequently more complex and sensitive ethical issues which arise" (Dodds et al., 1994: 4–5).

In 1999, in response to recommendations in the 1996 *NHMRC Report*, a new *National Statement* attempted to provide guidelines to cover all research including humans. It drew on principlism, and based its default view of research on the rolling out of a pre-designed series of research questions using a hypothetico-deductive model. Drafted by the National Health and Medical Research Council, the *Statement* was endorsed by the Australian Research Council (ARC), the Australian Vice-Chancellors' Committee, and endorsed or supported by the various Australian academies including the Academy of the Social Sciences in Australia. The circumstances of these endorsements merit attention.

When the Australian Health Ethics Committee had almost completed the revision of the NHMRC *Statement on Human Experimentation* around health research, it became aware that the Australian Research Council was developing ethical guidelines for the conduct of non-medical research that the Australian Research Council funded. Teleconferences were arranged between representatives of the Australian Health Ethics Committee, the Australian Research Council, the Australian Vice-Chancellors' Committee, and the heads of the learned academies covering social sciences, the humanities, science and technological sciences, and engineering, and resulted in an adapted version of AHEC's draft that was endorsed by the Australian Research Council, the Australian Vice-Chancellors' Committee, and the academies. While this may have been intended to embrace the social sciences, some academy members criticized what they saw as inadequate consultation and negotiation. The process contributed to resentment at the imposition of a medical model of ethics review. Colin Thomson experienced the vehement expression of bitter resentment from some members of those academies at this decision, not only in the years following the 1999 *National Statement*, but even when he was chair of the Australian Health Ethics Committee during the development of the 2007 version of the *National Statement*.

Thus, although the 1999 *National Statement* covered social science research, social scientists were offered little opportunity to influence the content. Dodds (2000) was extremely critical of both the final text and the process of drafting. She concluded that the *Statement* "retains the medical bias of the earlier NHMRC Statement" (5), with non-medical interests "more or less tacked-on ... in its final stages" (19). Most obviously, all of the detailed examples provided in the document related to health and medical research.

Over time, the way some committees interpreted the *National Statement* incensed social scientists and researchers in the humanities. For example, Greg Bamber and Jennifer Sappey (2007: 34) suggested the requirement by some local committees that researchers of the workplace obtain written consent from various levels of management would have blocked the development of seminal studies in industrial sociology. Institutional review also risked eliminating from the discipline a tradition of independent analysis by subjecting researchers to the whims of managers keen to protect their own and their organization's interests, leaving industrial sociologists as "servants of power." Helen Johnson (2004), an anthropologist, questioned the assumptions of a medical model that imagined the Australian researcher as always in a position of power in relation to research subjects, a position she argued was poorly theorized, naive, blind to gender, and often contested by the women in New Caledonia with whom she worked. Robert Cribb (2004) pointed to an apparently "cavalier disregard for the specific vocabulary and research practices of the humanities" (45), while Kayt Davies (2011) compared her colleagues in the discipline of journalism to "slow boiled frogs in their acceptance of the discrimination against and/or limitations placed on their practice by the bureaucratic processes of some HREC committees" (166).

Among other changes, the 1999 *Statement* explored the use of deception, covert research, and research involving collectivities, allowed expedited review for minimal-risk research – though it provided mixed messages about the level of review required for different categories of risk (Parker et al., 2003) – and facilitated multicentre research (Alderson et al., 1995). Institutional Ethics Committees were renamed Human Research Ethics Committees (HRECs), and they were required to record their decisions and receive complaints. Human Research Ethics Committees were also required to contain at least one member "with knowledge of, and current experience in, the areas of research that are regularly considered" by that particular committee. This meant social scientists *could* be members of the committee; however, in practice, many committees already dominated by medical research paradigms could continue in that vein, each one doomed in the words of Lynn Gillam (1993) "to the murky waters of trying to assess the methodology of projects that it does not really understand" (12).

Under the 1999 *National Statement*, "institutions and organisations in which research involving humans is undertaken must individually or jointly establish, adequately resource, and maintain an HREC composed and functioning in accordance with this Statement" (NHMRC, 1999: s. 2.1). Not surprisingly, institutions reached very different decisions about what constituted "adequate" resources, and this might have accounted for some of the variation in the quality of advice and feedback researchers received from research ethics administrators and committees. Both researchers and administrators have complained about the capacity of the review process developed by institutions, though these have tended to be expressed in different ways, in terms of excessive delays and workloads, respectively (Gillam et al., 2006; Malouff and Schutte, 2005; Allen, 2004).

Importantly, the 1999 *National Statement* reflected a central feature of the previous two decades of human research ethics review in Australia. There was no clear articulation of institutional responsibility for the conduct of ethics review. The 1999 *National Statement* placed few obligations on institutions to exercise any oversight of the conduct of their Institutional Ethics Committees, beyond providing an annual report to the National Health and Medical Research Council on the functioning of their committees. The primary purpose of those reports was to continue the institution's eligibility to retain and receive NHMRC funds. Reports were confined to matters of membership and meetings, and their completion did not inform an institution about the committee's performance.

Local ethics bureaucracies may not have always had the resources or expertise to play the role required of them. Perhaps some universities saw the role of ethics administrators primarily as processors of applications and recorders of committee decisions. Although administrators have provided helpful advice to applicants, it is not necessarily reasonable to expect relatively junior general staff to develop university-wide policies or maintain HREC compliance with the *National Statement* in the face of committee opposition. One study described the ethics officer as the recipient of complaints from researchers but who, "is often not in position to deal with the person's problems or is not seen as having the authority to do so, and in fact often does not have the authority to deal with some of the issues" (Fitzgerald and Yule, 2004: 44).

In contrast, other universities have recruited ethics managers with responsibility for developing institutional policy, sometimes in concert with senior administrators, as well as for supervising the work of more junior ethics officers and general staff. In such a system, administrators have the authority to act proactively and can provide detailed and constructive advice to researchers and members of the committee.

However, since the establishment of Institutional Ethics Committees was instrumental to ensure funding eligibility, there was little need or incentive for institutions to do more than maintain them. As a consequence, each Institutional Ethics Committee tended to exercise autonomy and develop its own modus operandi influenced by the views and attitudes of its members. Neither the National Health and Medical Research Council nor any other national body exercised any oversight of committee practice; there was no attempt to develop benchmarks, and there was widespread inconsistency. Between 1991 and 1999, the National Health and Medical Research Council did conduct annual workshops for members of Institutional Ethics Committees but these provided a forum for opinion and debate rather than an occasion for benchmarking and the development of standards of decision-making.

Throughout the two decades since the NHMRC's research funding policy had spawned the growth of Institutional Ethics Committees in universities and the subjection of social science research to ethics review, there was no national body with dedicated functions and membership to guide and inform the ethics review of social science research. The National Health and Medical Research Council had imposed on universities the requirement to conduct ethics review of all human research but had merely changed the formal scope of its one-page *Statement on Human Experimentation*. Somewhat bafflingly, the Australian Research Council, the national body that funded social science research, appeared to play no role at all beyond its endorsement of the 1999 *National Statement*; the NHMRC's dedicated committees – the Medical Research Ethics Committee (MREC) and the Australian Health Ethics Committee – never had authority, responsibility, or appropriate membership to develop informed guidance.

Little has been written about the work of these NHMRC committees, and it would be tempting to exaggerate their importance. However, the AHEC's ability to fulfil its functions was questioned soon after it was established in 1991 (Bienenstock, 1993). Colin Thomson's own experience as a member of the Australian Health Ethics Committee between 1998 and 2002 and as chair from 2006 to 2009 was of a committee whose agenda included a range of other matters of health ethics in addition to research ethics. Indeed, few AHEC members had direct experience of human research ethics, whether as researchers or as HREC members.

Human research ethics occupied significant time of the committee only during the two periods of *National Statement* revision, 1997–99 and 2004–07. During these periods, the committee only had four face-to-face meetings of two days per year so that much of the detailed guidelines or advice drafting work was undertaken by subcommittees between meetings. As a result, discussion of issues concerning human research ethics was usually at a fairly high level of generality, and of principles rather than processes. Accordingly, the Australian Health Ethics Committee was not in a position to fulfil a leadership role that might have addressed an emerging adversarial culture.

It did however engage with Institutional Ethics Committees and their members. Annual workshops on research ethics, usually lasting one day, were conducted in most years but there was little other outreach activity and little development or leadership of benchmarking for IEC and later HREC performance. In 2003, 2005, and 2007, the Australian Health Ethics Committee organized national conferences on human research ethics accompanied by some training activities. These attracted more than 500 attendees each year and were well received. In 2004, the National Health and Medical Research Council conducted a one-day research ethics course on more than 20 occasions in capital cities and regional centres.

On several occasions, complaints about the conduct of Institutional Ethics Committees and Human Research Ethics Committees were referred to the Australian Health Ethics Committee, but AHEC members found that their statutory functions gave them no clear authority to intervene or take any corrective action. In 2004, the National Health and Medical Research Council invited the Australian Health Ethics Committee, the Australian Research Council, and the Australian Vice-Chancellors' Committee to create a joint working party to review and, where necessary, revise the *National Statement*. As a result, the working party included five people with a background in the social sciences or humanities. For the first time, therefore, social scientists were included from the beginning in the redrafting process. A new *National Statement on Ethical Conduct in Human Research* was published in 2007.

The 2007 version of the *National Statement* updated and extended the previous *Statement* and represented an attempt to correct both some of the mistakes and some of the mistaken applications of the 1999 document. It certainly provided some well-prepared social scientists with additional tools for challenging the decisions of those Human Research Ethics Committees that had proved incapable of handling qualitative or emergent research designs (Cordner and Thomson, 2007). For instance, committees that had insisted all researchers obtain signed consent forms found the new *National Statement* entirely unsympathetic to their stance. The definition of research participant was narrowed, and participants were only to be afforded the respect and protection from harm that is due to them. So, covert research was recognized as justified in some circumstances, which opened up the possibility of preserving traditional approaches in industrial sociology, for example. Indeed, the new *National Statement* removed the centrality of the Human Research Ethics Committees in undertaking research ethics review by authorizing institutions to establish review processes that were commensurate with risk and devolved to a point that could be more responsive to distinct disciplinary traditions and practices.

It also extended the remit of the review process to all of the humanities and the creative arts. Clearly a vast improvement for social scientists on the 1999 version; nevertheless, the document revealed, in much of its terminology, its origins in the medical research tradition so that many social scientists remained unconvinced the *National Statement* might meet the needs of their disciplines. Anthony Langlois (2011), a political scientist and head of his own institution's Human Research Ethics Committee, wrote of concerns that the arrangements governing research ethics would lead to "research findings being potentially skewed; research going underground or being undertaken in ways which diverge from what has been approved by committees; self-censorship; disengagement from institutional research governance procedures; the generation of risk for researchers who are operating outside institutional approvals because they feel they 'have to'; the construction of unnecessary prejudice against the legitimate aims of research ethics review procedures; and, finally, and most disturbingly, important and legitimate research not being undertaken" (141).

The 2007 *National Statement* authorized institutions to establish less formal procedures than an HREC meeting for the review of research involving no more than low risk to participants. The ability and willingness of institutions to take advantage of this has been uneven. In the instance where they have been implemented, they have not always resulted in simpler or faster review. Further, where review remained necessary, structures built around the new *National Statement* failed to recognize the shift in thinking suggested by the document. For example, the National Ethics Application Form (NEAF) was developed to limit the need for Human Research Ethics Committees to ask for additional information and for researchers to rewrite their proposal each time they have applied to a new Human Research Ethics Committee. However, the National Ethics Application Form constructed particular kinds of medical research practices as standard, and social scientists found their conventional practices had to be defended as departures from the norm. For example, in some Australian and, in particular, some Indigenous cultures, failing to name sources is both a mark of disrespect and a sign of poor research practice (see also chapter 9 by Julie Bull in this volume): "the knowledge authorities that we work with insist that they are identified as the source of their comments. That is a fundamental ethical consideration of Yolŋu knowledge work. Truth claims are assessed in the first instance on the basis of the claimants' right to speak. So de-identification compromises our ability to assess the evidence" (Christie et al., 2010: 70).

Yet the National Ethics Application Form assumed participant anonymity and, while Michael Christie and his colleagues noted that the Human Research Ethics Committees at his university had accepted that participants could be named, other committees sought repeated assurances that researchers have thought through the consequences of identifying participants and have sought informed consent to do so. In a world of regulation constructed around medical research, social scientists have become angry and frustrated, arguing that their disciplinary traditions and methods do not fit the expectations of unsympathetic regulators and poorly drafted regulations.

Counterproductive Regulation

Australian social scientists have played an important role in considering the counterproductive results that can emerge from poorly conceived and poorly executed regulation. In 1995, Peter Grabosky developed a typology for counterproductive regulation, identifying how processes of escalation, displacement, over-deterrence, the provision of perverse incentives, and the opportunity costs of securing marginal compliance can act to scupper regulatory initiatives or cause collateral damage. Grabosky (1995: 352) blamed such failures on bad science, bad planning, implementation failure, and bad politics. So, a regulatory regime is unlikely to achieve its stated objectives if politically compromised, poorly informed regulators, in poorly coordinated and under-resourced systems do not understand what is causing the harm they sought to remedy or fail to appreciate the impact that intervention in one sphere may have on another. In addition, antagonistic or apparently unreasonable approaches to regulation can provoke defiance and "cultures of resistance." He challenged regulators to "anticipate negative consequences, to prevent them if possible, and where not, to minimize their impact" (365).

The nature of regulation in the field of research ethics has attracted criticism in Australia from researchers and administrators. Even people who have played a key role in the development and review of regulatory structures have expressed their concerns publicly. For example, in a 1991 lecture, Philip Pettit (1992: 11) counselled against the dynamics associated with the evolution of research ethics policy. He suggested that the growth of regulation might result in a reduction in the kinds of research sanctioned. If research ethics committees only attracted opprobrium when they made mistakes that allowed harmful research, and if they did not have to face an appeals procedure, they would inevitably increasingly err on the side of what they regarded as caution: "as time passes, ethics committees are bound to take a more and more restrictive shape" (11). Pettit warned that committees might feel the need to interfere in the conduct of research to justify their own existence. If there were no countervailing pressures, they would keep doing so, escalating their intervention, even if researchers censored their own proposals in order to avoid rejection. He was particularly concerned that increased regulation would provoke resistance to research ethics review among resentful and alienated researchers. Among other things, Pettit (1992: 18) proposed that academic disciplines should develop a "culture of research ethics" through education, discussion at professional gatherings, and administrative procedures for addressing complaints that could exist independently of regulatory bodies.

Pettit was a member of the Australian Health Ethics Committee between 1994 and 1996. In 1998, as described earlier in this chapter, his ideas were developed further. Don Chalmers and Philip Pettit (1998) argued that any system for the regulation of research ethics should have as its goal the facilitation and encouragement of ethically informed research "generating an awareness of ethical concerns in the research community at large and ... displaying a posture of trust in that community" (81), working to support "all those meritorious projects, and only those, that meet certain ethical standards" (80). Drawing on the work of Ian Ayres and John Braithwaite (1992) and Peter Grabosky (1995), Chalmers and Pettit (1998) argued that any system that relied heavily on inspection and policing would fail to achieve these goals. As a result, they reasoned that regulators should be alert to the dangers of the following scenarios: ethics reviewers see research as the concern of researchers, and ethics as their own concern, and so do not worry about the effects of their reviewing on research activity; ethics reviewers are unwilling to contemplate a "steady state" in which research generally satisfies the accepted ethical standards and ethics committees play an ever more passive role; researchers respond to this indifference, and this incremental creep, by adopting a resistant posture. Reflecting on his experience on his university's ethics committee at Alberta, Kevin Haggerty (2004) describes this phenomenon in the Canadian context, calling it "ethics creep": "a dual process whereby the regulatory structure of the ethics bureaucracy is expanding outward, colonizing new groups, practices and institutions, while at the same time intensifying the regulation of practices deemed to fall within its official ambit" (34).

In 2002, the *Monash Bioethics Review* invited researchers to assess the strengths and weaknesses of the structure regulating research ethics in Australia. By that time, there were more than 220 committees in operation, with more than 2,000 members (Breen, 2002; NHMRC, 2004). Once again, Susan Dodds (2002: 45), who was then chair of the research ethics committee at her university, launched an attack on the AHEC-mandated structure, this time focusing on the workings of local ethics review committees that she portrayed as facing a "resource crisis," operating with limited support from both their host institutions and the Australian Health Ethics Committee, and encountering mounting workloads, the majority "wilting under the mountains of paper." According to Maureen Fitzgerald and Elisa Yule (2004), meetings of some ethics committees regularly lasted six to seven hours. Some members of local ethics review committees voiced concerns about the heavy workloads faced by committees in the NHMRC Stakeholder Evaluation of HRECs in 2002 (Taverner Research Company, 2002). Although Dodds' portrayal was contested by AHEC's chair in 2002, Kerry Breen (2002) did acknowledge at the NHMRC Ethics Conference in Canberra in 2003 that ethics committee workloads had been subject to criticism.

In the same issue of the *Monash Bioethics Review*, Paul McNeill (2002) suggested that some ethics committees had responded to these pressures by becoming more bureaucratic, "blindly following rules, with little regard to whether or not the outcome is beneficial" (72). Previously a supporter of the ethics review process, McNeill warned the process had shifted its attention from ethics to regulation and control, reflecting a need to meet institutional requirements of risk management.

Paul Komesaroff (2002), director of the Monash Centre for the Study of Ethics in Medicine and Society, explored a slightly different line of criticism. He applauded the flexible and context-specific nature of the local ethics committees, noting that they enabled institutions to find ways of resolving disputes, allowing negotiated compromises, and permitting decision-making to be responsive to specific cultural needs. However, these successes had been attained at some cost. Komesaroff was troubled that researchers often felt "alienated from the review process" (69) and by the wide and apparently gratuitous variation in decisions between different ethics review committees (Jamrozik and Kolybaba, 1999). He attributed these failures to a lack of training for and communication among ethics committees.

There is little reason to believe that these problems have diminished since 2002. In the late 2000s, Marilys Guillemin and her colleagues (2012) interviewed 34 HREC members and 54 health researchers in Melbourne. Their work revealed that some ethics committee members and researchers believed that Human Research Ethics Committees were over-protective of both research participants and of the institutions that hosted the Human Research Ethics Committee, and they concluded that this behaviour may be damaging relations between researchers and ethics regulators and reducing levels of mutual trust. Researchers tended to generalize from their individual poor experiences with research ethics committees: "Researchers who had experienced notably difficult issues with an HREC over a particular application, either because of delays or their personal treatment, said that it was very difficult to put these experiences behind them" (Gillam et al., 2009: 7.14).

In many ways, Chalmers and Pettit's concerns expressed 15–20 years earlier remained true. The decades from 1984 laid the foundations of practice in human research ethics review – or, rather, allowed individual ethics review committees to establish their own practices, unconfined by national, regional, or even institutional constraints. For most of this time, the absence of any such constraint resulted in idiosyncratic, inconsistent decisions against which there was little recourse within or beyond the institutions in which the ethics review committees worked.

It was within this context that the three of us – Mark Israel, Gary Allen, and Colin Thomson – have operated as researchers, managers, and research ethics regulators and sometimes in a combination of these roles. The three of us have been members of Human Research Ethics Committees and have contributed to national regulation. We have also each come to question the role that the structures and practices have played in contributing to the growth of an adversarial culture in regulating research ethics. And given our diverse backgrounds, we have reached our current views through very different routes.

In 2003, two of Australia's leading criminologists, Don Weatherburn and John Braithwaite, commissioned research to identify whether their colleagues were regularly experiencing difficulties obtaining clearance for their research. The project received 50 written comments and interviewed almost 50 criminologists, other researchers, and administrators. Several criminologists had served on Human Research Ethics Committees, including some who had chaired such committees. Mark Israel (2004) was engaged to complete the report. Some criminologists reported they found the process of ethics review in Australia to be constructive. They appreciated the assistance of those ethics committees that used their expert knowledge of the research environment to draw attention to aspects of research design that could be changed to better protect participants. Despite this, many researchers identified systemic difficulties in the process of ethics review. First, they were frustrated by a *National Statement* that did not seem to take into account the conditions under which criminologists tended to operate. Second, they were deeply troubled by the operations of some autonomous HREC members who seemed to be over-controlling on the basis of limited expertise; acting slowly, secretly, and arbitrarily; and exercising unfettered discretion according to their own interpretations of what some researchers saw as amorphously expressed standards.

The combination of difficulties posed by the *National Statement* and Human Research Ethics Committees meant that, even in institutions where Human Research Ethics Committees were seen as supportive, researchers still experienced frustration. One researcher who had chaired his faculty's research ethics committee remarked that "the bureaucratic apparatus ... so consume[s] and alienate[s] many researchers that they see the ethics process as an unnecessary obstacle to doing research. Even turning from poacher to gamekeeper, I underestimated the antagonism felt by many researchers to the process" (David Dixon, University of New South Wales, email to Mark Israel, 6 Oct. 2004). Although researchers complained that Human Research Ethics Committees were becoming more intrusive, there was little consensus on why this might be happening. Some criminologists and, indeed, some heads and former heads of Human Research Ethics Committees were concerned that committees were losing their focus on ethics and were drifting towards increasingly conservative positions, over-rigidly applying poorly drafted rules to achieve technical compliance and risk management. In doing so, some Human Research Ethics Committees appeared to be straying from the requirements of the *National Statement*. As a result, at various times senior criminologists were able to place very little trust in the processes of the Human Research Ethics Committee at major research universities in almost every state. Some researchers interpreted this as the growth of an ethics industry that was being used by some administrators to create power bases and mark out territory through their control of Human Research Ethics Committees. One criminologist remarked that the Human Research Ethics Committee at his university had to comment on every project, regardless of the level of risk: "they can't help themselves."

Gary Allen has worked as a research ethics officer for more than 15 years. A congruence of factors contributed to his reflecting on the pressing need for a new approach to research ethics review. In the early 2000s, he reached the view that the "problem" was not that some researchers were not engaging with research ethics arrangements, but lay in a systemic flaw in the dominant approach to the governance of research ethics, which had the primary objective of policing researcher compliance with the national and institutional ethics arrangements. At best, this approach encouraged researchers to outsource their ethical responsibilities for the design and conduct of research to the bureaucracy of ethics review. At worst, this approach triggered a dissonance between actual ethical conduct in research and the bureaucracy of ethics review, and was consequently not effectively safeguarding the rights and welfare of research participants nor managing institutional risk (Allen, 2011). At the same time Allen was working on his doctorate, relocating to another university where he was to implement a reform of that institution's research ethics arrangements in the face of "mounting researcher disquiet" (Allen, 2004), and participating in a philanthropic program in Vietnam to establish research ethics arrangements that were culturally relevant and had a goal of facilitating ethical excellence in research.

These projects, combined with his academic research, suggested a need to break with established approaches to research ethics governance.

The intellectual work that members of Human Research Ethics Committees must perform is not simple. They are expected to discern whether each of a series of general ethical principles is satisfied in the design and proposed conduct of research projects presented for ethics review. The task involves applying a set of rules to facts and drawing conclusions about compliance. As an academic lawyer working within this environment, Colin Thomson concluded the model appeared more legal than ethical and risked turning an exercise that should promote reflection and deliberation into the mechanical application of precedent. A recurrent device in research ethics training, and one that all three authors have used in their work, is the creation of case studies that are deliberately flawed so as to highlight ethical issues that an ethics review committee would be expected to identify along with the appropriate corrections to require of the researcher. However, Colin Thomson reached the painful conclusion that an inadvertent but obvious outcome of this practice was that ethics regulators were being socialized to approach *all* research projects presented for review as if they had hidden flaws and that the measure of whether an ethics review committee has fulfilled its responsibility was therefore based on whether or not it had identified problems and sought changes in the proposed research.

Responding to the Adversarial Culture

Each of us has worked to reform existing guidelines and structures for research ethics review while, at the same time, arguing against the appropriateness of basing the need for and the development of ethics review on historical medical research malpractice. Having operated within our own institutions and having advocated for change within our professional networks and organizations as individuals, we found ourselves being asked to help a range of public and private educational institutions and hospitals, as well as state and federal government departments and agencies. We were drawn to work together by projects that required a set of knowledge, skills, and capacities that none of us had alone. Although we have followed different paths in recognizing the existence and structural causes of this adversarial culture, we each had reached similar conclusions and began to formulate similar responses. Our approach is based on building trust between researchers and administrators of research ethics review, shifting the focus from enforcing compliance to facilitating the capacity of researchers to act ethically (Cunningham and Schneider, 2001), and recognizing the importance of encouraging reflective practice in context over a mechanical adherence to following rules that do not fit the situation.

Building Trust

In 2003, Griffith University instituted an internal review of its ethics regulatory process that had been sharply criticized by some senior researchers for institutionalizing systemic problems (Allen, 2004). The report was highly critical of its existing processes (Griffith University, 2003): "The design of the current system for ethical review does not manage ... risks in a systematic manner. This is not unique to Griffith or a reflection on any of the stakeholders. The current processes were conceived in a much less complex regulatory environment with emergent problems and perceived failings symptomatic of a process under substantial stress from an ever-increasing volume of projects requiring ethical review and an ever-increasing regulatory burden" (2).

In response to the recommendations of the review report, the university made significant changes to its research ethics review process. The most important change entailed shifting away from an approach that focused on enforcing researcher compliance with regulatory standards and absolute rules to an approach that facilitated research and supported and drew on the expertise of the institution's researchers.

The university also sought and subsequently listened to the views of researchers and participants. Resource material and processes have continued to evolve in response to this feedback. The university established a proportional ethics review process, with three levels of ethics review that matched the paperwork, review, and processing time to the level of risk and ethical sensitivity of the planned work. For some research, especially for social science and fine arts work, this resulted in more than 85 per cent of projects qualifying for expedited review, with a review decision being communicated to applicants in fewer than 10 days. Benefits have not been limited to only a reduction in frustration and delays for researchers, but also the university's research ethics committee can now allocate sufficient time and attention to matters of genuinely higher risk and ethical sensitivity.

With the release of a booklet-based research ethics manual, the university moved away from absolute and universal rules towards helping researchers work through the design and justification of strategies appropriate to each specific research project. The university also appointed a network of academic staff to serve as Research Ethics Advisers (REAs). The Research Ethics Advisers have been a source of education and advice on both ethical conduct and regulatory compliance to graduate students and their supervisors, early career researchers, and other researchers in their academic areas. The network represents a distributed approach to the ownership of ethics expertise as a research design, conduct, and quality concern, rather than just the purview of central research administrators and the institution's research ethics committee. Research Ethics Advisers both support an approach to research ethics by researchers focused on reflective practice and provide discipline-specific expertise to the human research ethics committee, enhancing communication among applicants, administrators, and committee members.

Several Australian universities have sought to adopt and adapt the Griffith approach, and on some occasions, we have been asked to advise on managing change and to provide training. While Griffith University has been generous in sharing its experience and materials, the model requires long-term political and financial support from senior administrators. The adopting institution must create clear policy statements, fund the development of appropriate and responsive supporting resources, enable a respectful dialogue between researchers and ethics regulators, ensure ongoing training and support is provided, and formally recognize the workload placed on various parts of the university. Some institutions that have appointed Research Ethics Advisers have not been able to take advantage of them in the absence of other parts of the structure.

The Commonwealth Scientific and Industrial Research Organisation (CSIRO), Australia's national science agency, is one organization that has integrated some elements of the Griffith approach into its structures governing research ethics. Although the Organisation's focus is on the biophysical sciences, up to 5 per cent of its researchers are anthropologists, sociologists, psychologists, and economists who work with scientists in multidisciplinary teams to analyse the connections between natural, agricultural, industrial, and urban ecosystems and social and economic processes both inside and outside Australia. These teams also explore community and agency perspectives on climate change and energy technologies, and study the interactions between humans and technology in order to create new tools and platforms for information and communication technologies.

Its increasing engagement in social science research motivated the Commonwealth Scientific and Industrial Research Organisation to adopt clear processes to assure its work meets the highest scientific and ethical standards. CSIRO already followed the requirements of the *National Statement* for health and, with the expansion of the remit of the *National Statement*, sought to extend its processes to social science and multidisciplinary approaches. Given the Organisation's long history, it became important to develop coherent and persuasive argument to justify the introduction of new layers of bureaucracy around research ethics for social sciences. This was partly achieved by an unambiguous expression of commitment to the ethical conduct of human research from senior administrators. However, those responsible for introducing the new regime worked hard to persuade researchers they were making their lives easier rather than harder, supporting better research design, and adding value to their work. So, over the past decade, CSIRO has worked to establish an integrated approach to research ethics for social scientists. The system includes the creation of supporting resources, proportional and expedited processes of ethics review, and a capacity for executive and administrative action outside of HREC meetings. As part of the introduction of systems governing research ethics, we were contracted to work with the manager for social responsibility and ethics and provide training for both CSIRO's researchers around Australia and members of the Organisation's new Human Research Ethics Committee. Together, we sought to extend the ability of researchers to engage with ethical issues in social science research and encouraged the newly established Human Research Ethics Committee to build a sense of common purpose with researchers, avoiding mistakes known to have occurred elsewhere in Australia. Where possible, we also encouraged CSIRO to reduce the workload for researchers and regulators by creating bilateral agreements with other organizations so that multisite projects did not require multiple reviews.

FACILITATING REFLECTIVE PRACTICE

Social scientists can only benefit from the creation of an environment in which researchers operate ethically, and review mechanisms are conducted by respected, knowledgeable, and experienced people who help researchers develop better practices. However, while some Australian social scientists have considerable experience in negotiating both ethical dilemmas and HREC requirements, other researchers do not always have a ready understanding of the ideas behind national regimes of regulating research ethics. Many scholars do not have much experience or have little confidence in engaging with Human Research Ethics Committees. Where disciplines have failed to integrate material on ethics and ethics review into undergraduate and postgraduate courses, these skills must be learned on the job. As a result, some applications for ethics review submitted by social scientists are underprepared (Fitzgerald and Yule, 2004).

One strategy for providing education about research ethics in Australia is to offer clear, unequivocal directions by identifying the relevant provisions of the *National Statement* and considering how these provisions are likely to be interpreted by Human Research Ethics Committees. However, restricting guidance to bureaucratic compliance has serious limitations as prescriptive approaches to ethics and ethics education stand in fundamental opposition to moral thinking (Bauman, 1993). In addition, such approaches are fraught with practical problems as they assume a universalist approach to ethics, replace responsibility with compliance, and underprepare researchers for the complexities of decision-making in context (Israel, 2015). Rather than relying on the deceptive assurances of ethical codes, our institutions, organizations, regulatory regimes, and research disciplines should encourage theoretically informed, self-critical, perceptive approaches to moral matters that stimulate the moral imagination, recognize ethical issues, develop analytical skills, elicit a sense of moral obligation and personal responsibility – and that tolerate disagreement and ambiguity. In addition, student-centred learning incorporating role-playing, small-group discussion of targeted case studies, debate, simulation, and field experiences should provide students with concepts and skills and nurture the attributes that will allow them to handle moral issues independently and competently. Several institutions have created online research ethics education programs, and the open resource at Macquarie University is one of the few tailored to at least some parts of the social sciences (see Schrag, 2009). It is an area where local attention could be complemented by blogs – several of which already exist in research ethics – and massive open online courses (MOOCs) that share cutting-edge ideas about ethical conduct and regulation.

Our professional associations and learned academies should be more involved in generating and disseminating resources to promote reflection about research ethics. Several social science professional associations around the world have established ethics committees to police codes of ethics and act as a grievance body. The committees could play a more strategic role, developing and coordinating the various activities that an association takes up to support ethical practice, acting as a forum where ethical matters may be aired, tensions with regulatory systems monitored, and best practices collected in digital repositories and disseminated in ways that are sensitive to geography, discipline, and institutions. Associations may also find themselves in a position to act as advocates for methodologies that are threatened by bioethics-derived regulation. Our journals can also take some responsibility for communicating their contents to a wide audience – we applaud the case study and commentary approach of *Research Ethics* in the United Kingdom and the Educational Advantage initiative of the *Journal of Empirical Research on Human Research Ethics*, and attempted to create similarly thoughtful material by inviting multiple commentary on cases in the Appendix to Mark Israel and Iain Hay (2006) which will be reproduced and developed further on the Australasian Human Research Ethics Consultancy Services website (www.ahrecs.com).

CREATING GOVERNANCE ARRANGEMENTS THAT ARE FIT-FOR-PURPOSE

The three of us have also found that research ethics arrangements created to govern academic research did not fit well in other environments. In 2011 the Queensland Crime and Misconduct Commission (CMC) contracted us to help establish research ethics arrangements appropriate for the regulatory context in which they work and the nature of their work. The Crime and Misconduct Commission, now the Crime and Corruption Commission, is the State anti-corruption body mandated to tackle official corruption in the public sector, including the police and parliament, as well as to respond to organized and systemic crime. While the Commission has an investigatory function, research is often conducted by the Commission as the result of a regulatory requirement or directions from parliament.

Rather than enhancing the ethical credibility and justification of its research, the Commission had found the *National Statement* and university-based Human Research Ethics Committees imposed requirements that were largely unhelpful and impractical. The Human Research Ethics Committees were interpreting and operationalizing the *National Statement* in ways that were inconsistent with the Commission's statutory role. For example, some wanted to require that public sector officials could elect to use the process of informed consent to block research that the Crime and Misconduct Commission was mandated to undertake.

Research frameworks used by universities failed to recognize the kinds of harms and benefits that need to be judged in the contexts of public sector policy, and proved uncomfortable with the closer link between research findings and policy settings that might exist in a public sector body. In short, the Crime and Misconduct Commission found itself caught between its statutory responsibilities and arrangements governing research ethics that had never been devised with the work of public sector agencies such as the Crime and Misconduct Commission in mind. Despite these significant limitations and frustrations, the Commission wished to establish a robust approach to the ethical design, review, and conduct of its research work that was based on established best practices to safeguard the reputation of the organization and stand up to parliamentary scrutiny.

We assisted the Crime and Misconduct Commission in adopting a framework based on an organizationally and contextually relevant adaptation of the *National Statement*. The proposed proportional review framework had ethics review pathways that recognized the varying mandate held by individual projects (whether directed by regulatory or parliamentary requirement, or initiated by the CMC research directorate). It exempted from review some of the Commission's work such as intelligence gathering relating to an individual potential criminal matter. The ethics review arrangements included the participation of community members, experts, and public sector ethicists. The focus of these arrangements was to offer practical and valuable ethics advice to a research team, rather than to "approve," "ethically clear," or otherwise "police the compliance" of a project. Even though we recommended the adoption of a comprehensive framework of guidance material for research ethics, these were not to be treated as universal rules to be applied in an automatic and unthinking manner. Instead this framework was to provide resources to support the reflective practices of the CMC's research culture.

Creating a Voice for Social Scientists

Social scientists have rarely had the opportunity to influence the direction taken by research ethics guidelines in Australia. The one exception was in 2007 and, even then, members of the working party lacked the time and resources needed to generate an appropriate evidential base on which new policy might be based. There is plenty of scope for greater engagement with those who will be asked to draft new regulations for research ethics. There are a few strategies that might make this task easier in 2016 as we revise the *National Statement*. We have already pointed to the role our national professional associations might play. However, there is also the possibility of mobilizing our international networks to identify those jurisdictions that are more receptive to imagining better practices for research ethics review. Social scientists in other countries might then point to these developments to "ratchet up" (Braithwaite and Drahos, 1999) the quality of regulatory practice elsewhere. For example, we were able to use the Canadian *Tri-Council Policy Statement: Ethical Conduct for Research Involving Humans* (CIHR et al., 2005) and the *Research Ethics Framework* of the Economic and Social Research Council in the United Kingdom (2005) to counter a tendency to over-generalize obligations of beneficence and non-maleficence on the basis of principles developed to meet the needs of medical research. As a result, the 2007 *National Statement* indicated research undertaken in the social sciences may legitimately and deliberately work to the detriment of research subjects. In addition, the creation of ethics guidelines for indigenous research drafted by indigenous people in Australia, New Zealand and Canada offers opportunities to other indigenous communities to resist universalist, bioethics-derived codes (Australian Institute of Aboriginal and Torres Strait Islander Studies, 2011).

International declarations may confer greater legitimacy on those who are arguing for parallel changes in national guidelines for research ethics. In the field of health research ethics, publication ethics, and research integrity, international groups have chosen to draft statements that set international benchmarks. Statements such as the *Singapore Statement on Research Integrity* (2010) and the *International Ethical Guidelines for Biomedical Research Involving Human Subjects* issued by the Council for International Organizations of Medical Science (CIOMS, 2002) have then been used in those environments with few and/or poor guidelines to criticize unethical behaviour and encourage governments, organizations, and researchers to develop more comprehensive codes and guidance and to mould the direction those regulations take.

The Ethics Rupture gathering of more than 30 academics in Canada in 2012 (van den Hoonaard, 2013a) offered an opportune moment for social scientists to create a similar document that might prompt new debates about the ethical conduct of research and its regulation. With this in mind, we initiated and played a significant role in drafting the *New Brunswick Declaration*. The final document represents a collective effort; nevertheless, our aim in introducing the *Declaration* was to articulate a series of positive statements to support a constructive dialogue among various groups with an interest in nurturing ethical research and complementary regulatory practices. The *Declaration* needed to reflect the concerns of signatories without over-generalizing from the frequently negative experiences of a particular jurisdiction or institution at a specific time. Constructed to be aspirational, the authors of the *Declaration* avoided excessively burdensome commitments difficult to sustain over time. The *Declaration* (van den Hoonaard, 2013b) articulates many of the themes key to tackling the adversarial culture, including: "Encouraging a variety of means of furthering ethical conduct involving a broad range of parties" (Article 4); "Encouraging regulators and administrators to nurture a regulatory culture that grants researchers the same level of respect that researchers should offer research participants" (Article 5); and the need to "Commit to ongoing critical analysis of new and revised ethics regulations and regimes" (Article 6). In the Australian context, the *Declaration* provides a platform for critiquing existing frameworks and practices regulating research ethics and for promoting reform. There may have been opportunities to influence the rolling review of the 2007 *National Statement*.

Conclusion

In the face of national guidelines and local processes for research ethics review that frequently demonstrate little understanding of the practices and traditions of social science, researchers have complained about the governance of research ethics in Australia for a considerable period of time. The adversarial culture that has developed in Australia is frustrating for many regulators, researchers, and participants. This adversarial culture has ensured the loss of important opportunities to engage in original and significant research. Most bizarrely it has meant researchers have been forced to use research methods deemed to be legitimate rather than creating new practices to meet fresh intellectual, practical, and ethical challenges (Dyck and Allen, 2012). The growth of the adversarial culture should not have surprised anyone – its origins were identified by senior academics engaged in developing regulations – and was a predictable result of a failure to consult with researchers, a lack of regulator resources, and a gap in expertise in key parts of the regulatory structure.

This story, however, is too simple and too defeatist. It masks some of the shifts that have occurred in national guidelines and some local ethics review processes. It intimates there is little that researchers can do to work with – rather than against – research ethics regulators and administrators. We think this would be a mistaken conclusion. Although colleagues have traced the rise of the ethics review bureaucracy in other jurisdictions (Schrag, 2010; Hamilton, 2002, 2005), and its attendant net-widening and mesh-thinning, the adversarial culture serves the interests of very few people in the long run. It is time to plot its demise. During the last decade, as researchers, regulators, and bureaucrats, the three of us have been able to influence the redrafting of the *National Statement*, help some institutions that already had Human Research Ethics Committees to improve their practices, and assist others introducing ethics review to avoid the mistakes of the past. Finally, we have also been able to shape the beginnings of an international platform that may help social scientists act collectively to foster the ethical imaginations of our disciplines and create more appropriate processes of research ethics review. This work may not make the headlines in our disciplines; better news rarely does.

NOTE

A shorter version of this chapter appeared as Mark Israel, Gary Allen, and Colin Thomson (2014), "The Rise and Much-Sought Demise of the Adversarial Culture in Australian Research Ethics," in Mark K. Dixon and Erich von Dietze (eds.), *Australasian Ethics Network 2013 Refereed Conference Proceedings*, 12–27. https://www.aenconference.com/uploads/AEN_Conference_2013_Proceedings.pdf

REFERENCES

Alderson, Priscilla, Mary Madden, Ann Oakley, and Ruth Wilkins. (1995). "Access and Multi-Centre Research." *Monash Bioethics Review, Ethics Committee Supplement.* 14 (4): 18–22. http://dx.doi.org/10.1007/BF03351194
Allen, Gary. (2004). "The Governance of Research Ethics: Legitimacy and Facilitating Excellent Research." Paper presented at the Australian Research Management Society Conference, 15–17 Sept., Fremantle.
– (2011). "Resourcing Practice, Not Policing Compliance: A New Role for Ethics Committees and Administrators." Paper presented at the 3rd Annual Australasian Ethics Network Conference, 15–17 Mar., Brisbane.
Australian Health Ethics Committee (2002). *Ethical and Practical Issues Concerning Ashed Bones from the Commonwealth of Australia's Strontium 90*

Program 1957–1978. Advice of the Australian Health Ethics Committee to the Commonwealth Minister for Health and Ageing, Senator the Hon. Kay Patterson, Mar.

Australian Institute of Aboriginal and Torres Strait Islander Studies (AIATSIS). (2011). *Guidelines for Ethical Research in Australian Indigenous Studies (GERAIS)*. http://aiatsis.gov.au/research/ethical-research/guidelines-ethical-research-australian-indigenous-studies

Ayres, Ian, and John Braithwaite. (1992). *Responsive Regulation: Transcending the Deregulation Debate*. Oxford: Oxford University Press.

Bamber, Greg J., and Jennifer Sappey. (2007). "Unintended Consequences of Human Research Ethics Committees: Au Revoir Workplace Studies?" *Monash Bioethics Review* 26 (3): S26–36. http://dx.doi.org/10.1007/BF03351470

Bauman, Zygmunt. (1993). *Postmodern Ethics*. Oxford: Blackwell.

Bienenstock, John. (1993). *Report of an External Review of the National Health and Medical Research Council*. Canberra: AGPS.

Bouma, Gary D., and Kristin Diemer. (1996). "Human Ethics Review and the Social Sciences: Several Emerging Ethical Issues." *Monash Bioethics Review: Ethics Committee Supplement* 15 (1): 10–16. http://dx.doi.org/10.1007/BF03351195.

Braithwaite, John, and Peter Drahos. (1999). "Ratcheting Up and Driving Down Global Regulatory Standards." *Development* 42 (4): 109–14. http://dx.doi.org/10.1057/palgrave.development.1110096

Breen, Kerry J. (2002). "Improving Australia's Ethical Review Process: Slow and Steady Wins the Race." *Monash Bioethics Review, Ethics Committee Supplement* 21 (3): S58–62. http://dx.doi.org/10.1007/BF03351276

Chalmers, Don (2001). *Research Ethics in Australia*, vol. 2, *Ethical and Policy Issues in Research Involving Human Participants*. Commissioned Papers and Staff Analysis. Bethesda: MD, National Bioethics Advisory Commission.

Chalmers, Don, and Philip Pettit. (1998). "Towards a Consensual Culture in the Ethical Review of Research." *Medical Journal of Australia*. 168 (2): 79–82.

Christie, Michael with Yiŋiya Guyula, Kathy Gotha, and Dhäŋgal Gurruwiwi. (2010). "The Ethics of Teaching from Country." *Australian Aboriginal Studies* 2: 69–80.

CIHR et al. (Canadian Institutes of Health Research, Natural Sciences and Engineering Research Council of Canada, and Social Sciences and Humanities Research Council of Canada). (1998, with 2000, 2002, 2005 amendments). *Tri-Council Policy Statement: Ethical Conduct for Research Involving Humans*. Ottawa, ON: Interagency Secretariat on Research Ethics

CIOMS (Council for International Organizations of Medical Sciences). (2002). *International Ethical Guidelines for Biomedical Research Involving Human Subjects*. Geneva: Council for International Organizations of Medical Sciences.

Cordner, Christopher, and Colin Thomson. (2007). "No Need to Go! Workplace Studies and the Resources of the Revised National Statement." *Monash Bioethics Review* 26 (3): S37–48. http://dx.doi.org/10.1007/BF03351471

Cribb, Robert. (2004). "Ethical Regulation and Humanities Research in Australia: Problems and Consequences." *Monash Bioethics Review* 23 (3): S39–57. http://dx.doi.org/10.1007/BF03351415

Cunningham, Robert, and Robert Schneider. (2001). "Anti-administration Redeeming Bureaucracy by Witnessing and Gifting." *Administrative Theory and Praxis* 23 (4 Suppl): 573–88.

Davies, Kayt. (2011). "Journalism and HRECs: From Square Pegs to Squeaky Wheels." *Pacific Journalism Review* 17 (1): 157–74.

Dodds, Susan. (2000). "Human Research Ethics in Australia: Ethical Regulation and Public Policy." *Monash Bioethics Review, Ethics Committee Supplement* 19 (2): S4–21. http://dx.doi.org/10.1007/BF03351236

– (2002). "Is the Australian HREC System Sustainable?" *Monash Bioethics Review, Ethics Committee Supplement* 21 (3): S43–57. http://dx.doi.org/10.1007/BF03351274

Dodds, Susan, Rebecca Albury, and Colin Thomson. (1994). *Ethical Research and Ethics Committee Review of Social and Behavioural Research Proposals*. Report to the Department of Human Services and Health. Canberra: Commonwealth Department of Human Services and Health.

Dyck, Murray, and Gary Allen. (2012). "Is Mandatory Research Ethics Reviewing Ethical?" *Journal of Medical Ethics*. http://dx.doi.org/10.1136/medethics-2011-100274.

Economic and Social Research Council. (2005). *Research Ethics Framework*. Swindon: Economic and Social Research Council.

Fitzgerald, Maureen, and Elisa Yule. (2004). "Open and Closed Committees." *Monash Bioethics Review, Ethics Committee Supplement*. 23 (2): S35–49. http://dx.doi.org/10.1007/BF03351411

Gillam, Lynn. (1993). "But Is This Really a Matter for the Ethics Committee?" *Monash Bioethics Review, Ethics Committee Supplement* 12 (2): 9–14.

Gillam, Lynn, Marilys Guillemin, and Doreen Rosenthal. (2006). "'Obstructive and Power Hungry'?: The Australian Research Ethics Review Process." *Monash Bioethics Review* 25 (2): S30–8. http://dx.doi.org/10.1007/BF03351452

Gillam, Lynn, Marilys Guillemin, Annie Bolitho, and Doreen Rosenthal. (2009). "Human Research Ethics in Practice: Deliberative Strategies, Processes and Perceptions." *Monash Bioethics Review* 28 (1): 34–50. http://dx.doi.org/10.1007/BF03351308

Grabosky, Peter. (1995). "Counterproductive Regulation." *International Journal of the Sociology of Law* 23 (4): 347–69. http://dx.doi.org/10.1016/S0194-6595(05)80003-6

Griffith University. (2003). "Research Ethics Review: Internal Review." Unpublished report to Griffith University, Brisbane, 1 Aug. 2003

Guillemin, Marilys, Lynn Gillam, Doreen Rosenthal, and Annie Bolitho. (2012). "Human Research Ethics Committees: Examining their Roles and Practices." *Journal of Empirical Research on Human Research Ethics* 7 (3): 38–49. http://dx.doi.org/10.1525/jer.2012.7.3.38

Haggerty, Kevin D. (2004). "Ethics Creep: Governing Social Science Research in the Name of Ethics." *Qualitative Sociology* 27 (4): 391–414. http://dx.doi.org/10.1023/B:QUAS.0000049239.15922.a3

Hamilton, Ann. (2002). *Institutional Review Boards: Politics, Power, Purpose and Process in a Regulatory Organization.* Doctoral dissertation, University of Oklahoma.

– (2005). "The Development and Operation of IRBs: Medical Regulations and Social Science." *Journal of Applied Communication Research* 33 (3): 189–203. http://dx.doi.org/10.1080/00909880500149353

Israel, Mark. (2004). *Ethics and the Governance of Criminological Research in Australia.* Sydney: New South Wales Bureau of Crime Statistics and Research.

– (2015). *Research Ethics and Integrity for Social Scientists: Beyond Regulatory Compliance.* London: Sage.

Israel, Mark, and Iain Hay. (2006). *Research Ethics for Social Scientists: Between Ethical Conduct and Regulatory Compliance.* London: Sage.

Jamrozik, Konrad, and Marlene Kolybaba. (1999). "Are Ethics Committees Retarding the Improvement of Health Services in Australia?" *Medical Journal of Australia* 170 (1): 26–8.

Johnson, Helen. (2004). "Investigating the Dilemmas of Ethical Social Research." *Journal of International Women's Studies* 6 (1): 41–53.

Komesaroff, Paul A. (2002). "Response to Susan Dodds: Is the Australian HREC System Sustainable?" *Monash Bioethics Review, Ethics Committee Supplement.* 21 (3): S68–71. http://dx.doi.org/10.1007/BF03351279

Langlois, Anthony J. (2011). "Political Research and Human Research Ethics Committees." *Australian Journal of Political Science* 46 (1): 141–56. http://dx.doi.org/10.1080/10361146.2010.544287

Malouff, John M., and Nicola S. Schutte. (2005). ""Academic Psychologists" Perspectives on the Human Research Ethics Review Process.'" *Australian Psychologist* 40 (1): 57–62. http://dx.doi.org/10.1080/00050060512331317166

McNeill, Paul M. (1993). *The Ethics and Politics of Human Experimentation.* Cambridge: Cambridge University Press.

– (2002). "Research Ethics Review and the Bureaucracy." *Monash Bioethics Review, Ethics Committee Supplement* 21 (3): S72–3. http://dx.doi.org/10.1007/BF03351280

McNeill, Paul M., Catherine A. Berglund, and Ian W. Webster. (1990). "Reviewing the Reviewers: A Survey of Institutional Ethics Committees in Australia." *Medical Journal of Australia* 152 (6): 289–96.

– (1994). "How Much Influence do Various Members Have within Research Ethics Committees?" *Cambridge Quarterly of Healthcare Ethics* 3 (4): 522–32. http://dx.doi.org/10.1017/S0963180100005405

NHMRC (National Health and Medical Research Council). (1996). *Review of the Role and Functioning of Institutional Ethics Committees. Report to the Minister for Health and Family Services.* Canberra: Australian Government.

– (1999). *National Statement on Ethical Conduct in Research Involving Humans.* Canberra: Australian Government.

– (2004). *Report of the 2002–2003 HREC Annual Report Process.* Canberra: Australian Government.

– (2007). *National Statement on Ethical Conduct in Human Research.* Canberra: Australian Government.

Parker, Malcolm, Jim Holt, Graeme Turner, and Jack Broerse. (2003). "Ethics of Research Involving Humans: Uniform Processes for Disparate Categories?" *Monash Bioethics Review, Ethics Committee Supplement* 22 (3): S50–65. http://dx.doi.org/10.1007/BF03351397

Pettit, Philip. (1992). "Instituting a Research Ethic: Chilling and Cautionary Tales." *Bioethics News* 6 (2): 89–112. http://dx.doi.org/10.1111/j.1467-8519.1992.tb00189.x

Schrag, Zachary M. (2009). "Macquarie's Innovative Ethics Training." *Institutional Review Blog.* 17 April.

– (2010). *Ethical Imperialism: Institutional Review Boards and the Social Sciences, 1965–2009.* Baltimore: Johns Hopkins University Press.

Senate Community Affairs References Committee. (2004). *Forgotten Australians. Senate Community Affairs References Committee Report.* Canberra: Australian Parliament.

Singapore Statement on Research Integrity. (2010). Statement Prepared for Second World Conference on Research Integrity, 21–4 July 2010.

316   Mark Israel, Gary Allen, and Colin Thomson

Taverner Research Company. (2002). *NHMRC Stakeholder Evaluation 2002: Human Research Ethics Committees*. Canberra: Department of Health and Aging.

Thomas, David P. (2004). *Reading Doctors' Writing*. Canberra: Aboriginal Studies Press.

van den Hoonaard, Will C. (2013a). "The "Ethics Rupture" Summit, Fredericton, New Brunswick, Canada, October 25–28, 2012." *Journal of Empirical Research on Human Research Ethics* 8 (1): 3–7. http://dx.doi.org/10.1525/jer.2013.8.1.3

– (2013b). "The Social and Policy Contexts of the New Brunswick Declaration on Research Ethics, Integrity, and Governance: A Commentary." *Journal of Empirical Research on Human Research Ethics* 8 (2): 104–9. http://dx.doi.org/10.1525/jer.2013.8.2.104

16 Ethical Pluralism: Scholarly Societies and the Regulation of Research Ethics

ZACHARY M. SCHRAG

Kristen Perry wanted to do the right thing. "As an emerging researcher," she explained, "I at first was quite naïve about research ethics; without much critical thought, I accepted the ethical requirements set out by federal regulations and as applied by my institution. However, when one Sudanese youth refused to participate in my first study – simply because I was required to change his name, when he wanted to be identified – I began to question the appropriateness of ethical guidelines for research that are regularized and codified through university IRBs [Institutional Review Boards]" (Perry, 2011: 899). Eventually, she became interested enough in the problem to analyse IRB requirements at 32 research-intensive institutions. She found that "a strong orientation toward medical and experimental models of research" affects even those universities that have separate "nonmedical" IRBs (905).

As we consider alternatives to the present system of ethics review, we must ask how to move the promotion of research ethics beyond the medical orientation identified by Perry and so many other researchers in the humanities and social sciences. One possibility would be to find a greater role for professional scholarly associations. Associations know more about the ethics of particular forms of research than do national regulatory bodies. Yet, they generally lack power of enforcement. Shifting greater oversight responsibilities to these associations would mean rebuilding research ethics as a system based on trust.

The Claim of Universal Applicability

Today's system of research ethics review rests on the premise that a common set of ethical principles exists that are equally appropriate to any inquiry that requires human interaction, whether it takes the form of ethnography, surveys, psychological experiments, installing medical devices, dispensing drugs, or conducting cutting-edge genetic manipulation.

This premise was codified in 1978, when the US National Commission for the Protection of Human Subjects of Biomedical and Behavioral Research published its *Belmont Report*. That report recommended that research proposals be vetted for adequate informed consent, an "assessment of risk and benefits," and "fair procedures and outcomes in the selection of research subjects" (National Commission, 1979: 16, 18). The Commission based these requirements on the premise that "three basic principles, among those generally accepted in our cultural tradition, are particularly relevant to the ethics of research involving human subjects: the principles of respect for persons, beneficence and justice." By asserting that these principles are "relevant" to a category as large and unqualified as "research involving human subjects," this statement set a precedent for later assertions of a universal set of principles of research ethics (National Commission, 1979: 4).

One can understand the appeal of such an assertion. As ethicist Robert Veatch wrote in 1981, the "condition of universal applicability is so central to ethics that it is often incorporated into the very notion of what ethics means. When someone claims that a particular behavior in a particular circumstance is unethical, he is making a claim that he believes should be accepted in principle by everybody" (113).

Moreover, the 1970s were a particularly good time to be sceptical of the alternative to a universal ethics: a set of ethics established by specific groups of experts. In the wake of the Vietnam War, Watergate, and scandals involving research – most notoriously brought to light in 1972 concerning the Tuskegee Syphilis Study– Americans were looking for ways to rein in, not empower, alleged experts. As Veatch (1975) noted, the trend in research ethics review policy had been to give more and more authority to laypeople. A 1973 proposal – not implemented – would have limited researchers to one-third of the seats on an ethics review board, making an Institutional Review Board more like a jury of reasonable but inexpert citizens rather than an expert peer-review panel. And the US Congress confined researchers to a minority of the membership (5 of 11) on the National Commission itself. If research were to be governed by citizens, rather than researchers, it made all the more sense to establish universal principles that all citizens could accept.

In subsequent decades, policymakers have clung to the idea of a universal research ethics. Canada's *Tri-Council Policy Statement: Ethical Conduct for Research Involving Humans* rests on the belief that "three core principles – Respect for Persons, Concern for Welfare, and Justice ... transcend disciplinary boundaries and, therefore, are relevant to the full range of research covered by this Policy" (CIHR et al., 2010: 8). Similarly, the US Presidential Commission for the Study of Bioethical Issues (2011) asserted that current federal rules "reflect widely accepted principles of ethics ... rooted in longstanding values that find expression in many sources of moral philosophy; theological traditions; and codes, regulations, and rules." The Commission conceded, "Medical research that poses risk of physical injury rightly raises more concerns than does routine social survey research, for example." But it insisted, "The same ethical principles govern all of these activities, and serve as enduring guideposts that must not be ignored" (3).

Institutions also promote the idea of a universal research ethics. Almost every college and university in the United States that receives federal funds for human subjects research (HSR), for example, embraces the *Belmont Report* as its statement of ethics. And hundreds of those institutions require faculty and student researchers to complete the Collaborative Institutional Training Initiative (CITI) program, an online training system that also asserts a universality of ethical principles. "Researchers in the social and behavioral sciences and humanities attest, correctly, that the development of the regulations was driven by abuses in biomedical research," CITI concedes. "However, the current regulations reflect and embody the ethical principles described in the *Belmont Report* and these principles have broad applicability" (Bankert et al., n.d.).

Some scholars applaud such moves, arguing that disciplines can learn from each others' ethical standards (Aagaard-Hansen and Johansen, 2008). But what if some citizens – and researchers – object to a proposed ethical standard? Veatch (1981) noted that if people reject a purported universal claim, "they have either misunderstood the facts, are thinking of a somewhat different circumstance, or have made an error in moral judgment" (113) That is, either they are stupid, morally obtuse, or they know something the ethicist does not.

Unsurprisingly, critics of the ethics review system claim to belong to the third category. Researchers in public health, quality improvement, and the social sciences argue that they have ethical duties that do not always match those embraced by biomedical researchers. Serious ethical reflection, not ethical obtuseness, has led them to rebel.

Anthropologist Rena Lederman (2007) expresses the problem with particular eloquence: "The consistency-seeking logic of bureaucratic oversight persistently refuses to recognize diverse professional ethical standards *as ethical*, suspecting them instead of self-interest. However, readers should not confuse the simulation of compliance with cynicism on the part of researchers concerning their own actual ethical practice: *far from it*. It is, however, this very chasm between regulatory ethics (as too often enacted in IRB reviews) and the divergent practical realities of principled, upstanding research in this or that field that has led to widespread cynicism concerning IRBs" (315).

In her musings about what institutional structures might better recognize the legitimacy of diverse standards and practices, Lederman (2007) notes that "disciplinary communities ... have – in part through their professional associations – long-standing although certainly imperfect histories of active concern for and engagement around ethical research practice" (322).

Indeed, professional associations have played uneven roles in the development and operation of policies for protecting human subjects of research. In the United States and the United Kingdom, associations representing the humanities and social sciences have struggled to be heard, while in Canada they have had more success (Schrag, 2010; Stanley and Wise, 2010; Palys and Lowman, 2011; van den Hoonaard, 2011). It may be useful to consider the ways in which associations can be most helpful.

Articulating Ethical Pluralism

Scholarly associations have for decades worked to articulate ethical standards. They have done this not so much to shape public policy – for that outcome is uncertain at best – but to help their members act in ways that will bring credit to their disciplines and satisfy researchers' own consciences.

The most visible efforts are the publication of ethics codes, some of which have been in place for five decades, originating during the same time that the United States government was beginning to require research ethics review. These codes sometimes summarize proper behaviour in a few simple phrases. A draft code circulated by the American Anthropological Association (AAA), for example, promised "core principles ... expressed as concise statements which can be easily remembered for use by anthropologists in their everyday professional lives" (AAA, 2012).

In practice, it is unlikely that many scholars memorize or carry around laminated copies of these codes to be consulted in moments of moral doubt. And some of their most useful sections may concern mundane professional norms – such as the difference between a work that is "forthcoming" and one that is "in press" – rather than agonizing moral dilemmas. Yet these codes can do important work in helping researchers think about the ethics of their profession.

Some of the benefit comes from the very process of crafting a code. For example, the Linguistic Society of America (2008) has hosted a robust online discussion of the proposition that "linguists have a responsibility to protect and respect their research participants." Commenters have explored the possible meanings of such a statement in various contexts. Does an armchair researcher working with published texts have the same responsibilities as someone doing fieldwork? Can the approval of a community be solicited when one is recording the language of an emigrant from that community?

Another striking recent example is the decision by the American Anthropological Association (2010, 2011a) to solicit comments by posting draft principles on a blog. Not all principles received equal attention. The proposition, "There is an ethical dimension to all our professional relationships," received only two comments, neither substantial. But earlier and meatier propositions (especially the first, "Do no harm") provoked dozens of thoughtful comments. For those who do not know what they think till they see what they say, being prodded to write such comments is itself a benefit.

Yet the American Anthropological Association comments also revealed sharp disagreements among anthropologists about some basic premises, exposing the diversity of circumstances that exist even within a broadly defined scholarly discipline. Several commentators embraced the proposed principle of "do no harm," or some variant, such as "intend no harm." But others pointed out that in a world of conflict, helping one person often means harming another. "Do no harm is fine as a principle of medical practice," wrote Murray Leaf, "where you are working with a single individual. It is nearly meaningless when you (we) work with human communities, in which what is good and what is harm is usually in contention. As some of these posts suggests, what we do is often a matter of helping some while undermining the position of others. No harm at all, in such a context, would almost always be also no help at all – and no effect at all" (AAA, 2010).

Such disagreements cast doubt on the very idea of a disciplinary ethics code. As Patty Gray commented on the AAA blog,

> The circumstances of anthropological research done for corporate or marketing purposes is going to involve a slightly different set of ethical issues than anthropological research done for the purpose of discovering new knowledge about human beings and their lived experience, and sharing that knowledge in venues such as teaching, scholarly publications and academic conferences, popular communication (non-academic writing, public lectures, etc.). If you try to mix together these rather different "flavours," you are just going to get a mess that no one can swallow. I would rather see you serve them all up with their own individual integrity and let their nuances show through. (AAA, 2010)

Professional organizations have embraced such nuances in other contexts. For example, the American Historical Association, the National Council on Public History, and the Organization of American Historians have called on departments and institutions to recognize the variety of forms – not just books and articles, but museum exhibits, work at historic sites, new media, and the like – when making decisions about promotion and tenure. One can imagine similar acceptance of diversity for research ethics, though the result would bear little resemblance to the *Belmont Report*.

One long-standing grievance among social scientists is the concept of informed consent embedded in the *Belmont Report* and comparable documents based on biomedical ethics. Many social researchers have complained that formal criteria and procedures for obtaining informed consent – as expressed, for example, in 45 Code of Federal Regulations 46.116 (1991, the "Common Rule") – can destroy needed rapport between researcher and participant and can effectively silence those defined as "vulnerable" because they do not conform to an imagined norm. For some recent examples, see Mustanski (2011), Perry (2011), Ritterbusch (2012), and Swauger (2011).

Professional associations can help amplify these concerns. For example, 22 research organizations made submissions in response to proposed changes to US regulations for ethics review, which resulted in the *Social and Behavioral Science White Paper on Advanced Notice for Proposed Rulemaking (ANPRM)*, published by the American Educational Research Association (AERA, 2011). The *Social and Behavioral Science White Paper* notes that "current regulations as well as the proposed changes continue to assume a one-dimensional mental model of written consent at one point in time," and recommend that revised rules "set forth what needs to be accomplished through the consent process and the alternative approaches to obtaining meaningful consent, rather than emphasizing the default of written forms as the requirement" (AERA, 2011).

A more delicate issue concerns critical inquiry: the notion that some researchers *deliberately* harm those they study, for example, by exposing wrongdoing. As political scientist Anthony Langlois (2011) has written, "For a series of types of political research (and indeed for other activities which today are increasingly counted as research outputs when they are engaged in by academics, such as journalism), causing harm (or at least discomfort) may be the whole point of the exercise." He offers such examples as "research about political corruption, human rights abuses, the influence of unions or industry barons over policy, branch stacking, political intrigue, and so on" (150).

Professional associations have been wary about being so blunt, though the Oral History Association website does feature Linda Shopes's (2007) essay contending that "historians' deepest responsibility is to follow the evidence where it leads, to discern and make sense of the past in all its complexity; not necessarily to protect individuals. In this we are more like journalists and unlike medical professionals, who are indeed enjoined to do no harm." For social policy research, argue Paul Spicker and David Byrne (2010), "the ethical objective is not to minimise avoidable harm; it is to ensure that any adverse consequences will be legitimate and defensible" (13).

The second edition of the Canadian *Tri-Council Policy Statement: Ethical Conduct for Research Involving Humans* (CIHR et al., 2010) fudges this issue. On the one hand, it states, "Researchers and REBs [Research Ethics Boards] should aim to protect the welfare of participants, and, in some circumstances, to promote that welfare in view of any foreseeable risks associated with the research." Yet – presumably addressing projects like those mentioned by Langlois – it also acknowledges, "Some research, involving critical assessments of public, political or corporate institutions and associated public figures, for example, may be legitimately critical and/or opposed to the welfare of those individuals in a position of power, and may cause them some harm ... Such research should be carried out according to the professional standards of the relevant discipline(s) or field(s) of research." Thus, the *Tri-Council Policy Statement* effectively relies on professional bodies to articulate standards that complicate its own sweeping claims.

Telling Stories

The American Anthropological Association also suggests in its discussions another role for professional organizations as sources of an alternate form of ethical guidance, one relying less on abstract, prescriptive codes and more on examples and storytelling. In the course of debating "do no harm," researchers discussed work they and colleagues had done with American Indians, Iraqi sheiks, and Muslim Thais, among other groups, and used those experiences to weigh the utility of the proposed principle. "I work," wrote sociologist Bryan Bruns, "in conjunction with communities and a government agency, to design and support a process in which communities are likely to, in a reasonably democratic way, act to restrain the behavior and thereby reduce the benefits of a few people (upstream irrigators, large landowners) who currently take advantage of others, it's not clear how a principle of 'do no harm' would allow any practical engagement" (quoted in AAA, 2010).

Criminologist Michael Rowe (2007) agrees about the need for specificity. "It is the nature of ethnographic research that the principles contained in methodological textbooks or professional codes of conduct will be stretched and perhaps distorted as they are applied in dynamic situations," he writes. "If an absolute code of ethics is not feasible, researchers must be prepared to be reflexive in terms of ethical dilemmas and the methodological difficulties experienced in securing informed consent and meaningful access to research subjects" (48).

One means to such reflexivity is the telling of stories. People have been using stories to encourage ethical reflection and behaviour since before Jesus told his first parable, and law schools and business schools have for decades used cases to teach professional reasoning. Since at least the 1970s, some instructors of practical ethics have used cases to raise students' ethical sensitivity, knowledge, judgment, and will power, according to Michael Davis (1997).

Stories of research with human participants can be particularly compelling, especially when they describe relationships that develop over time and overflow the boundaries of research alone. Historians Tracy K'Meyer and Glenn Crothers (2007) have written about arguments they had with a woman in her late 80s about which subjects should be discussed in a recorded interview. Leila Rupp and Verta Taylor (2011), professors of feminist studies, have explained "the benefits and ethical dilemmas of going back or staying in the field" – i.e., keeping in close touch with the people they have studied once the initial research is complete – by telling the story of their evolving friendship with a group of Florida drag queens. In a heartfelt narrative, anthropologist Jonathan Stillo (2011a) has described getting a Facebook message from the mother of a young woman he had interviewed before her early death from tuberculosis; what should he tell the mother about her daughter's "life full of sickness and suffering"?

These narratives do not offer easy answers, and they often cast doubt on the formalized procedures of regulatory ethics. "I think at this point we have a system of ethics approval which is designed by clinicians and enforced by lawyers for the protection of hospital and university endowments in a litigious society," laments Stillo (2011b). "It is the worst of possible worlds." Geographer Amy Ritterbusch (2012), after describing in moving terms her efforts to offer lasting help to the people she studies, concludes, "Although well intentioned, 45 CFR 46 [the core US regulation] is a bureaucratic discourse that positions youth in problematic ways and is out of place in the world of Bogotana street girls" (18).

Putting aside for the moment debates about the future of scholarly publishing, scholarly associations' journals, newsletters, and other publications offer researchers the chance to record and disseminate such stories and ethical reflections (and to get credit from hiring and promotion committees for doing so). Some associations have gone further, collecting case studies into volumes for easy reference (APA, 1973). A task force of the American Anthropological Association, which published such a book in 1987, has proposed that a new collection be produced and periodically updated (AAA, 2011c).

Stories are helpful in educating both novice and experienced researchers in research ethics – if they are the right stories. The standardized CITI training required by many universities, for example, offers cautionary tales of alleged misbehaviour. When written by people who lack nuanced understanding of the dilemmas involved, such training can infuriate rather than educate. As one psychologist noted of the market-leading CITI program, "the attempt to create some sort of parallelism in the presentation (Tuskegee = Milgram? Nazis = Zimbardo?) is inaccurate and misguided, and does a disservice to the legacy of important social/behavioral research" (Srivastava, 2009).

But the same format can work well when used by scholars attuned to disciplinary norms. In 2009, ethnographers at Macquarie University in Australia created an online module called "Human Research Ethics for the Social Sciences and Humanities." Portions of the training system recapitulate the largely irrelevant history of medical research ethics that form the core of more standardized curricula. But the module also offers stories of dilemmas faced in recent years by ethnographers. And rather than demand simplistic multiple-choice answers, it often asks readers to reflect on the possibilities. "Say you are doing research on cigarette smoking," it asks, "but as you talk to the smokers, they start telling you about the illicit drugs they use. What do you do?" (Wynn et al., 2009)

At Princeton University, historians Angela Creager and John Haldon (2011) designed a two-day course on research ethics – including human subjects issues – for graduate students in history and the history of science. Publications of the American Historical Association (AHA) were one source among many used in the seminar. So were detailed accounts of specific controversies, such as historians' testimony in lawsuits about tobacco liability and sex discrimination. The American Historical Association played a further role by publicizing the course in its magazine, *Perspectives on History* (Creager and Haldon, 2011).

De-emphasizing Enforcement

Devolving ethical oversight to scholarly associations would come at a cost. For one thing, it would require work by the leadership of those associations to compile stories and guidance. (Some of this could be done in time saved not fighting the expansionist ethics review system.) More significantly, though, embracing pluralism would mean de-emphasizing the enforceability of ethical standards. If a question has many right answers, it is harder to punish someone for making the wrong choice.

Some advocates of ethics codes – whether established by governments or scholarly bodies – see them largely in terms of enforcement. As Joan Cassell and Sue-Ellen Jacobs (1987) explain, "On occasion, the concept of 'ethics' is used as a weapon: my beliefs differ from yours, therefore you are unethical. Anthropologists who speak of ethics in this sense wish to improve or, at the least, reprove the behavior of others. A 'Code of Ethics' in their view is a mechanism to help regulate the behavior of those with whom they disagree."

Some scholars today hold this attitude. "Is there no way that a new ethics code can be enforced?" asked Les Sponsel of the draft code of the American Anthropological Association: "Otherwise, what percentage of the membership pays any attention?" (AAA, 2011b). Barry Bainton went further, saying, "If the profession or its authorized representative which imposes the code on its members is unwilling to enforce the code and/or to back its members by defending them in court if necessary to uphold the code, then the ethical code is a sham" (quoted in AAA, 2011a).

Such critics have a pessimistic view of human nature; they might consider other situations in which people willingly embrace unenforceable standards. Each year Americans leave tips in restaurants, taxis, etc. totalling an estimated $42 billion, though it is only custom – not law – at play here (Templin, 2008). But sceptics are also drawing on the examples of such professions as law, medicine, and engineering, in which serious misconduct can lead to the revocation of a licence to practice.

In fall 2000, Sponsel and a fellow anthropologist, Terry Turner, encouraged the American Anthropological Association to investigate allegations that geneticist James Neel and anthropologist Napoleon Chagnon had committed various atrocities while studying the Yanomami of Venezuela. Sidestepping its ethics code's statement that the American Anthropological Association "does not adjudicate claims for unethical behavior," the Association established a task force to conduct an "inquiry" into "charges" against Neel and Chagnon. In part because it lacked clear procedures for conducting an investigation, the task force mishandled its assignment, failing even to invite Chagnon to defend himself. In 2005, the AAA membership voted to rescind the Association's acceptance of the task force report (AAA, 1998; Dreger, 2011).

No comparable scandal led the American Historical Association – around the same time – to end its 15-year experiment in adjudicating formal complaints against its members. Rather, the AHA Council found that the process of responding to complaints had been "complicated and time-consuming" yet "had virtually no public impact on the profession" (AHA, 2003). The Society of American Archivists (2009) has pointed to that experience in deciding to keep its own code "aspirational."

But just because professional organizations *themselves* have disavowed enforcement does not mean that their standards are unenforceable; institutions – particularly universities – have relied on disciplinary standards when investigating claims of research misconduct (not necessarily involving human subjects) by faculty members.

For example, universities have relied on the AHA's *Statement on Standards on Professional Conduct* (http://www.historians.org/pubs/free/ProfessionalStandards.cfm) to evaluate researchers' behaviour.

In 2002, Emory University commissioned a committee of outside scholars to investigate charges that Professor Michael Bellesiles had engaged in "intentional fabrication or falsification of research data" while writing his controversial 2000 book, *Arming America: The Origins of a National Gun Culture*. Finding Emory's own statement of Policies and Procedures to be "basically designed for the investigation of alleged misconduct in the life and physical sciences," the investigating committee instead relied on the standards set forth by the American Historical Association in its determination that Bellesiles had fallen short of professional norms (Katz et al., 2002). Technically, this determination was not an act of enforcement, but Bellesiles resigned his post not long after the investigative report was published (Emory University, 2002). Thus, by articulating the standards expected of its members, the American Historical Association had helped hold one of its members accountable. In a less visible, more recent case, an Arizona State University committee consulted the AHA standards when investigating allegations of plagiarism by a history professor there (Ryman, 2012).

One problem with this hybrid model – in which an association establishes standards but the university does the investigation – is that scholars sometimes work together in interdisciplinary teams. Whose ethics shall rule? It strikes me that this is not so great a challenge. Outside universities, different professionals – such as lawyers and accountants – frequently collaborate yet remain bound to their specific professional codes.

A greater problem may be that not all professors are members of a scholarly association with an ethics code. For example, Robin Mathy has repeatedly accused Michael Bailey of the Northwestern University Department of Psychology of violating the code of ethics of the American Psychological Association (Mathy, 2008; see also Svitek, 2011). Does it matter that Bailey is not a member of that Association?

An even trickier and more notorious case concerns Ward Churchill, a professor of ethnic studies at the University of Colorado, Boulder, who was accused of various acts of research misconduct (none concerning human subjects research). The university required all of its researchers to meet the standards of the National Science Foundation – whether or not they were engaged in science. The NSF standards, in turn, defined research misconduct as "a significant departure from accepted practices of the relevant research community" (Colorado Conference of the American Association of University Professors, 2012: 55). But what was the relevant research community in Churchill's case? An investigative committee noted the lack of a "statement of shared standards for the field of ethnic studies" and reasoned that "since the allegations considered here are in large part historical" it should use the American Historical Association's Statement on Standards of Professional Conduct (University of Colorado, Boulder, 2006: 10). Churchill objected: "I'm an Ethnic Studies scholar. I always have been." Indeed, he argued that ethnic studies had emerged to challenge the "the white supremacist triumphalism of the consensus narrative" that, he suggested, the AHA had helped perpetuate (Churchill, 2008: n216).

Such disagreement about appropriate standards is bad enough in a case of alleged plagiarism and fabrication, and it would be worse in a case involving allegations of improper treatment of research participants. If we do not want all scholars to be judged by the medical ethics of the *Belmont Report*, yet not all scholars belong to disciplinary societies with clear codes of conduct concerning research with people, how do we hold scholars to account?

One possibility would be for universities to broaden the list of ethics codes they recognize. Current regulations in the United States require institutions receiving federal human research funds to adopt "a statement of principles governing the institution in the discharge of its responsibilities for protecting the rights and welfare of human subjects of research conducted at or sponsored by the institution" (45 CFR 46.103). Though the regulations offer flexibility – even allowing institutions to formulate their own statements – in practice almost every US institution adopts the *Belmont Report* to meet this requirement.

Under present rules, universities could instead list several codes – *Belmont*, the anthropologists' code, the linguists' code, the historians' code, the participatory action research code, etc. – while still insisting that every affiliated researcher adhere to at least one. This would require both traditional scholars affiliated with organizations and non-traditional scholars like Churchill to articulate their responsibility to the people with whom they interact, without expecting them to follow all the procedures – and embrace all the values – of medical experimenters. Columbia University has pioneered this approach, freeing oral history projects from the jurisdiction of Institutional Review Boards but demanding that they adhere to the guidelines of the Oral History Association (Columbia University, 2007). Similarly, universities could accept a list of recognized curricula – including those developed by professional organizations – rather than the CITI program now commonly used.

A more important step is to move away from reliance on threats. Scott Burris (2008) has proposed, "Depriv[ing] IRBs of the power to independently stop or alter a study at all, placing a burden on the IRB to make a case for changes to a higher authority (such as a university administrator). Such constraints would, in practical terms, require the IRB to persuade the investigator through discussion that a study had ethical problems. This would not only be likely to reduce erroneous changes but also give the researcher the opportunity to take part in ethical deliberation as an autonomous agent" (70).

Similarly, Greg Koski, former director of the US Office of Human Research Protections has called for a shift to "a paradigm of professionalism," relying on education and certification, rather than prior restraint of proposals, to protect the rights and welfare of research participants (Dahl, 2012).

By articulating standards, collecting stories, and crafting ethics curricula, professional organizations could promote ethical research without entering the morass of pseudo-judicial investigations. To do so, they will need policymakers who welcome them as partners rather than regarding them as intruders.

REFERENCES

Aagaard-Hansen, Jens, and Maria Vang Johansen. (2008). "Research Ethics across Disciplines." *Anthropology Today* 24 (3): 15–19. http://dx.doi. org/10.1111/j.1467-8322.2008.00585.x

AAA (American Anthropological Association). (1998). *Code of Ethics of the American Anthropological Association*. http://www.aaanet.org/issues/policy-advocacy/upload/ethicscode.pdf

– (2010). *Ethics Task Force – Draft Principle: Do No Harm*. http://blog.aaanet. org/ethics-task-force/ethics-task-force-first-principle/

– (2011a). *Ethics Task Force – Draft Principle: Balance the Responsibility*. http:// blog.aaanet.org/ethics-task-force/ethics-task-force-fourth-draft-principle/

– (2011b). *Complete Draft Principles Released by Ethics Task Force*. http://blog. aaanet.org/2011/06/30/complete-draft-principles-released-by-ethics-task-force/

–(2011c). *Final Report of the Task Force for Comprehensive Ethics Review*. http:// www.aaanet.org/cmtes/ethics/upload/AAA-ETF-Final-Report.pdf

– (2012). *Principles of Professional Responsibility*. http://ethics.aaanet.org/ ethics-statement-0-preamble/

AERA (American Educational Research Association). (2011). *Social and Behavioral Science White Paper on Advanced Notice for Proposed Rulemaking (ANPRM)*. http://www.regulations.gov/#!documentDetail;D=HHS-OPHS-2011-0005-1102

AHA (American Historical Association). (2003). "Press Release: AHA Announces Changes in Efforts Relating to Professional Misconduct." 3 May. http://www.historians.org/press/PR_Adjudication.htm

APA (American Psychological Association). (1973). *Ethical Principles in the Conduct of Research with Human Participants. American Psychologist* 28 (1): 79–80.

Bankert, Elizabeth, et al. (n.d.) "History and Ethical Principles – SBR." *CITI Program*, www.citiprogram.org

Bellesiles, Michael A. (2000). *Arming America: The Origins of a National Gun Culture*. New York: Knopf.

Burris, Scott. (2008). "Regulatory Innovation in the Governance of Human Subjects Research: A Cautionary Tale and Some Modest Proposals." *Regulation & Governance* 2 (1): 65–84. http://dx.doi.org/10.1111/j.1748-5991.2007.00025.x

Cassell, Joan, and Sue-Ellen Jacobs (eds.). (1987). *Handbook on Ethical Issues in Anthropology*. American Anthropological Association. http://www.aaanet.org/committees/ethics/toc.htm.

Churchill, Ward. (2008). "The Myth of Academic Freedom: Experiencing the Application of Liberal Principle in a Neoconservative Era." *Works and Days*. 26/27 (51/52,53/54).

CIHR et al. (Canadian Institutes of Health Research, Natural Sciences and Engineering Research Council of Canada, and Social Sciences and Humanities Research Council of Canada). (2010). *Tri-Council Policy Statement: Ethical Conduct for Research Involving Humans*. 2nd ed. Ottawa: Interagency Panel on Research Ethics. http://www.pre.ethics.gc.ca/eng/policy-politique/initiatives/tcps2-eptc2/Default/

Colorado Conference of the American Association of University Professors. (2012). "Report on the Termination of Ward Churchill." *AAUP Journal of Academic Freedom* 3 (1).

Columbia University. (2007). *Columbia University Institutional Review Board Policy: IRB Review of Oral History Projects*. http://www.columbia.edu/cu/irb/policies/documents/OralHistoryPolicy.FINAL.012308.pdf

Creager, Angela N.H., and John F. Haldon. (2011). "Designing a Responsible Conduct of Research Course for Historians." *Perspectives on History* (Nov.).

Dahl, Dick. (2012)."The Future of Human Subjects Research Regulation." *Harvard Law Today*. July. http://today.law.harvard.edu/the-future-of-human-subjects-research-regulation/

Davis, Michael. (1997). "Developing and Using Cases to Teach Practical Ethics." *Teaching Philosophy* 20 (4): 353–85. http://dx.doi.org/10.5840/teachphil199720445

Dreger, Alice. (2011). "Darkness's Descent on the American Anthropological Association: A Cautionary Tale." *Human Nature (Hawthorne, NY)* 22 (3): 225–46. http://dx.doi.org/10.1007/s12110-011-9103-y

Emory University. (2002). "Oct. 25: Michael Bellesiles Resigns from Emory Faculty." http://www.emory.edu/news/Releases/bellesiles1035563546.html

K'Meyer, Tracy E., and A. Glenn Crothers. (2007). "'If I See Some of This in Writing, I'm Going to Shoot You': Reluctant Narrators, Taboo Topics, and the Ethical Dilemmas of the Oral Historian." *Oral History Review* 34 (1): 71–93. http://dx.doi.org/10.1525/ohr.2007.34.1.71

Katz, Stanley N., Hannah H. Gray, and Laurel Ulrich. (2002). *Report of the Investigative Committee in the Matter of Professor Michael Bellesiles.* Emory University. http://www.emory.edu/news/Releases/Final_Report.pdf

Langlois, Anthony J. (2011). "Political Research and Human Research Ethics Committees." *Australian Journal of Political Science* 46 (1): 141–56. http://dx.doi.org/10.1080/10361146.2010.544287

Lederman, Rena. (2007). "Comparative Research: A Modest Proposal Concerning the Object of Ethics Regulation." *PoLAR: Political and Legal Anthropology Review* 30 (2): 305–27. http://dx.doi.org/10.1525/pol.2007.30.2.305

Linguistic Society of America. (2008). "2. Responsibility to Those We Study." *LSA Ethics Discussion Blog.* 28 July. https://lsaethics.wordpress.com/2008/07/28/2-responsibility-to-those-we-study/

Mathy, Robin M. (2008). "Cowboys, Sheepherders, and 'The Man Who Would Be Queen': 'I Know' vs. First-Order Lived Experience." *Archives of Sexual Behavior* 37 (3): 462–5, discussion 505–10. http://dx.doi.org/10.1007/s10508-008-9335-z

Mustanski, Brian. (2011). "Ethical and Regulatory Issues with Conducting Sexuality Research with LGBT Adolescents: A Call to Action for a Scientifically Informed Approach." *Archives of Sexual Behavior* 40 (4): 673–86. http://dx.doi.org/10.1007/s10508-011-9745-1

National Commission (National Commission for the Protection of Human Subjects of Biomedical and Behavioral Research). (1979). *The Belmont Report: Ethical Principles and Guidelines for the Protection of Human Subjects of Research.* DHEW Publication No. (OS) 78–0012. Washington, DC: US Government Printing Office. (First published 1978).

Palys, Ted, and John Lowman. (2011). "What's Been Did and What's Been Hid." *Reflections: The SoL Journal* TCPS2 (Jan.): 18. http://www.sfu.ca/~palys/PalysLowmanCommentsOnTCPS2-2011.pdf

Perry, Kristen H. (2011). "Ethics, Vulnerability, and Speakers of Other Languages: How University IRBs (Do Not) Speak to Research Involving Refugee Participants." *Qualitative Inquiry* 17 (10): 899–912. http://dx.doi.org/10.1177/1077800411425006

Presidential Commission for the Study of Bioethical Issues. (2011). *Moral Science: Protecting Participants in Human Subjects Research.* Washington, DC. http://bioethics.gov/sites/default/files/Moral%20Science%20June%202012.pdf

Ritterbusch, Amy. (2012). "Bridging Guidelines and Practice: Toward a Grounded Care Ethics in Youth Participatory Action Research." *Professional Geographer* 64 (1): 16–24. http://dx.doi.org/10.1080/00330124.2011.596783

Rowe, Michael. (2007). "Tripping Over Molehills: Ethics and the Ethnography of Police Work." *International Journal of Social Research Methodology* 10 (1): 37–48. http://dx.doi.org/10.1080/13645570600652792

Rupp, Leila, and Verta Taylor. (2011). "Going Back and Giving Back: The Ethics of Staying in the Field." *Qualitative Sociology* 34 (3): 483–96. http://dx.doi.org/10.1007/s11133-011-9200-6

Ryman, Anne. (2012). "ASU History Professor at Center of Plagiarism Debate." *Arizona Republic*, 6 May. http://www.azcentral.com/arizonarepublic/news/articles/2012/04/26/20120426asu-professor-plagiarism-debate.html

Schrag, Zachary M. (2010). *Ethical Imperialism: Institutional Review Boards and the Social Sciences, 1965–2009.* Baltimore: Johns Hopkins University Press.

Shopes, Linda. (2007). "Oral History, Human Subjects. and Institutional Review Boards." (This material revises and expands upon Linda Shopes, "Negotiating Institutional Review Boards," AHA Perspectives Online 45 (3), Mar. 2007.) http://www.oralhistory.org/do-oral-history/oral-history-and-irb-review/

Society of American Archivists. (2009). "Enforcing Ethics." http://www2.archivists.org/news/2009/enforcing-ethics

Spicker, Paul, and David Byrne. (2010). "Unethical Guidelines." *Policy World.* (Winter/Spring): 12–14.

Srivastava, Sanjay. (2009). "Milgram Is Not Tuskegee." *The Hardest Science*, 8 July. http://hardsci.wordpress.com/2009/07/08/milgram-is-not-tuskegee/

Stanley, Liz, and Sue Wise. (2010). "The ESRC's 2010 Framework for Research Ethics: Fit for Research Purpose?" *Sociological Research Online* 15 (4): 12. http://dx.doi.org/10.5153/sro.2265

Stillo, Jonathan. (2011a). "The Trobriand Islanders Never Friended Malinowski on Facebook." *Cacaphony*. https://web.archive.org/web/20111203011159/http://cac.ophony.org/2011/11/30/the-trobriand-islanders-never-friended-malinowski-on-facebook

– (2011b). "Research Ethics in Impossibly Unethical Situations." *Cacaphony*. https://web.archive.org/web/20120128183101/http://cac.ophony. org/2011/12/21/research-ethics-in-impossibly-unethical-situations/

Svitek, Patrick. (2011). "Northwestern Copes with Fallout, Attention from Sex Toy Demo (Updated)." *The Daily Northwestern*, 1 May.

Swauger, Melissa. (2011). "Afterword: The Ethics of Risk, Power, and Representation." *Qualitative Sociology* 34 (3): 497–502. http://dx.doi. org/10.1007/s11133-011-9201-5

Templin, Neal. (2008). "Tipping Point: What It Takes to Make Your Waiter Like You." *Wall Street Journal*, 23 Oct.

University of Colorado, Boulder. (2006). *Report of the Investigative Committee of the Standing Committee on Research Misconduct at the University of Colorado at Boulder Concerning Allegations of Academic Misconduct Against Professor Ward Churchill*. https://rclinton.files.wordpress.com/2006/05/ wardchurchillreport.pdf.

van den Hoonaard, Will C. (2011). *The Seduction of Ethics: Transforming the Social Sciences*. Toronto: University of Toronto Press.

Veatch, Robert M. (1975). "Human Experimentation Committees: Professional or Representative?" *Hastings Center Report* 5 (5): 31–40. http://dx.doi. org/10.2307/3561227

Veatch, Robert M. (1981). *A Theory of Medical Ethics*. New York: Basic Books.

Wynn, L.L., and H. Paul Mason, and Kristina Everett. (2009). *Social Sciences Ethics Training – Macquarie University*. http://www.mq.edu.au/ethics_ training/

17 Research Ethics Review and Compliatorianism: A Curious Dilemma

ANN HAMILTON

The current system of research ethics review presents a curious dilemma. The system, despite its inherent contradictions, continues to grow as an agent of social and academic control, while failing researchers in social science. Yet these researchers have rarely offered any substantial resistance to the IRB (Institutional Review Board) process. This chapter is an attempt to unlock this dilemma by seeking the source of this lack of resistance, how this flawed system endures, and why. Finally, an exploration of the long-term consequences, particularly for social science, of allowing the system to continue and expand unimpeded is offered.

Is There a Purpose of Ethics Regulation That Benefits Social Research?

Anyone stepping into the world of research ethics review will realize that such a world is, as C.K. Gunsalus says, "rooted in scandal" (2002: para. 2). Almost invariably, scandals draw us in, bugs to incandescent light, into notorious medical and psychological research. And it is these inflammatory cases that regulators use to justify monitoring all research that relies on the public purse.

A visitor to the world of research ethics review also quickly realizes that the "ethics regime" has not only failed to keep pace with the diverse methodologies as practised by researchers, but also has cornered social science research into a biomedical paradigm. Thus, this regime touches all manner of research, whether social science or biomedicine, therapeutic or non-therapeutic, and involving all levels of "risk" even when there is no – or next to no – risk. The research ethics regime works in large part to the detriment of social science research. It raises unanswerable questions: What problems are we solving? Who is being harmed? Where is the need for these rules? Where is the empirical evidence that rules *work*? What is the *point* of this system? Why pollute an overcrowded system with low-risk proposals involving surveys, interviews, and observations? The American Association of University Professors (AAUP, 2013) recommends that "if a research project would impose no more than minimal risk of harm ... it *therefore* should be exempt from the requirement of IRB approval ... We use 'exempt' in its commonsense meaning, as we put in our 2006 report and repeat now: 'straightforwardly exempt, with no requirement of IRB approval of the exemption'" (7, emphasis added). Seven years elapsed between these two AAUP reports, and the same statements remain relevant. No changes toward a more relevant system are in place.

Mark Sheehan (2013), associate editor of the *Journal of Medical Ethics*, writes, "A common defence of the general scepticism [of Research Ethics Committees] is to suggest that risk of harm should be the criterion which determines the need for review ... [O]nly if your research poses significant risk of harm to subjects should it be reviewed" (485; see also Shamoo, 2007). Sheehan then concisely lists questions that are immediately raised: Who determines the appropriate level of risk? Who determines whether proposed research is above or below the required level? Sheehan concludes, "Without substantial argument, it is not at all clear that these questions should be answered by the researcher or can be decided in advance or according to a pre-set schema" (485). Rules that require future telling are folly. One can make the argument that the entire research ethics review system – and indeed many regulatory systems – are *simulations*, as described by Jean Baudrillard (1983). One could also argue that the "Common Rule" (45 CFR 46, 1991) is a similar instance of social-level delusion, detached from nearly all research realities, a Baudrillardian seduction into simulation. We act as if the Common Rule itself constitutes protection.

Regulation, I contend, has been turned upside down. Regulations are rooted in what people value. That behaviour is subsequently standardized into codes of conduct. Rules reflect the values found in the lifeworld. Rules are a derivative of values. In regulatory arrangements, that logical process is reversed – and ineffective.

Compliance to the code of federal (or other) regulation is *incidental* to the moral composure of researchers; it is the *moral* code of the individual that guides behaviour. As Greg Koski, the first director of the US Office of Human Research Protections (OHRP), acknowledges, "Scientists, not university review boards, bear primary responsibility for protecting human subjects" (as quoted in Brainard, 2000: A21). Ron Iphofen, in Chapter 20 in this volume, observes, "No matter what formalized and perfected ethics review structures are established there is really only one guarantor of ethical practice – the researcher. Ultimately it is the researcher in the field who knows when ethical practice is going on and when it is being threatened."

So, in the context of the protection of human subjects, procedural rules do not replace values. As procedural rules are substantially less salient than values, rules are most often unnecessary. In fact, rules are often not even *known*, as demonstrated in the numerous researcher nightmares about having gathered suddenly unusable data. These disruptions to research are not imposed because of harms to participants, but rather because of a lack of awareness of the local IRB interpretation du jour. The harm, therefore, is inflicted on an ill-fitting *process*, not on research participants. For people who have moral values – including the overwhelming majority of social researchers – these procedural rules do not matter. Circumvention of rules may even become the norm but is of little consequence in the lifeworld because it is not *rules* but moral *values* that prevent harm to research participants. Conversely, if an individual does *not* have moral values, these procedural rules will not produce ethical behaviour.

In many respects, oversight by the research ethics regime is a moot point. Virtually no direct oversight of social research by ethics committees occurs, and based on the lack of problems, harms, and lawsuits, no direct oversight is needed. And, in the most practical sense, all that is available from researchers *in reality* is a blanket assurance that the research is being conducted according to the proposal approved, which is considered to ensure ethical behaviour. Even though each proposal must be submitted and approved separately, without oversight, ethics board approval is tantamount to saying, "You must tell us a plausible story (in a format we call a *proposal*) about what you are up to and the story submitted must address everyone's liability concerns." With the absence of oversight by ethics review committees, one could logically and reasonably question the usefulness of such a system.

Rules without oversight are, at their essence, voluntary guidelines. Why don't we point this out? Why don't we remind ourselves and ethics regulators about the lack of harm with social research participants? Why don't we question a cumbersome and harmful solution in the absence of a problem? The application process is not voluntary, but the execution of the protocol always is. Researchers are required to complete this process, but are then left on their own to implement the research as described in the protocol submitted. Outside the world of the research ethics regime, laws have been long in place to protect individuals from invasion of privacy and libel and/or slander, and to provide remedy to participants damaged because of information they provided to anyone, including researchers. What more is needed?

Risk Assessment and Exemptions from the Ethics Review Process

If (1) ethics review is necessary, (2) if the current system works, and (3) if the true purpose of ethics review is protection of human participants in research, then why are not all researchers required to comply? Exceptions to the ethics review process are granted summarily for graduate and undergraduate students, unaffiliated researchers, expatriate researchers, unfunded researchers, journalists, historians, and others. How can the ethics regime claim to protect research participants when these and similar exemptions are commonly granted? If the focus were truly on protecting participants, the source of the funding would be irrelevant, along with the academic rank of researchers, the geographic location of study participants, and other details. "We seem confused," says Gunsalus (2002: para. 14), "about whether it is the nature of the interaction or the place where it occurs that makes an activity research – why else would anybody believe that a newspaper reporter who interviews people and publishes stories about them isn't doing research, but that a journalism professor and students performing the same tasks are doing research?" (See also Kerr, 2006.)

If one could argue that only research for therapeutic purposes should be screened for ethical guidance, then surely research for non-therapy should qualify for wholesale exemption – exemption from review *and* from the application process. Research in the humanities and the social sciences is typically not for therapeutic purposes and should be entirely exempt. A visitor to the realms of ethics review would quickly realize that the research ethics regime is in place to protect universities from lawsuits, to protect the flow of federal funds, and to protect the process itself. The process is designed to answer the conjuring of lawyers with vivid imaginations and an abundance of too-much-has-and-might-go-wrong stories (see Stark, 2007, quoting Edward Rourke).

Detrimental Effects of Regulations in Social Science and in Moral Behaviour

When we perpetuate compliatorianism in the face of no evidence of need, and in spite of federal exemptions, contemporary scholars are not leaving the academy in better shape than we found it. At some point it became acceptable – in fact, the preferred behaviour – for faculty to acknowledge to students and colleagues that many research proposals would produce great research, involve excellent methodologies, would be timely, and deal with important topics, but they would *never* get past an Institutional Review Board. Abandoning timely studies about important topics because they can't get past an ethics review board is a dangerous conclusion to accept, especially when this censorship of thought and deed is considered normal, inevitable, and even effective and virtuous – the *right* thing to do. This consent-without-resistance, especially in low-risk environments, this perpetuation of an inappropriate system is compliatorianism.[1]

As analysed in numerous works (e.g., van den Hoonaard, 2011; Hamilton 2002, 2005), the system of research ethics review is having a deleterious effect on the missions, purposes, and methodologies of the social sciences and humanities. Contemporary students often express wonder about how, in the classical age of ethnography, researchers were *allowed* to conduct their research. We should be asking why similar studies today are *not* exempt from a process that begs the question of need.

Warnings about this general problem – i.e., faculty losing control of the academic aspects of the university – have been issued for at least 100 years: Charles Osgood, called "the dean of Princeton humanists," stated in 1914, "Perhaps no more important question could be investigated now than that of the faculty's power to govern the purely academic functions of the college or university ... [this power] declines in many institutions to almost nothing ... [and is] more gravely menaced every year" (quoted in Delgado, 2004). The moment at which syllabi became viewed as legal documents rather than academic ones is clear evidence that Osgood was – and remains – right.

Muted Resistance

Given the factors described above, why are researchers not mounting resistance? In the social sciences alone, complaints have appeared in more than 325 publications (van den Hoonaard, personal communication,

2013). Even on the medical front,[2] researchers have been voicing serious complaints, citing the loss of lives when Institutional Review Boards are too slow in approving research proposals. Conflicts of interest are not adequately considered – and these situations produce much greater risk than social research, not only for participants in research, but also for members of society in general, as when a medicine or medical device is approved and then harms and even kills patients.

Many social scientists argue that the need for regulation of research ethics is highly exaggerated; some say the need for regulation does not exist. However, the fact that far too few researchers have openly challenged this unworkable system is an even bigger problem. Robert Dingwall (this volume) says, "There is now a broad consensus ... this model ... is not suitable for application to the social sciences." No less significant is that "the growing documentation of these failings has had little impact."

Searches of Google, the Office of Human Research Protections, the *Chronicle of Higher Education*, the American Association of University Professors, and Westlaw, using keyword combinations such as Institutional Review Board, lawsuit, social science, humanities, privacy, survey, interview, observation, and other terms, and including at least the past 11 years, yielded no information relevant to the so-called *problematique* issues ginned up by rule enthusiasts – compliatorianists including regulators, university lawyers, and researchers themselves. One cannot find, in the United States, lawsuits involving surveys, interviews, or observations.[3] Clearly, very few protection issues exist with these types of data gathering. Why are we constructing this elaborate system to solve problems that do not exist? Why accept, reinforce, or perpetuate the regulation of research ethics when it jeopardizes academic freedom and free inquiry, and provides no benefits to research participants? What about the debilitating effect of research ethics review on the social sciences? Moreover, even if there were problems, why do we think Institutional Review Boards can solve them? How would the Institutional Review Board even *know* if a problem exists? Why do we create and maintain the illusion that this process of ethics review is about protecting human research participants?

Examples of Inexplicable Compliatorianism

The Tale of the Questionnaire Administered to Graduating Students

The *Chronicle of Higher Education* reported in 2004 about a questionnaire given to approximately 15,000 graduating students at 125 medical schools. Federal regulators deemed the questionnaire, administered by the Association of American Medical Colleges, to be exempt under the education provision in that the study was designed to improve educational offerings (Borror, 2004). The survey included questions about satisfaction with curriculum and career plans, but also about sexual/verbal harassment and about the amount of debt students had amassed. These two latter areas of questioning were deemed to require IRB review as the answers might harm students in terms of employability or reputation, especially given that more than half the students voluntarily identified themselves on the survey form. Two levels of compliatorianism were displayed as a result. First, the response of the Association of American Medical Colleges was that they would eliminate the questions altogether. Why? Sexual/verbal harassment, especially when students are involved, and debt loads are highly important – to parents, students, faculty, administrators, and taxpayers. Second, the Association and six medical schools, even with the questionable items removed, all told federal regulators they would still submit the questionnaire to each of their separate Institutional Review Boards and that they would probably submit an annual version of it, too (Brainard, 2003, 2004). Why? The research is exempt. Proceed.

The Myth of Voluntariness

I am intrigued by the large number of researchers in the United States, Canada, and elsewhere who often indicate that the research ethics review system only applies to government-funded studies, subsequently describing their own participation as somehow "voluntary." Technically speaking, ethics review for research not funded by government *is* voluntary, but practically speaking, it is not. An overwhelmingly common institutional (i.e., local) interpretation of (federal) rules is that if *any* government funds come into the institution, *all* research involving humans must undergo ethics review. This is certainly an unfortunate interpretation that obliterates the fact that the ethics review system does not apply to non-funded research. Federal regulators readily admit they have no authority to insist that studies they do not fund be reviewed. "We humans exaggerate the extent to which our actions are voluntary and rationally chosen – or, put differently, we all understate the power of the situation" (Zimbardo, 2007: B7). Such taken-for-granted expectations feed into compliatorianism. I argue this is most frequently invisible; it isn't *understated* – it is *absent* from discussion.

Lisa-Jo van den Scott (chapter 12 in this volume) writes, "Researchers not only believe they are unable to challenge institutional hierarchies, but also lack the skills to approach their work with a revolutionary mindset aimed at overturning long-existing hierarchies of credibility in the field site, in publishing, and in teaching."

So, the ethics review process is voluntary for the institution (in the cases of non-funded research), but is not voluntary for the researcher. One look at an institution's ethics review rules and the processes for gaining an exemption, and the mirage of voluntariness rapidly disappears.

The Compliance Parable

In an advice column in the *Chronicle of Higher Education*, Karen Markin provides a splendid example of constructing, perpetuating, reinforcing, and defending the IRB system. She opens with the question, "How is it that you can do human-subject research without ever seeing, touching, or talking to another human being? If you can't answer that riddle, you could conduct an entire research project and [still] be forbidden to publish the results" (Markin, 2005: para. 1). This is an enthusiastic, even cheerful use of fear to justify an absurd regulatory mutation. Markin continues constructing, reinforcing, and perpetuating the system, stating, "Blame it on the federal government, which provides much of the money to conduct the research and therefore sets the rules" (para. 4). She invokes fear, explaining that institutions take the ethics regulations seriously because "failure to comply can hit them in the pocketbook through loss of grant dollars ... It's important for you to take them seriously also, or your project could be delayed or terminated ... Plus, any bad publicity resulting from an allegation ... could certainly dim your prospects for promotion and tenure" (para. 4). Her views suggest entrenchment, reinforced and sustained through career-ending, doom-filled scenarios, offered perpetually. One graduates and strives for promotion and tenure. An individual in academia succeeds if and when IRB members allow it. Markin, when discussing exemptions, adds, "It is not up to you to make that determination ... At most institutions, to say that a project qualifies for exempt review does not mean that no review is necessary. It means that, after you have submitted the necessary forms, an authorized official decides that no further review of your project is required" (para. 12). Very Oz-esque. She reinforces and repeats the notion that "whatever your thoughts on the wisdom of current practices, be aware that these boards are powerful" (para. 15). Suggesting strongly that you are powerless, Markin concludes, "So play it safe in terms of both your own research agenda and the well-being of society." Such a commonly held perspective escalates the play-it-safe, follow-the-rules mentality as a moral virtue.

Defaults as Deep Structure

Full-board review, written and signed consent forms, data sharing and/or public archiving of data are default settings in typical research ethics review systems. IRB members normalize these unseen templates of life, the hegemonic reality. Default positions on the part of researchers involve compliatorianism – the process is unquestioned, treated as inevitable, and even virtuous. Research ethics review regimes view the questions themselves as rebellion, as wrong and unethical. In the end, persistent questioning threatens careers.

Reasons for Perpetuating the System

Change typically meets resistance and this is especially true of bureaucrats. A common criticism of bureaucracies is they are ill-equipped to handle issues of the day (or the volume of the week). Life outpaces rules. The lifeworld is dynamic and ambiguous. Life involves liquid targets and local phenomena; values are liquid and local, as is the *implementation* of rules (see Hamilton, 2002). Although thresholds vary for the dysfunctional aspects of the IRB (or any) regulatory system, eventually nearly all individuals will describe some aspect of the system as deficient, absurd, frustrating, unreasonable, etc., whether they are regulators, regulatees, or regulatands.

IRB processes have not changed substantially for more than 30 years – with one important exception: mission creep, as described by several authors in this volume. With myriad problems recognized by all concerned – federal regulators, researchers, members of ethics boards – and, ironically, the fewest problems with participants themselves who are ostensibly the reason for this ever-widening review process, why has there been no movement toward the better system that these stakeholders envision?

First, the research ethics regime feeds the public demand for accountability. Mark Sheehan (2008) states, "Although there is an important connection between public trust and public accountability, we should not mistake such systems of accountability for trust" (633; see also

Manson and O'Neill, 2007). An unwarranted belief that rules plus compliance equals protection is prevalent; this is similar to the argument that if a car makes a noise, it can be fixed by turning up the radio.

Second, regulators are part of an ever-expanding bureaucracy, becoming increasingly professional, and career-minded. To exempt entire categories of research, in the view of some ethics regulators, is to open the door for their own exit into irrelevance. This hardly matters, though, given the pervasive and enthusiastic yet inexplicable cliff jumping of researchers.

Third, hypothetical situations form the basis of liability issues. Lawyers are prominent in decision-making groups involving rules, and rules therefore focus more on protecting institutional reputation than on any aspect of research itself, including the protection of human participants.

Fourth, a primary function of bureaucracy is control and power. Stanley Deetz (1995) suggests, "Cultural fragmentation and dispersion ... function to control and make productive resistance difficult" (166). Divide and confuse. And Theodor Adorno (1989b) points out, "When details come to seem the strongest reality of all, on account of their tangible immediacy, they blind the eye to genuine perception" (269). This is perhaps why ethics review so often takes the form of a micro-focus on copy-editing informed consent documents.

Fifth, complying with federal rules seems significantly more important than protecting research participants. One can find this missing-the-forest blindness in the response to OHRP sanctions in 2000 by University of Oklahoma President David Boren who spoke of the goal of becoming a "model of compliance" rather than a model of protection (see Gillham, 2000: 206; see also Schneider, 2000, for comments from University of Pennsylvania officials in a similar predicament).

Sixth, researchers themselves want to be colonized by the research ethics regime.

Social science researchers participate in, allow, stand by, watch, aid, and abet regulators and other compliatorianists in a system that requires rights to due process and provisions for open meetings be suspended (see Sheehan, 2008, regarding the pros and cons of open ethics committee meetings). With respect to open meetings, "At some universities investigators are asked – and in some instances, required – to attend the meetings at which their studies are reviewed ... For NIH [National Institutes of Health] scientists through the 1960s, the idea of evaluating a study without the investigator present was unthinkable because, the theory went, the investigator knew the research methods and the study population better than anyone else" (Stark, 2007: 405). With the researcher present, concerns can be made clear, and relevant responses can be made; much more reasonable than a form letter offering a few sentences about reasons for denial or requirements for changes in the proposal.

Seventh, how is it that Institutional Review Boards – bodies obsessed with making and following rules – so effortlessly ignore such fundamental rules as due process and the provision for open meetings? The American Association of University Professors states, "No provision is made in the regulations for an appeal process ... An IRB may demand that a change be made in a research protocol as a condition of approval ... Prospective researchers are given an opportunity to try to convince the IRB that the change need not be made, but scheduling difficulties often cause lengthy delays; and in any case, unless the prospective researcher is able to convince the IRB to rescind its demand, the IRB's demand settles the matter" (AAUP, 2006: para. 6–7).

Eighth, many novice social researchers have no logical choice but to accede to IRB demands; publications, promotions, and the granting of tenure are contingent on grant monies and publications, and these are inextricably linked to IRB approval. For now, at least, very few of these new researchers will choose to gamble with their careers by protesting IRB processes or by encouraging their future students to resist the system. *Compliatoria* has become a place with deep roots.

Ninth, a system of "vertical ethics" (a term coined by van den Hoonaard, 2011) promulgates the ethics regime through departments, universities, journals, etc. R. Douglas Hurt, head of the Department of History at Purdue University in 2006, said he "felt compelled to issue a memo telling [graduate students incorporating oral history into their research] to cease that research until they were sure they had IRB clearance" (quoted in Howard, 2006: para. 42). So Hurt's students were advised to stop all their projects and wait for the Institutional Review Board to decide what they can do in spite of clear federal exemptions. Hurt continued, "What I'm dealing with is the art of the possible at the moment ... This is the playing field that we have to operate in because the IRB is not going to budge on this" (quoted in Howard, 2006: para. 43).

A Discursive Ideology

Following Michel Foucault (1972), rhetorical strategies and practices maintain a position of dominance, and through their use a hegemonic ideology must be constructed, renewed, reinforced, and continually defended. These *discursive formations* constitute a common mechanism in universities for constructing, renewing, reinforcing, and defending ideologies. This shapes students in certain directions, teaches them to obey orders, and to pledge allegiance. But when major institutions clash, the veneer cracks, giving us an opportunity to first reveal and then reduce compliatorianism. However, we seldom consider the larger system that produces those clashes.

A bias toward compliance permeates the system in part because of this notion of participant protection, and also because it is easier, safer, and substantially preferred, generally, to conform than to rebel. Theodor Adorno (1989b: 268) states, "The whole [system] survives only through the unity of the functions which its members fulfill. Each individual without exception must take [on] some function ... to prolong ... existence; indeed, while [the] function lasts, [we are] ... taught to express ... gratitude for it" (268).

Incumbents in the system perceive rules as desirable, and following even bad rules as morally right. They see that adhering to rules is *equal to* protecting research participants. These concepts in research ethics review are central to the operation of compliatorianism. Alfred Schutz and Thomas Luckmann (1973) suggest, "In contrast to specific experiences, [these] fundamental structures do not enter into the grip of consciousness in the natural attitude" but they are "a condition of every experience of the lifeworld." They are somewhat like breathing. These experiences enter "the horizon of experience ... each experience 'obviously' or 'self-evidently' has an unchangeable spatial, temporal, and social arrangement" (103).

SunWolf and David Seibold (1998) provide a relevant example about juries and nested values: "The rule that 'the law should be followed' interpenetrates with the social rule that 'people should not report the transgressions of a friend'" (303). In our own experiences we may recall times when we have felt the law was followed but justice was not served, or that certain rules are not fair or not fairly imposed. Theodor Adorno (1989a) tells us, "Conformity has replaced consciousness" via the "culture industry," that is, models in the media about how to dress, think, behave, etc. "The concepts of order which [the culture industry] hammers into human beings are always those of the status quo. They remain unquestioned, unanalyzed, and undialectically presupposed, even if they no longer have any substance for those who accept them" (133). "Domination," according to Dennis Mumby (1987), "involves getting people to organize their behavior around a particular rules system" (115). Foucault, it seems, agrees when he advances the idea that power is a set of relationships that people hold with the texts that constitute organizations to which they belong, and which affect their lives, as in the case of IRBs. Foucault's idea that the more invisible power is, the more effective it is resonates with Mumby's statement about domination. Normative social structures are, according to Jacques Derrida (1981), products of systems privileging unity and identity over separation and difference. Privileging unity and identity has relevance to the *invisible side of a fully functioning* IRB regulatory system – compliatorianism, that is, the self-regulatory behaviour of researchers themselves, facilitating and legitimizing the power of the system, especially in the indoctrination of students. Even though faculty members may frequently badmouth Institutional Review Boards and ethics review processes, these criticisms constitute the "potato chips" of complaint: empty calories, empty words.

The ideas that rules are good and that following rules is good are obvious, particularly on the part of local regulators who see and entrench blind compliance as virtuous, and mission creep as inevitable and necessary. They are well rewarded for it, signalling no end to the system, no end to expansion, no end to the addressing of non-existent problems, and no end to the idea that the system solves problems.

Researchers are not encouraged to engage in *whying* and the subsequent casting off of rules and procedures adopted from non-substantiated fear through the use of a very few sensational occurrences. Kirsten Bell (this volume) discusses our "academic passivity and our tendency to accept systems of audit and accountability" that do not fit in social science. "There is a persistent temptation to apply procedures, methods, claims, and more recently, regulation developed for the medical sciences to social sciences. The IRB system is often nonsensical when applied to social research; the rules are not right or wrong, but irrelevant" (Hamilton, 2005: 5). Rena Lederman (chapter 2 in this volume) explains that social researchers "are faced with a no-win situation: either misrepresent their research plans by expressing them in alien, ultimately misleading terms (an ethical dilemma itself) or change their preferred research practices to fit regulatory assumptions about what (all) research is or should be like."

Srivastava (2009) reminds us, "The attempt to create some sort of parallelism in the [CITI] presentation (Tuskegee = Milgram? Nazis = Zimbardo?) is inaccurate and misguided, and does a disservice to the legacy of important social/behavioral research" (as quoted in Schrag, this volume). How long will the research ethics review system punish Milgram? How long will it punish social scientists because of Milgram, a psychologist after all?

Viewed cynically, the producers of this punishment (in this case, mostly lawyers on behalf of administrators) constrain the potentially adverse effects of research. Many cadres of well-meaning people are following without question rules that, from our perspective, make no sense. Can one even more cynically aver that lawyers also contribute mightily to fostering mistrust of researchers on the part of ethics regulators, as that keeps both ethics regulators and lawyers in business?

The Common Rule (45 CFR 46, 1991) seduces federal and local regulators and researchers into believing that if the rules are followed, protection of participants in research is guaranteed (see Baudrillard, 1988, esp. 149–65). The concern is not whether the *entire* IRB system is a simulation or not. Rather, the concern is the various ways in which specific *procedures* are simulated. The level of detachment among federal research ethics regulators, research ethics regulations, local interpretations of regulations of research ethics, actual researchers, the researched, and their local environment is an example of simulation.

So (process-based) compliance has replaced (purpose-based) protection as the most salient set of research ethics issues – a simulation in which the process obscures the purpose. However, in the IRB system researcher assimilation, in a sense meant by Baudrillard (1983), is nearly complete in that *compliance* is held as equal to *protection* and as virtuous and inevitable, and that federal law is considered to be a foundation – a place to erect even more evaluations, approvals, processes, and rules. Compliance, though itself often highly difficult, remains the path of least resistance. Assimilation into the research-ethics regulatory system *seems* inevitable, adding to the likelihood that it will be.

Michel Foucault (1980) describes *specific intellectuals* as ordinary people who understand their circumstances and have the ability to express themselves independently of the *universal theorizing intellectual*. Opposition to existing structures occurs, according to Foucault (1980), not through assumption of the role of the universal intellectual but through that of the specific intellectual. Earning respect on one's own terms, or the demonstration of one person making a difference are examples: "Not in the modality of the 'universal,' the 'exemplary,' and the 'just-and-true-for-all,' rather within specific sectors, at the precise points where their own conditions of life or work situate them" (126). Moreover, according to Foucault, this specificity is the level at which criminals challenge prison conditions, welfare workers and clients seek to change bureaucracies, government contractors with security clearance challenge secrecy and war policies, doctors challenge insurance companies, consumers organize against corrupt corporations, and, most relevant here, the regulated challenge regulators, and faculty challenge administrators.

Following the liquid-and-local line of argument, "specific researchers give specific power(s) to specific regulators at specific times. They don't have to. They do. They may (falsely) believe they have no choice. But, ... they ... do" (Hamilton, 2002: 216).

Researchers are too often discouraged from engaging in selective ethics, situational leadership, anecdotal evidence, gut feelings, or even merit raises. In the busy lives of scholars, the ease and safety of research ethics review dogma is preferable to time-consuming, risk-bearing rebellion, but this preference, for a growing number of social scientists, comes at too high a price.

NOTES

1 *Compliant* refers to a specific response to a specific stimulus. *Compliatorianism* is a mindset, an ideology, pervasive and invisible. The term is used to bring to the surface SINS (structures, institutionalizations, naturalizations, simulations) in the ethics review system. New terms are useful; the use of familiar words positions one to stay in familiar places.
2 See, e.g., the blog, "Suffocated Science."
3 Two cases in Canada should be mentioned: At Simon Fraser University in 1994, a criminology graduate student, Russell Ogden, was asked by a court to divulge confidential information in a matter involving a death while he was researching assisted suicides of persons with HIV. The student defended the case successfully, but only after a long struggle, and without the aid of the university's REB (Research Ethics Board). More recently, in 2014, a case at the University of Ottawa involved two professors in criminology who were asked by police to surrender interview data that could potentially have a bearing on a legal case. Despite the University's agreement to conform to this request, a Quebec court upheld the researchers' (and the REB's) position that such a request would violate any promise of confidentiality.

REFERENCES

Adorno, Theodor. (1989a). "The Culture Industry Reconsidered." In S.
    Bronner and D.M. Kellner (eds.), *Critical Theory and Society: A Reader*, 128–35.
    New York: Routledge.
– (1989b). "Society." In S. Bronner and D.M. Kellner (eds.), *Critical Theory and
    Society: A Reader*, 267–75. New York: Routledge.
AAUP (American Association of University Professors). (2006). *Research on
    Human Subjects: Academic Freedom and the Institutional Review Board*. http://
    www.aaup.org/report/research-human-subjects-academic-freedom-and-
    institutional-review-board
– (2013). *Regulation of Research on Human Subjects: Academic Freedom and the
    Institutional Review Board*. http://www.aaup.org/file/IRB-Final-Report.pdf
Baudrillard, Jean. (1983). *Simulations*. New York: Semiotext(e).
– (1988). "Simulacra and Simulations." In M. Poster (ed.), *Jean Baudrillard:
    Selected Writings*, 166–84. Stanford: Stanford University Press.
Borror, Kristina. (2004, 3 Aug). "Letter to OHRP." http://www.hhs.gov/ohrp/
    detrm_letrs/YR04/aug04a.pdf
Brainard, Jeffrey. (2000, 21 July). "Will a 'Fresh Face' Bring a New Approach
    to Federal Protection of Human Subjects?" *Chronicle of Higher Education* 46:
    A21.
– (2003, 23 July). "Survey of Medical School Graduates Raises Privacy
    Concerns, Group Says." *Chronicle of Higher Education*. http://chronicle.
    com/article/Survey-of-Medical-School/111528/
– (2004, 24 Sept.). "Privacy Concerns Spur Plan to Revise Questionnaire for
    Medical-School Graduates." *Chronicle of Higher Education* 51 (5): A23.
Deetz, Stanley. (1995). *Transforming Communication, Transforming Business:
    Building Responsive and Responsible Workplaces*. Cresskill, NJ: Hampton Press.
Delgado, Ray. (2004, 7 Apr.). "Advisory Board Marks 100 Years of Faculty
    Power." Stanford University News Release. http://news.stanford.edu/
    news/2004/april7/adboard-47.html
Derrida, Jacques. (1981). *Positions*. Chicago: University of Chicago Press.
Foucault, Michel. (1972). *The Archaeology of Knowledge and the Discourse on
    Language*. Translated by A.M. Sheridan Smith. New York: Pantheon.
– (1980). *Power/Knowledge: Selected Interviews and Other Writings, 1972–1977*.
    New York: Pantheon.
Gillham, Omer. (2000). "Medical Study Inquiry: OU Forges Ahead to Put
    Study Problems Aside." *Tulsa World*, 23 July.
Gunsalus, C.K. (2002, 15 Nov.). "Rethinking Protections for Human Subjects."
    Chronicle of Higher Education 49 (12): B24.

Hamilton, Ann F. (2002). *Institutional Review Boards: Politics, Power, Purpose and Process in a Regulatory Organization*. Doctoral dissertation, University of Oklahoma.

– (2005). "The Development and Operation of IRBs: Medical Regulations and Social Science." *Journal of Applied Communication Research* 33 (3): 189–203. http://dx.doi.org/10.1080/00909880500149353

Howard, Jennifer. (2006). "Oral History under Review." *Chronicle of Higher Education* 53 (12): A14.

Kerr, Robert L. (2006). "Unconstitutional Review Board? Considering a First Amendment Challenge to IRB Regulation of Journalistic Research Methods." *Communication Law and Policy* 11 (3): 393–447. http://dx.doi.org/10.1207/s15326926clp1103_4

Manson, Neil C., and Onora O'Neill. (2007). *Rethinking Informed Consent in Bioethics*, 154–182. Cambridge: Cambridge University Press. http://dx.doi.org/10.1017/CBO9780511814600.008

Markin, Karen. (2005, Aug.). "Playing It Safe with Research Risk." *Chronicle of Higher Education* 12. http://chronicle.com/article/Playing-It-Safe-With-Resear/44920/

Mumby, Dennis. (1987). "The Political Function of Narrative in Organizations." *Communication Monographs* 54 (2): 113–27. http://dx.doi.org/10.1080/03637758709390221

Schneider, Alison. (2000, 6 Nov.). "University of Pennsylvania Settles Lawsuit over Gene-Therapy Death." *Chronicle of Higher Education, Daily News*.

Schutz, Alfred, and Thomas Luckmann. (1973). *Structures of the Life-World*, vol. 1. Evanston, IL: Northwestern University Press.

Shamoo, Adil. (2007). "Deregulating Low-Risk Research." *Chronicle of Higher Education* 53 (48): B16.

Sheehan, Mark. (2008). "Should Research Ethics Committees Meet in Public?" *Journal of Medical Ethics* 34 (8): 631–5. http://dx.doi.org/10.1136/jme.2007.022574

– (2013). "Do We Need Research Ethics Committees?" *Journal of Medical Ethics* 39 (8): 485. http://dx.doi.org/10.1136/medethics-2013-101686

Srivastava, Sanjay. (2009, 8 July). "Milgram Is Not Tuskegee." *The Hardest Science*. https://hardsci.wordpress.com/2009/07/08/milgram-is-not-tuskegee/

Stark, Laura. (2007). "Victims in Our Own Minds? IRBs in Myth and Practice." *Law & Society Review* 41 (4): 777–86. http://dx.doi.org/10.1111/j.1540-5893.2007.00323.x

SunWolf, and David R. Seibold. (1998). "Jurors' Intuitive Rules for Deliberation: A Structurational Approach to Communication in Jury

Decisions Making." *Communication Monographs* 65 (4): 282–307. http://
dx.doi.org/10.1080/03637759809376455

van den Hoonaard, Will C. (2011). *The Seduction of Ethics: Transforming the
Social Sciences*. Toronto: University of Toronto Press.

Zimbardo, Philip (2007, 30 Mar.). "Revisiting the Stanford Prison Experiment:
A Lesson in the Power of Situation." *Chronicle of Higher Education* 53(30),
B6–7.

18 Enriching Ethics Review Processes in the Spirit of Participatory Dialogue

KATE HOLLAND

This chapter presents two strategies for improving research ethics review regimes with the purpose of working to overcome barriers posed by ethics review boards. Barriers are frequently based on assumptions board members make about participants, researchers, and the risks of research. In particular, I discuss the rationale for and benefits of (1) involving members of participant groups, community organizations, or advisory groups and (2) elevating the expertise of disciplinary peers in the review process. These practices, notwithstanding challenges, have great potential to enrich existing processes of research ethics review and, in some cases, improve existing procedures through modifying, replacing, or eliminating those that do not work. The chapter also provides an overview of some of the problems with systems of research ethics review identified by scholars from many countries, along with an explanation of the framework for ethics review of human research in Australia. I follow this by relating my own ethics review experience, arguing the vital need to integrate participant and peer review into the research ethics review process. On a broader scale, one needs to see a shift of moral reasoning in the ethics review process – one that requires greater public participation, recognition of the partiality and conflicting interests of current systems of ethics review (in particular, the biomedical model that underpins the current system), and encouragement of participatory dialogue (Eckenwiler, 2001).

As a PhD student, I proposed to interview people who may have had a diagnosis of mental illness. The University Human Research Ethics Committee (HREC) rejected the proposal. It expressed concerns related to participants' capacity to consent, their safety (and my own), and to my lack of clinical expertise.[1] My research in the area of media studies and health communication proposed to explore the ways people interpret and negotiate health information in their everyday lives. This research required my talking with people, including those who have health conditions, and involved qualitative research methods such as interviews. The research was not medical research and did not involve experimental procedures or treatments.

Problems with Existing Processes of Research Ethics Review

The expanding role of research ethics committees beyond their original purpose has been captured in terms such as *mission creep, ethics drift,* and *bureaucratic creep* (Fitzgerald, 2004; Gunsalus et al., 2007). Kevin Haggerty (2004) has argued that researchers in the social sciences and humanities are witnessing the emergence of a host of new fetters on knowledge production that are constraining scholarly research and structuring what truths can be spoken and by whom. He coined the term "ethics creep" to encapsulate the dual process by which the system of regulating research ethics "is expanding outward to incorporate a host of new activities and institutions, while at the same time intensifying the regulation of activities deemed to fall within its ambit" (391). A shift in the role of ethics committees from assessing risk to humans and assuring informed consent to protecting the institution from damage has been identified (Lincoln and Tierney, 2004: 228). Research ethics committees are increasingly giving attention to liability and legal issues – risk management for the institution and the researchers involved (Fitzgerald, 2004: 1) and, it seems, other topics overwhelmingly irrelevant to protecting participants and to the type of research proposed.

Researchers in the humanities and social sciences worry that the current framework guiding research ethics is incapable of assessing and responding to qualitative and/or interpretive research proposals, significantly disadvantaging such research (Lincoln and Tierney, 2004; van den Hoonaard, 2002). Even though the risks of qualitative, non-medical research are minimal compared with the physical or psychological harm brought on by biomedical procedures, drug trials, and other experimental conditions, abuses or failures in the biomedical realm contribute to a disproportionate level of largely irrelevant processes of ethics review related to the social sciences and humanities (Fitzgerald, 2005; van den Hoonaard, 2001). Researchers have identified the "just in case" mentality of many ethics committee members, driving decisions based on hypothetical worst-case scenarios and a better-safe-than-sorry posture (Haggerty, 2004: 412). But safe from what? Fitzgerald et al. (2006: 390) describe this as the "what if" narrative – developing hypothetical scenarios that take on lives of their own among members of ethics review committees. According to Kevin Haggerty (2004), the regulatory structure undergoes an "expansionist dynamic" (401) partly because it is difficult to predict the physical and psychological effects of participating in research. Thus, he concludes, "Pronouncements about 'risk' of research projects are more akin to a subjective imagining of potential scenarios unconstrained by empirical evidence" (402).

Ethics creep threatens academic freedom, constrains knowledge production contributing to information deficits for citizens, discourages and frustrates researchers, creates unnecessary work for ethics review committees and diverts their attention from the necessary scrutiny of biomedical research, and results in refusals to approve research that poses difficult but important questions (Haggerty, 2004; Schrag, 2011).

The System Governing Human Research Ethics Review at Australian Universities

In Australia, the *National Statement on Ethical Conduct in Human Research* (NHMRC et al., 2007) provides the overarching framework that governs research involving humans. The *National Statement* has been jointly developed by the National Health and Medical Research Council (NHMRC), the Australian Research Council (ARC), and the Australian Vice-Chancellors' Committee (AVCC). This revision of the previous 1999 *National Statement* reflects the evolving nature of research ethics review in response to the emergence of new technologies and research procedures, as well as concerns about ethics creep. The chair of the *National Statement* working party for the revised statement acknowledged, "In trying to make the national statement genuinely applicable to the gamut of human research, the working party has been acutely aware of the need to avoid 'ethics creep'" (Cordner, 2006: para. 12).

The 2007 *National Statement* requires universities to establish their own Human Research Ethics Committees (HRECs) and to implement procedures for ethics review. It includes provisions for institutional administrators to establish new and/or alternate ethics review processes for research involving low risk, and lists four forms this level might take (though institutions are not limited to these): (1) by the head of department; (2) by a departmental committee of peers; (3) through a delegated review with reporting to a Human Research Ethics Committee;

or (4) by a subcommittee of the Human Research Ethics Committee (NHMCR et al., 2007: 79). The *National Statement* also contains provisions for Human Research Ethics Committees to exempt from ethics review research deemed to constitute negligible risk.[2] Included in the minimum requirements for the composition of an ethics committee are at least two laypeople not affiliated with the institution and who are not currently engaged in medical, scientific, legal, or academic work; at least two people with current research experience relevant to the proposal under review who may be recruited as the need arises from an established pool of inducted members; at least one person with experience in professional care; and at least one lawyer. The committee must have at least eight members (NHMRC et al., 2007: 81).

The *National Statement* leaves room for flexibility and, therefore, ethics review processes vary from university to university. While some have one research ethics committee that reviews research proposals from all academic disciplines, others have implemented subcommittees that review applications that involve minimal risk. Some universities have separate committees or mechanisms in place to review biomedical research and humanities and social sciences research. The practice of having distinct disciplinary or departmental panels, also the case in other countries (Stark, 2007), confirms that different ethical issues are raised by medical research and research in the humanities and social sciences. However, it does not address the criticism, which Mark Israel (2005) has made in Australia, that if the National Health and Medical Research Council were serious about creating a general framework for research ethics, it would not use a biomedical base as its starting point.

Personal Encounter with Research Ethics Review or *Creep*

In the course of having my own doctoral project proposal rejected by a university ethics committee, I discovered how common the frustration with ethics review processes is among researchers in the humanities and social sciences. Rather than acquiesce to the committee's concerns (Holland, 2007), I changed my research so as not to conduct interviews. I have since learned that this is a disturbingly common experience and can be particularly difficult for graduate students and other researchers in the early stages of their careers (see van den Scott, chapter 12 in this volume).

The suggestion of including members of proposed participant groups or communities in processes of ethics review stems directly from my experiences with the ethics review committee as a student.

During the course of my research and immersion in the field, I met two people who were involved as both activists and academics in the mental health "consumer" movement in Australia. Our conversations touched on topics such as the importance of consumer/survivor perspectives, human rights, valuing "madness," and challenging medicalization.[3] In response to the ethics review committee's concerns about my original research proposal, Dr David Webb, one of these people, said, "Us mad folk are having these conversations (I don't like the word 'interview') all the time – and yes, there is risk in living in this world – but no, it is not OK for ethics committees to deny us this 'dignity of risk' that is a part of life that we are all entitled to" (personal communication, 2 Nov. 2006).

In relation to this insight, my doctoral thesis critically analysed the ethics review committee's concerns in the context of ethics creep and writing on post-psychiatry, calling for a more inclusive agenda in the field of mental health (Bracken and Thomas, 2005). I argued that the biomedical basis of existing systems of ethics review poses a potential threat to non-medical, qualitative research in this area, as well as the participatory and decision-making rights of those within the participant groups, that is, the consumer/survivor/ex-patient community (Holland, 2007; Morrison, 2005).

Shifting the Form of Moral Reasoning Guiding Ethics Review Committees

The conception of moral reasoning that underpins existing processes of ethics review requires the members of ethics committees to adopt the guise of "disinterested parties" and to imagine the perspectives of research subjects (Eckenwiler, 2001: 41). Often members of ethics committees have little, if any, knowledge of the people who may participate in and/or be affected by research. Together with a lack of understanding of emergent qualitative research approaches, and the worst-case-scenario framing mentioned above, this is a recipe for an overly cautious and restrictive research ethics review system.

Lisa Eckenwiler (2001: 40–2) calls for a new style of moral reasoning to guide committees in reviewing research ethics. She critiques the form of moral reasoning that underpins the traditional review of research involving humans, noting that it favours medical scientists and health care providers who are privileged for their presumed capacity to adopt and maintain a stance of alleged objectivity, in addition to having knowledge of disease processes. The conception of moral reasoning that dominates the research ethics review system is one in which those involved in deliberations are required to suppress their subjectivities. The review system renders the notion of expertise by lived experience as inferior, subjective, anecdotal, and/or value-laden – all the things that "expert knowledge" is assumed to be free of. In contrast, and consistent with the views expressed by Eckenwiler, Brian Wynne (1996: 75) emphasizes the need to problematize expert knowledge as culturally validated rather than *naturally* given. Laypeople bring different values and sophisticated forms of knowledge to their decisions about risk, often challenging expert assumptions based on their practical knowledge and lived experiences. It is critical that this knowledge is respected. Eckenwiler (2001) calls for ethics review committees to adopt a form of dialogical reasoning that attends to the "particularities of persons and of social and institutional contexts" (63). A dialogic or relational approach to research ethics involves embracing the "messy and diffuse" micropolitics of research wherein the roles and identities of all research participants are formed and reformed in the situated contexts in which research is carried out (Halse and Honey, 2007: 344–5).

Approaches in qualitative, ethnographic, and action research typically emphasize the knowledge and expertise of research participants (or partners as they are sometimes called). It is this situated knowledge and the practices of the participants that researchers seek to understand. Researchers often take the lead from the communities they are interested in by asking them to identify areas of research need, and involving them in the design, execution, and dissemination of the research. This is the case with action research, service user–led research, and other methods centred on community participation and empowerment, such as community-based participatory research (CBPR). Although these methods are not without ethical dilemmas of their own, they do highlight inadequacies in current systems of ethics review, especially those that do not account for the interests and needs of participant communities and systems that are inappropriate to the particular research methods proposed.

Rationale and Practicalities of Participant Involvement in Research Ethics Review

A number of researchers have identified the need for greater involvement of prospective research communities or participants in the processes of ethics review to ensure that decisions about research are responsive to the attitudes and concerns of the people being studied (Hadskis, 2007; McDonald and Cox, 2009). Nancy Shore et al. (2011: 362) highlight the growing number of community groups in the United States who are implementing processes of research ethics review that operate independently or in conjunction with Institutional Review Boards (IRBs). Their survey found that most of these groups were motivated by the desire to influence how research was conducted in their communities and to serve in a protective role, rather than to set the research agenda. Participant involvement in research ethics review can be particularly important when participants are vulnerable and their agency is typically ignored in the review process or considered only in relation to informed consent (London, 2002: 1079). Although informed consent is an area that requires sensitivity, Leslie London submits that elaborate consent procedures "may simply be inappropriate in their assumptions and expectations of what research participants would see as important protections of their rights" (1080). In relation to mental health, Stephen Tee and Judith Lathlean (2004: 539) argue that one of the barriers to obtaining ethics approval is the assumptions made about the vulnerability of users of mental health services based on limited understandings of diagnostic labels. Researchers can overcome these barriers by routinely involving users of mental health services during ethics approval procedures (542). Such participatory practices are likely to enhance the quality and relevance of research and the credibility and overall quality of the decisions made by research ethics committees.

The emerging practice of research ethics consultation illustrates the attempts in the wider research community to augment existing processes of ethics review. Describing the approach implemented at Stanford University, Cho et al. (2008) say the consultation service, an adjunct to the Institutional Review Board, is designed to make ethics advice available to biomedical researchers throughout the research process (4). According to Cho et al., research ethics consultation has the overarching goal of maximizing benefits and minimizing potential harms of research (5). Unlike ethics review committees, these forms of consultation do not have decision-making authority, but are designed to advise and collaborate, with more time and resources to devote to complex ethical analysis on a case-by-case basis when needed (9). David Fleming and Don Reynolds (2008) argue that "research ethics consultation services will be even more valuable to the research communities they serve if they are directly responsive and accountable to human-research participants" (24). In the context of genetics and mental health research, though also pertinent to other types of research, Downie and McDonald (2004) argue, "Given that those who experience the brunt of adverse effects from improperly conducted research projects are the participants, there is certain compelling logic to suggesting that REBs [Research Ethics Boards] should seek input and the expertise of those who have experiences with health research involving human subjects as participants" (166–7).

How then might participant involvement work in practice? What are the potential challenges? In discussing the composition and competence of research ethics committees, Jocelyn Downie (2006) suggests that greater emphasis should be given to the voice of research participants (92). However, she is uncertain about whether their inclusion on committees is the best way to achieve this. This caution is perhaps warranted. Jill Thompson et al. (2012: 8–9) found that patients and public participants involved in health research decision-making processes readily deferred to the expertise of health professionals and did not see their roles as being on a par with them. Some censored their own behaviours, concerned about how they would be perceived by health professionals. The tendency for participants to mirror professional viewpoints in their approach to research is a concern if it means grassroots experiential voices are seen as less credible within such research settings (4). Enabling potential research participants to consider research proposals independently of experts or existing committee structures may be one way to ensure that they are not inhibited from freely sharing their views.

Michael Hadskis (2007) describes the role of participant representatives as, "most fundamentally, speaking to the core ethical issues associated with the research project under review from the perspective(s) of the community from which the participants will be drawn" (167). He writes, "Research boards would profit from participant representatives weighing in on the relevant communities' perception of just how harmful *they* regard possible negative consequences of participation or their position on the conditions precedent for their acceptance of potential harms" (168, emphasis added). He suggests participant representatives could also offer information about "a community's attitude or attitudes toward certain types of research" (168).

It is, of course, centrally important to recognize diversity within participant groups and that multiple advisers may be required to capture the differing perspectives and interests within a participant or community group. As Lisa Eckenwiler (2001) argues, "We must acknowledge pluralism within groups, as well as the fact that people tend to have multiple community or group affiliations" (53). A practical solution to the issue of representation could be to recruit participant representatives from a variety of existing advocacy or community groups, health care consumer organizations, civil rights groups, community advisory boards, and the like (Hadskis, 2007: 170–1). This would improve the existing system, so long as there is sensitivity to the interests of individual participants and the constitution of such groups to ensure an informed response to their advice. At the same time, concerns about the representativeness of participants and community members should not be used to block this form of involvement, as the same criticism could be directed at committees as they are currently constituted.

The kind of involvement aligns most closely with community members bringing their experiential knowledge to the research ethics review process. In the case of health issues, this might include having a particular illness or treatment, or using a particular health service. Researchers are increasingly recognizing patient involvement in clinical research, including community and patient representatives engaging in ethics review processes to educate others about patient experiences. A study may have an impact on their day-to-day lives. Patients/consumers may also have experience as participants in research projects, on the basis of which they can say something about the impact of specific issues such as recruitment, consent processes, and the way information about a project is presented to participants.

The rationale for involving members of participant groups in processes of research ethics review aligns closely with that of community-based participatory research, designed to produce research that is relevant and sensitive to communities. This approach would suggest some level of community involvement in assessing the ethical dimensions of proposed research. Indeed, community-based participatory research, as with other user-led research, involves community members at several stages of research: initiating research ideas and projects; data collection, interpretation, and analysis; and dissemination of findings (Flicker et al., 2007). Recognizing that existing systems of ethics review are focused primarily on issues related to the individual, Steven Gilbert (2006) has proposed the development of an environmental health and community review board to more adequately incorporate consideration of the impact of research on a community. This is just one of many suggestions for bringing research ethics review processes in line with the needs of affected communities.

Patient and public involvement in various aspects of health research offers a potential source of guidance for involving participants in ethics review of both health-related and other research. Such involvement could take the form of being a member of a research advisory group and reviewing documentation related to research projects, such as information sheets, consent forms, and research protocols (Thompson et al., 2012: 5). Consumer panels used by funding bodies to involve consumers in decision-making processes about the funding of health research might serve as a useful model (O'Donnell and Entwistle, 2004). In response to the NHMRC 2004 *Model Framework for Consumer and Community Participation in Health Research* (in partnership with the Consumers Health Forum of Australia), Carl Saunders et al. (2007) state, "At a minimum, the framework is intended as a resource to provide advice and practical information to support and promote consumer participation in research in Australia" (2). The Cancer Council NSW, through its *Consumer Involvement in Research Project*, has sought to operationalize this framework with the aim, among others, of identifying the type of education that may be required to enable consumers to participate in the review of research grants, and establishing a consumer panel whose members could review and rank grant applications in accordance with specific criteria (Saunders et al., 2007). One initiative involved adding a consumer level to the review process whereby consumers would assess a proposal based on value measures they themselves identify. This serves as an adjunct to the scientific review by providing a more informal and unrestricted atmosphere in which participants can communicate openly and not feel intimidated about lacking scientific expertise. As Carl Saunders et al. note, "Their 'expertise' is their ability to provide an informed consumer perspective to the decision-making process" (3). There are other examples of members of community research panels working alongside health professionals and academic researchers in the cancer research community to "peer review and discuss research proposals in light of their understanding from the perspective of a patient or carer" (Collins et al., 2005: 116).

Increasing emphasis on the importance of consumer and community participation in health and medical research provides the larger context for involving prospective participants in research ethics review (Boote et al., 2002). Involvement in research is generally recognized by policymakers and service providers as a way of ensuring the quality of the research, creating partnerships between researchers and consumers, empowering consumers, and ensuring that research is conducted ethically. It would be paradoxical if consumer/service user involvement in research and other forms of research governance described above were *not* paralleled by a presence in the process of research ethics review or, indeed, if the ethics review process itself functions as an obstacle to greater participation of citizens in research (Staley and Minogue, 2006: 99).

For participant involvement in ethics review processes to be taken seriously in the context of health and other types of research, there must be recognition of the diversity of approaches to research and the forms of research relationships that they create. Health is not just about the absence or treatment of disease. Health research is undertaken by a wide variety of academic disciplines and consumer organizations where greater emphasis is given to subjective illness experiences, social determinants of health, and issues of prevention and health promotion within public health (Boote et al., 2002). Much of this research is qualitative in nature and, as such, does not raise the kind of ethical issues pertinent to clinical trials or other medical interventions. Research ethics committees must ensure that they avail themselves of the expertise necessary to be able to adequately review such research proposals. As experts in their own experiences of illness and health services, it makes sense for members of potential participant groups to be involved in this process. They are well positioned to identify and weigh the risks and benefits of research as well as understand how perceived risks could be mitigated. Furthermore, the practices of ethics review committees should not "curtail researchers' capacity to engage with and learn about research participants before beginning the research" (Halse and Honey, 2005: 2154). Members of ethics review committees must recognize that involving prospective participants (such as users of health services) in the planning stages of research should not require ethics review. Furthermore, research participants are active in negotiating their involvement in research, including protecting their own interests, and would likely welcome the opportunity for more dialogue with researchers (McDonald and Cox, 2009: 8). This interaction enriches the entire experience for those involved in the research.

Given the scope of research conducted within universities, it is unrealistic to expect research ethics committees to include representatives from all potential participant groups. New processes external to the university would need to be established to facilitate participant involvement in ethics review. This could mean an extension to the purview or mission of existing organizations, the establishment of dedicated research participant ethics advisory groups or panels, or a combination of both (Hadskis, 2007: 171). If the focus of research is a particular community, a community advisory board could be given a central role in the ethics review process (Strauss et al., 2001: 1941). For participants who are more dispersed, attempts should be made to draw on the perspectives of groups and individuals with knowledge of and/or experience relevant to participants. As Hadskis (2007: 174) suggests, public information initiatives could be used by ethics review committees to explain the types of research they review and to invite people to register their interest in being involved. Whatever form these processes take, they should retain a dialogic spirit, and participants should not be locked into only being able to provide advice on certain predetermined issues at predetermined times. It is also important to be conscious of perceived tokenism and the risk of bureaucratizing a process that would better serve its purpose by retaining flexibility. I am not suggesting that all research proposals would need to be subject to this form of ethics review process; it is likely to be particularly pertinent when researchers and ethics review committees disagree in their views of risks and/or the decision-making capacities of prospective participants. And, over time, members of research ethics review committees may feel freer to exempt rather than creep, if they see how other boards handle certain protocols (especially exempting certain types of research) with no ill effects.

The rationale for involving prospective participants in review processes should not be understood as primarily a protective one, rather it is grounded in the belief that participants have a substantive contribution to make to the design, execution, and reporting of research. Once these ethics review advisers or advisory groups or panels are in place, researchers could consult with them as they formulate their research proposals and complete the ethics review application process. Researchers can report to review boards about having sought and taken the advice of such a group in putting their research proposal together. This may reduce the instances of ethics review committees raising concerns about imagined risks to imagined participants, and may facilitate more frequent expedited reviews. In other cases, it may be possible that this type of (informal) ethics review could replace more formalized (and less relevant) processes of ethics committee review. In the event that an ethics committee has concerns about a particular research project, it may be useful for the researcher to seek the input of advocacy or consumer groups in responding to the review, which might include identifying where a committee's concerns are unwarranted or even contrary to the interests of the prospective participants and their communities. Members of research ethics review committees should also seek the expertise of such groups to ensure that their own determinations are relevant and sensitive to the communities whose interests they seek to serve and protect.

Rationale and Practicalities of Discipline-Level Research Ethics Review

Lending greater weight to the knowledge and expertise of disciplinary peers offers another possible alternative to current structures and processes of research ethics committee review. This suggestion has been canvassed in varying forms by several scholars (e.g., Gunsalus et al., 2007). In its 2005 response to the draft *National Statement* the Academy of the Social Sciences in Australia endorses and encourages the establishment of subcommittees related to discipline areas, organizational structures, or types of research; some Australian universities have adopted this model. This reflects the understanding that what it means to act in an ethical way is defined within researchers' communities of practice (Jacobson et al., 2007: 6). Parallels exist between these suggestions and those made by Iain Hay (1998) when discussing ethical strategies for geographers, though he is referring to the formation of a committee of one's research peers as well as their co-participants (subjects) as a way of dealing with complaints of unethical behaviour: "This composition places the onus on individual researchers to take into account the moral beliefs and expectations of their co-researchers, whilst also admitting into review procedures some knowledge about prevailing research practicalities, practice, and standards" (71).

A hybrid committee such as this, or even a less formal structure, could make ethics review a particularly valuable aspect of the research process, as it should be, rather than one that is approached with a sense of unease, frustration, and futility (Jacobson et al., 2007: 4–5). However, one must be mindful of Jocelyn Downie's (2006: 83–4) comment that assignment to disciplinary-level peer review should not be an arbitrary process because a discipline itself offers no inherent guarantee that research does not raise ethics concerns or would not benefit from a wider, more inclusive and diverse level of reviewer input. I suggest that discipline-level review would strengthen and lend greater substance to the ethics review process precisely because those doing the review would have expertise and an interest in the area of research – whether it is the proposed methods, the theoretical perspectives taken, and/or the prospective participants. To involve researchers from the same disciplines or methodological traditions in discussing research purposes and common ethical questions that arise and providing feedback to each other (Jacobson et al., 2007: 6) just makes sense, practically and intellectually. It is a system that is already in place and working (in the very highly related case of academic publishing). Given that this is the type of peer review process that academic researchers are most familiar with as they submit grant applications and research and other manuscripts, it makes sense that it could also apply to research ethics. In response to concerns or objections that disciplinary peers will be unlikely to make adverse rulings about their colleagues' proposals, while this is a possibility, it is also likely that peers will want to ensure that research conducted within their disciplines and fields of research is well-designed and reflective of current thinking and practice. How we conduct research with people and the findings that research produces are, after all, likely to reflect and provide benefits to scholars as well as participants and the wider community. Moreover, research that harms participants or squanders resources would negatively affect the entire discipline.

Discipline-level review might involve, in the first instance, researchers seeking ethics approval or some form of endorsement from the disciplinary-level committee or peer group they identify as having the necessary expertise to address the research proposal. This group could approve the research based on an assessment that the researcher has addressed relevant ethical issues and has the necessary skill and support to conduct the research. Alternatively, the discipline-level review may identify aspects of the research that should receive further consideration and offer advice in that regard. Many forms of research are suited to this type of review and the ethical conduct of research would not suffer as a result. Although not appropriate to all types of research, this discipline-level review should be an available alternative to full-committee review.

Discussion: The Case for New Approaches to Research Ethics Review

Universities are not likely to disable existing ethics committee structures and review processes. Therefore, the focus on ways the current processes can be improved, including other forms of review such as participant-level review and peer involvement, may be a more direct route to a better review system. The need for more flexibility with regard to the information and documentation required by ethics review committees is obvious. Rather than requiring researchers to respond to mandatory questions grounded in preconceptions about the research process that are irrelevant, allow researchers to submit a narrative about their intended research, using the existing procedures for expedited review. The narrative would address the fulfilment of identified ethics requirements, but would not require an illusion, that is, the completion of full details about the future, all on a one-size-fits-all form (Jacobson et al., 2007: 6). In the event that completing existing application forms is required, provisions must be made for researchers to complete them to the best of their ability and to provide further explanation as to why they are unable or unwilling to complete other aspects. These documents can be prepared in consultation with prospective participants, peer groups, and board members.

The obvious assumption is that participant and peer involvement would improve research ethics review, but caution is needed to ensure that this involvement does not increase difficulty for researchers to conduct research. If not properly instituted, the research ethics review process may become more onerous than it currently is, by increasing the number of perspectives and inherent differences of opinion, vested interests, and egos involved. It is important that individual researchers, in collaboration with participant groups and disciplinary peers, retain the responsibility to design and conduct research according to their expertise and that they be trusted to put in place appropriate mechanisms to carry out their research in a way that does not harm or threaten the participants involved or the interests of universities and funding agencies. Collaborating with prospective participants in developing research projects is a common practice that many researchers welcome. However, a range of factors influence researchers' decisions about what to research, why, and with whom, and it may not always be feasible or desirable to consult with prospective research participants and/or communities. The intent, therefore, is not to arm ethics review committees with another hoop through which to require researchers to jump but, rather, to encourage a participatory-dialogic process – whether it be between researchers and potential participants, researchers and their peers, researchers and members of ethics committees, or other stakeholder combinations – a process of ethical *reflection* that is arguably preferable to current processes of ethics *review*.

Another concern is that the proposals could be seen as shifting the burden of ethics review to already overworked academics (in the case of discipline-level processes) or people with existing health problems (in the case of health research). The researcher may erroneously assume that members of potential participant groups want to, or indeed, should be involved in research ethics review when this may not be the case. This necessitates reflexivity about the motives and representativeness of participants who choose to be involved in research *and* research-ethics review processes (Hogg and Williamson, 2001). Care is needed to ensure that those involved in ethics review do not undermine the views and experiences of other potential research participants in a way that is antithetical to its intent. There is no reason to believe that, as with ethics committee members, members of participant groups will not also engage in imagining harms of research to others whose knowledge and experience may well differ from their own. They may, however, provide different reasons for their views, which would themselves need to be subject to scrutiny, just as the decisions of ethics review committees should be. The issue of shifting some of the responsibilities of researchers and ethics committees onto third parties who may be equally constrained in their capacity to serve as liaisons among researchers and communities must also be considered by the parties involved. It is equally important that these forms of involvement do not stifle research – those who do not want to be cast in an unflattering light or who simply do not like the proposed research must not have the only nor the final word. The focus must be on better understanding rather than on another stage to get approval.

Objections to peer and participant involvement centre on concerns about whether members of participant groups or disciplinary peers can exercise impartiality in the ethics review process. Yet, as others have argued, the existing process of ethics review is replete with partiality and personal bias (Eckenwiler, 2001: 43). An argument could be made that members of certain prospective participant groups, as laypeople, lack the necessary knowledge and skills to make sufficiently informed and substantiated contributions to the ethics review process; that they lack research literacy required to understand the research process and to engage with researchers. This is the kind of attitude that underscores the need for participants and/or peers to be incorporated into processes of ethics review. This mentality must be challenged, not simply to better reflect the humanities and social science disciplines and their associated epistemological and methodological orientations, but also to better account for and respond to community expectations and to put into practice the rhetoric of consumer/community involvement.

Additional levels of bureaucratic oversight are difficult, time-consuming, and frustrating for researchers and regulators including members of ethics review committees and university administrators. A key concern in literature critical of formal ethics review processes is that what should be a *process* becomes a formulaic box-ticking exercise as researchers are required to communicate with ethics review committees through ill-fitting, often irrelevant application forms. Greater involvement of participant and disciplinary peers in the review process is likely to facilitate more informed considerations of the ethical issues and dilemmas present in a given proposal. The key point about participant and peer-level ethics review is that these processes rest on an understanding of ethics as integral to the research process itself, rather than something done prior to research and/or separate from the various ethical considerations that one experiences in their everyday lives. In this regard, the process need not be formalized or routinized within existing systems of research ethics review, rather existing systems must be flexible enough to accommodate participant and peer involvement. Scholars to a greater or lesser extent are already engaged in discussions with peers and members of potential participant groups in conceptualizing and designing research projects. It follows that researchers can integrate these practices into the ethics review process and (eventually) offer them as a basis for exemption of studies involving minimal and low risk. Clearly, elevating the role of participants and disciplinary peers within ethics review processes, and responding to concerns raised by them, will be aided by further empirical research into ways members of the community understand and evaluate risks and ethical issues generally, and in relation to different types of research specifically. Talking to members of advocacy groups and the wider community about their views on being involved in processes of research ethics review is also a fruitful area of inquiry.

Conclusion: Changing the Way We Think about and Do Research Ethics Review

Several scholars have identified the need to expand the dialogue about ethics, not just in terms of bringing more perspectives into the conversation, but also in terms of understanding the situated nature of ethical dilemmas involved in researching human experiences. This involves accommodating multiple epistemologies, attending to the particularities of participants and researchers, and viewing ethics as an "ongoing process of critical reflection, action, and accountability throughout the research" process (Halse and Honey, 2005: 2158). Christine Halse and Anne Honey (2005) write, "Thinking of research ethics as a continual process of collaboration would open up opportunities to dissolve the (mis)conception that ethics approval means ethical research; to erase the differential power relationships among researchers, ethics committees, and participants; and to interrupt the mechanisms that make researchers complicit in the 'othering' of research participants" (2159).

Changing the way we think about ethics involves changing the way ethics committee members think about research, researchers, and research participants. This involves embracing complexity and ambivalence and recognizing that rather than ensuring ethical research, the assumptions made by members of ethics committees may actually be a barrier to it. Existing processes of ethics review tend to be concerned more with the risks of research than its benefits, and with creating and deciding based on worst-case scenarios rather than participatory dialogue, and in the face of overwhelmingly common (non-harmful) outcomes. It would be desirable for the focus of ethics review to shift from vulnerability to potentiality with respect to participants and the benefits of research. This requires understanding that notions of vulnerability and expertise are not fixed but rather dependent on the circumstances in which we find ourselves in life as in research. The first aspect of elevating and, in turn, respecting the autonomy and expertise of potential research participants involves recognizing their capacity and right to decide to participate in research or not, and to stop participating at any time they choose. This recognition goes hand in hand with trusting researchers to be conscious of and to react appropriately to ethical issues that may arise during the course of their research activities (see Hamilton, chapter 17 in this volume).

It is difficult to suggest alternative processes of ethics review with too much specificity because ethics guidelines must be interpreted in the context of actual research (Hammersley, 2006). Many outstanding questions remain: how these review mechanisms would work in relation to existing structures of ethics committees, at what points potential participants should be invited to be involved, how to identify members of a potential participant group, and how to ensure there is enough diversity without making the process overly cumbersome. There are clearly many scholars engaging with these issues, and it is my hope that this chapter provides an impetus for others to consider how participant and peer-level review might work in their disciplines.

To conclude, within policy and academic discourse regarding research and research ethics in Australia and elsewhere, support for increased community, public, and consumer involvement in research is growing. As evidenced by the 2012 Ethics Summit, many ideas for improvements and alternatives in the research ethics review process are circulating. The ideas discussed in this chapter are efforts to capitalize on these tendencies with a view towards ensuring that *ethics review* systems are *ethical*. These ideas are intended to facilitate more informed review of emergent qualitative research designs and to address the problem of ethics review committees imagining harms – to the detriment of many forms of mostly benign research. Proposals to elevate the expertise of participant groups and disciplinary peers in research ethics review are underpinned by a desire to affirm scholarly responsibility for maintaining ethical research practices in response to the issues raised within their specific fields of research, and ensure that the voices of people affected by and included in research are heard – when research proposals are developed, reviewed, and executed, rather than having ethics review committees make decisions based on hypothetical, worst-case assumptions. These practices also have the potential to reduce the workload and increase the legitimacy of ethics review committees, bring researchers and communities closer together, and increase the impact of social research.

NOTES

1 I have documented my response to the committee's concerns elsewhere (Holland, 2007).

2 Section 2.1.6 of the *National Statement* says, "Research is 'low risk' where the only foreseeable risk is one of discomfort. Where the risk, even if unlikely, is more serious than discomfort, the research is not low risk." Section 2.1.7 says, "Research is 'negligible risk' where there is no foreseeable risk of harm or discomfort; and any foreseeable risk is no more than inconvenience. Where the risk, even if unlikely, is more than

inconvenience, the research is not negligible risk" (NHMRC et al., 2007: 18). Yet, as Kevin Haggerty (2004) has suggested, perceptions of risk, as with harm, may be limited only to the imagination of members of ethics committees, and questions are legitimately raised about where the line distinguishing *minimal* from *greater than minimal* risk in research is drawn in practice. The *National Statement* leaves *discomfort* and *inconvenience* open to expansive interpretation by local university ethics committees.

3 In the area of mental health, in addition to many diagnostic categories, there are important differences in the way people identify themselves and their relations with mental health services and psychiatry. In Australia, *consumer* is the term most widely used in policy documents describing the importance of people with first-hand illness/health experiences in health policy, services, and research. However, I use the term with caution because I recognize that many users of mental health services or people who have experienced psychiatry and the mental health system resist such a label in favour of terms such as psychiatric system *survivor* or mental health *service user*.

REFERENCES

Boote, Jonathan, Rosemary Telford, and Cindy Cooper. (2002). "Consumer Involvement in Health Research: A Review and Research Agenda." *Health Policy (Amsterdam)* 61 (2): 213–36. http://dx.doi.org/10.1016/S0168-8510(01)00214-7

Bracken, Patrick J., and Philip Thomas. (2005). *Postpsychiatry: Mental Health in a Postmodern World*. Oxford: Oxford University Press. http://dx.doi.org/10.1093/med/9780198526094.001.0001

Cho, Mildred K., Sara L. Tobin, Henry T. Greely, Jennifer McCormick, Angie Boyce, and David Magnus. (2008). "Strangers at the Benchside: Research Ethics Consultation." *American Journal of Bioethics* 8 (3): 4–13. http://dx.doi.org/10.1080/15265160802109322

Collins, Karen, Tony Stevens, and Sam H. Ahmedzai. (2005). "Can Consumer Research Panels Become an Integral Part of the Cancer Research Community?" *Clinical Effectiveness in Nursing* 9 (3–4): 112–18. http://dx.doi.org/10.1016/j.cein.2006.08.001

Cordner, Christopher. (2006). "Towards Healthy Research." *The Australian*, 23 Aug.

Downie, Jocelyn. (2006). "The Canadian Agency for the Oversight of Research Involving Humans: A Reform Proposal." *Accountability in Research* 13 (1): 75–100. http://dx.doi.org/10.1080/08989620600588969

Downie, Jocelyn, and Fiona McDonald. (2004). "Revisioning the Oversight of Research Involving Humans in Canada." *Health Law Journal* 12: 159–82.

Eckenwiler, Lisa. (2001). "Moral Reasoning and the Review of Research Involving Human Subjects." *Kennedy Institute of Ethics Journal* 11 (1): 37–69. http://dx.doi.org/10.1353/ken.2001.0003

Fitzgerald, Maureen H. (2004). "Big Basket or Mission Creep?" *Professional Ethics Report* 17 (2): 1–3.

– (2005). "Punctuated Equilibrium, Moral Panics and the Ethics Review Process." *Journal of Academic Ethics* 2 (4): 315–38. http://dx.doi.org/10.1007/s10805-005-9004-y

Fitzgerald, Maureen H., Paul A. Phillips, and Elisa Yule. (2006). "The Research Ethics Review Process and Ethics Review Narratives." *Ethics & Behavior* 16 (4): 377–95. http://dx.doi.org/10.1207/s15327019eb1604_7

Fleming, David A., and Don Reynolds. (2008). "Being Directly Responsive and Accountable to Human-Research Participants." *American Journal of Bioethics* 8 (3): 24–5. http://dx.doi.org/10.1080/15265160802109447

Flicker, Sarah, Robb Travers, Adrian Guta, Sean McDonald, and Aileen Meagher. (2007). "Ethical Dilemmas in Community-Based Participatory Research: Recommendations for Institutional Review Boards." *Journal of Urban Health* 84 (4): 478–93. http://dx.doi.org/10.1007/s11524-007-9165-7

Gilbert, Steven G. (2006). "Supplementing the Traditional Institutional Review Board with an Environmental Health and Community Review Board." *Environmental Health Perspectives* 114 (10): 1626–9. http://dx.doi.org/10.1289/ehp.9005

Gunsalus, C. Kristina, Edward M. Bruner, Nicholas C. Burbules, Leon Dash, Matthew Finkin, Joseph P. Goldberg, William Greenough, Gregory Miller, and Michael G. Pratt. (2007). "The Illinois White Paper – Improving the System for Protecting Human Subjects: Counteracting IRB 'Mission Creep.'" *Qualitative Inquiry* 13 (5): 617–49.

Hadskis, Michael R. (2007). "Giving Voice to Research Participants: Should IRBs Hear from Research Participant Representatives?" *Accountability in Research: Policies and Quality Assurance* 14 (3): 155–77. http://dx.doi.org/10.1080/08989620701455209

Haggerty, Kevin D. (2004). "Ethics Creep: Governing Social Science Research in the Name of Ethics." *Qualitative Sociology* 27 (4): 391–414. http://dx.doi.org/10.1023/B:QUAS.0000049239.15922.a3

Halse, Christine, and Anne Honey. (2005). "Unraveling Ethics: Illuminating the Moral Dilemmas of Research Ethics." *Signs (Chicago, Ill.)* 30 (4): 2141–62. http://dx.doi.org/10.1086/428419

– (2007). "Rethinking Ethics Review as Institutional Discourse." *Qualitative Inquiry* 13 (3): 336–52. http://dx.doi.org/10.1177/1077800406297651

Hammersley, Martyn. (2006). "Are Ethics Committees Ethical?" *Qualitative Research* 2: 4–8.

Hay, Iain. (1998). "Making Moral Imaginations: Research Ethics, Pedagogy, and Professional Human Geography." *Philosophy and Geography* 1 (1): 55–75. http://dx.doi.org/10.1080/13668799808573632

Hogg, Christine, and Charlotte Williamson. (2001). "Whose Interests Do Lay People Represent? Towards an Understanding of the Role of Lay People as Members of Committees." *Health Expectations* 4 (1): 2–9. http://dx.doi.org/10.1046/j.1369-6513.2001.00106.x

Holland, Kate. (2007). "The Epistemological Bias of Ethics Review: Constraining Mental Health Research." *Qualitative Inquiry* 13 (6): 895–913. http://dx.doi.org/10.1177/1077800407304469

Israel, Mark. (2005). "Research Hamstrung by Ethics Creep." *The Australian*, 12 Jan.

Jacobson, Nora, Rebecca Gewurtz, and Emma Haydon. (2007). "Ethical Review of Interpretive Research: Problems and Solutions." *IRB Ethics and Human Research* 29 (5): 1–8.

Lincoln, Yvonna S., and William G. Tierney. (2004). "Qualitative Research and Institutional Review Boards." *Qualitative Inquiry* 10 (2): 219–34. http://dx.doi.org/10.1177/1077800403262361

London, Leslie. (2002). "Ethical Oversight of Public Health Research: Can Rules and IRBs Make a Difference in Developing Countries?" *American Journal of Public Health* 92 (7): 1079–84. http://dx.doi.org/10.2105/AJPH.92.7.1079

McDonald, Michael, and Susan Cox. (2009). "Moving toward Evidence-Based Human Participant Protection." *Journal of Academic Ethics* 7 (1–2): 1–16. http://dx.doi.org/10.1007/s10805-009-9082-3

Morrison, Linda. J. (2005). *Talking Back to Psychiatry: The Psychiatric Consumer/Survivor/Ex-patient Movement*. New York: Routledge.

NHMRC et al. (National Health and Medical Research Council, Australian Research Council, Australian Vice-Chancellors' Committee). (2007). *National Statement on Ethical Conduct in Human Research*. Canberra: Australian Government.

O'Donnell, Máire, and Vikki Entwistle. (2004). "Consumer Involvement in Decisions about What Health-Related Research Is Funded." *Health Policy (Amsterdam)* 70 (3): 281–90. http://dx.doi.org/10.1016/j.healthpol.2004.04.004

Saunders, Carl, Sally Crossing, Afaf Girgis, Phyllis Butow, and Andrew Penman. (2007). "Operationalising a Model Framework for Consumer and

Community Participation in Health and Medical Research." *Australia and New Zealand Health Policy* 4 (1): 13. http://dx.doi.org/10.1186/1743-8462-4-13

Schrag, Zachary M. (2011). "The Case against Ethics Review in the Social Sciences." *Research Ethics* 7 (4): 120–31. http://dx.doi.org/10.1177/174701611100700402

Shore, Nancy, Ruta Brazauskas, Elaine Drew, Kristine A. Wong, Lisa Moy, Andrea Corage Baden, Kristen Cyr, Jocelyn Ulevicus, and Sarena D. Seifer. (2011). "Understanding Community-Based Processes for Research Ethics Review: A National Study." *American Journal of Public Health* 101 (S1): S359–64. http://dx.doi.org/10.2105/AJPH.2010.194340

Staley, Kristina, and Virginia Minogue. (2006). "User Involvement Leads to More Ethically Sound Research." *Clinical Ethics* 1 (2): 95–100. http://dx.doi.org/10.1258/147775006777254489

Stark, Laura. (2007). "Victims in Our Own Minds? IRBs in Myth and Practice." *Law & Society Review* 41 (4): 777–86. http://dx.doi.org/10.1111/j.1540-5893.2007.00323.x

Strauss, Ronald P., Sohini Sengupta, Sandra Crouse Quinn, Jean Goeppinger, Cora Spaulding, Susan Kegeles, and Greg Millett. (2001). "The Role of Community Advisory Boards: Involving Communities in the Informed Consent Process." *American Journal of Public Health* 91 (12): 1938–43. http://dx.doi.org/10.2105/AJPH.91.12.1938

Tee, Stephen R, and Judith A Lathlean. (2004). "The Ethics of Conducting a Co-operative Inquiry with Vulnerable People." *Journal of Advanced Nursing* 47 (5): 536–43. http://dx.doi.org/10.1111/j.1365-2648.2004.03130.x

Thompson, Jill, Paul Bissell, Cindy Cooper, Chris J. Armitage, and Rosemary Barber. (2012). "Credibility and the 'Professionalized' Lay Expert: Reflections on the Dilemmas and Opportunities of Public Involvement in Health Research." *Health* 16 (6): 602–18. http://dx.doi.org/10.1177/1363459312441008

van den Hoonaard, Will C. (2001). "Is Research-Ethics Review a Moral Panic?" *Canadian Review of Sociology and Anthropology La Revue canadienne de sociologie et d'anthropologie* 38 (1): 19–36. http://dx.doi.org/10.1111/j.1755-618X.2001.tb00601.x

– (ed.). (2002). *Walking the Tightrope: Ethical Issues for Qualitative Researchers.* Toronto: University of Toronto Press.

Wynne, Brian. (1996). "May the Sheep Safely Graze? A Reflexive View of the Expert-Lay Knowledge Divide." In Scott Lash, Bronislaw Szerszynski, and Brian Wynne (eds.), *Risk, Environment and Modernity*, 44–83. London: Sage.

19 Rupturing Ethics Literacy: The Ethics Application Repository (TEAR)

EMMA TUMILTY, MARTIN B. TOLICH,
AND STEPHANIE DOBSON

"Genius!" That is how the senior author responded to The Ethics Application Repository (TEAR), an open access online repository of ethics applications donated by scholars and funded by a three-year grant from the Royal Society of New Zealand (contract no. U001125). At the time Emma Tumilty was a research administrator in the School of Physiotherapy at the University of Otago advising postgraduate and novice researchers in preparing research proposals including ethics review applications. Immediately, she knew The Ethics Application Repository was a rupture in the normal process of ethics review. The Ethics Application Repository would aid student researchers facing enrolment deadlines and academics constricted by funding timeframes. Neither group could afford the delays caused by conditional board approval (requiring follow-up work) or even rejection (requiring full re-submission) of their ethics applications. Yet conditional approval, for novice researchers especially, was often the outcome bringing frustration and additional pressures to an already stressful environment. Research shows that few applications to ethics review committees submitted by novices are approved on their first reading, leading to multiple re-submissions and delaying the commencement of research (Lincoln and Tierney, 2004).

Reasons for these slow outcomes are often matters of communication. Guidelines included on ethics review committee websites written to aid researchers in presenting and explaining ethically sound projects to IRBs leave many questions unanswered, especially for the inexperienced researcher. To cover all areas of research, guidelines sacrifice depth for range, and there is an expectation that gaining ethics approval takes months. Research ethics guidelines often do not include reference to qualitative methodologies such as ethnography, photo voice, or participatory action research (Boser, 2007). Students, therefore, gain no feeling for both the committee's potential concerns with their work or for the level of detail required to explain it. Anecdotal evidence in New Zealand suggests that some graduate supervisors get Master's students to avoid IRB review and conduct secondary analysis (i.e., analysis of data already collected requiring no further ethical review). These latter students fail to learn how to think ethically. What they do learn is ethical cynicism: ethics review committees are to be avoided whenever possible.

Thus, the ill-defined (and continually moving) IRB goalposts are aimed at blindly by applicants guessing about the level of information the committees require and how it should be presented. Committee preference and decision-making appears mercurial due in part to the lack of transparency and the fact that, for example, 90 per cent of ethics committees in the United States meet behind closed doors (Stark, 2012). Knowledge transfer is a process that can only occur post-submission because of the way ethics review committees review applications – notification of requested changes arrive in brief written summaries. IRB letters requesting changes offer little explanation or justification, leaving researchers feeling misunderstood and frustrated. Equally, researchers often describe their work inadequately (thick with scientific detail, but light on contextual information and practical descriptions) failing to realize the disservice they are doing themselves by frustrating a busy committee with a high workload. Tolich has experienced this first hand when, as an IRB chair, he tried to describe qualitative research to a committee of IRB chairs, but was told qualitative research applications read as jargon (Tolich and Tumilty, 2013). This example shows that rather than purposeful obfuscation, applicants are unable to recognize what details and descriptions are required for the ethics review of their project in part because of a lack of direction by ethics review committees. When completing an IRB application, novice researchers face a blank page and are forced to reinvent the ethics wheel from scratch. This creates a fear of dealing with the processes around ethics rather than engaging in thinking about ethical principles.

Within the senior author's School of Physiotherapy the only tools available to minimize undesirable outcomes were the use of accumulated extra information gleaned through multiple application reviews and the practice of informal application sharing between supervisors, students, and peers. These informal sharing practices using limited applications (i.e., within a single department) may unintentionally contribute to subsequent applications sharing similar language – producing the perceived "jargon" referred to earlier. Therefore, The Ethics Application Repository,[1] with applications across multiple fields and methodologies, to be used as a resource freely and openly by all, seemed for the senior author like a "clouds parting before the sun" moment and so The Ethics Application Repository began.

The repository bridges the chasm between applicant researcher and the ethics review committee, allowing novice researchers access to best practice examples not only of how to conduct research ethically, but also how to explain it competently to an ethics review committee. Its goal is to redistribute privilege allowing novice researchers to gain a better understanding of application processes, beyond theory, when relating ethical principles to their work. The TEAR rupture creates the open dialogue and knowledge transfer currently lacking. In power terms, The Ethics Application Repository is one step towards levelling the field in two broad areas. First, it significantly demystifies ethics review processes providing a range of successful applications, and second it showcases best practice and demonstrates the creative ethical empiricism inherent in good research design, practice, and responsibility.

Rupturing Ethical Literacy

Just as the invention of the printing press allowed literacy to proliferate in the fifteenth century by removing the privilege of copying texts from scribes (and the associated cost of buying scribe-written texts), so the Internet is providing a vehicle for the sharing of knowledge and information globally and freely (Winston, 2010). Much like an open access journal, The Ethics Application Repository accepts submissions and selects them based on their quality but, unlike a journal, the entire collection is open submission and free access. By donating their work, scholars are not only sharing their knowledge, but are showcasing the ethical practice underlying their research. Recent research shows there is a correlation between the level of ethical reporting (description of details related to the ethical practices in one's research) and the quality of the research conducted (Ruiz-Canela et al., 2001).

Educational theory supports the use of exemplars and case studies in learning new forms of thinking and reasoning (Barrows and Feltovich, 1987; Norman, 2005). It is something well used in the medical/health professions where students are required to learn "clinical reasoning," a complex skill learned through interpreting theory in practice (Barrows and Feltovich, 1987; Norman, 2005). The development of skills can be aided through reading and analysis of exemplars and case studies. Similarly, ethical reasoning requires the interpretation of principles in practice and therefore the use of exemplars seems obvious. At present, novice researchers are expected to pick up ethical reasoning almost intuitively. Provided with generic guidelines, the ability to decide ethical practice is seen as common sense – researchers figure it out, some faster than others. Guidelines provided are often rooted in traditional biomedical research and are broad to ensure widest applicability. Students with a project outside this traditional model are more likely to encounter problems. Vulnerable participants, novel and qualitative methodologies, as well as new areas of research frequently encounter issues on the way through the ethics review process. The Ethics Application Repository reduces this cycle of trial and error, providing a means to conceptualize simple principles in complex situations with an eye to best practice.

Stage One: Proof of Concept

The Ethics Application Repository was developed in stages. The initial proof-of-concept stage (Tolich and Tumilty, 2013) involved developing the website, sourcing donations (22 initially submitted, eight of which met donor criteria and were uploaded). The first eight submissions fitting the TEAR donor criteria were qualitative, yet their subject material and methodologies are eclectic. The donations are organized as accessible resources. Upon entering the home page the user has the option to browse the site according to specific categories:

- *Communities and collections*: children's research; innovative methodologies; Internet research; participatory action research; social sciences
- *Issue date*: date of ethics application submissions, detailing the name(s) of the contributor(s) and the title of the research
- *Author*: displays the list of senior academics who have provided submissions
- *Title*: displays the title, issue date, and author name(s) of each ethics application
- *Subject*: displays the full breadth of the subjects and topic areas covered in the totality of TEAR contents.

Using any of these subgroupings will bring up the related, accessible contributions in order of their relation to the category.

Following the initial set-up, Stage Two, a stakeholder consultation, was conducted to investigate whether or not The Ethics Application Repository was necessary, applicable, and acceptable (Mahadkar et al., 2010; European Commission, n.d.). Stakeholders included graduate students, academics, and ethics committee members.

Stage Two: Stakeholder Consultation

Graduate students in the area of sociology and education at various New Zealand universities were consulted through an informal discussion in two focus groups and three subsequent informal face-to-face interviews. The students were purposively recruited through posters as persons more likely to conduct research using vulnerable populations and qualitative methods – often contentious ones – such as those uploaded to the TEAR site. The discussions were preceded by a presentation about The Ethics Application Repository, and time was allotted for students to go online to explore The Ethics Application Repository.

Overwhelmingly, the students responded to The Ethics Application Repository positively: "Wow" or "brilliant," but with some room for improvement – specifically, in layout, navigation, etc. (Focus Group 1). An education graduate student applied some learning theory, seeing current practice with IRB review as "sink or swim," whereas The Ethics Application Repository had a "scaffolding" effect (Focus Group 1, Student Participant 2). These students described The Ethics Application Repository as a form of sharing best practices and stated the need was evident to have something like this in ethics education, given sharing best practice examples was frequently and successfully used in other disciplines and areas.

The postgraduates also reflected on current practice. Time constraints with ethics applications was a major theme emerging from the focus group, as was the graduate students' empathy for isolated distance postgraduate student learners writing an IRB application: "I'm lucky I have people I can go to, but equally some people are distance-learners and don't have that ... and they need something else" (Focus group 1, Student Participant 3).

Some of these novice researchers, who had not yet completed an ethics application or even knew what an ethics application was, were somewhat overwhelmed when they saw the extent of the ethics applications on the TEAR site and were hit by the "enormity of the task" (Focus Group 1, Student Participant 1). These students also grasped the issues of applying abstract theory to practice, such as the use of a phone script to establish the safety of a participant who could possibly be in a domestic abuse situation in order to minimize participant risk (Focus Group 1, Student Participant 1).

All students interviewed one-to-one were PhD candidates, and many of them mentioned they had not had to prepare nor submit a proposal to an ethics review board for their Master's degree research and were struggling with the decisions of the ethics review committee for their PhD project. For these students, committee decisions had been contradictory, were out of touch (choosing to enforce a decision not necessarily in touch with the population they were protecting), and behind the times (decisions regarding the accessing of Facebook, for example) (Interviewees 3, 2, and 1, respectively).

Aside from comments about their experiences during the process and their general approval of The Ethics Application Repository, these students also provided constructive suggestions. These included additional material that could be added to aid those using the resource such as explanations detailing what changes, if any, applicants had to make to their applications in order to gain approval (Focus Group 1). Students also wondered if unsuccessful applications could be added to show what *not* to do (Focus Group 1, Participant 3). The addition of a collection for research in the area of disability was also welcomed enthusiastically (Focus Group 1, Student Participant 4).

In its current form, The Ethics Application Repository does not include examples of unsuccessful applications. Restrictions imposed as part of the ethics approval that The Ethics Application Repository operates under (University of Otago Human Ethics Committee no. 12/014), prohibits this. However, further development of the website to include space for notes regarding the applications by the applicants and information about the path to approval is being incorporated as well as site statistics (regarding most viewed and/or recently uploaded applications, for example).

Members of the focus groups and interviewees confirmed that sharing ethics applications was current informal practice and that The Ethics Application Repository is a broader, more accessible, and possibly more applicable form of this practice. This feedback, albeit limited, was encouraging and showed from the students' perspective that there is a need and that The Ethics Application Repository is seen as an appropriate and welcome solution.

Consultation with academics, administrators, and IRB members revealed further support for The Ethics Application Repository with many wondering why it did not already exist. "What a great idea and resource!" (personal communication between 2nd author and an ethics committee member). They saw The Ethics Application Repository as a step forward, and some recognized that the site was not only beneficial to students, but also to academic supervisors, advisers, researchers, and ethics committee members as well (IRB member's informal email). In general, they agreed that the sharing of exemplars moved ethical knowledge from being held by a few to being shared by many. Academics and others in this category were initially approached to share their applications and appeared to have no issue with donating applications, further supporting the idea that ethics applications can be open and transparent without negative effects (Tolich and Tumilty, 2013).

Aside from postgraduate students learning how to present their research plans and ways of incorporating good ethical practice into their research projects, The Ethics Application Repository is seen as useful to IRB members, teachers of research methods, and even experienced faculty. As the focus groups showed, The Ethics Application Repository does build on the common practice of supervisors sharing their own ethics applications with their graduate students, but The Ethics Application Repository is this practice writ large. Tolich, with 20 years of experience in graduate student supervision – a decade of that spent serving on ethics review committees – is doubtful about whether he could advise a graduate student who wishes to research identity in chat rooms or Facebook in appropriate ethical procedures and documentation. Among the goals of The Ethics Application Repository is pooling resources and facilitating sound ethical practice by allowing both novice researchers and their supervisors (who may be novices on a specific topic) to learn how scholars have previously approached ethics review, allowing researchers to better protect their research participants from harm (Tumilty, 2012). Not only can those completing ethics review benefit from The Ethics Application Repository, but those IRB members conducting ethics review, instructing others, or exploring ethical practice will also find value in it.

IRB members unfamiliar with a certain methodology (e.g., auto-ethnography, photo voice, chat room ethnography) or complex topics (i.e., any research involving children or the iterative nature of community-based participatory action research where participants are co-researchers) or obscure jargon (lived experience, saturation and process consent) can read how experts have described their experiences. This action promotes ethics review committees as educational institutions, arguably something they are not currently or historically.

If ethics review committees were educational institutions, they would have identified and posted common problems and their solutions and have supplied templates of appropriate permissions for others to mirror. Examples of strategies used to ensure safety both in complex situations such as data archiving or studies involving vulnerable participants, as well as models of best practice for frequently occurring issues could be identified and pooled as is the case with data-sharing initiatives (Van Den Eynden, 2008; Van Den Eynden and Corti, 2009). The Ethics Application Repository transforms the process between applicant and committee members from one of gatekeeping to one of learning through the use of successful applications.

Research methods teachers mine The Ethics Application Repository and encourage their graduate and undergraduate students to experientially follow narratives that blend theory, ethical principles, and methodologies. In addition, data researchers may mine the TEAR archive itself for use in secondary analysis, for example, studying the nature of informed consent forms and processes across ethics review committees, or the ways Indigenous consultation (with Māori, Aboriginals, First Nation Canadians, Native Americans, and other groups) is conducted.

Little existing instruction is available about how to complete ethics applications, producing unnecessary frustrations for both the researcher and the ethics review committee. The only resources available are an incomplete set of official guidelines, restricted access to supervisor exemplars, and an application form that too frequently baffles novices and experienced researchers alike. Applicants working in isolation must reinvent the wheel. The Ethics Application Repository is an agent of change by providing exemplars of how researchers have successfully presented their projects, including relevant ethical considerations, to ethics review committees. It also provides opportunities to research ethics review committees. Does The Ethics Application Repository improve the quality of ethics applications? Does it make more applications approved at first review? Does The Ethics Application Repository reduce the number of applicants required to re-submit their applications? Does it help prevent unnecessary delays in gaining ethics approval? We do not know, but we hope that The Ethics Application

Repository will bridge a divide not only between the ethics review committee and researchers but also among members of ethics review committees, researchers, and participants. Ethics review can become an educational institution through transparency, knowledge sharing, and open dialogue.

Stage Three: Expansion

The Ethics Application Repository has expanded the proof-of-concept stage growing from eight to 25 applications, with new applications being vetted and accepted continuously. The larger the collection of exemplars, the more useful The Ethics Application Repository becomes. Ongoing calls for donations will be a key activity of future TEAR development.

This expansion has drawn praise from Laura Stark (2013) who recognized The Ethics Application Repository as a means to combat the propensity of ethics review committees to rely on local precedents to make decisions about applications rather than on published ethics codes. By sharing ethics applications, researchers locate their own precedents to assist ethics review committees in reviewing their applications consistently.

Stage Four: Donations

Stage Four of The Ethics Application Repository is currently underway, systematically targeting researcher networks in one of the five topic areas where qualitative researchers have fraught relationships with ethics review committees. The first target is Internet research (the future and cutting edge of IRB review). In the future other special collections focused on children (traditionally a contentious topic due to the vulnerability of participants), community-based participatory research, and innovative methodologies (photo voice, auto-ethnography) will be studied.

Intellectual Generosity

During Stage One, Tolich called for submissions from professionally known academics with diverse research backgrounds. Donors approached were asked to provide only their formal ethics application, but most of the current donors also sent appendices relating to their project. This proved a serendipitous gold mine of information, as most donations have multiple appendices. A photo-voice project by Moshoula Capous Desyllas involving sex workers in Portland, Oregon, provides nine documents. These include the information sheet, recruitment flyers (two), telephone recruitment scripts, project summary handouts, curriculum training workshop for use of cameras, tips for using cameras in research, and a photograph release form. These documents serve as useful guides on both an information and process level. While the TEAR users may utilize examples of forms and scripts to help inform the development of their own planned documents, they may also stumble across documents related to processes they had not even considered, which they can then adapt and include where necessary and appropriate.

In the IRB application form, Moshoula Capous Desyllas placed limits on what her informants could or could not photograph. Desyllas stated there were risks involved in taking photos within this situation (including distress, discomfort, loss of privacy, etc.), and to avoid these risks participants are advised (through a form) that researchers must obtain verbal consent before taking photographs and, because of the illegal nature of sex work (in the applicant's country), no photographs would be accepted for the research project that depicted illegal acts. The various appendices provided valuable information that inexperienced researchers may overlook in the drive to gather data. Inexperience necessarily entails unknown unknowns.

The ability to read other applications at least gives novice researchers a starting point for mapping these unknown unknowns. For example, in a submission by Stephanie Wahab, studying violence in transitional housing, she proactively acknowledged that past violence is not the only research question, but violence may occur at any time during the research and participation may, in itself, lead to risk. In the telephone scripts submitted, she outlines a process to ensure that her participants are safe and if this is not the case, what should be done to correct the situation. This is done by telling participants what scripted answers they can use to reply that would sound innocuous to anyone listening in, but that would indicate to the researcher that the participant requires assistance, or that the present moment is not a good time for discussing the project. This proactive telephone script will not be found in any research methods textbook, but something similar should be developed in all research involving vulnerable people.

When TEAR developers sought formal ethics approval, Tolich learned that his ethics review committee feared researchers would cut and paste applications, contributing to a dumbing down of ethics (Tolich and Tumilty, 2013). Prohibitions against cutting and pasting cannot be too rigid, particularly considering that informal practices of sharing ethics applications occur regularly. The Ethics Application Repository provides a carefully structured repository of applications with the requirement for users to respect the intellectual property of the contributors while, at the same time, having access to resources that provide invaluable guidelines for students, faculty, and IRB members. The abundance of appendices either as telephone scripts or photo release forms in the current submissions means that best practice can more easily be replicated. Replicating and adapting a well-executed phone script, for example, does not lessen the ethical enquiry and thinking required to undertake ethics review, whether one is the researcher or the reviewer. Recognition of a need for certain safety measures in any given study, and adapting best practice to suit a specific project requires insight and analysis.

Currently, The Ethics Application Repository has a largely sociological and qualitative focus, but the senior author whose background is in health science instantly recognized that the usefulness of The Ethics Application Repository is translatable. Not only is more qualitative research being undertaken by health researchers as the view of health has moved from a purely biomedical model, but the complexities of health care issues in the twenty-first century mean interventions no longer come in magic bullets; multifaceted forms of interventions and investigations are required. This in turn often creates ethical intricacy – projects that require more in-depth and deliberate ethical consideration as they involve more complex situations, relationships, and participant needs.

Ethical intricacy in the past has generally been resolved through time-consuming trial and error in the ethics review process. This process can be opaque and idiosyncratic (Stark, 2012) with little room for dialogue and knowledge sharing. When stakeholders listed above were approached to comment about The Ethics Application Repository, they responded with almost instinctual approval and wonderment at why such a repository did not already exist. Based on this, one can assume at least two things: (1) the sharing of ethics applications by researchers is not seen as risky, and (2) figuring out best practice for ethical conduct in research is not as self-explanatory as we might like to believe. The Ethics Application Repository exposes applications, laying them bare for all to see, as shared knowledge artefacts rather than privately owned documents. TEAR developers and users assume that reading multiple examples of successful IRB applications on specific topics can promote best practice for novice researchers and others allowing them to compare and contrast their project with donated exemplars.

Stage Five: Evaluation

Stage Five of the TEAR project is contemporaneous involving ongoing review of The Ethics Application Repository from both external professionals and existing donors. In what follows, an academic who has had nothing to do with the setup of The Ethics Application Repository provides a review of its strengths and weaknesses. Dobson, a postdoctoral fellow in social anthropology at Otago University found the site accessible with room for improvement.

Functionality is good, according to Dobson; regardless of search criteria, retrieval of the material is clear and easy to access. When a user accesses a particular contribution, it is clearly described in terms of keywords, abstract, and in which TEAR collection it is listed.

Dobson also states that each contribution provides valuable ethics resources for use by other researchers. A broad range of research projects are available, and the collection is multidisciplinary. The resources available offer a guide for others in terms of writing ethics applications, designing information sheets and consent forms, and pre-empting potential issues associated with researching sensitive topics. This is another valuable aspect of The Ethics Application Repository – each contribution is described by subject and broad area, providing potential guidelines for a particular body of research.

Dobson considers the site to be innovative and current, allowing full, user-friendly access to complex ethics applications. The Ethics Application Repository invites others to donate their material to continue the growth of both the number of holdings and users, and it draws from a broad range of research projects that encourage interdisciplinary access and dialogue, as well as being of interest to a wide range of academic researchers. Each contribution is uncensored, allowing significant engagement with potential issues, as well as providing access to documents associated with the contributions. Some contributions explicitly address details about ethical concerns associated with social research, and different methodologies are showcased, providing researchers with examples of various methodological and ethical designs for particular research projects. TEAR's Members Code of Practice requires all users to respect the contributions available and protects the intellectual property of the donors to The Ethics Application Repository.

Dobson's suggestions triangulate with the feedback received in Stage Two from graduate students, academics, IRB members, and administrators. Specifically, The Ethics Application Repository draws from a broad geographic range of institutional review boards. Detailing different ethics processes from conception to acceptance more fully, for example, in the form of flow charts or timelines, might further elucidate these processes. Ethics application processes could be further demystified with step-by-step resources that would raise awareness of the procedure from beginning to end. Some contributions detail sensitive information with potentially difficult scenarios, and potential responses to such scenarios. It would be helpful for contributors to submit an optional follow-up to discuss difficulties they encountered and how they dealt with them. Situations in which researchers run into difficulty can be avoided, and empirical examples of problem solving and best practice would be invaluable in building knowledge about appropriate research design and practice. An online discussion board for researchers might be a useful progression for the site. Such a forum might enable junior and senior researchers to discuss relevant ethical issues and build on the notion of The Ethics Application Repository as a resource that encourages dialogue, transparency, and academic community building.

Dobson's feedback provides the TEAR team with a considered view of what is being done well and what can be done better. Various factors influence IRB decision-making and its consistency (Pritchard, 2011), but the availability of past decisions or other decisions rendered by other ethics committees involving projects unfamiliar to a particular committee is clearly beneficial.

Conclusion

The Ethics Application Repository is an innovative and helpful online resource that encourages open access and transparency in terms of ethics review processes. Acquiring ethics approval for research can be a daunting exercise and The Ethics Application Repository goes some way towards simplifying this complex area by providing examples of successful ethics applications.

The Ethics Application Repository is most useful in its capacity to provide real life ethics applications for a range of research approaches.

These examples highlight multiple ethical issues and areas of interest for researchers, showcasing successful ethics applications and researchers' experiences with ethics review committees. The contributions available also engage with particular methodologies and approaches for particular research projects, ostensibly providing guidelines for developing methods and potential ethical issues and concerns for a given research area.

The Ethics Application Repository may be extended in the future to include a discussion forum and a source of practical resources regarding ethics review processes. Providing material so applicants can better understand the requirements of research ethics review and can explore best practice will make the process of applying to an ethics review committee one characterized by less anxiety and by more informed and ethical research design.

NOTE

1 See www.tear.otago.ac.nz/

REFERENCES

Barrows, Howard S., and Paul J. Feltovich. (1987). "The Clinical Reasoning Process." *Medical Education* 21 (2): 86–91. http://dx.doi.org/10.1111/j.1365-2923.1987.tb00671.x

Boser, Susan. (2007). "Power, Ethics, and the IRB: Dissonance Over Human Participant Review of Participatory Research." *Qualitative Inquiry* 13 (8): 1060–74. http://dx.doi.org/10.1177/1077800407308220.

Desyllas, M.C. (2013). "Using Photovoice with Sex Workers: The Power of Art, Agency and Resistance." *Qualitative Social Work: Research and Practice*. http://dx.doi.org/10.1177/1473325013496596

European Commission. (n.d.). *Code of Good Practice for Consultation of Stakeholders*. Brussels: Directorate-General for Health and Consumers. http://ec.europa.eu/dgs/health_food-safety/dgs_consultations/docs/code_good_practices_consultation_en.pdf

Lincoln, Yvonna, and William G. Tierney. (2004). "Qualitative Research and Institutional Review Boards." *Qualitative Inquiry* 10 (2): 219–34. http://dx.doi.org/10.1177/1077800403262361

Mahadkar, Sameedha. S., Grant R. Mills, and Andrew D.F. Price (2010). "Stakeholder Consultation Review: A Comparative Analysis." In *Proceedings of the HaCIRIC International Conference 2010: Better Healthcare Through Better Infrastructure, 22–4 Sept., Edinburgh, Scotland*, 28–41.

Norman, Geoffrey. (2005). "Research in Clinical Reasoning: Past History and Current Trends." *Medical Education* 39 (4): 418–27. http://dx.doi.org/10.1111/j.1365-2929.2005.02127.x

Pritchard, Ivor A. (2011). "How do IRB Members Make Decisions? A Review and Research Agenda." *Journal of Empirical Research on Human Research Ethics* 6 (2): 31–46. http://dx.doi.org/10.1525/jer.2011.6.2.31

Ruiz-Canela, López M., Jokin de Irala-Estevez, and Miguel Ángel Martinez-Gonzalez. (2001). "Methodological Quality and Reporting of Ethical Requirements in Clinical Trials." *Journal of Medical Ethics* 27 (3): 172–6. http://dx.doi.org/10.1136/jme.27.3.172

Stark, Laura. (2012). *Behind Closed Doors: IRBs and the Making of Ethical Research.* Chicago: University of Chicago Press.

– (2013). "Managing Local Precedents – Three models: Challenges of Multisite, Multidisciplinary Studies" National Academies of Science. http://tvworldwide.com/events/nas/130321/

The Ethics Application Repository (TEAR). http://www.tear.otago.ac.nz/

Tolich, Martin, and Emma Tumilty. (2013). "Making Ethics Review a Learning Institution: The Ethics Application Repository Proof of Concept – tear.otago.ac.nz." *Qualitative Research.* http://dx.doi.org/10.1177/1468794112468476

Tumilty, E. (2012). "Replacing Ethical Review Fear with TEAR (The Ethics Application Repository)." Paper presented at the Postgraduate Research Student Conference: Politics and Politics, July, Dunedin, New Zealand.

Van Den Eynden, Veerle. (2008). "Sharing Research Data and Confidentiality: Restrictions Caused by Deficient Consent Forms." *Research Ethics Review* 4 (1): 37–8. http://dx.doi.org/10.1177/174701610800400111

Van Den Eynden, Veerle, and Louise Corti. (2009). "Tensions between Data Sharing and Data Protection in Research with People." *SRA News,* 12–15 May.

Winston, Robert. (2010). *Bad Ideas? An Arresting History of our Inventions.* London: Bantam Press.

20 Professional Research Ethics: Helping to Balance Individual and Institutional Integrity

RON IPHOFEN

... one of the greatest gifts one generation can give to another is the wisdom it has gained from experience.

Andrew Zuckerman, *Wisdom*

We're much closer together in the world today than we ever were in the past. Given that it is a much smaller world, we are in a much stronger position to shape that world ... One way of doing that is to draw lessons from the European Union (EU). The EU is the best example in the history of the world of conflict resolution.

John Hume, a Northern Ireland politician elect as a Member of the EU Parliament

Throughout my career I have been dedicated to applied social science. I have an abiding interest in what good can be done by our work, how our research can help people and societies improve themselves. It is this concern with a special form of impact that led to my interest in research ethics: How we can we be sure we are doing the right things in the right way? I have also been concerned with finding ways to advise colleagues about best practice and so, in this chapter, too, I hope my approach is as pragmatic as possible.

Some years ago I saw a need to argue for improved professional oversight of social science research. I tried to make the point that behaving ethically while producing high-quality social research requires ongoing awareness of the ethical consequences of one's work (Iphofen, 2004). This must be embedded in initial research training and reinforced through continuous professional development. The wealth of experience establishing ethical research standards in social science was being applied disparately – to some extent it still is. I advocated that the social science professions regulate themselves properly before inadequate regulation is imposed by external agencies or, worse still, in response to case law. My argument was not seriously taken up and, since then, the feared regulation – ethics creep in the form of formalized regulation of research ethics particularly within universities in the United Kingdom – has grown, and given the evidence produced by many attendees at this New Brunswick Summit of 2012, that regulation has indeed been inadequate and frequently irrelevant.

In this chapter I explore one particular avenue to improving regulation – the role of professional associations. Clearly, a balance must be struck in the forms of regulation, but far better we regulate ourselves than allow others to regulate more crudely and in their own interests.

Assumptions

Some essential premises to my argument exist that I trust most colleagues would agree with. First, ethics is all about compromise – it is a balancing of the good against the bad. In research we typically see those as *potential* harms balanced against *potential* benefits. All research contains harm, because, to varying degrees, it is intrusive on the lives of others. And we can only speak in terms of potential because we cannot anticipate all the harms and benefits. We certainly hope that our desired benefits will come to fruition, so that the intrusion can be justified in terms of the benefits accruing to individuals, communities, and / or societies, and to our knowledge and understanding – that is, to social science.

No matter what formalized and perfected ethics review structures are established there is really only one guarantor of ethical practice: the researcher. Ultimately it is the researcher in the field who knows when ethical practice is going on and when it is being threatened. Given that research is a process rather than an event, ethical decisions necessarily must be taken in a dynamic context – once more placing the ultimate burden of responsibility on the field researcher.

If we think of ethics as relating to moral obligations to stakeholders, the researcher may be faced with a range of these including funders, commissioners, managers, supervisors, professional colleagues, and, of course, research participants. Stakeholders may reflect opposing tensions. For example, researchers' loyalties may be divided, say, between promises of confidentiality to research participants and the law when the participant discloses a breach of the law.

Formal ethics review is unlikely to disappear or even lessen substantially. Indeed, I have seen enough worrying proposals and practices to argue that it should not disappear. As a mentor for the Social Research Association (SRA) in the United Kingdom, I have come across examples of threats, bribery, corruption, physical and psychological injury, barely justified deception, and a range of pressures being put on researchers by employers, managers, and funders to contravene other fundamental standards of proper behaviour. Such behaviour rarely makes headlines because the consequences affect only small communities of interest and do not typically entail large amounts of money when compared with abuses in the financial sector, pharmaceutical companies, or agri-industry. But there is enough going on to be concerned about and it is in all our interests, as practitioners, research participants, and the beneficiaries of social research to ensure that harmful practices are minimized in scope and degree.

I have also witnessed some atrocious forms of ethics review. For example, a graduate student's proposal was rejected by a National Health Service (NHS) multicentre research ethics committee (MREC) on the grounds that the covert observation on which the design was based was considered by them to be inherently unethical – thus disallowing any form of covert research. I have witnessed researchers' colleagues sitting as panel members using the opportunity to attack publicly their colleagues' proposals with proposers leaving the room in tears when faced with the hostile atmosphere of the review. I have seen a professorial colleague discredit submissions from colleagues within the same department to curry favour for other reasons with the chair of the research ethics committee. And one ethics committee routinely deferred to the opinions of a clinical psychologist who would criticize proposers' methodologies and insist on modification as a condition of ethics review approval – even when the methodology (the "science") was supposed to be beyond the panel's remit.

Thus, while I share the frustrations that have led to critical publications about ethics-review processes and panels, I believe it is vital to avoid a mutually maligning discourse that creates more stubborn resistance on both sides. I like to think that most panel members are well intentioned most of the time, and it may be that we have to focus more on the pressures brought on by the institutionalized setting than on the individuals striving to do their best within it.

Moreover, I would argue that most review obstructions occur when the distinction between the governance of research and independent ethics review is lost. All too frequently ethics review panels take more concern over corporate liability and image than reflecting independently on any anticipated threats to the integrity of a study. There is an instinctive risk *aversion* rather than a cultivated risk *awareness* on the part of members of ethics review panels. Researchers are often implicated in unethical practice by the institutional constraints they experience – pressures to ensure the data are gathered, results are analysed, and publication ensured (Iphofen, 2011: chapter 12). The ethics review process must be arranged to minimize such infrastructural pressures.

So my central assumption, again something I am sure we can all agree on is this: ethics review can and should be improved, and the gist of my argument here is that both individual researchers and their professional associations have a significant role to play in ensuring that improvement and, further, in the practice of ethical research in general.

European Context

To strengthen the case for the role of professional associations in ethics review, the experience of the European Commission (EC) illustrating international trends and pressures is useful. Partly as a consequence of funding regimes, but also for sound reasons of comparative methodology, research organizations have become more internationally oriented. National and international variations in research standards and applicable laws pose difficulties for researchers. Embedded cultural assumptions in different countries about the nature and purpose of social research may fundamentally alter the status of social scientific knowledge. For example, perspectives on how respondents are treated; how data are generated, handled, and transferred; and the ownership of intellectual property have for some time been evolving in Europe. Currently, we are awaiting new regulations – not just directives – for data protection. So while there is pressure for harmonization on one level, there remain considerable variations in culture and accepted practice. It is what some globalization scholars have referred to as *glocalization*. But at the administrative level of ethics review within the Commission such differences must be reconciled face to face during the ethics review. Evaluation panels (ethics review boards) are asked to achieve a consensus in their recommendations and reports to ease the ability of researchers to respond to them.

The trend towards institutionalized research governance in higher education has offered no guarantee that high standards will be set, and the same may be true of the highly bureaucratized EC processes with mechanisms that do not necessarily guarantee safeguards for the public nor ensure the quality of research as indicated in the previously stated assumptions. Even within the European Commission, ethics review can be confused with risk assessment, damage control, and corporate indemnity.

A project to develop professional and ethical guidelines for the conduct of socioeconomic research across Europe (2000–04) raised some interesting issues (see http://www.respectproject.org/main/index.php for the specific case described here.) The project proposal arose as a result of management consultants posing as social researchers and winning large EC research tenders but producing low-quality work that was threatening to discredit social science in general. The proposal for implementation of ethical standards was not welcomed within certain organizations (e.g., those perceived or that perceive themselves as being more scientific), and so the proposal was to some extent sidelined into a sector not directly helpful to social science research (then called Information Societies Technology or IST). The developers of the proposal were unable to broaden the brief to include professional standards affecting socioeconomic research generally since this is managed within the EC directorates. This work, reported in 2004 (Iphofen et al., 2004), had some subtle and indirect influence in taking ethics review forward in the European Commission in spite of resistance to a broader-based research ethics review from the biomedical scientists who wished to retain power over their own jurisdiction. So ethics debates remained ghettoized in disparate subject areas, and sharing best practices across disciplines and professions became dependent on the will and skills of researchers and their personal and professional networks.

Subsequently, within the European Commission there appeared to be some moves from the Directorate General for Research and Innovation to support more social science and humanities (SSH) funding – a recognition of parallel research problems across disciplines. Commissioned discussion papers on the social sciences and humanities and representations to the Science and Society Committee (in which all European nations are represented) also demonstrate this interest. Growing funding calls for multidisciplinary, problem-focused projects, the application of appropriate generic research standards, and a concern for the assessment of societal impact is further evidence of this.

It is thought that the social sciences and humanities have been poorly understood in terms of ethics review, and attempts are being made to improve regulation in part to increase funding for the social sciences and humanities. At the same time there is resistance to heavy-handed ethics review and concern about fair and accurate review processes that accommodate and appreciate the diversity of social science and humanities methodologies. In fact, this seems to be a global concern – to avoid the gold-standard mentality imported from the biomedical sciences. Three development projects focused on responsible research and innovation were conducted during 2011–12. A series of documents, discussion papers, and guidance documents were produced that included explanations about the nature of social science and humanities methodologies, typical ethical dilemmas that arise, and how these projects might best be reviewed. (The reports can be accessed via the SINAPSE website: https://europa.eu/sinapse/sinapse/index.cfm.)[1]

Now most proposals go through a multidisciplinary ethics review process that cuts across the science disciplines. A recent review panel I chaired, for example, included a geneticist, an anthropologist, a psychologist, a biomedical researcher (with a law degree), a pediatrician, and a medical ethicist. Of course the process is challenging, especially in gaining adequate understanding from non-SSH researchers about designs and methods in social science and humanities research and, for example, alternate methods for obtaining valid consent from research participants.

But with the best of intentions review practices can become "routinized" within evaluation panels as reviewers of research ethics become familiar with European rules and regulations and tend to apply them in a formalized manner. So, standardized responses to "gaps" in ethics risk estimates by proposers are adopted and advised. A "standard text" document with carefully worded, often legally inspired phrases is used when researchers leave perceived gaps in their proposals. For example, when animal experimenters fail to refer to well-established regulations called the "3 Rs" (reduction, refinement, and replacement); when imaginative nanotechnology researchers fail to acknowledge that they cannot fully anticipate potential risks of their work; or when data protection regulations nationally and internationally are widely adopted, requiring institutions to have identifiable data controllers. So for reasons of administrative convenience a standard text is returned to the proposer explaining precisely what must be addressed in order to gain board approval. There is even a provision to audit projects with regard to their ethical practices, but this is rarely applied because it is impossible in terms of money and time. Most attempts to monitor what researchers are actually doing, rather than what they say they are going to do fall by the wayside.

Consequently, as with assembly-line, standardized operations in general, there is a danger of traction in research ethics review – both on the part of members of ethics review panels and researchers who might be beginning to learn the correct phraseology and forestall the formulaic response. This could be seen as a checklist mentality, but it is not the fault of checklists per se rather a state of mind that sees ethics review as an obstacle to be overcome – as obstructive rather than constructive, unnecessarily complex, bureaucratically unwieldy, and worst of all, undemocratic as it represents narrow, often unspecified sectional, organizational interests and concerns rather than protection of research participants and facilitation of the advancement of science in general.

A new development in the system is the spread of ethics review into European Demonstration (ED) projects. Unlike traditional research projects aimed at generating basic knowledge, the European Demonstration projects aim to use available knowledge to transform research results into practice. The objective is to demonstrate the viability of a new technology along with its economic advantages under realistic conditions. This can be taken in a broad sense and, for example, can show the potential for increased competitiveness for European industries, can enhance efficiency of public services, increase quality of life, and improve public perception and understanding of new biotechnologies.

Currently, I serve as chair of the ethical advisory group for a demonstration project undertaken to provide a set of procedural tools to improve urban transport security (see http://www.secur-ed.eu/).[2] Participants include public transport stakeholders and security firms across Europe as well as university-based research technologists. An interesting feature is how low ethical awareness is among the stakeholders. The tasks of the advisory group have grown as gaps in their knowledge of informed consent, data protection, personal data, visual recognition, GPS personal tracking, etc. have emerged. So, although it is not strictly a research project, this demonstration project has confronted many of the same dilemmas researchers confront generally, but dilemmas that industry representatives have apparently not had to consider thus far. Also interesting is the new set of tasks that has been added to the project – an assessment of societal impact. It appears that social-level impact (in addition to impacts on participants) has become an ethical issue; it is most certainly an area of knowledge that social scientists ought to be contributing to.

The Role of Professional Associations

These particular examples of European developments are offered to illustrate the increasing complexity of researchers' experiences. And although there may be very minimal dangers to the participants in most social research activity, this should not mean researchers should lessen their consideration for the participants. More seriously, the growth of multidisciplinary research implicates social scientists in bio-medical, genetic, and/or nanotechnology projects in which risks are higher. Researchers themselves must take responsibility for conscience and quality, but there is a key role for professional bodies to be educa-tive, informative, and supportive of maintaining standards and raising ethical awareness as the research environment becomes increasingly complex.

Problems and prospects exist for any field of activity adopting a "pro-fessional" status and all that goes with it. Enhanced recognition typi-cally endows economic and political advantages, but it also requires establishing more formal accreditation and validation processes to determine what constitutes a professional. A lengthy literature in occu-pational sociology exists that suggests *profession* is a variable property of occupations dependent on the possession of certain attributes (see Table 20.1, below). These attributes can only be applied descriptively; they do not explain why one occupation comes to be regarded as a distinct profession while another does not. This appears to depend on combinations of economic and cultural values of the society in which the occupation operates. Moreover, those who have studied these attri-butes extensively appear to find no reason for ranking any one attribute over any other (cf. Freidson, 1970a: 4), although the professional desig-nation does appear to depend on the quantity of attributes overall. The attributes reflect the structural and attitudinal components of behav-iour deemed appropriate to the practices of a particular occupation. Thus, the occupations of medical practitioner and lawyer are generally considered to be professions because they possess a large number of these attributes.

It is evident from Table 20.1 that social scientists possess most of these attributes, although some may be hotly debated within each discipline.

Table 20.1. Attributes of Professions

Ethical service orientation to others
High occupational autonomy
Control over admission to profession inheres in professional body
High work satisfaction
Prolonged training, specialized abstract knowledge
Professional body governs training
Stringent professional norms, self-enforced
Non-standardized, individualized product or service
Work as a central life interest (commitment)
Ability to deflect criticism over bad outcomes
Free of lay evaluation and control (self-policing)
High prestige accorded by non-professionals
Social control based on expert knowledge
Strong affiliation with profession (solidarity)
Strong identification with and commitment to profession
Subordination and control of clients
Terminal occupation (lasts for life)
Universalistic, objective, ethically neutral relationship with clients
Commands high-calibre students
Control of professional body over relevant legislation
Stringent socialization of students into profession
Exercise of moral authority to influence social change
High power
High income
Control over licensure
Licensure by state or government

Sources: Attributes drawn from Braude (1975: 103–11), Cockerham (1995: 188), Freidson (1994: 122–3), Godfrey (1999), Macdonald (1995: 6–7,169), and Mumford (1983: 249–54).

Professional associations must become a source of unity from within, which is preferable to external impositions of law. Of course, the first limitation on social science as a profession is the diversity of disciplines, each with a desire to maintain its autonomy. On the one hand, professional associations can aid development by encouraging open debate about the role and effectiveness of the professional contribution to knowledge and scientific progress. On the other hand, professional power is formal, bureaucratized, and stable, being vested in "relationships between positions rather than [in] relations between specific persons" (Dornbusch and Scott, 1975: 37). In practice the actual power given to any individual professional will depend to some degree on the size of the organization (Godfrey, 1999).

Eliot Freidson distinguished client-dependent from colleague-dependent medical practice (1970b: 91–3) and showed how this influenced the emerging sense of professional responsibility in medicine. Freidson has observed (about medicine) that attempts by professions to dictate the manner in which their expert knowledge will be applied are, in fact, based on power and privilege rather than on expertise (1970a: 382). Such a view has led to attempts to reduce the power of medical professionals throughout the twentieth century. Consequently, there is a need for caution about how professions are regulated. Onora O'Neill (2002) in the Reith Lectures on Trust pointed out that a culture of managerial accountability undermines the very goal it is seeking: a more responsible professional. Excessive regulation and concerns for the auditing of minute detail can lead to a lowering of service quality. Instead she argued for "intelligent accountability" and an established and reliable form of professional self-regulation. In that connection, Anthony (2007: 12) suggests "people who are sufficiently informed to judge performance and independent enough to be objective; and [who can] ... communicate their assessments to the wider public in intelligible form." However, with increasing concern about the protection of the public, the maintenance of safe practices, and the avoidance of litigation, it may be that additional qualifications act as indicators of standards and competence.

Professional associations are well positioned to build and promote a culture of ethical practice linking both traditional and innovative methodologies. They can offer educational programs specific to methods favoured by the discipline and that raise awareness of the forms that members of ethics review committees are likely to encounter. This education is best offered by professional associations rather than the organizations within which the review occurs or within employing organizations because they inevitably contain conflicts of interests, cannot be genuinely independent, and frequently lead to protection of institutional processes rather than ethical principles. Moreover, organizations are less likely to protect whistleblowers, a position that is not in the best interest of free, independent, and ethical enquiry.

Professional associations can guide their members through the procedures and processes of ethics review and warn against common obstacles to particular methods. Indeed, a key professional device for enhancing ethical awareness is expert mentorship – the sharing of experiences and solutions to problems. Advice and guidance can be offered through forums. For example, in the United Kingdom the Social Research Association, the Market Research Society, and the British Psychological Society offer such support. From their professional associations researchers can glean ways to articulate their approach, to develop rationales for particular methodologies, and to deal with anticipated difficulties. The more articulate they become, the better they can argue a case in review. Encouraging social science researchers to serve on ethics review boards is an important way to develop better understanding about how the review boards operate. This is not a question of knowing the enemy or of poacher-turned-gamekeeper. Rather it is a way to see how institutional pressures affect research practices and finding ways to confront and overcome them. These experiences gained while serving on an ethics board can then be shared with the professional association membership, improving the system for researchers, ethics board members, and research participants.

Reviewers on ethics panels should apply the following critical questions to any proposed research:

Who is doing it? Consider researchers' competence by reviewing CVs, the institutions in which they work, credentials (or notoriety) of those organizations, and assessment of their prior work in the field.
Why are they doing it? What is the purpose? Is the research demonstrably worth doing?
How are they doing it? What is the method? Both of the above dimensions come together in this balancing dimension: The balance between the intellectual/scientific freedom necessary for researchers to explore the world as they see fit, and the collective responsibility to protect research participants.

And to improve the ethics review process, these same questions should be asked of the ethics review board or panel:

Who is doing it? Who are the board members? What skills and experience do they have?
Why are they doing it? What motives do they have? What are their aims and intentions?
How are they doing it? What are the processes and procedures? What mechanisms exist for improving the system? For appealing board decisions?

This is a plea for enhanced transparency of the operations of research ethics review. Professional associations can use their power to ask such questions and to demand transparency in the ethics review process. At the same time, given that the researcher in the field is the ultimate arbiter of ethical judgment, it is vital to recognize and value her or his need for professional independence. This includes the need for flexibility in method and design and allowance for adjustments in the field. Changing both ethical and methodological decisions while research is going on is frequently needed, and researchers must be able to make such revisions at any time they are necessary during the course of the research. Changes in the external environment, public attitudes, socio-political climate, and other situations contribute to unexpected changes in research design.

Members of research ethics review panels and researchers alike must recognize that vast differences of opinion about both ethics and methods exist. Such differences are contested and refined by members of professional associations. Reasoned argument and debate must be a full part of ethics committee deliberations, with respect for contested variations in approach. Competent researchers will have good reasons for their ethical and methodological choices – and they should be able to articulate them in a critical but supportive arena. At the same time, when ethics reviewers have objections, those objections must be based on adequate grounds and the ethics board members must articulate the objections fully.

The ideal ethics review process involves reviewers who accommodate the fact that research frequently requires taking risks and chances and should be risk *alert* but not *averse* to risk. Research activities (especially innovative ones) and outcomes may require relaxing or shifting cultural norms and values; members of research ethics review panels must be knowledgeable and experienced in ethics and familiar with a broad range of methodological issues and practices. Maintaining an accessible record, or collective memory, of previous decisions and rationales is central. Again, this is a logical role for professional associations – they can cultivate and nurture independent thought and judgment that is the essence of ethical decision-making. After all, the ultimate purpose of research ethics review is the *minimizing* of harm.

As the EC example illustrates, what lies behind the larger European Union mission is an attempt to move beyond the local to establish and sustain more universal principles and values. No institution could be better positioned to debate and resolve differences in perspectives on standards than a professional association built around commonality of theory and method. In effect, the New Brunswick Summit provided the opportunity to explore international perspectives.

Professional Codes and Ethical Guidelines

A major debate within professional associations involves the degree of power the organization should have to sanction members based on violations of ethics codes or guidelines. What powers of exclusion, reprimand, or proscription can be applied by the professional association to any member who transgresses? Some associations have disciplinary committees that can exclude or punish members who bring the association into disrepute. Others argue that ethics guidelines function better aspirationally, as educative prescriptions that advise researchers about ethical behaviour, assisting their judgments, and ultimately relying on the individual researcher to make ethical choices.

It is important to note that these codes and guidelines are typically constructed on the basis of a normative prescription – duty-based rather than rights-based morality. For example, one could conceive of an alternate guidance structure based on rights; it would be much harder to apply as rights are more difficult to define and operationalize and, in practice, are more inclined to conflict with each other. Thus, no individual person is viewed as having a right to have her or his data protected. Rather, the data controller is instructed to protect data in particular ways – it is by these collective means that individuals are protected.

From a rights perspective it would be nice to argue successfully that the public has a right to adequate information about, say, new scientific discovery, new technologies, even the social reality we share. It would be good to ensure the public was adequately informed and professional codes often strive to encourage researchers to take such responsibility. But researchers have little control in disseminating findings. It is unfair to admonish researchers for failing to publicize a message that other, more powerful interests resist circulating. The comparison of rights-based and duty-based moralities illustrates the inherent tensions among ethical principles. The writers of codes and guidelines continually try to reconcile those tensions – the right of a participant to be informed is contradicted by the right for data sources to remain unnamed.

Considerable progress is being made towards establishing a consensus approach to ethical values, principles, and practices in social science research (Iphofen, 2010). In 2013, the UK Academy of Social Sciences secured funding and sponsored a series of symposia that included many social science disciplines and were designed to lead to a statement of common practices or standards to publicly demonstrate the care that social scientists routinely take in doing the right things in the right way. Again, there is a role for the unifying character of professional associations.

Conclusion: A Comment on "Democratic" Practice

The concerns of participants at the New Brunswick Summit about undemocratic practices, ethical imperialism, and ethics creep are clear. A response to this critique depends on the view one holds of how democracy *should* operate and how it *actually* operates. All scientists including social scientists necessarily work in a pluralist political context in which power is unevenly distributed. The power of individuals is limited by context – the power of researchers to freely investigate and the power of participants to be investigated or not are bound by norms and institutional constraints.

Institutions and organizations do have a right, indeed a responsibility, to protect themselves. Organizations are accountable to owners and other stakeholders. At the same time, researchers have a duty to tell the best truth they can find, and their rights and responsibilities must be linked to that larger aspiration. It matters because, if things go wrong, everyone suffers – either as participants or as researchers if the field becomes so contaminated that people will not want to get involved in future research. If we are clear about the issues raised here, we are best able to manage the process as researchers and sustain ethical social science practices.

As members of democracies, contributors to this volume challenge aspects of the systems of institutional research ethics review – arguing for acknowledging the integrity of researchers and their ability to conduct research in a responsible manner. In terms of moral philosophy, this is akin to adopting a virtue ethics stance. So a responsible researcher is a virtuous researcher able to produce "good work" (Reeves and Knell, 2006). But this uneven distribution of power means the individual researcher is vulnerable to numerous forms of institutional oppression. Without the power of a supportive organization a researcher's virtues may not be easily recognized. With membership and/or participation in a professional association, the researcher gains status and the collective power of a community of like-minded individuals. With professional support mechanisms in place, we are better able to reassure the public and institutional regulators that what is promised can be delivered. This is even more the case in the increasingly complex research settings today.

What we can hope for in ourselves as researchers is an autonomous, thinking professional with finely honed critical skills who is able to offer a full rationale for the methods proposed and can explain how they can minimize harm to participants while pursuing their valued scientific goals.

NOTES

1 The reports can be accessed via the SINAPSE website: https://europa.eu/sinapse/sinapse/index.cfm
2 See http://www.secur-ed.eu/

REFERENCES

Anthony, Sandy. (2007). "Moving Forward: Making Regulation Work." *U.K. Medical Protection Society Casebook* 15 (1): 10–13.

Braude, Lee. (1975). *Work and Workers: A Sociological Analysis*. New York: Praeger.

Cockerham, William C. (1995). *Medical Sociology*. 6th ed. Englewood Cliffs, NJ: Prentice-Hall.

Dornbusch, Stanford M., and W. Richard Scott. (1975). *Evaluation and the Exercise of Authority*. San Francisco: Jossey-Bass.

Freidson, Eliot. (1970a). *Profession of Medicine*. New York: Harper and Row.

– (1970b). *Professional Dominance*. Chicago: Aldine.

– (1994). *Professionalism Reborn: Theory, Prophecy and Policy*. Chicago: University of Chicago Press.

Godfrey, Eric P. (1999). "Small College Teaching as a Profession." In E.P. Godfrey (ed.), *Teaching Sociology: The Small College Experience*, chapter 25: 171-182. Washington, DC: American Sociological Association.

Iphofen, Ron. (2004). "A Code to Keep Away Judges, Juries and MPs." *Times Higher Education*, 16 (Jan.): 24.

– (2010). "Do the Right Thing – Unite." *Times Higher Education* 14 (Jan.): 27.

– (2011). *Ethical Decision Making in Social Research: A Practical Guide*. London: Palgrave Macmillan. http://dx.doi.org/10.1057/9780230319219

406   Ron Iphofen

Iphofen, Ron, Sally Dench, and Ursula Huws. (2004). *An EU Code of Ethics for Socio-Economic Research*. Brighton: Institute for Employment Studies (IES). www.respectproject.org

Macdonald, Keith M. (1995). *The Sociology of the Professions*. Thousand Oaks, CA: Sage.

Mumford, Emily. (1983). *Medical Sociology: Patients, Providers, and Policies*. New York: Random House.

O'Neill, Onora. (2002). *Autonomy and Trust in Bioethics*. Cambridge: Cambridge University Press.

Reeves, Richard, and John Knell. (2006). "Good Work and Professional Work." In John Craig (ed.), *Production Values: Futures for Professionalism*, 211–18. London: Demos.

Final Thoughts

So Where from Here? Finding Paths through the Bramble of Research Ethics Review

ANN HAMILTON AND WILL C. VAN DEN HOONAARD

In our concluding chapter we express the collective worries brought to our attention by the contributors in *The Ethics Rupture*. They point to the symptoms of an intense ethics rupture that currently prevails in university research ethics regimes, to the continuing effects of such a rupture, and to illusions that keep the rupture afloat. While uncertain about the eventual fate of the research ethics review regimes, this chapter includes certain abiding characteristics of an unruptured system. Finally, we offer specific insights about possible outcomes if researchers in the social sciences opt to stay within the current system of ethics review, as well as discussion from those who foresee the dismembering of the system.

The Symptoms of the Ethics Rupture

The audit culture has seized many public institutions and entangled them in going beyond their original mandates. The ethics review regime was born in the audit culture and has become a signal accomplishment. The growing power and authority of the ethics review boards – identified variously as ethics creep, mission creep, ethics drift, and similar terms – has made this system more and more difficult for researchers to question. How is it that even a researcher's *questioning* the ethics decision-making of board members is considered to be stepping out of line? Fear-based, anxiety-driven, and career-ruining possibilities perpetuate both researchers' nightmares and urban legends – the same few stories about controversial research conducted by Stanley Milgram, Philip Zimbardo, even sometimes William F. Whyte and Erving Goffman drive regulation. New experiences emerge that affirm that "ethics drift" is real, threatening the mission of social scientists. And, as Robert Dingwall points out (chapter 1), the proliferation of people professionally vested in the research ethics review system makes it more difficult to dislodge or even contain the system.

Researchers in the social sciences, a solid and steady stream of them, offer constructive critiques of the ethics review system, discussing numerous benefits to researchers, participants, and regulators alike in bringing ethics review processes closer to the world of social science and the methods employed in social research, especially when data gathering involves surveys, interviews, ethnographic fieldwork, and other observational methods. Aggravatingly, policymakers focused on regulating fail to listen to the social science community; when they do invite formal comments – a rare event occurring in approximately 20-year intervals – the process is long and results in little if any change.[1]

The lack of self-critical, reflective components in the system of research ethics review, including the lack of the most fundamental legal precedent of providing due process to appeal ethics board decisions, reinforces the prevailing system regardless of the problems created and in spite of the many consistent urgings for change.

Part of the regime's malaise is that local ethics review panels – e.g., in the United States, where they are called Institutional Review Boards (IRBs) – make decisions that are stricter than necessary when it comes to reviewing survey, interview, fieldwork, and observational research methods, rather than favouring federal rules that allow exemptions. As Dingwall (2008) explains, concerning the United Kingdom, "In 2006, the Economic and Social Research Council announced a new 'Research Ethics Framework' for social science research, which offered greater flexibility, but universities did not take advantage of the flexibility" and are therefore maintaining a stricter system (4). This pattern is similar in many countries including those discussed in this volume: Australia, New Zealand, Brazil, Italy, England, Scotland, the United States, and Canada, as well as the European Union.

Local managerial domination (Alvesson and Deetz, 1996) leads ethics review committees to exempt themselves from federal rules. This managerial domination is central to the existing situation in which debates about ethics regulation are silenced, treated as reckless, dangerous, and – perhaps most significantly – as futile. Researchers are encouraged to "realize" (and accept) that they have everything to lose and nothing to gain in working to modify, improve, or even eradicate a system that affects them so completely. Why do we allow this structure to remain intact? To solidify and entrench itself?

Although the regulatory system is cohesive in its authority, it is still uneven in places – and we hope that this unevenness can provide a better space for social research, as the various chapters in this volume have suggested. Israel et al. (chapter 15) note this unevenness in their examination of the research ethics review process in Australia. In Canada, some of our contributors agree that the amendments in the second edition of the *Tri-Council Policy Statement: Ethical Conduct for Research Involving Humans* (*TCPS* 2) (CIHR et al., 2010) seemed to have moved forward in recognizing the aims and language of social science research, but it is as yet too soon to know whether those changes have worked themselves into the sinew of ethics review committees. Kirsten Bell (chapter 10) and Igor Gontcharov (chapter 13) conclude the amendments have not gone far enough. It is worth noting that, regardless of any changes, there are always inconsistent decisions within the same national ethics regime, between local ethics review boards and federal regulations, and even within the same particular board over time.

Further, researchers in the social sciences recognize that a class system pervades academia and formal systems of research ethics review. C.K. Gunsalus (quoted in Brainard, 2003) confesses that she has "a hard time saying to my colleagues in history that what you do is not research ... [which] tends to reinforce an existing 'class system' in academe, in which some biomedical researchers view their studies as methodologically more rigorous than the work of historians."

Continuing Effects of the Rupture

In this chapter and throughout this volume, we editors and the contributing authors have considered the effects of hyper-regulation, demonstrating the numerous harms stemming from the over-regulation of social science research. We have already pointed out that ethics regulators at the federal level allow for numerous exemptions that members of local ethics review panels overwhelmingly ignore. We have brought forth problems with the lingering biomedical lexicon, which is ill-fitting and irrelevant to social science research, and discussed regulatory ideologies – especially the idea that *something* must be wrong or dangerous in every proposal without evidence to support that contention. We've discussed the presumption that compliance equals protection, and a strong case has been made that the system of research ethics review in social science begs the question of need, and, finally, that local boards view stricter-than-federal rules as desirable.

So much is at stake for the social sciences if current processes are allowed to continue, especially if we are unable to analyse and understand the processes of research ethics review. Gag orders, a common aspect of legal proceedings, will extend to correspondence between ethics review committees and researchers. They impinge on freedom of knowledge and on the spread of important knowledge for researchers and the ethics review community as a whole.

Without fundamental changes, the social sciences will continue to be pauperized in their richness of perspectives and homogenized in terms of their methodologies. Students will lose their historical sense of their disciplines, and their theoretical bearings.

More and more research will occur within this ill-fitting legal framework, and research that focuses on deviance and illegalities is endangered, headed for the history books. "Many social researchers," Zachary Schrag (chapter 16) reminds us, "have complained that formal criteria and procedures for obtaining informed consent ... can destroy needed rapport between researcher and participant and can effectively silence those defined as 'vulnerable' because they do not conform to an imagined norm." The bending of research toward the demands of research ethics review committees means that some social science methods are becoming homogenized while also pauperizing the social sciences as a whole: standardization is at the core of any bureaucracy, and therefore the system of research ethics review is not equipped to differentiate among the social sciences.

Robert Dingwall (chapter 1) discusses the inconsistent application of regulations, and significantly, he also points out that the freedom of creative artists and journalists – and by extension researchers – is a central pillar of democratic societies. "Where we are dealing with change and instability," Dingwall asserts, "a society's ability to respond will be strongly influenced by the degree to which its institutions can successfully innovate. Academic freedom is one of the preconditions of that adaptability."

We, as social scientists, have a responsibility to explore social structures and must preserve the right to conduct these explorations even when that exploration affects those in authority (see Marco Marzano, chapter 5), including ethics review boards themselves. As we know, rights and responsibilities are inextricably linked, as are responsibility and authority. And, it is clear in this context that meeting responsibilities requires the authority to do so. Although the costs of entry for artists and journalists are relatively low, as Dingwall argues, and pre-emptive review is rare, the same is not true for researchers in the social sciences. The research ethics review system – lagging behind the real research world of innovation and discovery – has become illusory. In the absence of substantive change, we pretend.

Certain identifiable trends in research ethics review serve to destabilize the system. Periodically, new objects of what merits ethics review gain currency, only to disappear or even gain more prominence in ethics debates.[2] Ethics review committees have recently inserted themselves into research conducted abroad, have insisted on internal confidentiality in focus groups, have required lock and key to protect field notes, and the destruction of interview transcripts, or alternately, have insisted that researchers forever archive data, and the list goes on. These requirements sometimes have bona fide roots in ethical reflection, but because these interventions are unevenly established across the research ethics regime, scholars find themselves inadvertently out of step with sudden changes that are frequently temporary. These idiosyncrasies come and go from committee to committee, vary from time to time, and from committee membership to committee membership. Even within particular topics of research such as "intimate" research or in-class research, one finds newly emerging and highly disparate processes of research ethics review. Cautionary notes and rumours abound. The only certain outcome from these committee behaviours is the uncertainty of them. The negative effects on social science, however, are clear.

Trends occur in research generally, and research ethics panels must first acknowledge and eventually contend with them. What is one to make of "go-along ethnography," "clinical ethnography," "collaborative research," and "ethnodrama," "auto-ethnography," or "visual anthropology?" If even researchers have trouble configuring the precise nature of each of these methodological approaches, one can hardly expect research ethics committees to keep themselves current on these emerging approaches. And, of course, all will need to consider whether these new areas acquire new ethical complexions or whether it is sufficient to cast them into a more familiar, traditional concept of research. Social researchers, and society at large, are suffering because written informed consent documents and full-board review are the default settings for researchers using low-to-no risk methods that are, nevertheless, not accommodated within the current system of research ethics review.

Some regulatory trends have an iterative effect. For example, the birth of member checking (Sandelowski, 2008) rests with feminist social researchers who wished to narrow the gap between researchers and research participants. Member checking delineates a wide variety of uses, but the principal one involves researchers checking or validating the information in interviews and sometimes requiring the interview participant to approve the typed transcript (see also Shokeid, 1997) to reframe their research. Today, research ethics committees regularly invoke this approach in the belief that interview transcripts should be an exact rendering of what transpired in interviews (see Kirsten Bell, chapter 10). All of this seems to make sense, but traditionally member checking was invoked in particular circumstances – not across the board of all interview research. When we read Natasha Mauthner's chapter (11) about the legal mandate to archive interview data in the United Kingdom, one could not help but think that legislators, too, hold this narrow view of how researchers use data.

These disturbances are not new to historian Zachary Schrag who produced an important book (2010) on the history of ethics review in the United States.[3] Research ethics committees offer very little, if any, opportunity for the critical inquiry that many social science scholars take seriously. What is more, Schrag avers, ethics committees look through the historical lens of medical research abuses. Suspicion and hostility might be the hallmark of how ethics review committees approach disciplines unfamiliar to committee members.

Illusions That Keep the Rupture Afloat

As in all things social, including the highly charged setting of research ethics review, it is no surprise that illusions and fictions abound. Many contributing authors demonstrate here how a number of these illusions and fictions are created and sustained. In great part these illusions keep the entire system of ethics review afloat. Illusions abiding in the system of research ethics review include, particularly, the idea of *participants* as constructed by regulators; the illusion of a universal ethics code; the illusion that rules, if followed, constitute protection; and illusions about knowledge, consistency, and control within the system.

The "Human Participant"

The social creation of the *human participant* is similar to operationalization in that the created entity is far removed from reality. As Igor Gontcharov explains in chapter 13, *participant* is not the proper term for those observed by unobtrusive researchers who render no treatment; he argues that we must stop using that term when a person does not participate in anything except everyday life. Gontcharov argues that "the term research *subject* is politically obsolete" in the social sciences: "The concept is historically conditioned and possesses negative connotations. In this respect, the task of the word *participants* is to change the mindset of both researchers and human subjects, and to empower humans involved in research." It is unreasonable to think that these tasks can be accomplished by changing a single word while leaving problems firmly intact. And, it is not likely a universal term exists within the plural world of social research. This change in labelling appears to be much ado about very little: the adoption of *participants* may be seen as an attempt to evade existing problems, a distraction parading as change (see Kirsten Bell, chapter 10).

In the same vein, Heather Kitchin Dahringer (chapter 7) points out that research via the Internet does not necessarily involve "participants" insofar as the research process is very frequently unidirectional. With the obvious exception of those who participate in interactive online research, people online are overwhelmingly operating in public arenas and their identities are not known to the researcher – two key elements explicitly selected by federal regulators as exempt from review. As Patrick O'Neill, a psychologist, remarks in chapter 6, individuals under study "are participants only in a rather euphemistic sense." Ann Hamilton discusses in her 2002 dissertation another problem: That the term "participant" includes interviewees, survey respondents, the observed (who undergo no treatment), *and* clinical *patients* adds to the notion that there is no difference among these types of participation, and, following that, a single set of rules is adequate. One term to describe all participants is not adequate, as it makes no distinction among diverse forms of treatment. This difficulty is substantially bigger than labelling and creating distractions – for decades, regulators and others have argued that one universal code of ethics exists and should be followed.

"Universal" Ethics Codes

The reader would likely be astounded, as we would be, if a single code of ethics could indeed govern such disparate social sectors as the civil service, the oil and gas industry, and non-profit organizations. Yet, nearly identical processes of research ethics review are now required for such widely different approaches as clinical trials, some research in the humanities, genome research, social science studies, oral history, community studies, surveys, psychology, and autobiographical writing, to name only a few. Even the name of a guiding ethics review document in the United States – the "Common Rule" – entrenches this idea.

The belief in "universal ethics codes," however, has two faces, and both are fictive. On the one hand, policymakers and others falsely hold that a single ethics code can and should consistently apply across the entire spectrum of all research. The argument goes something like this: ethics should permeate all we do, and ethical principles apply across all situations, at all times, and for all people. Although many of us may agree with such assertions, it is a matter of *relevance* in the case of the system of research ethics review. The rules and concerns in biomedicine are not the same rules and concerns that are relevant in survey research. We do not advocate a lack of ethics in research; we advocate a lack of interference in low- and no-risk social research. On the other hand, there is the fiction that these "universal" ethics codes remain untouched or pristine when they pass through the bowels of a bureaucracy that Nathan Emmerich (2013) of Queen's University in Belfast describes as the "practical machinery." Rena Lederman, in discussing "rationalizing difference," in chapter 2, directly addresses the active role of bureaucracy in the United States. This "practical machinery" contorts "universal" ethics codes into meaningless-yet-required processes that even regulators do not recognize as being related to federal laws and guidelines before local interpretations further convolute and distort them.

Nathan Emmerich (2013: 5) recently advanced our understanding by pointing out that it is not stated universal truths that decide whether particular research initiatives are ethical (or not); it is ethics as promulgated by members of Research Ethics Boards. Drawing on the findings of Laura Stark (2011), Emmerich avers that members of these committees typically draw on their own personal, professional, and disciplinary knowledge and experiences – frequently a narrow band of specialized knowledge – to determine the ethics of the broad range of social research. When we see that ethics committee members rely on old cases and previous judgments, we know that "universal" ethics codes have given way to local, particular interpretations – illusions produced by members of ethics review committees who too frequently know too little about the proposed methods, and who operate under the assumption that this lack of knowledge does not matter.

Illusion of Rules as Protection

As Hamilton (2002) argues, "We have developed an unwarranted belief that rules plus compliance equals protection" (45). Many contributors to this volume point out that research ethics board members frequently focus on informed consent documents – requiring written documents, editing and re-editing those documents – perhaps as compensation for the lack of direct oversight, and to inject themselves, with a rather loud voice, into research activity in which they never participate, activity they only imagine. Zachary Schrag (2011) reinforces the idea that "even rules that seem to protect vulnerable groups may threaten vulnerable individuals" (126). The hyper-regulation of protected classes contributes to researchers' avoidance of studying these groups and dehumanizes the people in those groups, stripping them of the right to decide whether or not to participate in research, or even to oppose the idea that they are vulnerable. The stated purpose for research ethics regimes is to reduce risk to research participants, but fear of litigation has supplanted protection. Robert Dingwall (chapter 1) and Patricia and Peter Adler (chapter 3), as well as other contributors to this volume write that the protection of research participants is less important to ethics committees than the protection of institutions. Moreover, the system is entrenching itself in other areas: grant requirements and academic publications are now purveyors of ethics in research. Institutions engage in "reputation management" that, according to Dingwall, stands at the heart of research ethics review.

Other Illusions

Illusion of knowledge. Lisa-Jo Kestin van den Scott (chapter 12) explains that the Collaborative Institutional Training Initiative (CITI) tests for students and other researchers have the stated purpose of increasing knowledge about conducting ethical research. However, the perceived "true legal role of the boards," along with attempts to frame the Institutional Review Boards as interested in ethics rather than liability, "produces comments from students about how their intelligence has been insulted." Moreover, the CITI tests further this by "test[ing] the students on history that, from the perspective of social scientists, seems largely irrelevant to their field and studies. Many graduate students see the process of CITI testing, along with the entire process, as a charade."

The indoctrination of generations of students and researchers into a flawed system of research ethics review that is entrenched as required, as necessary in spite of being irrelevant, and cumbersome without benefit, and the *acceptability of accepting* all this is an even more insidious illusion.

Illusion of consistency. Considerable research exists about research ethics committees and their pronounced lack of consistency in the decisions rendered, not only across ethics review boards, but even within the same board over time as membership changes. Further, what might seem to be obvious areas of knowledge or experience for members of ethics boards, such as defining "minimal risk" and "low risk," or establishing what constitutes a "sensitive" question or "discomfort" are areas of broad inconsistencies and inconsistent results from ethics boards are frequently insurmountable to social researchers who try to address them. Patrick O'Neill (chapter 6) writes, "Researchers who must have several ethics boards approve a project are often frustrated by the difference of opinion among boards. Some believe that formal accreditation of ethics boards will help to make decisions more consistent – many Institutional Review Boards in the United States are accredited, Research Ethics Boards in Canada are not." O'Neill points out that in the study conducted by Seema Shah et al. (2004), "all 188 chairs making wildly inconsistent judgments did come from *accredited* Institutional Review Boards" (O'Neill's emphasis).

Illusion of control. Several contributing authors here aver that direct oversight of social research is impossible except in the rarest of circumstances. Regulators of research ethics do not know what happens in the field; all they can assure are promises of compliance, but not the actual *experience* of compliance. Rules in any system cannot account for every situation, and enforcement of rules is never complete. For members of research ethics committees and regulators to act as if they control, or even *know* what occurs in the research environment is illusory. What the ethics review committee knows about the studies they approve is vastly limited. And we must acknowledge, as Ron Iphofen writes in chapter 20, "There is really only one guarantor of ethical practice – the researcher. Ultimately it is the researcher in the field who knows when ethical practice is going on and when it is being threatened." This is an example of what Hamilton calls the "liquid and local" nature of making rules and of following them. To think that ethics review boards control what researchers do beyond submitting paperwork is an illusion.

General Characteristics of an Unruptured System

The richness offered by the chapters in this volume enables us to sketch several paths for leading especially social scientists from the bramble of the research ethics review system. On the most general, cultural level, a number of scholars offer sage advice about what it takes to create a collaborative culture focused on sharing information, with or without research ethics review, for survey interview, fieldwork, and observational methods.

A fundamental shift from an adversarial culture (Israel et al., chapter 15) to one that eschews "mutually maligning discourse" (Iphofen, chapter 20) is required for a promising culture of research. Whether this shift falls inside or outside the research ethics regime is not of particular significance. What matters is that all parties – regulators, researchers, student researchers, research participants, and society at large – stand to benefit from a collaborative research culture.

Mark Israel et al. (chapter 15) point out this adversarial culture leads to difficulties associated with such us-against-them positioning. The failure to include researchers in the rule-making processes, as well as a lack of limited regulator resources, and a lack of expertise within the system have contributed substantially to this predictable outcome.

To develop a culture of collaboration, trust must be at the forefront of one's aims (see work by Dingwall, chapter 1; Israel et al., chapter 15; and Schrag, chapter 16). Trust requires forgetting the disparaging past (Bell, chapter 10) and taking an a-historical approach when considering the ethical nature of one's research. Such a culture will nurture researchers to search not only for the truth, but also to speak the truth (Marzano, chapter 5), untrammelled by convention or tradition. Trust should encompass the understanding that researchers know the ethical dimensions in their field (Adler and Adler, chapter 3; and Hamilton, chapter 17). That administrative staff members working with research ethics committees are labelled *compliance officers* is an exaltation of regulation and an impediment to developing collaborative thinking that benefits all stakeholders.

Part of adopting a non-adversarial, ethical culture of research requires the recognition of disciplinary diversity. The disciplines cannot be treated alike (Lederman, chapter 2), and we should fervently embrace pluralism (Schrag, chapter 16). Along with many authors in this volume, Jennifer Howard (2006) encourages social scientists to join research ethics committees to help the committees educate themselves, suggesting that "to come across a humanist on an IRB is as startling as spotting a peacock in a flock of robins" (para. 34).[4]

Collaboration is suggested not only among ethics review committees and researchers, but also among disciplines: social scientists can reject "scientific colonialism" (Mauthner, chapter 11) and should be aware that their frames of reference may include the "colonized mind" as a repository of constructs from the biomedical paradigm (Hamilton, chapter 17). Certainly, as Julie Bull (chapter 9) avers, researchers must decolonize their methods if they wish to proceed with the study of Aboriginal groups, especially groups that are on the road to extinction. We may not have another two or three decades to repair this rupture.

New ideas are churning the sediments of the research ethics culture. Now is the historical moment for change (Bell, chapter 10; Guerriero, chapter 14). The mood in the United Kingdom is no less restive or urgent in the call for change. The three 2013 Ethics Symposia in London (2013)[5] arose from a growing concern that "has sprung up all over the world lately regarding the governance of research ethics and whether regulations to govern them are inappropriately designed." Indeed, according to the authors of the Symposia report, "some researchers view regulation as anti-democratic and a barrier to their academic investigations, something that could hold important studies back." Through its thematic *Generic Ethics Principles in Social Science Research*, the authors, with a note of optimism, write, "The Academy of Social Sciences is joining the international debate in the hope of raising awareness and discussing the possibility of articulating a consensus about research ethics that would be respected among all those affected." The problem appears particularly pronounced for those at the start of their careers, who may find it difficult to establish job security and are often under more scrutiny, and punished more severely and publicly, than established, insulated scholars.

Researchers in the social sciences are not standing alone when responding to the need and time for change. Medical researcher Simon Whitney, author of *The Python's Embrace* and an article with the same title (2012), recently created a blog with a no-less certain title: *Suffocating Science: Research Ethics Committees, Institutional Review Boards, and the Crisis in Ethics Review* (http://suffocatedscience.com/). Historian Zachary Schrag (chapter 16) has a long-standing blog, *Institutional Review Blog: News and Commentary about Institutional Review Board Oversight of the Humanities and Social Sciences* (http://www.institutionalreviewblog.com/). As a sign of the times, the Canadian Panel on Research Ethics

(PRE) and the US Office of Human Research Protections (OHRP), agencies that oversee their respective countries' research ethics regimes, initiated discussions in 2011 and 2013, respectively, about the next stage of such reviews. In the United States, the National Research Council (2014) produced a report proposing revisions to the "Common Rule." One can readily see that if the Office of Human Research Protections would incorporate them, and local research ethics review committees would follow them, the social sciences would be substantially reinvigorated in the United States. Perhaps, as Kirsten Bell (chapter 10) writes, the time has finally come.

Two options stand before us. Option A is a restructured system of research ethics review; option B involves dismemberment of the system as applied to social science research.

Option A: Working within a Restructured System

The world offers, as demonstrated here, a diverse regulatory system of research ethics review. Many researchers are optimistic that the current system of research ethics review can adapt to the needs of social scientists. Emma Tumilty, Martin Tolich, and Stephanie Dobson (chapter 19) and Ron Iphofen (chapter 20) have been working on a modus vivendi designed to reconcile conflicting demands, ultimately acknowledging that the ethics regime is a worthy one to follow, demonstrating the importance of keying the ethics of research into existing formal structures of national policies. They seek piecemeal solutions to reforming the ethics regime, tinkering with proposals to change some of the foundational features, whether they pertain to mandatory written informed consent documents or the need for researchers to specify in advance of collecting data the precise nature and purpose of their plans and analysis.

A most promising segment for change in the ethics review system touches the area of the kinds of research that should be excluded from the reach of ethics review committees. Following federal exemptions at the local level would reduce the workload of ethics committees, allowing them more time to consider research that actually poses a threat to the welfare of research participants. National-level systems of research ethics review specify the kinds of human "research" that should be exempt from ethics review, but those exemptions are few in number in the local context. The crystallization of local ethics committees and ethics mission creep has led to ever-narrowing boundaries for exemption.

The contributors to this volume have called for a series of disciplines and/or methods beyond oral history to be exempt from review, namely, those employing surveys, interviews, observations (Lederman, chapter 2), research involving no or low risk (e.g., Dingwall, chapter 1; Bell, chapter 10; Hamilton, chapter 17), research that does not involve therapeutic procedures (Hamilton, chapter 17), unfunded research (Adler and Adler, chapter 3), or some aspects of online research where privacy is no longer possible anyway and certainly beyond the control of researchers (Dahringer, chapter 7). Behind these clear evocations is the belief that the institutionalization of irrelevant processes and paperwork should be resisted, a broadly held view and one that is likely shared by researchers and ethics board members alike, even when not articulated.

The contributors to this volume have voiced concerns about ethics review committees' curtailing researchers' capacity to engage with and learn about research participants before officially starting the research. Particularly in community-participatory research, researchers must collaborate with potential participants to write a proposal that at least resembles what the researcher is likely to encounter in the field. To restrict the ability of researchers to collaborate with participants when planning research makes no sense. Kate Holland (chapter 18), Patricia Adler and Peter Adler (chapter 3), Rena Lederman (chapter 1), and others describe such exploratory work as a necessary part of research, grounded in the belief that participants have a substantive contribution to make to the design, execution, and reporting of research. Potential participants can inform and educate researchers as they formulate research proposals and complete the ethics review process, and researchers can provide information about this collaboration to members of research ethics committees, which may reduce board concerns about imagined risks to imagined participants.

Those who have worked with (or within) ethics review committees will have realized that much hinges on ideology and language. One can be stymied by the use of particular words that trigger certain decisions in a particular direction. When a researcher proposes to conduct interviews and mentions that they may have a "therapeutic" effect, an ethics committee member (who may be a counsellor, for example) will throw words of caution and perhaps even deny permission to conduct the interviews. It is also sometimes extraordinarily difficult for members of ethics review committees to move beyond the medical paradigm of research (Schrag, chapter 16). And, as discussed, terms vary greatly across disciplines: "analysis" is different from discipline to discipline, and "observation" means watching people in one context but may mean drawing blood in another.

Kate Holland (chapter 18) sees community-based research as a promising area for change. Because the received code of ethics excludes any consideration of community-based research, policymakers are more open to this new venue of ethics in research. If one were cynical one could claim that a new venue offers a new means for research ethics committees to stretch their powers and bureaucratic control. Still, this approach furthers hope for welcome changes in ethics codes, especially the relaxing of ethics review requirements for community research and similar endeavours.

In addition to actually serving on ethics review committees, social researchers must encourage educational presentations that put researchers in a more positive light than when they are under fire defending a rejected or mangled proposal in a regulatory context. Academic departments and professional associations that are related in methodologies can make interdisciplinary presentations to the research ethics committee. This would not only save time, but also and more significantly perhaps, would model collaboration in the ethics context for the committee. As the education model grows deeper roots, seeds of collaboration are sown, rather than fear, in the minds of students and other researchers. The contributors to this volume provide evidence that the ethics review system is already moving toward a focus on education (see Lederman, 2007). Perhaps the best evidence that migration from regulation to education and collaboration is occurring is the establishment of The Ethics Application Repository (TEAR). This project, described by Tumilty et al. (chapter 19), is a valuable resource for both researchers and ethics board members. The applications, board responses, and relevant correspondence contributed to the repository provide examples of proposals that can guide researchers in writing their applications, and the resources in the repository can also provide members of ethics committees with evidence they need to exempt certain forms of research. Providing evidence and reasons for decisions creates a more comfortable ethics review environment for both researchers and regulators, positioning The Ethics Application Repository as a very important resource itself, as well as being important as a model for scholarly associations and others who wish to develop similar ways of sharing knowledge. The Ethics Application Repository is collaboration-in-action.

Kate Holland (chapter 18) specifically suggests that ethics review committees should encourage a narrative approach in sorting through such issues as informed consent. Narratives are a better approach to explaining specific ethics issues in the proposed research and how they will be addressed in specific terms. Narratives create fewer illusions than when researchers are asked to provide full details of future events in a one-size-fits-all standardized format. Citing Jacobsen et al. (2007), Holland suggests that researchers should not be required to give the full account before the research begins: "Just one example is Memorial University of Newfoundland, which used this approach to process ethics applications – with positive outcomes including the creation of a common striving among both the board members and researchers" (Interview R118, 2 Aug. 2003: 2).[6] There is another important benefit to this education orientation: reconfiguring the nature and strength of relations among members of research ethics committees, members of professional association, and researchers. Current attitudes of committee members toward researchers too frequently involve scepticism and suspicion. This appears to be an outgrowth of the regulator mindset that holds if regulation is needed it is because there are bad researchers out there who must be stopped. Inherent in legitimate (i.e., needed) regulation is a problem that must be contained, reduced, eliminated. Some of the contributing authors here have argued that approaching researchers in this way is itself unethical.

One hopes that the more than 325 publications and presentations critical of processes of research ethics review will gradually have an impact. *The New Brunswick Declaration: A Declaration on Research Ethics, Integrity, and Governance* (see Appendix A), developed at the 2012 Ethics Summit in Fredericton, New Brunswick, sets out new concepts and relationships among members of ethics committees, researchers, and others involved in research – a relationship that reduces the wholesale negative, unhelpful, imposing manners of research ethics committees (see van den Hoonaard, 2013a, 2013b; Hamilton, 2002). In short, ethics board members should treat researchers with the same respect that they expect researchers to extend to participants.

An opinion prevalent among contributors to this volume is that research ethics committees should refrain from interfering with the researcher's conception of methods and that professional and academic societies can be used to greater advantage in ethics review (Israel et al., chapter 15; Schrag, chapter 16; and Iphofen, chapter 20). Scholarly and professional associations are nearly uniquely suited to debate the most relevant ethical issues in a given field of study. They are also suited to educate researchers about the particular issues, including ethical ones, prevailing in their specific field, and to provide effective ways of managing risks based on relevant, real-world experiences. These are far more productive activities than perpetuating the illusion that regulation by people who know substantially less than researchers in the field benefits research participants or anyone else.

Ethics committees act *in loco parentis*, outwardly suggesting they are needed to watch over, with these parental eyes, the ethical well-being of everyone – and every institution – involved in human research endeavours. If the community of researchers wishes to embark on the process of gauging the performance of ethics review committees, it might be necessary to take an active stance toward evaluating ethics boards. While this approach seems counterintuitive to creating a non-adversarial culture, by avoiding ad hominum attacks, not inventing the motivations of ethics committee members, and by having board assessments as part of the routines of university governance can reduce conflicts. Zachary Schrag (chapter 16) encourages researchers to publish case studies (in fact, many have done so already). Israel et al. (chapter 15) propose that researchers should talk about the control and secrecy exercised by ethics review committees, while Patricia Adler and Peter Adler (chapter 3) urge exposing the "capriciousness, censorship, and ultimately restriction of valuable field research" and promote research about the ways ethics committees have become corrupt in exercising power. The Consortium of Social Science Associations (COSSA), Adler and Adler suggest, should develop explicit standards by which to judge the performance of ethics review committees. Similar points are raised about historians (Schrag) and anthropologists (Lederman, chapter 2).

Under these conditions, one hopes that ethics review panels would cease using "flawed" research proposals as lessons in workshops (Israel et al., chapter 15) and that mishaps in the past do not overwhelm either the research ethics committees or researchers (O'Neill, chapter 6). Along the same lines, as Lisa-Jo van den Scott articulates so well, one can also hope that the Collaborative Institutional Training Initiative (CITI) will find its way to a dustbin as it contains no relevant "training" component for social scientists.

We must set aside the illusion that research ethics committees must approve what researchers do, instead trusting researchers to handle moral issues in the field (Israel et al., chapter 15; Marzano, chapter 5; Iphofen, chapter 20). Such an action would be akin to policymakers welcoming researchers as partners (Schrag, chapter 16). For some (like Dingwall, chapter 1), "burdensome rules obstruct moral action" on the part of researchers. However, if ethics review committees do firmly believe that researchers are moral agents, they must put those beliefs into action by creating a shield law for researchers and promote the notion of a certificate of confidentiality (Adler and Adler, chapter 3) or, what Hamilton (2002) suggests, a blanket assurance for individual researchers similar to the ones arranged between the federal regulators and institutions. The contributors to this volume almost universally agree that ethics review committees should, and can under current rules, resist the hegemony of default settings including requiring written consent forms (instead of acknowledging that informed consent is a process rather than an event) and full-board review (as opposed to exemption being the standard for much of social research). Further, Marco Marzano argues that covert methods are necessary in some types of research and, therefore, must not be summarily disallowed. And, Lee Murray (chapter 8) reminds us, Canadian research ethics policies explicitly do not discourage research on controversial topics that challenge mainstream thought and that Research Ethics Boards should not discourage that research either.

Option B: Dispensing with the System

A bramble of history, well-intentioned ideologies, and unintended consequences fill the chronicles of research ethics review. The chapters in *The Ethics Rupture* not only underscore the inevitable entanglements of such a bramble, but also point to authentic efforts on the part of researchers to mitigate conflicts and create a livable system of ethics review, one appropriate to research in the social sciences and humanities. National regimes for regulating research ethics review seem immutable to any serious change – "unmeltable ethnics" in the words of Michael Novak (1972), and applied more recently to social research by Norman Denzin and Yvonne Lincoln (2000: 53).

National and local regulators have met with silence the innumerable scholarly works narrating the immediate and long-term shortcomings of processes of research ethics review. These processes are stagnating. For researchers in the social sciences an uncanny and debilitating resignation and compliatorianism have been the norm for too long. The Ethics Summit, the *Declaration of New Brunswick*, and now this volume have converged to nudge the research ethics review system off high-centre.

Our volume points to a plurality of ethics review processes and a plurality of affected disciplines, and to the importance of activism directed toward a better system for everyone involved. We certainly must stop vilifying those who propose changes to this flawed charade.

Proponents for dismembering the ethics review system point to the full inappropriateness of biomedical frameworks (in policy- and decision-making) as the anvil of the system – it has no relevance for the social sciences. It is better to dispense with the system. Zachary Schrag (chapter 16) describes, "One long-standing grievance among social scientists is the concept of informed consent embedded in the *Belmont Report* and comparable documents based on biomedical ethics." The heavy, impractical burden that research ethics committees must wrestle daily, along with the profound, negative impact on research in the social sciences, levies a further toll that seems unavoidable. Elsewhere, van den Hoonaard (2011) has argued that worldwide the systems of research ethics review costs at least $500 million in expenses. Is it time to jettison this system?

There is a moral strength that stands outside the prevailing research ethics regime. That strength can be found in the moral core of researchers and in the professional and academic organizations that represent them. With the focus revolving around institutional attempts to bring researchers to account, Ron Iphofen (chapter 20) nevertheless argues "for acknowledging the integrity of researchers and their ability to conduct research in a responsible manner. In terms of moral philosophy, this is akin to adopting a virtue ethics stance."

So ...

In the face of strong interests heavily vested in the research ethics review system itself and that any attempt at reform has been too easily dismissed as serving only researchers, we – social scientists – have begun to look at change from a different light. At the most basic level, we know it is essential to develop a collaborative culture of research, including ethics considerations – to replace the regulatory model. We believe the migration from regulation toward education has begun, and we have offered several examples, including most tangibly perhaps The Ethics Application Repository (TEAR). It is our hope – with this work and the work to come – to complete the migration to the collaborative culture, toward what we believe will be a safer and more vibrant social research environment.

NOTES

1 In 2003, Canada's Interagency Panel on Research Ethics (PRE) undertook
   a massive consultation with scholars and other stakeholders regarding
   the *TCPS 1* (CIHR et al., 1998), the results of which contributed to changes
   in the *TCPS 2* (CIHR et al., 2010). The Social Sciences and Humanities
   Research Ethics Special Working Committee of PRE organized three local
   consultations, received 56 submissions representing 60 departmental
   chairs, 1,400 faculty, and 5,000 members of the Canadian Association of
   Sociology and Anthropology, 47 academic departments, and nine REBs
   or offices of research services (PRE, 2003). Interestingly, at least two
   contributors to this volume (Bell and Gontcharov) conclude that for all this
   consultation, the changes were superficial, effective mostly at providing a
   distraction from more substantive issues.
2 In the past, one of us used "fads" to describe the temporary and
   capricious nature of objects that gain the attention of research ethics
   committees. Perhaps another term is more suitable. Can one describe
   an ethics committee's worry about the safety of researchers in the field
   as a "vogue"? It lasts for a long while, but it does move away from a
   committee's attention, only to be replaced by another "fashionable" event
   to place under the ethics review microscope. One area that is enduring
   is the preoccupation with written informed consent documents that are
   tangible, and easily manipulated, mostly meaninglessly, by anyone with a
   word processor.
3 While editing *The Ethics Rupture*, we have learned of *Protecting Research
   Confidentiality*, a fourth empirical book on the research ethics review
   process (Palys and Lowman, 2014).
4 During these past 20 years we often say and hear that social scientists
   must be adequately represented on review boards, and this suggestion is
   too often interpreted, reduced actually, to the idea that having one or two
   token members on an ethics board is what is being proposed. We say this is
   inadequate. A subcommittee, at a minimum, is needed for survey, interview,
   field, and observational research. With only one or two social scientists on a
   board, engaging in discussions with other members who know little about
   the methods proposed is not a formula for success. A subcommittee would
   produce more effective results for researchers, board members, and for
   participants. Of course, a logical place for these committees is likely within
   academic departments, as several contributors have suggested.
5 The Economic and Social Research Council, the British Psychological
   Society, the British Sociological Association, and the Open University
   supported the symposia.

6 Interview R118, 2 Aug. 2003, 2. This interview was part of the research that led to van den Hoonaard's ethnography on ethics committees (2011).

REFERENCES

Alvesson, Mats, and Stanley Deetz. (1996). "Critical Theory and Postmodernism Approaches to Organizational Studies." In Stewart Clegg, Cynthia Hardy, and Walter R. Nord (eds.), *Handbook of Organization Studies*, 191–217. Thousand Oaks, CA: Sage.

Brainard, Jeffrey. (2003, 21 Oct.). "Federal Agency Says Oral History Is Not Subject to Rules on Human Research Volunteers." *Chronicle of Higher Education Online*.

CIHR et al. (Canadian Institutes of Health Research, Natural Sciences and Engineering Research Council of Canada, and Social Sciences and Humanities Research Council of Canada). (1998, with 2000, 2002, 2005 amendments). *Tri-Council Policy Statement: Ethical Conduct for Research Involving Humans*. Ottawa: Interagency Panel on Research Ethics.

– (2010). *Tri-Council Policy Statement: Ethical Conduct for Research Involving Humans*. 2nd ed. Ottawa: Interagency Panel on Research Ethics.

Denzin, Norman, and Yvonne Lincoln. (2000). *Handbook of Qualitative Research*. Thousand Oaks, CA: Sage.

Dingwall, Robert. (2008). "The Ethical Case against Ethical Regulation in Humanities and Social Science Research." *21st Century Society* 3 (1): 1–12.

Emmerich, Natthan. (2013). "Between the Accountable and the Auditable: Ethics and Ethical Governance in the Social Sciences." *Research Ethics* 9 (4): 175–86. http://dx.doi.org/10.1177/1747016113510654

Ethics Symposia in London. http://www.bps.org.uk/news/academy-social-sciences-publishes-symposia-results-ethics

Hamilton, Ann. (2002). *Institutional Review Boards: Politics, Power, Purpose and Process in a Regulatory Organization*. Doctoral dissertation, University of Oklahoma.

Howard, Jennifer. (2006, 10 Nov.). "Oral History under Review." *Chronicle of Higher Education Online*.

Jacobsen, Nora, Rebecca Gewurtz, and Emma Haydon. (2007). "Ethical Review of Interpretive Research: Problems and Solutions." *IRB Ethics and Human Research* 29 (5): 1–8.

Lederman, Rena. (2007). "Educate Your IRB: An Experiment in Cross-Disciplinary Communication." *Anthropology News* 48 (6): 33–4. http://dx.doi.org/10.1525/an.2007.48.6.33

National Research Council. (2014). *Proposed Revisions to the Common Rule for the Protection of Human Subjects in the Behavioral and Social Sciences*. Washington, DC: National Academies Press.

Novak, Michael. (1972). *The Rise of the Unmeltable Ethnics: The New Political Force of the Seventies*. New York: Macmillan.

Palys, Ted, and John Lowman. (2014). *Protecting Research Confidentiality: What Happens when Law and Ethics Collide*. Toronto: James Lorimer.

PRE (Interagency Panel on Research Ethics). (2003). "Summary of Questions Asked in Relation to TCPS Sections." *Compendium of TCPS Interpretation Questions and Responses, September 1998–October 2002: Appendix 2*. Ottawa: Secretariat on Research Ethics

Sandelowski, Margarete. (2008). "Member Check." In Lisa M. Given (ed.), *The Sage Encyclopedia of Qualitative Research Methods*, 501–2. Los Angeles: Sage. http://dx.doi.org/10.4135/9781412963909.n257

Schrag, Zachary M. (2010). *Ethical Imperialism: Institutional Review Boards and the Social Sciences, 1965–2009*. Baltimore: Johns Hopkins University Press.

– (2011). Special Issue on the Regulation of Human Subjects Research. (Guest Editor). *Journal of Policy History* 23 (1).

Shah, Seema, Amy Whittle, Benjamin Wilfond, Gary Gensler, and David Wendler. (2004). "How Do Institutional Review Boards Apply the Federal Risk and Benefit Standards for Pediatric Research?" *Journal of the American Medical Association* 291 (4): 476–82. http://dx.doi.org/10.1001/jama.291.4.476

Shokeid, Moishe. (1997). "Negotiating Multiple Viewpoints: The Cook, the Native, the Publisher, and the Ethnographic Text." *Current Anthropology* 38 (4): 631–45. http://dx.doi.org/10.1086/204649

Stark, Laura. (2011). *Behind Closed Doors: IRBs and the Making of Ethical Research*. Chicago: University of Chicago Press. http://dx.doi.org/10.7208/chicago/9780226770888.001.0001

van den Hoonaard, Will C. (2011). *The Seduction of Ethics: Transforming the Social Sciences*. Toronto: University of Toronto Press.

– (2013a). "The 'Ethics Rupture' Summit, Fredericton, New Brunswick, Canada, October 25–28, 2012." *Journal of Empirical Research on Human Research Ethics* 8 (1): 3–7. http://dx.doi.org/10.1525/jer.2013.8.1.3

– (2013b). "The Social and Policy Contexts of the New Brunswick Declaration on Research Ethics, Integrity, and Governance: A Commentary." *Journal of Empirical Research on Human Research Ethics* 8 (2): 104–9. http://dx.doi.org/10.1525/jer.2013.8.2.104

Whitney, Simon N. (2012). "The Python's Embrace: Clinical Research Regulation by Institutional Review Boards." *Pediatrics* 129 (3): 576–8. http://dx.doi.org/10.1542/peds.2011-3455

Appendix

The New Brunswick Declaration

A Declaration on Research Ethics, Integrity, and Governance Resulting from the 1st Ethics Rupture Summit (Fredericton, New Brunswick, Canada)

The Ethics Rupture Summit was a gathering in October 2012 of researchers from Australia, Brazil, Canada, Italy, New Zealand, the United Kingdom, and the United States, who are committed to enhancing ethical research practice, and supporting innovative alternatives to the regulation of research ethics that might achieve this end.

As signatories of the New Brunswick Declaration, we:

1 Seek to promote respect for the right to freedom and expression.
2 *Affirm that the practice of research should respect persons and collectivities and privilege the possibility of benefit over risk.* We champion constructive relationships among research participants, researchers, funders, publishers, research institutions, research ethics regulators and the wider community that aim to develop better understandings of ethical principles and practices.
3 *Believe researchers must be held to professional standards of competence, integrity, and trust,* which include expectations that they will act reflexively and responsibly when new ethical challenges arise before, during, and long after the completion of research projects. Standards should be based on professional codes of ethical practice relevant to the research, drawn from the full diversity of professional associations to which those who study human experience belong, which include the arts and humanities, behavioural, health, and social sciences.

4 *Encourage a variety of means of furthering ethical conduct involving a broad range of parties* such as participant communities, academic journals, professional associations, state and non-state funding agencies, academic departments and institutions, national regulators, and oversight ethics committees.

5 *Encourage regulators and administrators to nurture a regulatory culture that grants researchers the same level of respect that researchers should offer research participants.*

6 *Seek to promote the social reproduction of ethical communities of practice.* Effective ethics education works in socially embedded settings and from the ground up: it depends on strong mentoring, experiential learning, and nurturance when engaging students and novice researchers with ethics in research settings.

7 *Are committed to ongoing critical analysis of new and revised ethics regulations and regimes* by highlighting exemplary and innovative research ethics review processes; identifying tensions and contradictions among various elements of research ethics governance; and seeing that every venue devoted to discussing proposed ethics guidelines includes critical analysis and research about research ethics governance.

8 *Shall work together to bring new experience, insights, and expertise to bear on these principles, goals, and mechanisms.*

Contributors

Patricia A. Adler ("IRBan Renewal") (PhD, Sociology, University of California, San Diego) is professor emerita of sociology at the University of Colorado. Her myriad research interests span social psychology, deviant behaviour, the sociology of drugs, sociology of children, sociology of sports, and sociology of work and leisure. Along with Peter Adler, her most recent work is *The Tender Cut: Inside the Hidden World of Self-Injury*. Together, they were the co-recipients of the 2010 George Herbert Mead Lifetime Achievement Award from the Society for the Study of Symbolic Interaction.

Peter Adler ("IRBan Renewal") (PhD, Sociology, University of California, San Diego) is professor emeritusat the University of Denver and is an expert in qualitative and ethnographic methods, as well as the sociology of children, sociology of sport, and deviant behaviour. Together with Patricia Adler, he is the author of an acclaimed textbook on field research methods in sociology, entitled *Membership Roles in Field Research*.

Gary Allen ("Australian Research Ethics Governance: Plotting the Demise of the Adversarial Culture") is Senior Policy Officer at Griffith University. He has a degree in education and a doctorate in social sciences. His work on the establishment of positive institutional research ethics arrangements was recognized with an Outstanding Doctoral Thesis Award from Queensland University of Technology. He has worked in the human research ethics area for almost two decades, with a number of research institutions, state and federal departments, private companies, and research ethics committees in Australia, Canada, the United Kingdom, and Vietnam.

Kirsten Bell ("The More Things Change, the More They Stay the Same: *TCPS 2* and the Institutional Oversight of Social Science Research in Canada") (PhD, Social Anthropology, James Cook University, Australia) is Research Associate, Department of Anthropology, University of British Columbia. Initially specializing in Korean new religious movements, today she works primarily on the anthropology of public health and biomedicine. She has published widely in these areas on an array of topics that include cancer, tobacco, addiction, genital cutting, and research ethics. Bell is the lead editor of the book entitled, *Alcohol, Tobacco and Obesity: Morality, Mortality and the New Public Health*, and she is currently an associate editor of the journal *Critical Public Health*.

Julie Bull ("A Two-Eyed Seeing Approach to Research Ethics Review: An Indigenous Perspective") (PhD cand., Interdisciplinary Studies/ Indigenous Research Ethics, University of New Brunswick) is an Indigenous scholar from NunatuKavut, Labrador. She teaches in the Aboriginsal Studies Program at the University of Toronto, is a research consultant at NunatuKavut Community Council, an ethics policy policy developer at the Native Council of Prince Edward Island, and a member of several local and national committees to advance research ethics policy for research involving Indigenous people. As a Vanier scholar, her research interests are rooted in Aboriginal health and education with a specific focus on research ethics and the governance of research involving Indigenous people.

Heather Kitchin Dahringer ("The Internet as a Stage: Dramaturgy, Research Ethics Boards, and Privacy as 'Performance'") (PhD, Sociology, Carleton University, Ottawa) is professor of sociology at Acadia University in Nova Scotia. She has worked with governmental panels and working groups on research ethics. She has served as a commissioned discussant of the Interagency Advisory Panel and Secretariat on Research Ethics. Her book *Research Ethics and the Internet: Negotiating Canadas Tri-Council Policy Statement* has heavily shaped the *TCPS 2*'s new language on ethical procedures for Internet research. She is currently working on a new book to be entitled, *Social Problems in Canada: Mapping Geographies of Violence*.

Robert Dingwall ("The Social Costs of Ethics Regulation") (PhD, Medical Sociology, University of Aberdeen) is a consulting sociologist and part-time professor of sociology at Nottingham Trent University. He has wide international experience in teaching and research, particularly in the study of law, medicine, science, and technology. This has focused mainly on issues about professions, work, and organizations, as well as writing on social theory, research ethics, and qualitative research methods. His academic recognition includes terms as editor-in-chief of *Sociology of Health and Illness* and *Symbolic Interaction*, and he has held office in the Law and Society Association, the American Sociological Association, and the UK Academy of Social Sciences.

Stephanie Dobson ("Rupturing Ethics Literacy: The Ethics Application Repository (TEAR)") (PhD, Anthropology, University of Otago) is currently a professional practice fellow at the University of Otago. Her qualitative research focuses on Muslim women in New Zealand. Her publications have examined Muslim women's perspectives and experiences in such areas as identity, multiculturalism, faith, religious interpretation, and diaspora.

Igor Gontcharov ("The Eclipse of 'Human Subjects' and the Rise of 'Human Participants' in Research Involving Humans") (LLM, PhD cand., Osgoode Hall Law School) is senior fellow, Critical Research Laboratory in Law & Society (CRL) at Osgoode Hall Law School, and a member of the University Health Network Rehabilitation Medicine and Science REB Review Panel. His research interests include risk policy harmonization in research involving humans, sociology and ethnography of law, and the regulation and governance of knowledge production. In 2010–11 he was a research fellow at the School of Law at Columbia University in New York City. In 2011–12 he was a convener of the "Emerging Scholars Workshop Series," the "Challenging Conventions!" speaker series, and a conference on Critical Legal Studies and Methodology, "Re-Igniting Critical Race," organized through CRL.

Iara Coelho Zito Guerriero ("Ethics in Social Science and Humanities Research: Brazilian Strategies to Improve Guidelines") (PhD, Public Health, University of Sao Paulo) has researched and worked in the human research ethics field for more than 15 years. She is a researcher at the Institute of Tropical Medicine, University of Sao Paulo. Currently she is in her second turn as a member of the National Commission on Research Ethics (CONEP/Brazil). Since 2013, she is chairing the CONEP working group that is developing the Brazilian guidelines on research ethics in the social sciences and humanities. Her interests in research are qualitative methodologies, research ethics, and research ethics boards.

Ann Hamilton ("The Ethics Rupture Summit in the Context of Current Trends in Research Ethics Review," "Research Ethics Review and Compliatorianism: A Curious Dilemma," and "So Where from Here? Finding Paths through the Bramble of Research Ethics Review") holds a PhD in human communication from the University of Oklahoma. She explores power structures in regulatory organizations, education and economic systems, and interpersonal relationships. She teaches courses in conflict management, crisis communication, leadership, communication theory, and sources and discourses of power. She is an editor, specializing in dissertations, books, and articles written by non-native speakers of English, and she develops curricula, individual courses, and printed and media materials for university, corporate, and government organizations.

Kate Holland ("Enriching Ethics Review Processes in the Spirit of Participatory Dialogue") (PhD, Communication, University of Canberra) is a senior research fellow in the News and Media Research Centre, Faculty of Arts and Design, University of Canberra. Her key research areas include communication and media studies, particularly the relationships between media and public understandings and responses to health issues. She has published qualitative research on issues such as mental illness, suicide, overweight and obesity, infectious diseases, media reporting guidelines, anti-stigma campaigns, the fatosphere, and conflicts of interest. Her interest in research ethics derives from her doctoral work from which she published "The Epistemological Bias of Ethics Review: Constraining Mental Health Research" (in *Qualitative Inquiry*, 2007).

Ron Iphofen ("Professional Research Ethics: Helping to Balance Individual and Institutional Integrity") (PhD, Health Care Professional Education, University of Wales, Bangor) currently acts as a scientific consultant on research ethics for the European Commission, evaluating the ethics of projects within the Framework Program 7 and Horizon 2020. He has written for and contributed to several Commission activities including a report on "Research Ethics in Ethnography and Anthropology," a talk to the Science and Society Committee on "Integrating Ethics in Policy and Project Design." He has recently completed chairing an ethics and societal impact advisory group on a major Commission-funded project on mass passenger transport security.

Mark Israel ("Australian Research Ethics Governance: Plotting the Demise of the Adversarial Culture") (Law, Cambridge University, and D.Phil., Oxford University) is Professor of Law and Criminology in the Faculty of Law at the University of Western Australia. He has published over 70 books, book chapters, and journal articles in the areas of political exile and migration, research ethics and integrity, higher education and research policy, criminology, and socio-legal studies. His work includes *Research Ethics and Integrity for Social Scientists: Beyond Regulatory Compliance*. He has undertaken research ethics-related consultancy for, among others, federal and state governments, higher education and health institutions, NGOs, and research agen cies in Europe, Asia, and Australasia.

Rena Lederman ("Fieldwork Double-Bound in Human Research-Ethics Reviews: Discplinary Competence, or Regulatory Compliance and the Muting of Disciplinary Values") (PhD, Anthropology, Columbia University) is professor of anthropology, Princeton University (where she has been a long-time IRB member). Her research interests include Melanesian gender, exchange, history and sociopolitical relations, but in recent years she has been engaged in the comparative anthropological study of (inter)disciplinarity, with special attention to research practices and ethics in the humanities and social sciences. She is editor of a special issue of *American Ethnologist* (2006) on the fraught relationship between ethnographers and IRBs, author of the chapter on "Ethics" in *Handbook of Sociocultural Anthropology*, and other works on disciplinary and regulatory ethics. She was co-chair of the American Anthropological Association's Committee on Ethics; and, with Lise Dobrin, she co-authored the American Anthropological Association's official commentary on the US Office of Human Research Protection's 2011 "Advance Notice of Proposed Rulemaking" concerning a general revision of the regulatory code governing human-subjects research ethics.

Marco Marzano ("Uncomfortable Truths, Ethics, and Qualitative Research: Escaping the Dominance of Informed Consent") (PhD, Political Science, University of Florence) is full professor of sociology, Department of Foreign Languages, Literatures and Communication Studies, University of Bergamo, Italy. Marzano has been working in the area of social research ethics since 2005, when he presented a paper to the First Congress of Qualitative Inquiry entitled "Toward Ethical Globalization?" Some of his recent publications on this topic include "Informed Consent, Deception, and Research Freedom in Qualitative Research" (in *Qualitative Inquiry*, 2007) and "Informed Consent" in the *Sage Handbook of Interview Research*.

Natasha S. Mauthner ("Should Data Sharing Be Regulated?") (PhD, Social and Political Sciences, University of Cambridge) is professor at the University of Aberdeen, Business School. She has written on the philosophy and ethics of data archiving and sharing in the social sciences with publications in the *Australian Journal of Social Research Methodology*, *Social Epistemology*, the *Australian Journal of Social Issues*, *Ethics in Qualitative Research*, and *Digital Qualitative Research Methods*. She was member pf the National Advisory Board for the UK's Economic and Social Research Council-funded Timescapes longitudinal qualitative study (2007–12), contributed to the Economic and Social Research Council National Centre for Research Methods Network for Methodological Innovation "New Frontiers for Qualitative Longitudinal Methods" (2012–14), was an "expert contributor" to the Nuffield Council on Bioethics' report, *The Culture of Scientific Research in the UK* (2014), and is member of the University of Aberdeen's Advisory Group on Research Ethics and Governance.

B. Lee Murray ("Research Ethics Boards: Are They Ready for Autoethnography?") (PhD, Nursing, University of Saskatchewan) is associate professor at the University of Saskatchewan, College of Nursing. She is also a clinical nurse specialist (CNS) in adolescent mental health, in particular suicidal adolescents and adolescents with developmental disabilities. Her clinical practice, research, and teaching are in the area of adolescent mental health, individual and group counselling, interprofessional practice, and school health in the context of the role of a mental health nurse in schools. She also has a great interest and curiosity regarding "mothering." To satisfy this curiosity, she uses autoethnography as methodology to explore the normative discourse of mothering in the context of her own experiences as a mother.

Patrick O'Neill ("Assessing Risk in Psychological Research") is a Canadian psychologist who received his BA from the University of Victoria and his Master's and PhD in Community-Clinical Psychology from

Yale University. His principal area of research and teaching is ethical decision-making, particularly in the context of psychological research and practice, with a special interest in qualitative research and community psychology. He has written extensively on ethical decision-making in psychology, and he is the author of the book entitled, *Negotiating Consent in Psychotherapy.* He was a member of the Panel on Research Ethics, which created in 2010 the 2nd edition of *Tri-Council Policy Statement: Ethical Conduct for Research Involving Humans.*

Zachary M. Schrag ("Ethical Pluralism: Scholarly Societies and the Regulation of Research Ethics") (PhD, History, Columbia University) is professor of history at George Mason University. Some of his recent publications include "The Case against Ethics Review in the Social Sciences" (in *Research Ethics*, 2011); *Ethical Imperialism: Institutional Review Boards and the Social Sciences, 1965–2009*; and "Ethical Training for Oral Historians" (in *Perspectives: Newsletter of the American Historical Association*, 2007). He was also editor of a special issue on human subjects regulations in several countries of the *Journal of Policy History* (2011). His first book is entitled, *The Great Society Subway: A History of the Washington Metro.*

Laura Stark ("The Language of Ethics: How Research Ethics Review Creates Inequalities for Language Minorities in Research") (PhD, Princeton University) is assistant professor at Vanderbilt University. She is the author of the book entitled, *Behind Closed Doors: IRBs and the Making of Ethical Research,* as well as several articles and chapters based on her observations of IRB meetings and new historical research on ethics. These pieces explore how members of human-subjects review boards make decisions and their unintended effects, and include "Reading Trust between the Lines: Housekeeping Work and Inequality in Human-Subjects Review" (in *Cambridge Quarterly of Healthcare Ethics*, 2013), "IRBs and the Problem of 'Local Precedents'"(in *Human Subjects Research Regulation*, 2014), "IRB Meetings by the Minute(s)" (in *Knowledge Making, Use and Evaluation in the Social Sciences*, 2010), and with Adam Hedgecoe, "A Practical Guide to Research Ethics" (in *Handbook on Qualitative Health Research*, 2010). Stark has served as an IRB member and as an embryonic stem cell research oversight committee member.

Colin Thomson ("Australian Research Ethics Governance: Plotting the Demise of the Adversarial Culture") (BA, LLB, LLM) is professor of law at the University of Wollongong where he is the academic leader for Health Law and Ethics in the Graduate School of Medicine. He was chair of the Australian Health Ethics Committee of the National Health and Medical Research Council (NHMRC) (2006–09) and a member of that committee (1998–2002). Between 2002 and 2006, he was the consultant on health ethics for the NHMRC. During this period, Thomson provided consulting services to the NHMRC, the NSW Health Department, and the NSW Department of Community Services. He currently chairs two research ethics committees.

Martin B. Tolich ("Rupturing Ethics Literacy: The Ethics Applications Repository (TEAR)") (PhD, Sociology, University of California, Davis) is sociology professor at the University of Otago and Marsden Grant Recipient 2012–14 to study "tensions in ethics review and indigenous (NZ) consultation." He is also chair of New Zealand's Health and Disability IRB (2004–08), in addition to eight other years on IRBs. Tolich's contribution is to discuss his work creating research tools to allow researchers to search through previous successful IRB applications and learn how to make effective research proposals by new researchers that will be more likely to meet IRB requirements.

Emma Tumilty ("Rupturing Ethics Literacy: The Ethics Applications Repository (TEAR)") (PhD cand., Bioethics, University of Otago) has been involved in health research practice, governance, and management. She is currently employed at Otago Polytechnic in the area of online/open education and is a member of two IRBs. Shehas been a volunteer on the TEAR project for two years and has presented and published on this work. Her research interests lie in the scope and nature of ethical review, as well as the relationship of research practices to social justice.

Will C. van den Hoonaard (co-editor) (PhD, Sociology, Univesity of Manchester) is professor emeritus, University of New Brunswick, and research associate at the Atlantic Centre for Qualitative Research and Analysis, St Thomas University, Fredericton. He has authored and edited a dozen books on a wide variety of topics, including the Dutch in New Brunswick, a fishing village in Iceland, the Baha'i community of Canada, ethics, and qualitative methodology. His most recent books include *The Seduction of Ethics: Transforming the Social Sciences*, *Essentials of Thinking Ethically in Qualitative Research*, and *Map Worlds: A History of*

Women in Cartography. A founding member of the Canada's Tri-Council Inter-Agency Advisory Panel on Research Ethics, he has also served as the first chair of the Special Working Group on the Social Sciences and the Humanities. In 2013, the Health Improvement Institute (Bethesda, MD) awarded him the Lifetime Achievement Award for Excellence in Human Research Protection.

Lisa-Jo Kestin van den Scott ("The Socialization of Contemporary Students by Ethics Boards: Malaise and Ethics for Graduate Students") (PhD, Sociology, Northwestern University), is Postdoctoral Fellow in Visual Sociology, Brock Studio for Narrative, Visual and Digital Methods, Brock University, St Catharines, ON, Canada. Her research works at the intersection of symbolic interactionism, urban sociology, and science and technology studies. She has authored work on the interaction of two knowledge systems in the Canadian Arctic, including Inuit identity work with their homes. She has published in *Journal of Contemporary Ethnography, Sociology Compass, American Behavioral Scientist, Symbolic Interaction,* and *Journal of Empirical Research on Human Research Ethics.* She serves as treasurer for the Society for the Study of Symbolic Interaction.

Index

Ogburn, W.F., 140
Ogden, R., 349n3
Olson, J.S., 221
On-line research. *See* Cyber research
Onyemelukwe, C., 257
Open University (UK), 429n5
Opt-out policy, 86
Oral history, 9, 14, 47, 60, 66n8, 67n13, 78, 200, 207, 329
Oral History Association, 60, 323; code of, 329
Organization of American Historians, 322
Organizations, scholarly and educational, 64
Osgood, C., 339

Paine, C., 135
Palen, L., 148
Palys, T., 20n7, 198, 264n8, 320, 428n3
Panopticon, 79
Parker, M., 289, 291
Parrhesia, 112–16; cf prophets and sages, 115; absence takes away the freedom to criticize, 116
Parry, O., 207–8
Participant observation, 33, 43, 47, 53, 81, 85. *See also* Ethnography/ers; Field research/work(ers); Observational methods
"Participant" vs "subject," 16, 241, 250–2, 258–63; semantics of, 252–3, 414–15; in cyber research, 136–7; not at home in any science, 262; sometime not clear who are, 128
Participants, 34, 223, 239, 256, 269–70, 301, 358–65, 385, 417; protection of, 77, 193, 211, 213–14; protecting vs risk management,

35; researcher's beliefs about, 272–3; rights of, 33; voice of, quieted by ethics review, 235
Participatory action research, 329, 377, 379
Passivity, academic, about ethics review, 199–200, 347
Paternalism, 35–6
Patient involvement, 262, 361–2
Patterson, K., 199
Paulsen, F., 30
Pauly, N., 103
Pauperization of social sciences, 18, 241, 412
Pels, P., 65n2
Penslar, R., 49
Performance management, 33
Perry, C.M., 207
Perry, K., 317, 322
"Personal," in virtual spaces, 67n13
Peters, T., 109
Petryna, A., 92
Pettit, P., 285–6, 296, 298–9
Petty, J., 103
Phenomenology, 198
Philip Morris International, 217
Philosophy, classical, 112
Photo voice, 377, 385
Photographs, 143, 385
Plagiarism, 46, 328–9
Plattner, S., 191
Plemmons, D., 15–16
Policy Framework on Research Data (UK), 210
Policy researchers/makers, 255–6; listen seldom to social scientists, 410
Political science, 74
Polsky, N., 80
Poole, R., 179

460   Index